Totalitarianism and Political Religion

Totalitarianism and Political Religion

An Intellectual History

A. JAMES GREGOR

STANFORD UNIVERSITY PRESS

Stanford, California

Stanford University Press
Stanford, California
©2012 by the Board of Trustees of the Leland Stanford Junior University. All rights reserved.

No part of this book may be reproduced or transmitted in any form or by any means, electronic or mechanical, including photocopying and recording, or in any information storage or retrieval system without the prior written permission of Stanford University Press

Library of Congress Cataloging-in-Publication Data

Gregor, A. James (Anthony James), author.
 Totalitarianism and political religion : an intellectual history / A. James Gregor.
     pages cm.
 Includes bibliographical references and index.
 ISBN 978-0-8047-8130-5 (cloth : alk. paper)
  1. Totalitarianism—History. 2. Fascism—History. 3. National socialism. 4. Religion and politics—History. I. Title.
JC480.G745 2012
320.53—dc23   2011036780

Printed in the United States of America on acid-free, archival-quality paper

Typeset at Stanford University Press in 10/13 Minion

This book is dedicated to DR. JAMES L. SIMONS, BRIAN CAIN, *and* MARK ST. LEZIN, *whose humanity and skill helped postpone the inevitable long enough to allow its appearance.*

Acknowledgments

In the fragmented, self-absorbed, and sometimes alienated academic world of the inexact sciences, we often overlook the reality that we are products of all the efforts of an incalculable number of influences, among them those who taught us, those who argued with us, and those tentative scholars we taught over the years. There is not space enough to individually cite all those who contributed to the work before the reader. It is perhaps enough to call up the generic memory of those good teachers at Columbia University—Earnest Nagel, and Arthur Danto among them—together with all those students who, over half a century, helped me sharpen my cognitive skills. My gratitude must be more specific when I allude to the content of my exposition. Then, I am obliged to refer to that critical tribe of professionals, contenders, and clarifiers from whom I have learned so much and who have influenced my intellectual life to the degree that traces of their work can be found everywhere in my own. Renzo De Felice, Ernst Nolte, and Richard Pipes must be counted among them. And there was Sidney Hook, Anthony James Joes, and Augusto Del Noce, together with Giuseppe Prezzolini, Ludovico Incisa di Camerana, Ugo Spirito, and Hervé Cavallera. They all assisted me in my effort to understand the ideas that shaped the world in which I have lived. After half a century of study and application, I have arrived at some tentative conclusions. Those that are plausible are the products of those good persons who instructed me by their works and their counsel. I am solely responsible for those ideas that are flawed.

Finally, I owe a special debt to the professionalism and thoughtfulness of Norris Pope, who shepherded the manuscript through the publication process, from its selection to its final appearance. To my wife, Professor Maria Hsia Chang, I am grateful for all kinds of good things: her advice and patience—and for the presence of all those special creatures that give so much meaning to our lives.

Contents

Preface   xi

1. Introduction   1
2. Hegelians after Hegel   29
3. Friedrich Engels and Karl Marx: History as Religion   58
4. Leninism: Revolution as Religion   87
5. Fascism: The Antecedents   115
6. Fascism: The State as Religion   142
7. The Religiopolitical Background of National Socialism   170
8. National Socialism: Race as Religion   199
9. Consolidation and Decay   226
10. Conclusions and Speculations   257

Index   287

Preface

The twentieth was perhaps the most destructive century in human history. Certainly, more lives and property were consumed through willful human agency during those years than in any other comparable period of time. Human beings killed each other, and destroyed things, with such serious application that the entire century bore a nightmare quality. Millions upon millions perished. Entire cities disappeared—and whole continents seemed shaken. At the end, millions of broken human beings returned to shattered homes—and only few really could remember what it had been all about. We were told it was all madness—as though that might serve as explanation. In fact, the tragedy deserves more of an accounting than that.

Surely it was a time of madness, but the unnumbered dead of the past century deserve something more than that simple affirmation. The work before the reader attempts to provide something of an interpretive story of that doleful time—its beliefs, its passions, and its temper. Amid all the other factors that contributed to the tragedy, there was a kind of creedal ferocity that made every exchange a matter of existential importance. The twentieth century was host to systems of doctrinal conviction that made unorthodox belief a capital affront, made conflict mortal, and all enterprise sacrificial. Such belief systems were predicated on moral persuasions so intense and inflexible that they could tolerate only an absolute unanimity of opinion within their sphere of influence. Nor was unanimity expected only in opinions held. Entire categories of human beings—conceived somehow "alien"—were condemned to destruction because of some indelible deficiency—membership in some offending economic class, or as product of a blighted biological provenance. Communities so circumstanced became jealous of their homogeneity, their infrangible unity. In such an environment, thought became "ideological," so that any opposition, no matter how temporary or trivial, appeared to threaten the extirpation of a faith, an insult to an entire manner of life.

The century saw the emergence of governments that charged themselves with the responsibility of governing lives in such fashion as to leave little to personal choice. Life was seen as willing service, implicit duty, spontaneous sacrifice, and selfless toil—and politics the infallible guide to it all. There were special books, written by special authors—that were to be venerated. There were Leaders, chosen by God or History—or both as one—who were Saviors, and Prophets, and All Seeing Sages. There were unitary political parties that were repositories of impeccable truth, sure science, and intuitive verities. There were guardians of it all—"vanguards," and "hierarchies," and "central committees," all equipped with answers to all the questions that have puzzled human beings since the beginnings of consciousness. And there were "New Men" who would people a redeemed creation.

In war and peace these political systems demanded more of their subjects than any other system of government in human memory. In war, there was a ferocity and an ardor rarely experienced. Millions gave themselves over to combat without reserve. Whole populations continued to fight when everything was lost. We have identified those systems so typified by a variety of names—as "dictatorships," as "despotisms," as "totalitarianisms," and sometimes, when passions somewhat abated, as "administered societies." Whatever the names given, there was something in such systems that was unique—that sometimes did not register among those who saw in them something "regenerative." That something was alive with a kind of fervor we have almost always identified with religion, spontaneous or institutional.

That is what this work has chosen to address: that clutch of ideas, identified as "political religion" that animates the systems considered. The presence of a political religion among all the other variables that shape events explains neither the history of those systems nor that of the twentieth century. The argument here is that the discussion of the role of political religion in such systems contributes to our general understanding of the complex period under consideration. The twentieth century was the product of so many contributing factors that no single insight could pretend to account for it all. The contention here is that a collection of beliefs, that share properties with the religions with which we have been familiar, operated in the twentieth century to make the contest of ideas and the challenge of arms more ferocious and destructive than they might otherwise have been.

We shall be concerned here with the history of such ideas. It cannot be an exhaustive history. That would exceed both the capacity of the author and the patience of the reader. Neither can it be a "true" account of the ideas of any of the authors to whom reference is made. It is not at all clear what the "truth" of any of the ideas of a political theorist might be—so many of their ideas defy any known process of confirmation. At best, what is attempted is to show that revolutionary leaders have referred to the work of political theorists and have drawn from that work certain implications. It is left to others to attempt to explain how and why ideas make human beings behave as they do—or in what circumstances such ideas become effective.

The work before the reader will attempt to deliver an account of the ideas that inspired many in the twentieth century, convincing them to live, to labor, to sacrifice, to obey, and to fight and die in their service. It will attempt to give dimension to the terrible tragedy of the twentieth century. It will be an account of secular faiths, bearing many names. It will speak of Marxism-Leninisms, of Fascism, and of National Socialism. Many have dealt with these ideologies as having the qualities of religion. It is hoped that this work contributes something to that important discussion.

A. James Gregor
Berkeley, California

Totalitarianism and Political Religion

CHAPTER ONE

Introduction

> The State is based on religion.... It is only when religion is made the foundation that the practice of righteousness attains stability, and that the fulfillment of duty is secured. It is in religion that what is deepest in man, the conscience, first feels that it lies under an absolute obligation, and has the certain knowledge of this obligation; therefore the State must rest on religion.... In this aspect, religion stands in the closest connection with the political principle.
> —Georg Wilhelm Friedrich Hegel[1]

Since time immemorial, thinkers have acknowledged, directly or indirectly, explicitly or implicitly, an intimate relationship between religion and politics. The relationship has not been characterized to everyone's satisfaction, but few have denied that it exists. Preliterate societies have rarely, if ever, attempted to consistently distinguish the sacred from the politically profane—and the fact is that the sacred and the political overlap in intricate fashion in the least, as well as in the most, advanced communities. In tribal societies, as in pharaonic Egypt and Imperial Rome, rulers were cloaked in the trappings of divinity. In modern times, the industrializing Japanese chose to imagine their emperors as linearly descended from the sun god.

[1] G. F. W. Hegel, *The Philosophy of History* (New York: Dover Publications, Inc.), pp. 50, 51; *Philosophy of Mind*, part 3 of *The Encyclopaedia of the Philosophical Sciences* (Oxford: The Clarendon Press, 2003), para. 552, p. 283; and *Lectures on the Philosophy of Religion* (London: Routledge & Kegan Paul, 1962), vol. 1, p. 102. Editors of Hegel's works in English have not consistently capitalized technical terms like "State," "Reason," and "Will" in their texts. The difficulty is, of course, not being able to identify their technical use. All nouns are capitalized in German, and in his narratives, Hegel never specifically signaled their technical use. Below, for the sake of consistency, technical terms will be capitalized throughout (even in English-language texts where they are not). The term "state" presents special problems. It is clear that Hegel spoke of a "proper" state that clearly required capitalization. The difficulty is trying to determine when he was speaking technically of the "Idea of the State" and when he was referring to the empirical states with which we are all familiar. To complicate the issue further, Hegel held that *all* states had something of the State in them, however transient and distorted—so that in speaking of states, one found embedded in them features of the State.

Among contemporary social scientists, there is easy talk of "civil religions," and "sacralized politics," by virtue of which politics in industrial democracies is imbued with some of the features of faith. Belief in the sacred is invoked to render business transactions more reliable, institutions more just, witnesses more truthful, and children more obedient. Belief in the divine prompts citizens to conform their conduct to public law, moral sanction, and collective conscience. Faith prompts individuals to sacrifice in the service of the community. Public ceremonies often take on the properties of worship, and things—flags, songs, and offices—become invested with special significance, requiring unusual deference and respect.

Although sometimes intricate and often inscrutable, the relationship between faith and politics in industrialized democracies is generally functional in character. In such environs, the profane allocation of responsibilities, for example, is often legitimated by invocations to one or another divinity through the swearing of oaths. Politicians speak, with easy familiarity, of "God," the "Almighty," and "Providence"—and their declamations are thereby held to be more binding.

Among citizens in industrial democracies, God is expected to provide stability and respect for law and common practice in peace, and protection and victory in conflict. All of which is advanced with sufficient imprecision to allow any and all citizens the freedom to choose their own divinity, as well as their own church affiliation. In general, "valid" laws are understood to somehow conform to some set of ill defined, but divine, enjoinments. All these forms of sacralization are readily recognized, granted, and, in general, considered benign, if not beneficent.

Conversely, throughout history there have been practices associated with sacralization that have been, and are, deplored: the ritual sacrifice of human beings to demanding deities; the insistence on absolute conformity to dogma; the attendant punishment of heresy; as well as the explicit or implicit call for the immolation of all that, and all those, considered offensive to powers transcendent.

It has been considered the unique accomplishment of the industrialized democracies to have rendered sacralization, at least in large part, inoffensive to modern sensibilities. Young men and women still imagine themselves directed by the Almighty to defend their countries with homicidal violence. Moral evil is still, more often than not, defined in terms of a decalog found in a revered text. Amid all that, individuals are allowed choices, and offenses to public morality and security are judged by regulations conceived fair rather than sacred. However it works, sacralization in industrial democracies is generally expected to contribute to the stability, promise, and predictability of organized society, redounding to the benefit of everyone.

Unhappily, over time, and most emphatically over the past two centuries, the sacralization of politics in modern settings has taken on ominous features. Since at least the end of the nineteenth century, political sociologists and theorists, in developing or industrialized countries, have chosen to identify a category of political movements and institutionalized systems of governance as "political religions."[2] Political religions are understood to be phenomena essentially peculiar, though not exclusive, to the twentieth century. Though secular in character, such "religions" are understood to share some properties of generic religion—properties conceived negative in import—fanaticism, intolerance, and irrationality.

Some contemporary political systems, industrialized or not, are avowedly religious—informed by legal systems that are dictated by revelation (a form of *jus divinum*)—in which, behaviors and systems of observances are prescribed in order to provide for collective and individual redemption and salvation. They are systems in which priests and prophets have an affirmed place. Such systems are overtly religious and license their political power through their candid and overt religiosity. Their populations are animated by faith, and infused by a sense of duty. Citizens perform individual and group rituals in order to evoke, maintain, and renew a sense of collective identity. The priests and prophets of such a system are the embodiments of an ineffable *charisma*, the proper recipients of adulation and unqualified obedience. "Islamic republics" are contemporary members of such a class.

All political systems, to some degree, feature at least some of those properties. As has been suggested, some of the symbols and rituals in industrialized democracies are treated with seemingly religious deference; presidents and political leaders in such systems certainly enjoy a measure of respect denied others. Nonetheless, analysts insist on the qualitative and quantitative differences between explicitly "politicized religions," as such, and the "civil religions"

---

[2] The nomenclature varies, but the content of the discussion is clearly recognizable. Some of the most illuminating discussion can be found in Gaetano Mosca, *Elementi di scienza politica* (Bari: Gius. Laterza & Figli, 1953), 2 vols., available in English as *The Ruling Class* (New York: McGraw-Hill Book Company, 1939), particularly chap. 7; see Gustave Le Bon, *The Crowd: A Study of the Popular Mind* (London: Ernest Benn Limited, 1952), particularly bk. 1, chap. 4; and Vilfredo Pareto, *A Treatise on General Sociology: The Mind and Society* (New York: Dover Publications, Inc., 1935), 2 vols., particularly vol. 1, chap. 4. Pareto's discussions concerning the relationship of religion to politics are engaging and instructive. Among the many modern and contemporary authors, the works of Emilio Gentile, *Politics as Religion* (Princeton: Princeton University Press, 2006); and Michael Burleigh, *Sacred Causes: The Clash of Religion and Politics, from the Great War to the War on Terror* (New York: Harper, 2006), recommend themselves.

of industrial pluralisms. There are clear differences between an unqualifiedly religious system that has assumed sovereign political power, and an industrial democracy animated by a "civil religion." There are manifest differences in allowable public conduct between religious systems that have assumed jealous political power and the systems that permit the religious pluralisms with which we are familiar.

What those differences imply for public policy and public conduct need not detain us here. For present purposes, it is important to acknowledge that there are also arresting qualitative and quantitative differences between avowedly religious systems, the civil religions of industrialized democracies, and the political religions of "totalitarianisms."

"Totalitarianism"[3] is a term that refers to a relatively distinct set of political arrangements that, while professedly secular, have an unmistakably religious cast. They are systems led by the inspired—those who are considered possessed of unassailable truths, as well as being invariably wise in calculation and correct in judgment. The leaders of such systems are spoken of as "charismatics"[4]—and generally assume leadership responsibilities for life. They are addressed, deferentially, as "The Leader," and their behaviors understood to fully embody the will of the community.

Of the movements they lead, each is infused by a faith that brooks no reservation or opposition; any suggestion of an alternative politics is abjured. In principle, such movements aspire to single party control. The aspiration is vindicated by a conviction that the charismatic leader and his party boast qualities that ensure flawless judgment and unmatched virtue. Obedience and sacrifice in the service of such leadership will assure the movement, and its party, merited success.

Because the instruments of special purpose, the movement, the party, and the state it constructs, conceive any opposition, however bland, to be indecent at best, and immoral at worst. Given the political environment of the totalitarian state, any opposition is held to be the product of either ignorance or malevolence—requiring alternatively reeducation or punishment.

---

[3] The literature devoted to "totalitarianism" is vast. Some of the more interesting examples, that are relatively easy to obtain, include Michael Geyer and Sheila Fitzpatrick, eds., *Beyond Totalitarianism: Stalinism and Nazism Compared* (New York: Cambridge University Press, 2009); Abbott Gleason, *Totalitarianism: The Inner History of the Cold War* (New York: Oxford University Press, 1995); Leonard Schapiro, *Totalitarianism* (New York: Praeger Publishers, 1972); and Ernest A. Menze, ed., *Totalitarianism Reconsidered* (London: Kennikat Press, 1981).

[4] Charles Lindholm, *Charisma* (Cambridge, Mass.: Basil Blackwell, 1990) is helpful in dealing with a difficult concept.

Animated by an irrepressible conviction regarding the rectitude of their cause, totalitarians feel compelled to marshal all others to their mission. Totalitarians tend to seek total control of all aspects of life lived and business conducted. Those ends are pursued through monopoly control of production and distribution, education and communication, as well as welfare and well-being. What results is a real or factitious sense of community—a seamless unity of all members of a body of believers—each prepared to obey and sacrifice in faithful service.

Clearly each such system differs in its particulars. Each leader will have unique properties; each movement its own belief system. Controls will vary in extent and intensity, and punishment in frequency and lethality. Nonetheless, the sense is that the twentieth century was host to a peculiar set of political systems that shared the general species traits of religious fundamentalism. They are not accounted religious. Many, if not most, claim to be antireligious and secular in principle. Many, if not most, disclaim interest in transcendent matters—in questions of immortality and final judgments. Nonetheless, the features of religion are unmistakable. Totalitarian systems are animated by "political religions"[5]—a concept with which the present discussion will occupy itself.

"Political religions" will be spoken of with the conviction that, in the course of discussion, the scope and reference of such a concept increasingly will become evident. The account will occupy itself with their intellectual origins, something of their history, as well as allusion to what is implied by their postures. In substance, the account will be, largely, an intellectual history of totalitarianism—as a peculiar political system that has taken on some of the distinguishing characteristics of what historically has been identified as religion—and which, because of the technological appurtenances of our time, has acquired the abilities to control, and shape to its purposes, entire, complex societies.

Ideologies

There are no generally accepted definitions for many of the most important terms, and their associated concepts, employed in studied social science discourse. Most terms are very loosely defined—but sufficiently understood

---

[5] Theologians have not succeeded in supplying a generally accepted definition of what a "religion" might be taken to be. In that, they are little different from intellectual historians or political theorists when they attempt convincing definitions of generally contested terms like "totalitarianism," "political," "democracy," or any number of other notions. For a discussion of some of the problems, see A. James Gregor, *Metascience and Politics: An Inquiry into the Conceptual Language of Political Science* (New Brunswick, N.J.: Transaction Publishers, 2003), chaps. 3, 4, and 8.

to allow a reasonably effortless exchange of ideas among the initiated. Thus, there are no generally accepted definitions for the terms "religion," "political," "democracy," or "totalitarianism." Nonetheless, we are perfectly comfortable speaking of "religion" as "that system of beliefs, together with those attendant rules and observances, dealing with things considered sacred." We speak of the "political" as any arrangement dealing with "the authoritative allocation of resources."

Certainly, such definitions leave a great deal to be desired. They are not sufficiently precise to rule out things seemingly, but not quite, the same. Such disabilities attend any effort at lexical definition of contested concepts. For present purposes, the intuitive sense of what "religion" or "politics" might mean is perfectly suitable. Much the same will be true of terms like "totalitarian" and "ideology." Their discursive treatment should make their meaning sufficiently transparent to support discussion.

Notwithstanding, some special attention here will be accorded "ideology"—to serve heuristic purpose in the discussion that follows. "Ideology," as a concept, will be forced to bear the weight of a number of distinctions important for any discussion concerning the relationship of religion to politics—when neither religion nor politics can be explicitly defined.

In social science exchanges, the term "ideology" is generally understood to refer to special formulations that, in their totality, are neither exclusively scientific nor religious. At the same time, it is held that ideologies may host elements of both. Unlike scientific products, and more like those of religion, ideologies entertain and advance moral judgments, recommendations, enjoinments, and imperatives. Unlike exclusively religious ideologies, secular ideologies make seemingly substantive scientific claims critical to their enterprise.[6]

As used here, the concept "ideology" covers all those theoretical formulations that pretend to explain the essence and workings of the world and the humans in it. Ideologies are variable in content and intent, but all imagine themselves delivering illuminating, and convincing, "perspectives on the world (*Weltanschauungen*)." Thus, we are accustomed to speaking of "religious," "Marxist," "racist," and "democratic" worldviews—and assume that each provides some comprehension of the world and its purposes different from any alternative. For any ideology to perform such tasks, it must contain at least three constituent claim components: empirical, logical, and normative. It must, in effect, share at least some of the major attributes of *science*.

Science is understood to deal with *empirical* claims—descriptive and predic-

---

[6] See A. James Gregor, *The Ideology of Fascism: The Rationale of Totalitarianism* (New York: The Free Press, 1969), chap. 1.

tive propositions about material "reality." In principle, we expect such claims to be subject to confirmation or disconfirmation by sensory evidence—simple and/or compound observations. In standard science, complex empirical propositions are threaded together by logical connectives and transformation rules in order to predict and explain events and features in the observable world. Of the logical connectives employed by science, it can be said the *logic* employed proceeds through valid forms to sound conclusion by virtue of explicit definition and rules of transformation. In part, scientific truth becomes a function of language itself. Mathematical truth claims fall into this category. One knows what constitutes a proof in mathematics, and validity in logic. Science has learned to map logicomathematics over the perceived world in order to render predictions possible.

It is intuitively clear that ideologies are both something less, and something more, than empirical and logical truth claims. While composed, in part, of empirical and logical claims, nothing in past history suggests that the falsification of any or all such claims would necessarily result in the renunciation of an ideology.

It is its *normative* character that clearly distinguishes ideology from science and establishes its affinities with religion. Normative pronouncements tender qualitative judgments—making attributions, for example, of goodness and beauty to things, behaviors, and experiences. Such pronouncements make claims for which no generally accepted truth conditions are available. In general, one simply does not know what evidence would provide the requisite warrant for the claim that a work is "beautiful," or a behavior "righteous." Unlike empirical and logical claims, such declamations are typified by emotive, imperative, and perlocutionary affect.[7] What they lack is empirical or logical license. It can be said that while ideologies, like science, make efforts to describe and explain the world, their principal function is to inspire transformative behavior—to prompt action. Their principal purpose is not to understand the world, it is to change it.

Ideologies, in effect, are very complicated artifacts. Curiously enough, those committed to one or another ideology spend surprisingly little time attempting to confirm or disconfirm its empirical claims. It would seem, for example, that by the twenty-first century Marx's followers would have established the empirical truth of the nineteenth-century claim that the "proletariat" has suffered "increasing emiseration" over time. And yet, no unequivocal confirmation has been forthcoming.

[7] "Perlocutionary" language involves speech that produces affect, and is expected to influence behavior and activity. See Gregor, *Metascience and Politics*, chap. 9.

In attempting to establish the truth of such a claim, for example, one is not certain who might count as a "proletarian." Nor is one equipped with a precise definition of what "emiseration" might imply, or how it might be measured. Given the vagueness and ambiguity, it is, in principle, impossible to confirm or disconfirm the truth of the Marxist insistence that the proletariat suffers increasing emiseration over time. None of that, in any way, seems to discourage Marxism's proponents.

The survivability of such formulations does not seem to depend on the logical or descriptive truth of its claims, but on normative affect. Ideologies are persuasive in ways other than logic and science are convincing.

Most founders of ideologies spend remarkably little time in trying to establish the truth of the empirical and logical components of their belief systems. National Socialist claims concerning the superiority and/or inferiority of one or another "race" defy confirmation. To pretend to establish the truth of such claims minimally requires a generally accepted definition of "race"—and some suggestion as to how "superiority" or "inferiority" might be recognized and measured. The failure to satisfy any of those requirements did little to diminish commitment by the followers of Adolf Hitler.

In fact, it has been the case that the proponents of one or another ideology will make every effort to avoid and/or obstruct attempts to determine the truth or falsity of any of its component claims. Some, for example, will specifically reject the standard procedures of confirmation or disconfirmation. There will be talk of a rejection of "bourgeois" or "Jewish" logic and science. Only the findings of "proletarian" or "Aryan" investigators could possibly be accommodated. Truth and untruth become hostage to methodological eccentricities.

In effect, it would appear that the formulation of empirical or logical truths is not the principal occupation of the ideologist. More than anything else, it seems that ideologies are formulations specifically designed to give expression to evaluative judgments—to prescribe and proscribe, to celebrate heroes and to deliver us from "monsters." Ideologies frame goal cultures for multitudes. They advance supportive and sustaining codes of conduct. At their best, "secular" ideologies are functional surrogates for traditional religion. Some ideologies appear as secular surrogates for religion because their advocates insist that the bulk of their constituent claims are empirical and/or logical. The majority of theological claims, on the other hand, are acknowledged to be "transcendental," intrinsically beyond the range of either empirical or logical evidence. Religious beliefs appeal to faith. Secular ideologists claim to be involved in an entirely different venture. They pretend to formulate and advance claims they hold "scientific."

Some have argued that the secular ideologies of our time, at least in part, are the result of the overall decline in faith, abandonment of belief in a world transcendent. With the commencement of the modern era there was a gradual, then increasingly accelerated, loss of faith in a supermundane reality. The Renaissance, the Enlightenment, and the advance of empirical science all contributed to the process. By the end of the eighteenth century, there were many who dismissed religious beliefs as superstition. At the same time, there were others who insisted that human beings could not be mobilized to collective purpose without appeals religious in character. What they proceeded to do was to put together belief systems that might serve in just such a capacity.

By the time of the French revolution, there were those who fabricated the requisite belief systems—which today are identified as "political religions." A political religion is a system of beliefs that rejects the notion that political power emanates from a divine source. Instead, a nation or its citizens are "sacralized" and made the repository of sovereign political power. Among later ideologists, there were those who were to recognize other sacralized bases of power: the state, a class, a race, or history itself.[8]

The most familiar of these modern ideologies insist on the absolute quality of the truths they dispense. Throughout the twentieth century, Marxists, Fascists, National Socialists, Maoists, and the followers of Pol Pot have all behaved very much as though possessed of revealed truth. They have behaved, in fact, as though they were communicants of a faith. They rarely, if ever, conceded difficulties in establishing the truth of their most fundamental claims; they poorly tolerated open inquiry; they dealt with any reservations concerning the truth of their claims as moral infractions; and they regularly treated those who attempted to reduce the vagueness and ambiguity of their pronouncements as heretics and apostates.[9] In effect, some of the major ideologists of the modern era have taken on the behavioral properties of the faithful—and the systems they construct, the institutional features of religious intolerance.

That there are no warranted sciences of metaphysics, universal ethics, or applied morality, is critical to present concerns. Throughout history, one of the most important functions of religion has been to explain the ultimate origin and goal of created beings—and thereby to specifically provide codes of

---

[8] See the entire discussion in Michael Burleigh, *Earthly Powers: The Clash of Religion and Politics in Europe from the French Revolution to the Great War* (New York: Harper Collins Publishers, 2005), particularly chaps. 1–6.

[9] The entire history of Marxism, as an ideology, is replete with instances of such treatment. There was not one major Marxist in the twentieth century who has not been charged with either heresy or apostasy. See the discussion in A. James Gregor, *Marxism, Fascism, and Totalitarianism: Chapters in the Intellectual History of Modern Radicalism* (Stanford: Stanford University Press, 2009), chaps. 3–7.

conduct, the grounds for moral judgment, the identification of infractions, the depiction of public purposes, as well as the prescription of individual and collective ends. When a subset of political ideologies expressly assumes such metaphysical and normative responsibilities, it can be spoken of as a "political religion."

It is important to recognize that some ideologies, however they characterize themselves, are essentially religious in character. They have assumed responsibilities that historically have been those of organized faith. Such ideologies, as a subset, pretend to the responsibilities of faith while, at the same time, concealing their expressly normative professions beneath the cover of economic, historical, biological, or philosophical "science." In traditional religion, enjoinments, injunctions, prescriptions, and proscriptions are warranted by appeal to sacred texts, revelations, epiphanies, and divinations. They are generally conceived binding because of the deep sentiments they inspire. However they choose to present themselves, political religions share many of the same features.

In many ways, traditional and political religions share properties. However disguised as exclusively empirical or logical, for example, political, like traditional, religions recommend, advocate, prescribe, and command behaviors. The agents in such systems almost always inspire awe, and the leaders, reverence. The systems strategically employ sign, symbol, and ritual—and the "truth" of doctrine rests on individual and collective faith. In both traditional as well as political religions, it is faith, not empirical or logical truth, which inspires loyalty, self-abnegation, commitment, and obedience.[10]

Political Philosophy and Political Religion

By the beginning of the nineteenth century the intellectual environment of Europe had been transformed. The Renaissance and the Enlightenment

[10] Most ethical systems, ideological or not, seem to ultimately appeal to self-interest—an interest for which no argument is necessary or required. Interest in one's self is unproblematic. In industrial democracies, the most palpable appeal is made to individual interests. Individuals are considered rational calculators prepared to negotiate in the pursuit of their concerns. They seek the best possible negotiable ends. Whatever normative elements animate such a process, they are self-affirming and unproblematic. One does not have to be convinced to seek a maximization of personal well-being. Appealing to personal interest, the allocation of benefits and the guidance of collective purpose is the result of negotiation between reasonable maximizers. The most fundamental claims that serve in the allocation of benefits or in the guidance of public purpose are made in terms of individual and collective interests that, in principle, can be measured and counted. When the most fundamental claims employed for such purposes cannot be so measured or counted, we are dealing with inscrutables that begin to take on the appearance of metaphysical claims that require grounds other than measuring or counting. These are the ideologies that attempt to warrant the political religions with which we are here concerned.

had altered cultural, religious, and political circumstances. In prior centuries, Christian Europe had held philosophy in thrall as its handmaiden—but by the seventeenth, philosophers pretended to intellectual independence. Thereafter, politics could no longer rest on indisputable religious truths but sought enabling principles.

In his time, David Hume (1711–1776) argued that once religion no longer provided the legitimating rationale for politics, political parties required some alternative. No political party could "support itself without a philosophical or speculative system of principles annexed to its political or practical one." He went on to suggest that the fabrication of such systems would result in their being "a little unshapely ... more especially when actuated by party zeal."[11] In effect, Hume intimated that the modern world had created conditions that gave rise to the need for ideological justification for political systems. Such alternatives would replace religion as the arbiter of collective purpose and as a guide to conduct. He had anticipated the advent of rationalizing ideologies and the birth of political religions.

More than that, Hume foresaw that such enabling speculative systems might well serve other than beneficent purposes. In his *History of England*, for instance, he spoke of circumstances in which "every man had framed the model of a republic; and however new it was, or fantastical, he was eager in recommending it to his fellow citizens, or even imposing it by force upon them"[12]—at disabling cost.

Hume was convinced that human beings were capable of fabricating "fantastical" systems, predicated on what were thought to be impeccable truths. He was equally convinced that in so doing they could hardly avoid gross error and moral infraction. He was prepared to argue that such secular surrogates of religious faith could only be flawed in substance and often deleterious in effect. He argued that there was no evidence that might confirm the infallibility of the truth claims of any system that human beings were prepared to invoke in order to influence conduct. His systematic skepticism was the ground of his tolerance, and of his common-sense humanity.

Hume's reasoned opinion was that *all* claims must be supported by best evidence—and that evidence changes with subject matter, time, and circumstance.[13] As a consequence, he held all claims to the possession of truth to be, in

---

[11] David Hume, *Essays Moral, Literary, and Political* (Indianapolis: Liberty Classics, 1985), pp. 465–466.

[12] David Hume, *The History of England, from the Invasion of Julius Caesar to the Revolution of 1688* (Indianapolis: Liberty Classics, 1983), vol. 5, p. 3.

[13] In dealing with basic epistemological issues, the English seemed prepared to be "commonsensical." Thinkers such as Francis Bacon and John Locke had early argued that the human mind somehow captured the properties of external materiality in sensory "representations"—to store

principle, contingent and corrigible. Tomorrow's evidence might well discredit today's truth. That he was tolerant followed from just such convictions. No truth could be so insulated from counterevidence as to be infallible. We forever must be prepared to abandon claims we believe true, and acknowledge the possible truth of claims we think false.

Hume was prepared to allow that in some domains of discourse it was difficult to establish truth or falsity with any conviction. Clearly, he felt that to be the case regarding matters of faith. At the same time, he was prepared to acknowledge that human beings gave evidence of needing faith in order to function properly. Thus, he was prepared to tolerate the general tenets of prereflective theism in the choice of individuals, but not their imposition on others. Hume held that because all belief systems are transient, none could be imposed, or impose itself, on others. Individuals should be free to follow the call of whatever faith—as long as it inflicts no harm on others.

His opinions fostered and sustained Hume's humanity. Given his skepticism, for example, he counseled against allowing a single dominant power to control a political system. No single agency could claim the right to impose its views on citizens. He recognized such a claim to undisputed control a self-evident threat to the free exchange of ideas, the freedom of choice, and the liberty of conscience. Hume proposed political arrangements composed of a number of independent, responsible authorities, each armed with the "right of lawful dissent"—in what is today identified as a pluralistic system of "checks and balances"—all animated by a civil religion.[14]

An argument can be made that such a view follows, at least in part, from an initial *individualistic* orientation peculiar to British empiricists. That is to say,

---

them in consciousness as "ideas." Humans would then employ reflective imaging and generalizations in order to formulate natural laws and predict material behaviors. All of that depended on best evidence, and was forever contingent. Attempts to understand a transcendent domain were left to the private reflections of individuals. British empiricism in general, and Hume, in particular, advocated a tolerant form of religious opinion that tends to be identified as deism—in which a "creator" was conceived initiating a law-governed system of things in which *persons* were destined to operate. It was a metaphysical system well adapted to the procedural democracy that is now identified with the politics of industrialized systems. See the interesting discussion in Bernard Bailyn, *The Ideological Origins of the American Revolution* (Cambridge, Mass.: Harvard University Press, 1967), particularly chaps. 1–3, 6.

[14] See the discussion in David Hume, *A Treatise of Human Nature* (Oxford: Clarendon Press, 1978), p. 564. For Hume, his *Treatise*, and his *An Enquiry Concerning the Principles of Morals*, served as the foundation of his political philosophy. His *Political Essays* (Cambridge: Cambridge University Press, 1994; edited by Kund Haakonssen) provides supplementary material that served Hume's purposes in attempting to make political discourse less divisive and sectarian. In the *Political Essays*, Hume speaks of the tolerance of diverse opinion, and of dispersing power throughout the political system.

British empiricists argued that at the very commencement of the search for truth, *individuals* observed external things—things that were solid and shaped, and which behaved in regular fashion. The epistemology of British empiricism was eminently "commonsensical."

On the Continent, things were fundamentally different—and political philosophy followed a different trajectory.[15] Again, epistemology lay at the center of concern; but there, a different pattern of argument was forthcoming, in part, out of specific philosophical developments[16]—and, in part, the result of the intense religious dialogue that engaged the attention of all.

In asking how human beings might come to know the essentials of an "external world," a world of "natural phenomena" that existed independent of human consciousness—and how one was to construe the relationship between the physical and the mental—Continental epistemologists followed a course different from that pursued by their colleagues across the Channel. The difference was partially the result of a special preoccupation among Continentals with how all of that was related to an omniscient, omnipotent, and omnipresent Creator.[17]

By the nineteenth century, that was the context in which all of Europe was prepared to systematically (i.e., philosophically) address theological and confessional controversies. The entire century was to be buffeted by questions that were inherently epistemological—yet not exclusively empirical or logical. One set of those questions turned on what a secular understanding of the reality of the world might be. Another attempted to deal with the supposed knowledge of an "other-worldly" domain that was supersensual and transcendent. Science was to grow out of the one, and modern theology out of the other. The distinction between the two was not always clear.

In general, philosophers on the Continent dealt with these matters in their own fashion. If epistemological pursuits were governed by common sense in the British Isles, that could hardly be said of ruminations on the Continent.

---

[15] Some have argued for a kind of Anglo-Saxon "exceptionalism"—with the English intrinsically "individualistic" and "libertarian." Rather than English empiricism giving rise to individual rights, individual rights gave rise to epistemological empiricism. See Alan Macfarlane, *The Origins of English Individualism: The Family, Property, and Social Transition* (Oxford: Blackwell, 1992).

[16] These included the opposition of the "rationalists" (Rene Descartes [1596–1650] and his followers) to British empiricism (Thomas Hobbes [1588–1679], John Locke [1632–1704], and David Hume [1711–1776]). In his *Lectures on the History of Philosophy* (New York: The Humanities Press, Inc., 1955), vol. 3, pp. 220–222, Hegel identified the works of Descartes and Locke as among the original sources of the metaphysics of his time.

[17] Frederick Copleston, *A History of Philosophy: Modern Philosophy* (Garden City, N.Y.: Doubleday and Co., Inc., 1960), vol. 6, provides a summary account. In this context, see Hegel's discussion with respect to Descartes in *Lectures on the History of Philosophy*, vol. 3, pp. 250–252.

Against the British empiricists, Immanuel Kant argued that among humans, all the complex cognitive activity of perception, representation, calculation, and judgment took place in an arena he identified as the "Transcendental Unity of Self-consciousness." *Consciousness*, rather than *persons*, was the touchstone of his system.

It became the case that many Continental thinkers commenced their inquiries not with individuals, but with consciousness. Consciousness was life's most immediate reality; "external things" were understood to be the result of consciousness collecting and organizing *phenomena* into universals, categories, sets, subsets, and variants. Without consciousness there could be neither "subjective" nor "objective" experience. Without consciousness, there could be neither "self" nor "other." There would be neither selves nor things. Our notions of self and the external world, it was argued, are constructed out of the immediacy of consciousness. *Idealism*, the conviction that the ultimate reality of existence, as well as the ground of knowing, was consciousness, had demonstrated a philosophical persistence on the European Continent.

For epistemological idealists, consciousness is the very substance of that which we claim to know. By commencing with that which we know with certainty—consciousness—we come to know the "external" world as its derivative. By starting from where we are—as consciousness—we begin to fathom how the "external world" is constructed out of its given elements. It was argued that we first create the world and then find ourselves in it. We discover that the world is *logical* because our consciousness is logical. We discover that the world is *mathematical* because our consciousness is mathematical. We discover traces of ourselves everywhere in the object world because *we* are its architect. Whatever we distinguish as "subjective" and "objective" within our experience, is the product of distinctions made in mind. The externalities of which we speak, the "things" and "processes" external to "us," are all possessed of the qualities of mind, and distinctions drawn in mind. German idealism thus understood the fabric of the world, in perhaps both ontological as well as epistemological senses, to be "spiritual" in essence, sharing all the fundamental properties of mind.[18]

In idealism, modern epistemology moved from the representative semirealism of Hume and Locke—that conceived individual selves observing an object world—to a constructive subjectivism—in which selves, in some sense or another and in communion, shaped their common world. Absolute idealism

---

[18] See Johann Gottlieb Fichte, *The Science of Knowledge* (London: Truebner & Co., 1889), as representative of this persuasion. When the term "mind" refers to the philosophical substratum of things, it will be capitalized.

arrived at an intellectual posture in which both the world and the thinking self were understood to be, in some substantial fashion, constructs of an inclusive, universal intelligence: Mind, Absolute Reason, or Absolute Spirit. It was no longer conceived that there were two orders of being—ideas and things, mind and matter—but rather, that all were one in Mind or Spirit.

In and through Spirit all the qualities of mind and matter were to be explained. Spirit enjoyed explanatory priority over the realms of nature and individual consciousness. Through sustained analysis, that conscious subjectivity with which philosophical idealism began, resolved the "externalities" of the "object" into an infinite consciousness, a pure "Idea." At that point all the various categories of unspirituality and imperfect spirituality were progressively subsumed, or sublated (*aufgehoben*), into Spirit as universal Purpose, as Absolute Idea, as infinite Mind—the ground of all possible Being.[19] It would be a comprehensive interpretation of experience; its object, the Whole, the Absolute, or God; its medium, thought; and its method, "totalistic" and "dialectical."[20]

Several things, important for present purposes, require emphasis. Granted that everything in the world displays the qualities of mind, it was equally evident to epistemological idealists that the world, even as we know it in the most ordinary sense, is much too grand, and much too complex, to be the product of any one *finite*, or any collection of finite, minds.

We regularly and systematically share intelligence with others, and they understand our logic, and our mathematics, and the regularities we record—through which, we come to know "reality." In some meaningful sense, we *all share a common consciousness*; we are *individual, particular*, only as members of some kind of vast *universal*. We are all, in some profound sense, *one*. We all share in some kind of epistemological and/or ontological cosmic consciousness that is anything but remote or mystic—since we participate in it every day. In every day of our lives we share in a complex, remarkable, and universal intelligence. We share a unity in *thought*. For absolute idealists, empirical individuals, and personal consciousness, are secondary, derivative of a larger Consciousness.

Out of that larger Consciousness, we proceed to fashion not only objects, but ourselves as well—persistent phenomena that manifest themselves according to rule, and which, on successive occasions, we can reidentify, count, and measure. In this recurrence of both ourselves and objects in time, we implicitly and explic-

[19] In this context, see the discussion in Hegel, *Philosophy of Mind*, para. 377 and *Zusatz*, together with paras. 379–381.

[20] Empirical science, as we understand it, would not be the "science" of which Hegel speaks. The "standard" science known to students is a product of understanding. It is not the "Total Knowing" to which Hegel addresses himself.

itly acknowledge a shared consciousness.[21] Out of such elements, and out of those issues, Georg Friedrich Wilhelm Hegel was to produce a system of reflections that were to shape the political and religious thought of the nineteenth and twentieth centuries. It was a system that spoke of "totalities," and of the "subsumption" of individuals into all inclusive "universals." It was a body of thought Hegel would leave as legacy to the revolutionaries of the nineteenth and twentieth centuries.

Georg Friedrich Wilhelm Hegel (1770–1831)

In the effort to trace the evolution of political religions in the modern period, some political theorists and intellectual historians have identified Hegel as one of the major inspirations of the intellectual rationale serving their advocacy, initiation, and cultivation.[22] If Hume, and the British empiricists, were advocates of pluralistic civil religions, Hegel and German idealists have been identified as the inspiration behind political "sacralization," and totalitarian political thought.

Of course, there have been political religions innocent of, or dismissive of, Hegelianism. Nonetheless, the system is instructive insofar as it provides considerable insight into what would make an ideology functionally suitable as a secular political religion in the twentieth century.

In itself, Hegelianism is an all but impenetrable philosophical system, for which there is no single universally accepted interpretation, much less an acknowledged roster of all its real or fancied social or political implications.[23] What will be attempted here will be the provision of an account that identifies a constellation of ideas prominent in the thought of Hegel that consistently or episodically appear in those ideologies of the twentieth century currently considered political religions. However incomplete or selective the account, it is not intended to be untrue to the complex beliefs left us by Hegel. It will be an attempt to make a plausible case for the pragmatic suitability of those beliefs as components of a totalitarian rationale.[24]

---

[21] For a convenient discussion of these themes, see Josiah Royce, *The Philosophy of Loyalty* (New York: Macmillan, 1918), part 1, chap. 1. A technical exposition can be found in Hegel, *The Phenomenology of Mind* (London: George Allen & Unwin Ltd., 1971).

[22] Karl Popper, *The Open Society and Its Enemies* (New York: Harper & Row, 1963), 2 vols.; L. T. Hobhouse, *The Metaphysical Theory of the State: A Criticism* (London: George Allen & Unwin, 1960); and Sidney Hook, "Hegel Rehabilitated?" and "Hegel and His Apologists," in Walter Kaufmann, ed., *Hegel's Political Philosophy* (New York: Atherton Press, 1970), pp. 55–70, 87–108.

[23] So complex and so impenetrable is his work that Josiah Royce could insist that "concerning Hegel . . . it is extraordinarily difficult to get or to give any general impressions that will not be seriously misleading." Josiah Royce, *The Spirit of Modern Philosophy: An Essay in the Form of Lectures* (New York: Houghton Mifflin Company, 1892), p. 190.

[24] There is no intent, here, to deliver a philosophically adequate version of Hegelianism. There have been many attempts at delivering just such a narrative, and by almost all accounts, there is no

In all of this, many of the issues involved turn on matters epistemological—on what is to count as *true* in any serious exchange. Empirical science, ideologies, traditional and political religions—all occupy themselves with claims to truth.

For Hegel, *true* knowledge was an exclusive product of Reason (*Vernunft*)—rather than the result of some process of empirical verification. Coming to *truly* know is a philosophic process involving an intricate analysis of the central properties of mind.[25]

For Hegel, serious philosophical inquiry reveals a world that, in its inmost essence, is *thought*—"thought which is at home with itself, and at the same time embraces the universe . . . and transforms it into an intelligent world."[26] That intelligible Reality, Hegel argued, has all the qualities of consciousness, and all the potentiality of Spirit.[27] It follows that Mind, rather than matter, was understood to be the essence of truth as well as the foundation of ontological Reality.[28]

Several things emerge from this special line of reasoning. Even in the most elementary knowing, knowing involves incorporating what is known into some more inclusive category. We begin to come to know ourselves only when we know ourselves as human, and we know ourselves as human only when we know ourselves as members of a subspecies, species, and genus. Coming to know particulars is a function of their seried inclusion in suitable categories—"universals." And we cannot truly know anything, Hegel argues, until what we know is lodged in an ascending series of subsumptions terminating in an all-inclusive Absolute Mind (or Spirit)—for Absolute Spirit was conceived "underlying all possible being and the world."[29]

Within such a conception, however difficult to immediately comprehend, Hegel argues that what ordinary thinking considers individuals or particulars cannot be fully appreciated, nor can empirical individuals achieve cognitive,

---

single rendering that satisfies all specialists. As far as Hegel's *true* political intentions, I will leave that for others to determine. There are competent attempts to find a more liberal purport in his writings. See, for example, the discussion in Herbert Marcuse, *Reason and Revolution: Hegel and the Rise of Social Theory* (New York: Humanities Press, 1954), part I; Shlomo Avineri, *Hegel's Theory of the Modern State* (New York: Cambridge University Press, 1972); Avineri, "Hook's Hegel," and Z. A. Pelczynski, "Hegel Again," in Kaufmann, *Hegel's Political Philosophy*, pp. 71–79, 80–86.

[25] Hegel's exposition of the "logic" of the world is found in his *Science of Logic* (London: George Allen & Unwin, Ltd., 1929), 2 vols.

[26] Hegel, *Lectures on the History of Philosophy*, vol. 3, p. 546.

[27] For that reason, Hegel could speak of his entire enterprise as a "theodicy," a vindication of God's attributes as they are manifest in the world. See ibid., and *The Philosophy of History*, p. 457.

[28] "In finite mind there is only the beginning of [a] return which is consummated only in absolute mind . . . in its absolute truth." Hegel, *Philosophy of Mind*, para. 381, Zusatz, p. 12. Consult the entire paragraph for a representative instance of Hegel's general treatment.

[29] J. N. Findlay, "Foreword" to ibid., p. x.

or "true reality," until *subsumed* under an appropriately inclusive universal.[30] In the pedestrian world of everyday affairs, what that meant to Hegel was that collectivities enjoy precedence over particulars, families over members, and religions over communicants. In terms of the specific world of politics, it meant that States enjoy precedence over individuals.[31]

The philosophically "proper State . . . consists in the thoroughgoing unity of the universal and the single." The State is an instrumentality for human beings who recognize themselves not as self-seeking individualists, but moral agents. As such, only the State could create the environment in which the individual would attain a "genuine individuality, and an ethical life"—for it is "the individual's destiny to live a universal life"[32]—and it is only the State, subsuming the individual, that affords the appropriate circumstance.[33] Only the unity and universality extended by the State provide the conditions in which individuals might realize the fullness of self—the satisfaction of life's ethical imperative.

In contradistinction to Hegelianism, the liberalism of the nineteenth century spoke of the authority of the state as the consensual result of cautious contract, entered into to afford security. The contract was a cautious one, because within liberalism, state authority was always understood to constitute a potential threat to the natural rights of the individual.[34] In explicit opposition,[35] Hege-

---

[30] The technical account of this process is advanced in Hegel, *The Phenomenology of Mind*.

[31] The theme of the subsumption of the individual to the universal is constant throughout Hegelianism. In discussing political constitutions, for example, Hegel spoke of the "really living totality" of the State as involving two "notions," those of *individuality* and *universality*, and characterized their proper relationship, in a proper State, as one of the *subsumption* of the former under the latter. Within the proper State, the individual is subsumed under the family, the corporation, religion, and the nation. See Hegel, *Philosophy of Mind*, para. 541, p. 269, and *Philosophy of Right* (Oxford: Clarendon Press, 1942), para. 258, p. 156. The entire sections on "Civil Society" and "The State" in *Philosophy of Right* recommend themselves.

[32] See the discussion in Hegel, *Philosophy of Mind*, para. 541, pp. 269–270. Hegel argued that many states were far from "proper States"—being simply mechanical means for maintaining a minimum degree of peace and stability.

[33] "The rational end of man is life in the state." Hegel, *Philosophy of Right*, para. 75, addition 47, p. 242.

[34] "'Liberalism' sets up . . . the atomistic principle, that which insists upon the sway of individual wills; maintaining that all government should emanate from their express power, and have their express sanction. Asserting this formal side of Freedom—this abstraction—the party in question allows no political organisation to be firmly established." Hegel, *The Philosophy of History*, p. 452.

[35] One need only read Hegel's Preface to his *Philosophy of Right*, and his last work on the English Reform Bill, to appreciate the grave reservations he entertained concerning what is today identified as "liberalism." As a consequence of his convictions, Hegel saw England as a political community in which "institutions characterized by real freedom" were notable in their absence. Hegel, *The Philosophy of History*, p. 454. He identified those who speak so grandiloquently of the defense of individual or "people's" rights as being advocates of "selfishness," bearing on their brow a "hatred of law,"

lianism understood the proper State to be a greater being, the more inclusive being, agent of a superpersonal Spirit in whom individuals, by escaping their narrow interests, find their fuller, more positive selves.[36] To accomplish that, individuals, as members of a proper State, are educated to "true," rather than "formal" or "subjective" freedom.[37] Instead of seeking the "natural freedom" of which liberalism spoke, members of a proper State found true freedom in fealty, obedience, and steadfastness. For Hegel, true freedom involves positive acts of self-determination, acting in conformity with one's most fundamental interests—and, because of his conception of the State, true freedom is achieved in obedience to law and authority, in compliance with collective norms,[38] and in committing oneself to productive purpose in the service of the community.[39] True freedom is to labor diligently to meet collective needs,[40] to extend succorance to others, to enhance agriculture and industry,[41] and to sustain and enhance the fabric of that rational life that is the State. In effect, true freedom is living an ethical life—satisfying the requirements of the moral idea—which can only be accomplished within the parameters of a proper State.

For Hegel, the self-realization of human beings as fully moral was possible only within the arrangements of a proper State. He understood the State to be "the organization and actualization of moral life," supplying the necessary conditions for the realization of one's full humanity.[42] As individuals we can only

---

seeing it only as a "shackle" on personal liberties—entirely incapable of recognizing in obedience to law the actuality of their very Freedom. Several things would seem to follow from such convictions. Hegel dismisses the notion that society and/or the State might be the consequence of a voluntary contract entered into by individuals living in "freedom" in the state of nature. "The error which first meets us is the direct contradictory of our principle that the State presents the realization of Freedom; the opinion, viz., that man is free by *nature*, but that in *society*, in the State—to which nevertheless he is irresistibly impelled—he must limit this natural freedom." Ibid., pp. 40–41.

[36] See Hegel, *The Philosophy of History*, pp. 439–441.

[37] "The Idea of the State in modern times has a special character in that the State is the actualization of freedom not in accordance with subjective whim but in accordance with the concept of the will, i.e. in accordance with its universality and divinity." Hegel, *Philosophy of Right*, para. 260, addition 154, p. 280.

[38] "Obedience" to law, we are told, "is itself the true freedom, because the State is a self-possessed, self-realizing reason—in short, moral life." Hegel, *Philosophy of Mind*, para. 552, p. 287.

[39] Hegel regularly alludes to production, including machine manufacture, for the satisfaction of individual and collective needs. See Hegel, *Philosophy of Right*, paras. 190–196, pp. 127–128.

[40] Hegel argues that there is no place for idlers in the proper State. Hegel, *The Philosophy of History*, p. 423.

[41] Hegel, *Philosophy of Right*, para. 204, p. 132.

[42] "The State is the actual existing realized moral life. For it is the Unity of the universal, essential Will, with that of the individual; and this is 'Morality.'" Hegel, *The Philosophy of History*, p. 38; see Hegel, *Philosophy of Mind*, para. 552, p. 283.

participate in meaningfulness, in reason, and purpose, by becoming one with the greater union that is the State. In that union, in its rational purpose, we find freedom and moral direction.[43]

More than that, Hegelianism argued that Spirit, in its articulation, employed States to its purpose. "Spirit," Hegel argued, "not merely broods *over* history as over the waters, but lives in it and is alone its principle of movement. . . . For Spirit is consciousness. . . . [and] Reason is in history."[44]

History, for Hegel, is "mind clothing itself with the form of events."[45] History is the story of the sequences involved in that complex and protracted process of the dialectical workings of the Absolute. The workings of the Absolute involve the lives of individuals and collections of individuals, both in time and at immediate levels of experience, as the "unconscious tools and organs of the world mind at work within them." History, in effect, is the record of God's work in time. "The History of the World, with all the changing scenes which its annals present, is [the] process of development and the realization of Spirit."[46]

When Hegel spoke of history, he did not pretend to occupy himself with the provision of an accurate chronicle of deeds, events, or states of society. He spoke neither as historian nor sociologist. He identified what he was doing as outlining a "philosophical history of the world"—an account that rested on his antecedent philosophical analysis—demonstrating that "the Idea is in truth, the leader of peoples and of the World; the Spirit, the rational and necessitate will of that conductor, is and has been the director of the events of the World's History." He went on to affirm that the intuition that "Reason is the Sovereign of the World; that the history of the world . . . presents us with a rational process" may be "a hypothesis in the domain of history as such, in that of philosophy it is no hypothesis. It is there proven by speculative cognition."[47] Thus, while it seemed evident that he thought that his history of the world would

---

[43] See *Philosophy of Mind*, para. 382, pp. 15–16. The concept "Freedom" serves as a technical term in Hegelianism, and requires some degree of explication, but it seems clear that possessed of its own dynamic, infinite and unconstrained in its proceedings, Spirit, as Mind, is uniquely characterized by Freedom.

[44] Hegel, ibid., para. 550, p. 281.

[45] Hegel, *Philosophy of Right*, para. 346, p. 217.

[46] Hegel, *The Philosophy of History*, p. 457. "The spiritual and the natural universe are interpenetrated as one harmonious universe, which withdraws into itself, and in its various aspects develops the Absolute into a totality, in order, by the very process of so doing to become conscious of itself in its unity, in Thought. Philosophy is thus the true theodicy . . . a reconciliation of spirit, namely of the spirit which has apprehended itself in its freedom and in the riches of reality." Hegel, *Lectures on the History of Philosophy*, vol. 3, p. 547.

[47] Hegel, *The Philosophy of History*, pp. 8, 9. Hegel insists that his thesis "has been proved in Philosophy," and was to be "here regarded as demonstrated." Ibid., p. 10.

provide plausible grounds for maintaining the truth of his central convictions concerning the role of Spirit in the life of humanity, Hegel directed his audience to his professional philosophical exposition for a *compelling* demonstration. He was convinced that he had delivered himself of an impeccable, metaphysical "Truth."

For Hegel, history is the necessary story of the passage of Absolute Mind in the world,[48] attired in the livery of nations, actuated by the State, and employing individuals as conscious or unconscious instruments.[49] Totally unaware of the more comprehensive design to which their actions contribute, most human beings pursue their interests and their claims with full volition and application. Only time reveals the true meaning of those actions—in the working out of universal History. It is only then, that it becomes clear that they have served the ends of Reason.

The course followed is necessary because guided by the inflexible dialectic of Reason[50]—and peoples and nations are the vessels, because only they can serve as host to the proper State. Individuals, singly or in communion, become its agents because only they can operate mechanically in the empirical world.

Beyond that, Hegel held that at critical junctures in history, some peoples, nations, and individuals serve as the primary movers of events. They find themselves at transformative intersections in the history of humankind—and while individuals dutifully serve the proper State with self-sacrifice and devotion,[51] the obligation to properly serve becomes particularly urgent at just those times. For a proper State, clothed in the garments of nationhood, is particularly "moral—virtuous—vigorous" when it is engaged in the realization of the "grand objects" of the World Spirit.[52] So occupied, it serves as a "vehicle for the contemporary development of the collective Spirit in its actual existence; it is the objective actuality in which that Spirit for the time invests its Will." Hegel

---

[48] "The History of the World, with all the changing scenes which its annals present, is this process of development and the realization of Spirit." Ibid., p. 457.

[49] While history is made by peoples and States, it is individual human beings, pursuing the passions, private aims, and the satisfaction of personal desires that constitute the effective springs of action. Peoples and States make history through the active energy of individuals who, in serving their own interests, fulfill the concealed purpose of Spirit. All actions, including world-historical actions, culminate with individuals as subjects giving actuality. They are the living instruments of what is in substance the deed of the world mind. Hegel, *Philosophy of Right*, paras. 344–348, pp. 217–218.

[50] For Hegel, Spirit, through Reason, was the "sovereign of the world," and "that the history of the world ... presents us with a rational process." He argued that "Spirit [is] the rational and necessitated will ... the director of events of the World's History." Hegel, *The Philosophy of History*, p. 8.

[51] Ibid., p. 30.

[52] Ibid., p. 74.

goes on to tell us that "against this absolute Will the other particular minds have no rights: *that* nation dominates the world"—and chosen individuals emerge as special deputies of the World Spirit. They make entrance on the scene as "World Historical Individuals," acting out the ultimate purposes of Reason.[53]

Those Great Men, chosen by History, are the representatives of their age; they are harbingers of a coming time. They often sense the magnitude of their responsibilities, and more often than not, intuit the spirit of a people and the temper of a nation. Moved by conviction, such men "may treat other great, even sacred interests, inconsiderably; conduct which is indeed obnoxious to moral reprehension. But," Hegel continued, "so mighty a form must trample down many an innocent flower—crush to pieces many an object in its path."[54]

Given the rationale, it is evident why those individuals who serve the Will of the World Spirit in the creation of new states, or who shape them in accordance with the ripeness of time, should be called "heroes of the epoch," or "World historical" figures. Nor is it difficult to understand why such individuals, occupying "a higher ground than that on which morality has properly its position," cannot be measured by ordinary standards of good or evil. "The deeds of great men, who are the Individuals of the World's History," can only be measured against "that intrinsic result of which they were not conscious." In effect, and in that measure, the conduct of the Heroes of History is beyond ordinary good and evil. We are told that the responsibilities and obligations that attach to the behaviors of ordinary mortals do not apply to such individuals. Ordinary moral claims do not bind them; those sorts of claims are irrelevant when "brought into collision with world historical deeds."[55]

It would seem that circumstances would have it that all must be prepared to perish before the march of those whose actions embody the Will of the World Spirit. For the World Historical Individual, it may appear that he is prepared to treat individuals as no more than means to ulterior ends. Yet that is only apparent. Ultimately, Hegel argues, all men share in the ultimate purpose, no matter their particular assessment of events, nor the price they must pay in its accomplishment. In the final analysis, all are participants in what Hegel identifies as "the cunning of Reason"—that cunning that harnesses the passions and the behaviors of all to the realization of its purpose.

All of this is found in the body of thought that Hegel left his heirs. It embraced a vision of humanity and its world so seductive that there were few in

---

[53] Ibid., p. 29; see *Philosophy of Right*, paras. 350–352, p. 219. Hegel warns such nations and such individuals that when such special periods run their course, the "universal Will steps forward . . . and delivers [them] over to its chance and doom." Ibid., para. 550, p. 281

[54] Hegel, *The Philosophy of History*, p. 32.

[55] Ibid., p. 67.

the nineteenth century who entirely escaped its influence. It was a vision of humanity and its world that cast its spell over the cultivated audiences of the most advanced industrialized and industrializing countries. Part of its fascination arose out of the aura of religion that hung about it. It is not clear, to this date, that its influence has entirely dissipated.

Hegelianism as Political Religion

In such a worldview, Reality—in nature and history—is the product of Spirit. For Hegel, Spirit, as the Absolute, becomes the creative source of all there is. Spirit creates and sustains Being—which, over time, articulates itself, into a universal of particulars. Spirit as the ground of Being, is the universal into which, in the final analysis, particularity finds completion. Spirit is the universal in which all particulars find their origin, as well as their immediate, and anticipate their ultimate, Being—all of which is essentially a philosophical theology.

Hegel never attempted to conceal the fact that his professional philosophy gave expression to all the categories of Christian faith. He held that the knowledge that found expression as feeling and faith in religion, found reasoned articulation in his philosophy. He told his audience that "the object of religion as well as philosophy is eternal truth,"[56] and that "philosophy is itself, in fact, worship; it is religion."[57] For Hegel, there was a form of thinking that systematically resolved itself into a totality which incorporated both philosophy and religion.[58]

In his mature system, it was evident that Hegel's conception of *Geist*, Mind or Spirit, was the lineal descendant of the Holy Spirit of Christianity. Mediated by the metaphysical world of idealism, Hegel saw the history of Spirit as the story, in time, of the Absolute—that infinite intelligence that is the existential universal of which we are all inextricably part.[59] For Hegel, the Absolute is the substance of our individual, transient being.[60] With the least reflection, we come to intuit the infinite Being behind the finite semblance.[61] It is an awareness that has lain at the foundation of religion since time immemorial.[62] For

---

[56] Hegel, *Lectures on the Philosophy of Religion*, vol. 1, p. 19.

[57] Ibid., pp. 20, 21, 26, 33, 43.

[58] Ibid., p. 19. In his early "Fragment of a System," for a variety of technical reasons, Hegel still entertained the reservations that found expression in his injunction that "philosophy...has to stop short of religion." By the time of his full maturity, however, it was clear that no such reservation was entertained.

[59] Ibid., pp. 23, 24, 30, 53.

[60] One of the better discussions of this reflection is found ibid., pt. I, sect. 3, 2.

[61] See Hegel's "Lectures on the Proofs of the Existence of God," ibid., vol. 3, pp. 155–367.

[62] See ibid., vol. l, part l, c,2, pp. 61–73.

Hegel, the figurative concepts of "God" and "infinity" affirm something of the nature of the Absolute we all sense—however dimly.[63]

Hegel engages his audience in an enterprise calculated to reveal something of the Absolute that governs all things. At the very commencement of his discussion of Universal History, Hegel argued that in order to come to know anything of the Absolute, one at least must first discern "the abstract characteristics of the nature of Spirit"; that would be followed by an account of the "means Spirit uses in order to realize its Idea"; and finally, he would speak of that "shape which the perfect embodiment of Spirit assumes—the State."[64] In effect, Hegel sacralized the State, made History its medium, and human beings its instruments. All of that constitutes the rationale on which Hegel rests his identification of the State as "divine," as possessed of "majesty and absolute authority."[65] In effect and in all its essentials, Hegelianism was a political religion.

For Hegel, the Spirit, in the process of its fulfillment, employed the State—marshalling human activity to its service. For Hegel, the State was the Spirit objectified—"Mind on earth (*der Geist der in der Welt steht*)." As such, in the course of its articulation, the Spirit manifested itself as the State.[66] The State, in turn, in calling individuals to its purposes, afforded them the opportunity for their full maturation as moral agents. Hegelianism was a doctrine designed to provide the criteria governing moral choice and the measure of ethical conduct.

The State as the embodiment of Spirit is a universal, composed of individuals as time and circumstances find them. In order to achieve the purposes of Spirit, the State must synthesize, "sublate," particular persons—enlisting their energies—making them one with the State—thereby conscripting them to the service of Spirit while enhancing, rather than diminishing, them.

It was in the State that individuals discovered the entirety of "that which is just and moral," for that could only be determined by recognition of the qualities of Spirit. And it was only in the State that individuals might attain that knowledge "through the forming process of education."[67] Its very nature

---

[63] "Spirit . . . exists only as activity; that is to say, in so far as it posits itself, is actual or for itself and produces itself." Ibid., vol. l, p. 74.

[64] Ibid., vol. I, p. 17.

[65] See the discussion in Hegel, "Preface" to *Philosophy of Right*, pp. 1–13 and para. 257, pp. 156, 157.

[66] For Hegel, the concept State embodies in it an awareness of the development of Spirit as the result of a necessity "already contained, in an ideal manner, in the germ and is brought forth by the germ itself, not by an alien power." In accounting for the articulation of Spirit, as State, in historic time, Hegel appealed to an explanatory principle that "involves . . . the existence of a latent germ of being—a capacity or potentiality striving to realize itself." Hegel, *Philosophy of Mind*, paras. 377, 379, pp. 1 and 5; *The Philosophy of History*, p. 54.

[67] Hegel, *Philosophy of Right*, para. 270, p. 165. Hegel was always careful to insist that the State and

requires that the State not only maintain individuals as citizens, securing their rights as actuality, promoting their welfare, protecting their families, but educate them to an awareness of their most fundamental interests, guiding each of them away from the exclusivity of self-interest, carrying them back into the moral life of "the universal Spirit."[68]

The State, as the Mind or Spirit objectified, in order to discharge its fiduciary obligations, must educate citizens to their obligations. That could only involve drawing out of each a "capacity to feel one with the Whole"—commencing with the primary family and concluding with the State—with morality rooted in "a feeling, a consciousness, and a will, not limited to individual personality and interest, but embracing the common interests of the members generally." It was only by acquiring that inward sense of sentiment and understanding that individuals could appreciate the reality of what Hegel identified as the "essential, independent, intrinsically universal Will" that should govern all of humanity's behavior.

Only that appreciation affords the requisite knowledge of "what Right really is." "Right" we are told can only be established by the abstraction "from inclination, impulse and desire as the particular; i.e., we must know what the Will is in itself.... What the Will is in itself can be known only when these specific and contradictory forms of volition have been eliminated."[69] And only in the conditions institutionalized by the fully formed, modern State can one abstract from the personal inclinations, impulses, and desires of individuals and determine what the true Will, in itself, might be.

It was that argument that rendered "the State ... the actuality of the ethical Idea"—for it was only within the State that "the particular self-consciousness," through the availability of security, property, and education, is raised "to consciousness of its universality."[70] That given, Hegel could then plausibly argue that it was only as a member of a proper State that the individual might rise to the possibility of a truly ethical life. The State, the agent of the Spirit's "self-actualization," is the means of human ethical fulfillment.

For Hegel, given its imputed essence, and its historic role, the State is conceived the embodiment of the "divine will, in the sense that it is Mind present on earth, unfolding itself to be the actual shape and organization of a world."[71]

---

religion shared identical responsibilities in that regard. Again, there is the distinction of the empirical "state" and the ideal "State." Empirical states often, if not inevitably, fall far short of the Ideal State. See the discussion in Hegel, *Lectures on the Philosophy of Religion*, vol. 1, pp. 247–258.

[68] Hegel, *Philosophy of Right*, para. 270, p. 165; *Philosophy of Mind*, para. 537, p. 264.
[69] Hegel, *The Philosophy of History*, pp. 42, 442.
[70] Hegel, *Philosophy of Right*, paras. 257, 258, pp. 155, 156.
[71] Ibid., para. 258, p. 156.

He goes on to argue that "since the State is Mind objectified, it is only as one of its members that the individual himself has objectivity, genuine individuality, and an ethical life. Unification pure and simple is the true content and aim of the individual, and the individual's destiny is the living of a universal life. His further particular satisfaction, activity and mode of conduct have this substantive and universally valid life as their starting point and result. Rationality, taken generally and in the abstract, consists in the thoroughgoing unity of the universal and the single."[72]

For Hegel, the modern State was "the totality of human life so far as it is the life of moral beings united in a community by tradition, religion, [and] moral convictions."[73] Under the superintendence of the State, educated to their responsibilities through the family, the church, and their participation in those "corporations" that minister to their material interests, individuals attain their fullness as human beings in Reason and Freedom—for to obey the State each obeys his or her most fundamental interests.[74]

The State proper, "in the form of an organic whole," is "thus the embodiment of rational freedom." It is "the totality—the soul—the individuate unity"—in which "it is not the isolated will of individuals that prevails; individual pretensions are relinquished, and the general Will is the essential bond of political union."[75]

Thus, Hegel could insist that in his "obedience to the laws of the State, as the Rational element in volition and action . . . man is free, for all that is demanded is that the Particular should yield to the General."[76] Possessed of such understanding, any rational person would choose morality and freely yield to the general Will.

Given those convictions, Hegel goes on to argue that "the State is the true form of Reality. In it the true moral Will comes into the sphere of Reality, and Spirit lives in its true nature."[77] Behind the specialized vocabulary, it is clear that Hegel was prepared to assign the State the responsibility of satisfying all of humankind's traditional religious needs.

---

[72] Ibid., paras. 257, 258, pp. 155, 156. Hegel argues that to achieve humanity, personality, individuals must be part of a collective, a family, a guild, a church. In them, individuals are inured to the responsibilities of collective life. Through such means "the State obtains as its members individuals who are already moral (for as mere *persons* they are not) and who, united to form a State, bring with them that sound basis of a political edifice—the capacity to feel one with a Whole." Hegel, *The Philosophy of History*, p. 42.

[73] Translator's Notes, Hegel, *Philosophy of Right*, note to para. 267, p. 364.

[74] See the discussion in Hegel, *Philosophy of Mind*, paras. 514, 515, 517, pp. 254, 255.

[75] Hegel, *The Philosophy of History*, pp. 46, 47.

[76] Ibid., p. 423. In the *Philosophy of Mind* we are told that the "good" is "the not particular but only universal of the will." Para. 509, p. 251.

[77] Hegel, *Lectures on the Philosophy of Religion*, vol. 1, p. 246.

Given his views, Hegel was convinced that philosophy and religion pursued the same purpose, were animated by the same energies, were made up of the same content, and were both occupied with knowledge of eternal Truth and infinite Being. Both spoke of the origins of the world, of its purpose, of humanity's place therein, and the moral obligations that flow out of that appreciation of Reality.

While religion might assume a special character and form, and faith may have its source in one's "deepest personal being," rather than detached reflection, philosophy was, nevertheless, "identical with religion." That allowed Hegel, with perfect consistency, to argue that the essence of the proper State is to be found in religion.[78] That which could be said of political philosophy, and the proper State, could, with equal cogency, be said of religion.

Thus Hegel avers that "in religion man is free before God; in that he brings his will into conformity with the divine Will, he is not in opposition to the supreme Will, but possesses himself in it." Given the identity of religion and philosophy, Hegel proceeds to maintain that there is, in fact, "but one conception of Freedom in religion and the State."[79] If conformity in the one meant Freedom, conformity in the other could mean no less.

"True religion," Hegel maintained, "sanctions obedience to the law and the legal arrangements of the State—an obedience which is itself the true Freedom, because the State is a self-possessed, self-realizing Reason—in short, moral life in the State."[80] So convinced of all that was he, that Hegel celebrated the fact that in post-reformation Europe "obedience to the laws of the State, as the Rational element in volition and action, was made the principle of human conduct. In this obedience," he insisted, "man is free."[81] The modern State, for Hegel, was "the actuality of concrete Freedom."[82]

These were the notions Hegel left as an inheritance to the intellectuals of the nineteenth century. It was a political religion so complex and obscure that it has produced a multiplicity of equally plausible, if widely variant, interpretations. There were the interpretations of "old Hegelians," "young Hegelians," and "neo-

---

[78] Ibid., 1, pp. 19, 20, 21, 33, 43, 54. "In a general sense, religion and the foundation of the State are one and the same; they are in their real essence identical." Ibid., p. 247.

[79] Ibid.

[80] Hegel, *Philosophy of Mind*, p. 286.

[81] Hegel, *The Philosophy of History*, p. 423.

[82] Hegel, *Philosophy of Right*, para. 260, p. 160. "The State is the actually existing, realized moral life. For it is the Unity of the universal, essential Will, with that of the individual; and this is 'Morality.' The individual living in this unity has a moral life; possesses a value that consists in this substantiality alone." Hegel, *The Philosophy of History*, p. 38. Freedom, for Hegel, was "nothing but the recognition and adoption of such universal substantial objects as Right and Law, and the production of a reality that is accordant with them—the State." Ibid., p. 59.

hegelians." There were those who devoted their time to an analysis of Hegel's religious convictions, others to the political implications of his account, and still others to his notions about anthropology. There were "radical" Hegelians, and "conservative" Hegelians. There were revolutionary Hegelians and reactionary Hegelians. Whatever they were called, or called themselves, they each understood Hegelianism in remarkably different fashion.

None of that is in dispute. What serves our purposes is the fact that with all the advantage of hindsight, there are identifiable components, however contested their interpretation, which fed into the political radicalism of the nineteenth and twentieth centuries. There was Hegelianism's studied rejection of the political liberalism that had grown out of that individualism and empiricism that had accompanied the British philosophical tradition. There was the haughty dismissal of uncertainty that typified much of that tradition. Much was made of the possession of "Truth"—and the obligations attendant upon that possession. There was much consequent talk of selflessness, sacrifice, duty, and obligation in a "new morality." There was the invocation of a sense of mission, and allusions to the purposes of "History," and the conception that human beings served as unknowing instruments of occult purposes. There was that "Will" that was the will of everyone—and then there were the "Heroes" of history, who fashioned states and made wars, and whose personal behaviors escaped the judgment of their peers. And there was the fact that all of it was wreathed in sentiment and faith, delivered in an account crowded with the expectation of the appearance of charismatic champions who would lead peoples and who would create new worlds—all couched in the language of matchless Truth, insistent morality, and religious conviction.

It was not so much a question of who interpreted Hegelianism correctly; it was more what might be fabricated out of its elements. Hegelianism, for all its impenetrable complexity, was so replete with stimulating fragments of thought, rich asides, and profound insights, that many in the nineteenth and twentieth centuries found their inspiration there—an inspiration that had about it more than a little of the liturgical quality of religious confession.

CHAPTER TWO

Hegelians after Hegel

The new philosophy... takes the place of religion and has the essence of religion within itself. In truth, it is itself religion.
—Ludwig Feuerbach[1]

Our religion does not involve a church, because it is more than that. It is a religion unconfined; it is the substance of our very lives.
—Moses Hess[2]

During the first half of the nineteenth century in Europe, philosophical, theological, and political issues came together in combustible mixture. After 1814, with the close of the Napoleonic period, conservatives sought to unscramble the results of the French revolution and Napoleon's shuffling of Europe's political, and by implications its social, arrangements. The efforts at restoration never really were successful, but they did provoke the response of "progressives."

From 1815 until the death of Hegel in 1831, all of Europe was restive. In France, the July revolution of 1830, in and of itself, was convincing evidence of that. In Germany, the entire period of disquiet opened with the Wartburgfest of 1817, signaling, as it did, the dissatisfaction of young intellectuals with the lack of national unity and political freedom. The Carlsbad decrees of 1819—that proscribed the activities of German student organizations, imposed supervision on intellectual life, and censored print communication—did little to placate those who sought greater political expression.

Throughout Germany there was agitation for a constitutional order that might promise greater protection for property rights as well as possibilities for the expression of popular opinion. The young Hegel shared in the sentiment. Some of his early writings have survived in which he praises the English system of taxation, advocates a reasonably well defined penal code, and recommends that government institutionalize a distinction between legislative and juridical

[1] Ludwig Feuerbach, *Principles of the Philosophy of the Future* (New York: The Bobbs-Merrill Company, 1966), para. 64, pp. 72–73.

[2] Moses Hess, *Die europäische Triarchie*, in *Philosophische und sozialistische Schriften 1837–1850* (Berlin: Akademie Verlag, 1961), p. 112.

functions—postures that, at that time, could only be identified as "liberal."[3] In 1802, at Jena, he authored "The German Constitution," an essay that remains perhaps the most liberal of his political reflections.[4]

Hegel, a student of philosophy with generous interests in history, politics, economics, and religion, having emancipated himself from prevailing Protestant orthodoxy, remained preoccupied with religious issues, focusing on the relationship between doctrinal beliefs and the social and political setting in which they articulated themselves. Throughout his life, a combination of religious and political interests was central to his work.

As Hegel matured, and the political, economic, and social conditions in Germany changed, his convictions became increasingly more traditional—and, in a significant sense, more conservative. By the time of his death in 1831, there were young scholars, directly or indirectly his students, who had begun to find themselves uncomfortable within the confines of the thought of the Master. The Bauers, Bruno and Edgar, Arnold Ruge, David Friedrich Strauss, Max Stirner, and Moses Hess were counted among them—to be joined, in time, by Ludwig Feuerbach.

The Young Hegelians

During the years between the Congress of Vienna and the death of Hegel, Germany had undergone significant change. The number of relatively independent patrimonial estates within the German Empire diminished from some three hundred to about thirty-seven—all reasonably well organized political entities, allowing varying degrees of popular representation. In many, case law was largely abandoned in the courts, to give place to a system of rational codes. By that time, a tariff union had been negotiated for all of Germany, and industry, based on the discoveries of applied science, gained a foothold and had begun to expand—particularly in the nation's west. Polytechnic institutions were founded and material interests jostled those of the "spirit."

In the course of all that, the church was seen by many as a critical collateral support of a state system increasingly perceived as unresponsive. As a result, those who sought reform of the state often directed their criticisms toward the church. More vulnerable than the state, the church, as an institution, became the object of searching and sustained criticism by a "progressive" minority. The

---

[3] See Shlomo Avineri, *Hegel's Theory of the Modern State* (London: Cambridge University Press, 1972), chap. 1; and T. M. Knox, "Hegel and Prussianism," in Walter Kaufmann, ed., *Hegel's Political Philosophy* (New York: Atherton Press, 1970), pp. 14–21.

[4] "The German Constitution" is found in G. W. F. Hegel, *Political Writings* (Translated by T. M. Knox. London: Oxford, 1964).

perhaps unintended consequence of such criticism was to undermine the substantive unity of the Hegelian legacy. For Hegel, political, philosophical, and religious convictions constituted a principled unity. His immediate followers explored its disaggregation.

For Germany's political reformers, the persistent demand for political liberty and protection for civil rights was left unsatisfied—with institutional religion conceived a benighted support of the unenlightened system, an opponent of progress and liberty. In effect, Germany's young Hegelians were rapidly moving away from anything that resembled the religious and political ideal embodied in the mature philosophy of Georg Wilhelm Friedrich Hegel.

By the time he wrote *The Philosophy of Right*, Hegel's political preferences were for a Prussia, ruled by a progressive monarch, administered by a class of efficient bureaucrats, who together would "universalize" a civil society of estates. Hegel anticipated that Germany's rulers would unite all the particular interests found among citizens into an abiding harmony. His preferred community would be one infused with, and sustained by, religious belief,[5] possessed of a sense of brotherhood, in which all dichotomies would be resolved.

It was to that vision of organized political life that some of Hegel's students raised objection. The fusion of religion and politics left many discomfited. There was a disposition to consider religious belief as somehow intellectually primitive. Less than rational, housed in state-supported institutions, religious beliefs seemed to represent everything that "progressives" held to be retrograde in a Germany undergoing fundamental change. They undertook searching criticism of the rationale upon which religious doctrine was predicated. They pursued a fundamental review of Hegel's assessments of the intrinsic character of religion and its relationship to right reason, philosophy, and the state. By the mid 1830s, those numbered among the Young Hegelians—while still considering themselves Hegelians—had begun to entertain increasingly anticlerical, antireligious, and antiauthoritarian opinions.

Among them, some were to have immediate impact on the intellectual convictions of the period. David Friedrich Strauss (1808–1874), disillusioned in his efforts to provide a rational basis for his Christian convictions, published his *Leben Jesu* (*The Life of Jesus*) in 1835. His book went a considerable distance in reducing to fable, myth, and metaphor the historicity of the Christian Gospels. Bruno Bauer, in turn, undertook a more rigorous critique of the evidentiary foundations of the Bible. By 1840, the entire enterprise had become a scandal.

---

[5] "Although the aspects of Religion and the State are different, they are radically *one*; and the laws find their highest confirmation in Religion." Hegel, *The Philosophy of Religion* (Translated by J. Sibree. New York: Dover Publications, Inc., 1956), p. 449.

The criticism of religion clearly had political implications, and was accompanied by a kind of provocative and inflammatory pamphleteering. By that time the "progressive" critics of Hegel were more and more frequently denounced as atheists and subverters of the state. They were no longer counted as "Young," but as revolutionary, or "Left," Hegelians.[6]

For the present account, it is important to note the Hegelian continuities found in the work of the immediate posthegelians. That the synoptic Gospels were the product of mythmaking and trope, shaping the consciousness of a community still immersed in Old Testament tradition, is less meaningful than the fact that Strauss understood Christianity to be the phased consequence of historical development.

To understand Christianity required comprehending each of its stages, cumulatively revealed as a sequence of empirical events. Strauss continued to understand history as the purposeful record of human behavior. In his *Die Christliche Glaubenslehre in ihrer geschichtlichen Entwicklung* (*Christian Teaching in Its Historical Development*),[7] published in 1840, Strauss argued that history is a record of the conquest of the human spirit over the recalcitrance of matter.

Within the chronicle of events recorded in conventional studies, philosophy reveals a meaningful pattern of conquest by the human spirit—radiating out over wider and wider reaches of social and political life. Events are arbitrary, their informing pattern is not. Taken together events are seen as constituents of a rational totality.

The immediately effective agent of such development is community, in each of which individuals function as unconscious bearers of maturing ideas. Personal interests become components of larger purpose in what is understood to be a complex dialectic of human maturation.

What appeared evident to most contemporaries was the fact that, throughout his critical writings, Strauss remained Hegelian insofar as his criticism of institutional religion was not intended as a renunciation of religion, as such. Rather, he was convinced that those cultural, legal, and political views that offended the sensibilities of the young Hegelians might be rendered more progressive by changes in the collective appreciation of religion and its role in history. For Strauss, ultimately, his critique of religion became its *humanization*;

---

[6] One of the better accounts, in English, of Left Hegelian thought is found in Sidney Hook, *From Hegel to Marx: Studies in the Intellectual Development of Karl Marx* (Ann Arbor: University of Michigan Press, 1962), together with the translation of Karl Loewith, *From Hegel to Nietzsche: The Revolution in Nineteenth-Century Thought* (Garden City, New York: Doubleday and Co, 1967), Part 2.

[7] The entire title is *Die Christliche Glaubenslehre in ihrer geschichtlichen Entwicklung und in Kampf mit der modernen Wissenschaft*.

he sought to render religion and philosophy less abstract, more directly applicable to human concerns. He wished to emphasize the connection of religious thought, and its philosophical analysis, to the existing circumstances of Germany in the throes of systemic change.[8] Germany was expected to change as its attitudes toward organized religion changed in the face of criticism. These were the themes, with variations and increasing emphasis, which were to recur among young Hegelians.

How infectious the criticism of institutional religion had become by the beginning of the 1840s is evident in the history of the work of Bruno Bauer (1809–1882), initially a conservative detractor of Strauss—ultimately to become a critic of what he interpreted as Strauss' theoretical timidities. Bauer was to undertake an intense methodological and substantive criticism of Strauss' work, not to defend the integrity of the Gospels, but to expose their lack of substance.

Bauer's *Kritik der evangelischen Geschichte der Synoptiker* (1841–1842) was a direct assault on the historical credibility of the synoptic Gospels—and a denial of the very historicity of Jesus. Thus, while Strauss could remain a Christian, however critical, Bauer could not. The incontrovertible implication of his position was antichristian—and if one consistently applied his method, one could only conclude with atheism.

From there, Bauer embarked on a profusion of "critical" studies of intellectual history—concluding with the conviction that Europe was on the cusp of a new era—that the very poverty of its cognitive efforts demonstrated that the Continent was scheduled to cede its dominance to another. For Bauer, epochs of transition evidenced a disintegration of political power, and a collapse of social mores. He saw in the Europe of his time all the earmarks of systemic involution. It had exhausted itself in insoluble contradictions. In true Hegelian fashion, he conceived "history" as having revealed all that. History had followed its ineluctable course, leaving revelatory traces in its wake.

However destructive his criticism of method and substance, Bauer forever retained his faith in history.[9] Like many of Hegel's students, Bauer looked to history to reveal something of humankind's ultimate reality. History, of all inquiries, was the source of Bauer's understanding of his times. This was so much in

---

[8] In 1845, Marx and Engels complained that "*real humanism* has no more dangerous enemy in Germany than *spiritualism* or *speculative idealism*," which fails to draw out *practical inferences* from speculations. Strauss was clearly considered one of the offenders. See Karl Marx and Frederick Engels, *The Holy Family or Critique of Critical Criticism,* in Marx and Engels, *Collected Works* (New York: International Publishers, 1975), vol. 4, p. 7; and Engels, "Rapid Progress of Communism in Germany," ibid., p. 240.

[9] See the summary account in Loewith, *From Hegel to Nietzsche*, pp. 107–108.

evidence that the young Marx, in his contemporary criticism, complained that Bauer had made "*history* . . . a person apart, a metaphysical subject in which the real human individuals are merely the bearers." Bauer, Marx complained, spoke of "history" as a self-conscious agent who would not be thwarted or "mocked." History, for Bauer, had "purposes" and advanced "truths."[10] History, the measure of time, in some inscrutable sense was transcendent; it was purposive; it possessed truths; it had cosmic goals to which individual lives were made subject; it had the critical traits of divinity; it was sacralized.

Like Strauss, and with many Hegelians, young and not so young, Bauer saw history, as divine subject, providing critical insight into the world. To so conceive history was a disposition that was widely shared by those who had learned philosophy at the feet of Hegel. One among them, who was to leave an indelible mark on the thought of the nineteenth century was Ludwig Feuerbach—"son of Hegel and father to Marx."[11]

Ludwig Feuerbach (1804–1872)

Until his thirtieth year, Ludwig Feuerbach[12] remained on the margins of the politics of his time. Born in 1804, he was seventeen when Hegel published his *Philosophy of Right*—which many consider his most conservative political treatise. Shortly thereafter, in 1824, Feuerbach became Hegel's student at the University of Berlin—where he was an ardent and dutiful disciple. Until as late as 1835, irrespective of some reservations, Feuerbach was to vigorously defend Hegel against "liberal" criticism.

By the middle years of the 1830s, Feuerbach had become convinced that critical thought had the responsibility of applying its insights to the immediate and practical problems of contemporary humanity. By that time, he was prepared to allow that Hegel's thought had been largely passive and retrospective—concerned with a kind of other-worldly reality to the exclusion of concrete application. Feuerbach sought to offer insights that were prospective in intent—in order to address immediate social and political problems and help shape the future of humankind. In 1839, he published his "Critique of Hegelian Philosophy"—signaling a measure of dissatisfaction with the system.[13] Two years later, as part of

---

[10] Marx and Engels, *Holy Family*, p. 79.

[11] As quoted in William B. Chamberlain, *Heaven Wasn't His Destination: The Philosophy of Ludwig Feuerbach* (London: George Allen & Unwin, 1941), p. 16.

[12] For useful summaries of Feuerbach's role in the evolving discussion, see Loewith, *From Hegel to Nietzsche*, pp. 69–80; and Herbert Marcuse, *Reason and Revolution: Hegel and the Rise of Social Theory* (New York: The Humanities Press, 1954), pp. 267–273.

[13] See the convenient summary in Werner Schuffenhauer, *Feuerbach und der junge Marx: Zur*

his general criticism of Hegelianism, he published his revolutionary critique of institutional religion, *The Essence of Christianity*[14]—to open a new, and potentially more revolutionary, chapter in German philosophy. In 1843, he sought to systematize his thought in his *Principles of the Philosophy of the Future*.[15]

Moved by the circumstances in which Germany found itself, surrounded by articulate critics of the "old philosophy," animated by the conviction that he was morally obliged to attempt to lift real burdens from real human beings in the real world, Feuerbach sought to redeem Hegelianism—by making it applicable to the world endured by ordinary mortals. Rather than dismissing the legacy of the immediate past, he saw his "new philosophy" as a way of achieving nothing less than "the realization of Hegelian philosophy"—just as he was to consider his critique of theology to be its fulfillment.[16]

The imperative that fueled Feuerbach's efforts was the "humanization" of Hegelianism—to make the system more responsive to human needs. He came to the conviction that to accomplish that involved making Hegelian thought relevant to the world human beings experienced in daily life. He sought Hegelianism's reform; and that turned on his conviction that he had discovered the "secret" that made of it an airy, detached abstraction—a body of thought that had little to say to the vast majority of suffering humankind. Feuerbach saw Hegelianism as a system whose announced purpose was the liberation of humankind—but which not only manifested itself as arcane, profuse, and impenetrably complex, but aloof as well.

In his effort to restore Hegelianism to its purpose, Feuerbach sought to bring it down to the level of ordinary people and things—to have it abandon its solitary preoccupation with uncertain concepts and abstract reasoning. Feuerbach sought to restore reality to the evanescence of Hegel's philosophy by "inverting" its conceptual language. To accomplish that, he proposed a critical review of all the pretended "realities" that stocked Hegel's philosophical universe.

The "Absolute" and "Spirit" were but two of Hegel's essential realities. Among a host of others, there was "Consciousness"; and there was "Reason" as well. Other diaphanous notions alienated those who tried to read Hegel's works. Feuerbach reasoned that something was fundamentally wrong with any exposition that only succeeded in confounding the understanding of those most well disposed.

Entstehungsgeschichte der marxistischen Weltanschauung (Berlin: VEB Deutscher Verlag der Wissenschaften, 1965), pp. 12–19.

[14] Ludwig Feuerbach, *The Essence of Christianity* (Translated by George Eliot. New York: Harper & Brothers, 1957).

[15] Feuerbach, *Principles of the Philosophy of the Future*.

[16] Ibid., paras. 20, 21, p. 31.

As a solution, Feuerbach suggested that one reflect on some of Hegel's pivotal notions—"Consciousness" and "Reason," for example. What immediately becomes evident, he maintained, is that "consciousness" does not stand alone. It is a *predicate*, a property, of something. "Reason" is a *predicate*, a property, of something. There is no "consciousness" or "reason" independent of an accommodating *subject*. He counseled his readers, that "[we] must always restore predicates to their proper subject, to render subjects, objects—thereby inverting speculative philosophy to reveal the pure, unvarnished truth."[17]

"The essence of the *Logic* of Hegel," Feuerbach argued, "is human thought made transcendent, set outside man." A real property of real people had been "reified"—rendered a subject in its own right—to subsist in abstraction beyond the world of ordinary thought.[18] "Thought," however, "is not the subject of itself," he continued, existing in an illusory, immaterial world, "but a predicate of a real being."[19]

"Where words cease," Feuerbach continued, "life first begins, and the secret of being is ... disclosed." Being is found in "particularity and individuality"—only particular individuals or things possess predicate properties—properties that define being. Those properties are sensed and distinguish themselves from thought. Whatever consciousness we have of being, Feuerbach reminded his readers, "is indeed always and necessarily bound to a definite content." Feuerbach concluded that before "being" became the Being of Hegel's Absolute, it referred to some determinate set of sensory events—"for the essential characteristic of an objective being, of a being outside thoughts or the imagination, is sensation."[20]

Somehow, Feuerbach insisted, human beings lost the awareness of the sensory, material reality of their lives and experience.[21] They became party to their own alienation and dehumanization. They became aliens in a world of their own unconscious creation.

---

[17] Feuerbach, "Vorläufige Thesen zur Reform der Philosophie," *Sämmtliche Werke* (Leipzig: Voss Verlag, 1846), vol. 2, p. 246. Karl Marx had read Feuerbach's works while still a student (see Marx's letter to Feuerbach, 11 August 1844, in Ludwig Feuerbach, *Briefwechsel* [Leipzig: Philipp Reclam, 1963], p. 183). In his preparatory work for his dissertation, Marx maintained that "common thought always has abstract predicates ready which it has separated from the subject. All philosophers have proceeded to render such predicates subjects." See Karl Marx, "Vorarbeiten zur Disseration," in Karl Marx, Friedrich Engels, *Gesamtausgabe: Historisch-Kritische Gesamtausgabe Werke/Schriften/Briefe* (Berlin: Marx-Engels-Verlag, 1927), vol. I, bk. 1, p. 119.

[18] Feuerbach, "Vorläufige Thesen," *Sämmtliche Werke*, vol. 2, pp. 246, 247.

[19] Feuerbach, *Principles of the Philosophy of the Future*, para. 51, p. 67.

[20] Ibid., paras. 7, 29, pp. 9, 44, 45. We are told that "being after its removal from all the essential qualities of the objects is only your conception of being—a being that is made up and invented, without the essence of being." Ibid., p. 42.

[21] "The new philosophy regards and considers being as it is for us, not only as thinking but as really existing beings ... as the being of the senses, perception, feeling, and love." Ibid., para. 33, p. 52.

What is evident in all of that is the fact that given these maturing convictions, Feuerbach's reform of Hegelianism inexorably led him to an uncertain form of epistemological materialism. The truth of all of Hegel's concepts were understood to originate nowhere else than in human life and experience. At the root of all the arcane architecture of Hegel's world—the reality of all the unreal phantoms that populate humankind's philosophical imagination—one finds human sensory experience. For Feuerbach, "only that is real, at least for man, that is an object of true and real activity."[22] The truth and reality of the world is in a life lived.[23] It is not consciousness that gives rise to life, but life to consciousness.[24]

For Feuerbach, the very evidence of being, the consciousness of existence, originates in sensory experience. By the time he wrote *Principles of the Philosophy of the Future* in 1843, he could affirm with confidence, that "the real in its reality ... is the sensuous. Truth, reality, and sensation are identical"—and the "substratum" of all that is *matter*.[25] Feuerbach's reform of Hegelianism seemingly had led him to a pedestrian form of realism.

Feuerbach appears to have been prepared to argue that we experience a material reality through sensation—and in the course of that experience consciousness formulates, and further experience confirms, truth claims. While "the secret of immediate knowledge is sensation,"[26] the truth of that immediate knowledge rests on some sort of intersubjective verification. Feuerbach argued, "[T]hat which I alone perceive I doubt; only that which the other also perceives is certain." Thus, by the time he published his *Principles*, Feuerbach appears to have settled on a criterion of truth that involved sensation as primary to a subsequent framing and tendering of truth claims—all subject to intersubjective confirmation. "The community of man with man," he contended, "is the first principle and criterion of truth and generality. The certainty of the existence of other things apart from me is mediated for me through the certainty of the

---

[22] Ibid., para. 25, p. 23.

[23] "A being that is not distinguished from thought and that is only a predicate or a determination of reason is only an ideated and abstracted being; ... in truth it is not being. ... If a mere determination of ideas constitutes the essence of being, how should being be distinguished from thought?" Ibid., para. 24, pp. 38, 39.

[24] "I do not generate the object from the thought, but the thought from the object; and I hold *that* alone to be an object which has an existence beyond one's own brain." Feuerbach, *The Essence of Christianity*, p. xxxiv.

[25] Feuerbach, *Principles of the Philosophy of the Future*, para. 32, p. 51. "The essential characteristic of an objective being, of a being outside thoughts or the imagination, is sensation. ... The image of this being apart from thought is matter—the substratum of reality." Ibid., paras. 7, p. 9 and 29, p. 45. The "[new philosophy] generates thought from the *opposite* of thought, from Matter, from existence, from the senses." Feuerbach, *The Essence of Christianity*, p. xxxv.

[26] Feuerbach, *The Essence of Christianity*, para. 38, p. 55.

existence of another human being apart from me."[27] True knowledge is a function of a sensory life lived in communion.

One commences with individual "sensuous perception," the elements of which are integrated into a common, "primary" observational language. That language serves as the foundation of those generalizations in thought[28] necessary to the descriptive and predictive claims of empirical science. The intersubjective confirmation or disconfirmation of those claims turn, once again, on direct or indirect perception.[29]

Feuerbach argued that all those gossamer "realities" found in the pages of Hegel's works were actually projections of just such a life sensed and abstracted—human properties and perceived phenomena made conceptual "realities"—lodged in featureless logical space. Feuerbach insisted that Hegel had employed some sort of word magic to make of human properties creatures in a world that transcended mortal experience. For Feuerbach, that was the "secret" of Hegelianism.

Feuerbach argued that to explain the process employed would be to appreciate the fact that Hegel's entire philosophy was a desperate attempt to make rational a system of religious beliefs that rested exclusively on blind faith and artless imaginings. In fact, Feuerbach's critique of Christianity, in his *Essence of Christianity*, was predicated on that conviction together with his argued analysis of Hegel's "secret."[30]

Feuerbach maintained that Hegel provided substance to religion by taking human properties, rendering them abstract, and projecting them upon imagined divinities beyond the reach of human observation. In the process, finite human reason became transcendental, omniscient Reason—and simple human awareness became cosmic Consciousness. Hegel took the fact that human beings occupy finite space—and projected that property into conceptual space, where it became a poorly conceived divine Omnipresence occupying *all* of space. In the course of all of this, human properties were diminished by comparison; as God was enhanced, humanity dwindled.

Feuerbach was equally convinced that "only in man's wretchedness does God have his birthplace. . . . God is what man would like to be."[31] In a clear sense, Feuerbach argued that religion and philosophy, at least in significant measure, were appeals for compensation on the part of human beings because of felt

---

[27] Ibid., para. 41, p. 59.

[28] "[Man] has relation to the object first through the senses, i.e., passively, before defining it in thought." Ibid., p. xxxv.

[29] Feuerbach, *Principles of the Philosophy of the Future*, paras. 43, 48, pp. 60, 64–65.

[30] See his letter to Otto Wigand, 5 January 1841, in Feuerbach, *Briefwechsel*, pp. 140–144.

[31] Feuerbach, *Principles of the Philosophy of the Future*, para. 29, p. 48.

deficiencies. Mortals enrich ethereal beings, because human lives are deficient and impoverished.³² By investing the Spirit with universal Reason, human beings acknowledge their impaired faculties. The God of virtue and the Spirit of infinite Reason are acknowledgments for felt deficiencies. Human beings find virtue in God and the Absolute because of its absence in their own lives. Religion and philosophy were compensatory products of felt need.³³

Given his analysis, the "secret" of religion, like the secret of Hegel's philosophy, is revealed as nothing other than the fact that human beings project their properties into a make-believe transcendence. Thus, the finite reasoning characteristic of ordinary mortals becomes an "ideated," transcendental Reason—and the limited creativity of individuals becomes Creation. Feuerbach informs his readers that "this is the mystery of religion—[man] projects his being into objectivity. . . . Theology and speculative philosophy make real beings and things into . . . predicates of a distinct, transcendent, absolute, i.e., abstract being." In effect, "Christians [have] made mental phenomena into independent beings, . . . in short, predicates of their own nature, whether recognized as such or not, into independent subjective existences. . . . Religion, at least the Christian, is the relation of man to himself, or more correctly to his own nature . . . viewed as a nature apart from his own. The divine being is nothing else than the human being, or, rather, the human nature purified, freed from the limits of the individual man, made objective—i.e., contemplated and revered as another, a distinct being."³⁴

Feuerbach spoke of human objectification and human alienation to explain religious beliefs. Over time, and as a consequence of some obscure imperative, human beings had palliated their sense of diminished selves by enhancing created divinities. They then further demeaned themselves by seeking some kind of redemption at the hands of those beings they themselves had invented. Rather than resolving their problems, the result was a still more emphatic sense of inefficacy.

Feuerbach's response to all of that was to recommend that human beings acknowledge the actualities of traditional religious belief. He was to argue that human beings would begin their redemption by recognizing that the awesome attributes of divinity, in the final analysis, were actually those of their own col-

---

³² "To enrich God, man must become poor; that God may be all, man must be nothing." Feuerbach, *The Essence of Christianity*, p. 26.

³³ "When . . . man has nothing else apart from himself, he searches and finds everything in himself; he posits in place of the real world the imaginary and intelligible world in which there is everything that is in the real world, but abstracted and imagined." Feuerbach, *Principles of the Philosophy of the Future*, para. 29, p. 45.

³⁴ Feuerbach, *The Essence of Christianity*, pp. xl, 14, 22, 29–30; see pp. 30–31.

lective nature. Feuerbach proposed the restoration to humanity of its alienated attributes. All the *predicates* that Hegel had assigned to the transcendental beings of his absolute idealism—Feuerbach would restore to earthly *subjects*. He would have them understand that the Consciousness of Hegelianism was to be seen as nothing other than the common consciousness of the species. The Reason of Hegelianism nothing other than the shared reasoning of humanity in its temporal and spatial entirety.

For Feuerbach divinity resides in the "divineness" of divine attributes—with a despoiled humankind their source. Feuerbach argued for the restoration to alienated humanity of those divine attributes. He sought the "redivinization," the "sacralization," of the human species. He saw the beginnings of human salvation in *the making of theology, anthropology*. Human energy, so long focused on worlds of obscure philosophical and religious vagaries, would return to serve the real needs of humankind.

Other than being simply injurious to human beings by confusing the nature and knowledge of reality, the old theology and the old philosophy deprived humanity "of the power of real life as of the genuine sense of truth and virtue," making obscure the actual dimensions of its material and spiritual impoverishment. For Feuerbach, religion was "the dream of the human mind," and as a consequence, the being of "real things" was seen only "in the entrancing splendor of imagination and caprice instead of in the simple daylight of reality and necessity."[35] Religious fictions render human beings passive in the face of privation and tolerant when subject to abuse. Institutional religion served as an opiate for suffering humanity.

As long as they remained confounded by the old religion and philosophy, one could hardly expect humans to address real issues. Embroiled in those projections that characterize theological and metaphysical thought, human beings become impotent in the face of real challenge.[36]

What is clear is that Feuerbach's most fundamental and constant concern was with the material, i.e., economic, social, and political conditions, which determine the quality of life of human beings. He saw his task as lifting from them the burden of religion and speculative philosophy so that human beings

---

[35] Ibid., pp. xxxix, 274. Feuerbach held an adequate understanding of philosophy, and the reality of empirical being, to be of critical concern. He maintained that "the question of being is indeed a practical question ... of life and death." Feuerbach, *Principles of the Philosophy of the Future*, para. 28, p. 43.

[36] "The more attributes ... I deny to [God], the more I set it apart from myself, the less power and influence I let it exercise on me, the freer I become of it. The more qualities I have, the more I am also for others, the greater is the circumference of my effects and influence." Feuerbach, *Principles of the Philosophy of the Future*, para. 16, p. 24.

might struggle to create conditions "providing a tangible, actual, political and social existence" that not only would ensure both bread and social equality,[37] but abate the wretchedness that made religion a compensatory necessity. He understood his critique of religion as the most practical and promising strategy through which political issues might be addressed. He conceived his "irreligiosity" as fundamentally "revolutionary." He was convinced that his efforts would contribute to the struggle against the inhumanity of the world in which he found himself. He fully anticipated that his theoretical notions would become revolutionary once they succeeded in inspiring masses.[38]

The philosophical notions in which he invested so much confidence rested on his convictions on the centrality of *sensation* in coming to know the world, on the *communal* grounds of truth, on *matter* as the substance of reality, and *socioeconomic needs* as levers of human behavior. Those were the elements that distinguished Feuerbach's philosophy from that of the idealists who preceded him. As differences they were, in themselves, important—but perhaps more so insofar as they served to redirect the thought of those who were to shape the future. That *matter*, rather than *consciousness*, was the ultimate reality of the world was to influence radical thought for the next century.

For Feuerbach, the explicit realization that the ultimate reality of the world was *matter* was essential to the liberation of thinking humanity.[39] That *consciousness*, with which idealism had forever occupied itself, was a *derivative* product of matter, of nature,[40] entirely altered the direction of German philosophy. Thereafter, much of German philosophy, particularly *radical* thought in Germany, ceded priority to sensation as the foundation of knowledge. Ideas were a function of sensation. "That which perception [gives] is appropriated by thought, and that which is the function and concern of the senses, of perception and of life, becomes the function and concern of thought. . . . The reality of the idea is . . . sensation."[41]

[37] Feuerbach, Preface to *Sämmtliche Werke*, vol. 1, pp. xiv–xv.

[38] See Feuerbach, in letters to Georg Herwegh, 3 September 1842, p. 165; Arnold Ruge, 10 March 1843 and (no date) June 1843, *Briefwechsel*, pp. 172, 176.

[39] "The world," Feuerbach informs his readers, "is matter"—and the "real" is "that which exists materially. . . . A being that only thinks, and thinks abstractly, has no conception at all of being, of existence, or of reality." Feuerbach, *Principles of the Philosophy of the Future*, paras. 6, 15, 26, pp. 7, 22, 40.

[40] "Hegelian philosophy made thought . . . into a divine and absolute being" when, in fact, we become conscious of things in thought only through the determinations provided by sensory experience. Absent those determinations, "thought," "consciousness," become "ideated" abstractions, entirely unreal. "The consciousness of being," for example, "is indeed always and necessarily bound to a definite [sensory] content." See ibid., paras. 23, 24, 27, pp. 36–37, 38, 42.

[41] Ibid., para. 29, p. 46.

Feuerbach conceived consciousness, thought, idea, subordinate to material reality. He understood them to be byproducts of life and living. The "real" is "that which exists materially"—consciousness is its "reflection."[42] "The self-consciousness of modern philosophy," Feuerbach affirmed, "is itself . . . only a being ideated and mediated through abstraction and thus a doubtful being. Certain and immediately assured is only that which is an object of the senses, perception, and feeling."[43] For Feuerbach, thought was a derivative product, a "reflection" of material reality. In the world of human beings, matter had priority.

In his maturity, he identified his epistemological materialism and its communal criterion of truth as indispensable for human beings—required to survive in the real world.[44] It was a realistic conception of human beings negotiating the demands of a material world—and it was the "very foundation of that natural science to which alone belongs the past, present, and future."[45]

Feuerbach was convinced that what his analysis had accomplished was not only to reveal the "secret" of both theology and philosophy, but that "the new philosophy is the complete and absolute dissolution, without any contradiction, of theology into anthropology." Correspondingly, "the new philosophy makes man—with the inclusion of nature as the foundation of man—the unique, universal and highest object of philosophy. It thus makes anthropology, with the inclusion of physiology, the universal science."[46]

The process Feuerbach described reflected conditions that prevailed in the world of human beings. The secret of religion was anthropology. The objects of human worship were fetishistic expressions of human properties—compensatory projections wrought from the wretched deficiencies suffered. For Feuerbach, "God" was the unhappy product of "man abstracted from himself."[47] Human beings find in God or the Absolute a fantastic, compensatory projection of their own flawed existence.[48]

---

[42] Ibid., para. 15, p. 22; and "Only through the senses, and not through thought for itself, is an object given in a true sense. The object that is given in thought or that is identical with thought is only idea." Ibid., para. 32, p. 51; see ibid., paras. 17, 22, pp. 26–30, 34–36.

[43] Ibid., para. 37, p. 55.

[44] It is not clear what Feuerbach intended with such a claim. Much of what he says is similar to the epistemological ruminations of prekantian British empiricists.

[45] Feuerbach argued that he extended credence to generalizations, particularly those that were metaphysical, only if they could be expressed as empirical, i.e., scientific, laws of nature. See his letter to Wilhelm Bolin, 1 July 1867, in *Briefwechsel*, p. 343; and "Empiricism or realism—by which is here understood generally the so-called real sciences, especially the natural sciences. . . ." Feuerbach, *Principles of the Philosophy of the Future*, para. 15, p. 22.

[46] Feuerbach, *Principles of the Philosophy of the Future*, paras. 52, 54, pp. 68, 70.

[47] Feuerbach, *The Essence of Christianity*, p. 31.

[48] "The yearning of man after something above himself is nothing else than the longing after

Feuerbach and the Religion of Man (Theanthropism)

Those were the thoughts Feuerbach left to his successors—who were to influence history in a more significant measure than he. They counted in their number some of the most important revolutionary thinkers of the nineteenth century.

Most of those elements of Feuerbach's thought that survived in the revolutionary thinking that succeeded him turn out to have been residual Hegelianisms. Although predicating cognition on the "common sense" primacy of sense perception, Feuerbach's rendering takes him in an entirely different direction than that pursued by British empiricists. The general context in which Feuerbach lodged his system was what he identified essentially as "historicophilosophical."

Feuerbach argued that the primary organon of cognition is individual sense perception—that *feeling* is the province of the *individual* self—but, as corollary of that, he argued that "*reason* is the self-consciousness of the *species*." That one can speak intelligibly of the "truth of nature" can only be a function of a "positing of the species." Without universal reason, the self-consciousness of the species, individual sense perception remains opaque and indecipherable, privative and dysfunctional.

For Feuerbach, "reason" was "the highest species of being.... Reason cannot content itself in the individual; it has its adequate existence only when it has the species for its object, and the species not as it has already developed itself in the past and present but as it will develop itself in the unknown future."

Feuerbach's entire conception of knowing was derivative of Hegel's epistemology. "What the individual man does not know and cannot do, all of mankind together knows and can do. Thus, the divine knowledge that knows simultaneously every particular has its reality in the knowledge of the species."[49]

Like Hegel, Feuerbach was persuaded that human beings were "species beings," and that the individual, alone, was an orphaned creature, without true knowledge, and without moral guidance. It was participation in a community over time that rendered the individual rational—an affirmation realized in history. In that sense, Feuerbach appeals to Hegel. It was Hegel who insisted that "the history of the world ... presents us with a rational process."[50] Feuerbach

---

the perfect type of his nature, the yearning to be free from himself, i.e., from the limits and defects of his individuality." Ibid., p. 281.

[49] Ibid., "Appendix," para. 4, pp. 285–286; see pp. xxxiii, xli; and Feuerbach, *Principles of the Philosophy of the Future*, para. 12, p. 17.

[50] Hegel, *The Philosophy of History* (New York: Dover Publications, Inc., 1956), p. 9.

proceeded with his work believing that not only would history reveal a pattern, but that pattern would be, in some indeterminate sense, not only rational, but moral as well. It was a process that ultimately would lead humanity, as species, to fulfillment and liberation. Feuerbach was a protagonist of the thesis that history pursued an informing, "dialectical" course—collective, moral, and rational.

Hegelian in inspiration, Feuerbach's historical method was deterministic. All of humankind's history followed a prefigured pattern—and, like Hegel, Feuerbach considered that his "new philosophy" was the *necessary* culmination of all antecedent philosophic thought. Feuerbach was convinced that his philosophy was the "precise, deductive" consequence of "historical necessity."[51] In his judgment, his thought captured the reality of a long sequence that until his time had been left abstract and insubstantial. Once revealed, it became clear that the prevailing state of humanity was the certain consequence of a protracted historical dialectic, destined to culminate in the liberation and fulfillment of humankind.[52]

One comes away from such reflections with the impression of a world in which material externalities, subtended by rational and moral purpose, impact human beings in determinate fashion, shaping their individual and collective lives. Human life reflects the rational and moral purpose of matter as matter reveals itself in history. Human thought, through all of cultural history, follows a pattern that is a reflection of the dialectical sequence intrinsic to the material history of sensuous life.

Such notions imply that humanity is the "unique, universal, and highest object" of created life.[53] We are left with reasonings that contend that the natural world of sensory perception, and, by implication, matter itself, are inextricably involved in human affairs. Feuerbach contends that historical sequences follow a predetermined, necessary pattern, intended to culminate in the redemption of suffering humanity.

It is evident that the "natural humanism" of Feuerbach was infused throughout with decidedly *religious sentiment*. Feuerbach was fully conscious of that. He consistently argued that his critique of traditional theology was calculated not to rid the world of religious sentiment;[54] it was to render it *anthropologi-*

---

[51] Feuerbach, *Principles of the Philosophy of the Future*, para. 31, p. 49; see paras. 19 and 20, p. 31.

[52] See Feuerbach, *The Essence of Christianity*, p. xxxiv; and Herbert Marcuse, *Reason and Revolution: Hegel and the Rise of Social Theory*, p. 268.

[53] Feuerbach, *Principles of the Philosophy of the Future*, para. 54, p. 70.

[54] "It was in no sense Feuerbach's intent to destroy religion. He sought, rather, to reconstruct it. Indeed he once referred to himself as a second Luther. . . . He did not proclaim the end of all religion, but only attacked the old in behalf of a new." Chamberlain, *Heaven Wasn't His Destination*, p. 59.

cal. The worship of a transcendental, abstract divinity was to give place to the worship of a suffering, but worthy, humanity.[55] The purpose of his "historicophilosophical analysis" was nothing less than to convince human beings that "man has his highest being, his God, in himself."[56] In effect, Feuerbach said of his "new philosophy" that "it takes the place of religion and has the essence of religion within itself. In truth, it is itself religion."[57]

For Feuerbach, human beings would find their salvation in Truth, and truth was a byproduct of life lived in common. He had argued that while sense perception was individual and personal, truth was a purchase of intersubjective confirmation. Like the truth of sense perception, the truth of human salvation was to be found in communion. While individuals were redeemed in their individuality, that redemption could only be accomplished in community, in the discipline of association. Feuerbach held that "the single man for himself possesses the essence of man neither in himself as a moral being nor in himself as a thinking being. The essence of man is contained only in the community and unity of man with man.... It is the truth," he continued, "that no being—be it man, God, mind, or ego—is for itself alone a true, perfect, and absolute being, that truth and perfection are only the connection and unity of beings equal in their essence. The highest and last principle of philosophy is, therefore, the unity of man with man."[58]

By 1844, Feuerbach had delivered himself of the substance of his "new philosophy." What was evident was its materialist, communitarian, and "communist" character. In the summer of that year, Feuerbach read, with enthusiasm, the volume *Guarantee of Harmony and Freedom* by Wilhelm Weitling—whom he proceeded to describe as a "prophet of the working class."[59] By that time, Feuerbach was an advocate of some form of "communism"—whose rationale included the conviction that the history of the world was the story of human redemption—governed by the logic of right reason and animated by moral imperative.

It was about the same time that the twenty-four-year-old Karl Marx wrote Feuerbach to inform him that in his, Marx's, judgment, *The Essence of Chris-*

---

[55] *Principles of the Philosophy of the Future*, para. 50, 52, 54, pp. 66, 68, 70. In this context, see the discussion in Sergei Bulgakov, *Karl Marx as a Religious Type: His Relation to the Religion of Anthropotheism of L. Feuerbach* (Belmont, Mass.: Nordland Publishing Company, 1979), particularly chap. 7.

[56] Feuerbach, Appendix, *The Essence of Christianity*, p. 281.

[57] Feuerbach, *Principles of the Philosophy of the Future*, para. 64, p. 73.

[58] Ibid., paras. 54, 63, pp. 70, 72.

[59] Feuerbach, letter to Friedrich Kapp, 15 October 1844, *Briefwechsel*, p. 195. See Wilhelm Weitling, *Garantien der Harmonie und Freiheit* (Berlin: Akademie-Verlag, 1955, originally published in 1842).

tianity, and *Principles of the Philosophy of the Future*, had, intentionally or unintentionally, supplied revolutionary communists with a philosophical foundation for their socialism. The young Marx was so overcome by Feuerbach's accomplishment, that he respectfully extended to him not only his most profound respect, but his love as well.[60]

In the course of that same letter, Marx expressed the Feuerbachian, and Hegelian, conviction that whatever else transpired, "history," itself, was "preparing the practical elements for the emancipation of mankind." The fascination with the function of history in the story of humanity's redemption was evident in the belief systems of the young Friedrich Engels as well.[61] At least for that reason, Feuerbach's characterization of history, moving at the necessary pace and deliberate determination of reason, struck response in both Marx and Engels. All—Hegel, Feuerbach, Engels, and Marx—shared an enduring faith in the dialectic of history.

Moses Hess (1812–1875)

The themes identified here in the work of Ludwig Feuerbach were not unique. Quite independent of any direct knowledge of the work of Feuerbach, Moses Hess, born in Bonn in 1812, was to engage the same elements in his *Die heilige Geschichte der Menschheit*—written in 1836 and published in 1837—before the appearance of Feuerbach's *Essence of Christianity*. The themes shared in the work of both thinkers were part of Germany's intellectual *Zeitgeist*.

In his *The Sacred History of Humankind*, written in his twenty-fourth year, Hess outlined his conception of history—a conception that grew directly out of his deepest religious convictions. His first work gave absolutely no evidence of any reticence in expressing what were traditional beliefs. Educated in Jewish orthodoxy, Hess' first major work reflected the tenets of the faith of his fathers. He saw history as an extension of the Old Testament, governed by "eternal and necessary laws" that made manifest the will of the Great God Jehovah. For Hess, "religion and history" were "inextricably related, the one," he maintained, "mak[ing] comprehensible the other." Convinced of the sacred lawfulness of

---

[60] Letter of Karl Marx to Feuerbach, 11 August 1844, in Karl Marx and Frederick Engels, *Collected Works*, vol. 3, pp. 354–355. In his letter, Marx informed Feuerbach that German communists in Paris, through the League of the Just, were systematically studying *The Essence of Christianity*. In order to make his books more readily available, Marx told Feuerbach that Friedrich Engels, another enthusiast, was supervising the translation of his works into English.

[61] Engels spoke of Hegel's *Philosophy of History* as "an enormous work"—out of which he "read ... dutifully every evening," the "tremendous thoughts" of which gripped him "terribly." "Letter to Friedrich Graeber," in Karl Marx and Frederick Engels, *Collected Works*, vol. 2, p. 490.

history, he informed his readers that "History is the science that succeeds in most illuminating the social and spiritual relations of human beings"[62]—a persuasion perhaps more Hegelian than it was Judaic.

As much as Hegel, Hess understood God's intention to have been that humanity, in the course of time, should achieve freedom and equality. The entire cosmic process invested in that purpose was law governed—and involved progression over reasonably discrete epochs. At the beginning of history, human beings participated unconsciously in the structured continuity, to only gradually develop a rational awareness of the entire divinely governed sequence.

For Hess, both divine intention, and the history in which it found expression, served distinctly human purpose. The history of humankind proceeds with metered measure toward a predestined conclusion—with development over time administered by "eternal and necessary laws." For Hess, history was understood to be "the mediated life of God"—the "conscious activity of the World Spirit."[63]

Humans, as they mature in time, learn to conform to the regularities governing history in much the same fashion that they have learned to obey the laws of nature. It is the will of God that manifests itself in natural and specifically historical regularities—and human beings, as rational agents, learn to conform to that will. "World history," for the young Hess, was a divinely inspired, willed, and goal-directed "unity, a totality, and a necessity." The ultimate freedom and equality human beings were destined to enjoy at the culmination of that history would be found in nothing other than "conscious obedience to God's laws."[64] Like Hegel and Feuerbach, Hess discovered reason and morality in history.[65] And like both, he insisted that whatever else it might be, history was a science, just as biology, physics, and geology were sciences—the proper object of systematic study—and subject to predictive regularity.[66] He went on to maintain that Hegel had recognized that history was the soul of philosophy and that reason was the essence of both. Granted that, the entailed logic allows human beings to anticipate futures. The dialectic of reason reveals the "logic" of science in general, and history in particular.[67]

[62] Moses Hess, *Die heilige Geschichte der Menschheit: Von einem Jünger Spinoza's*, in *Philosophische und sozialistische Schriften*, pp. 17, 42–43.

[63] Hess, *Die europäische Triarchie* (Leipzig: Otto Wigand, 1841), ibid., p. 80.

[64] Hess, *Die heilige Geschichte der Menschheit*, pp. 17, 42, 45, 48.

[65] Hess, *Die europäische Triarchie*, p. 84.

[66] Hess, *Die heilige Geschichte der Menschheit*, p. 42. Hess had found his rationale sustained by the argument in the volume by August von Cieszkowski, *Prolegomena zur Historiosophie* (Berlin: Vait und Co., 1838).

[67] Hess, *Die europäische Triarchie*, pp. 94–95. Hess maintained that Hegel's work was more a history than a philosophy. Cf. ibid., p. 86.

Like Feuerbach, Hess argued that the basic problem with Hegelianism was its abstract and detached character. He insisted that as long as philosophy remained abstract and detached, it would not be life relevant. Philosophy must inspire deeds. Life is activity, and if philosophy would serve life, it must foster action.[68]

For Hess, the world of the mid nineteenth century was beset by social "contradictions" that cried out for resolution. Like Hegel, Hess conceived "contradictions" providing the motive energy of history—moving humanity to that behavior calculated to satisfy the requirements of the inner logic of the dialectic. In Hess' judgment, the contradiction that demanded action in the Europe of his time, was that which manifested itself in the pauperism that afflicted the vast majority of the working population, opposed to the obscene opulence of the monied aristocracy. In his estimation, it was that central contradiction that fueled the dialectic of the period and gave direction to the actions of humankind.[69]

While the specific motive impulses of the dialectic remained uncertain in the writings of Hegel—for Hess, contradictions arose out of evident social and economic tensions. He traced the activity of humans working in association from the first fabrication of products to satisfy their personal needs in an environment of fundamental equality, to that stage in which violence, chicanery, and law compelled participants to accept an unequal redistribution of welfare and invidious distinctions of rank. The stronger arrogated goods to their own use—and fashioned laws to protect their purloined ownership. As humankind produced in greater and greater quantity and variety, the privileged wrested more and more for themselves, while the weak suffered in both real and relative measure.

Hess traced the development of productive forces to the point at which industry began to establish itself in society. He cited the founding and expansion of industry in the British Isles as an illustrative case in point. In England, because of prevailing property rights, machine production was concentrated in the hands of those privileged by birth and inherited wealth. Workers who previously had been independent yeomen and artisans were swept into shops dominated by machines and the masters of those machines. Monopolization of the land drove still more into the grip of factory labor. In the course of that ineluctable process, human beings were reduced to little more than appendages

---

[68] See Hess, "Gegenwärtige Krisis der deutschen Philosophie," "Philosophie der That," in *Philosophische und sozialistische Schriften*, pp. 170, 210–211, 219.

[69] See the entire discussion in Hess, "Zwei Reden über Kommunismus," *Rheinische Jahrbücher*, in *Philosophische und sozialistische Schriften*, pp. 348–359.

of machines in an obscure process they could hardly understand. Hess anticipated that the helplessness and the unendurable poverty of the vast majority of Britain's workers would precipitate revolution, first in England and then in those countries that shared similar economic systems.[70] The dialectic of history was the product of human choice in situations where outcomes were totally unanticipated and in which there were but few options.

Hess maintained that by the mid nineteenth century, history saw industry producing in such quantities, and in such variety, that humans, under the organized auspices of a rational state, might have all their physical and spiritual needs equitably satisfied. History had provided the conditions in which the divine promise of liberty and equality could be satisfied in abundance. Human beings could no longer avoid the responsibility of resolving all the contradictions that had tormented humanity since the beginning of time.

It was evident to Hess that history afforded guidance to human beings. What earlier had been the will of God or the World Spirit had become, by 1845, the workings of history. Driven by the evolving social and economic "contradictions" that had afflicted humanity since the first appearance of private property, and the egotism that was its product, human beings increasingly divined history's intentions. Maturing right reason obliged them to undertake the resolution of the glaring contradiction of poverty, injustice, and humiliation in the midst of wealth. Human beings were morally obliged to abolish the system of private ownership, sales competition, and antisocial egotism that had "wage slavery" and pauperism as their inevitable consequence.[71]

Hess argued that in those countries characterized by advanced industrialization, "One comes away from today's reality with the conviction that all the efforts made have been unable to rescue the majority of the unfortunates from a condition akin to slavery." In his judgment, the efforts at political reform in industrialized and industrializing countries produced, at best, palliatives. The situation had become unendurable—and gave every evidence of extending itself to the Continent. He went on to maintain that history made evident that the task of the time was to address man's inhumanity to man. A resolution of humanity's problems would be forthcoming only when the current "disorganized society" was transformed into an organic "unity in the state."[72]

[70] Hess, "Über eine in England bevorstehende Katastrophe," in *Philosophische und sozialistische Schriften*, pp. 183–185.

[71] Hess, *Die europäische Triarchie*, p. 96.

[72] Hess, "Die politischen Parteien in Deutschland," in *Philosophische und sozialistische Schriften*, p. 192. That was written in 1842, after Hess had made the acquaintance of Karl Marx in the summer of 1841. He had voiced essentially the same sentiments in 1841, in *Die europäische Triarchie*, p. 96, before making Marx's acquaintance.

By 1845, Hess had become an advocate for the creation of a communist society in which human beings would attain that fullness in freedom and equality that they had forever sought in the promises of religion.[73] By that time, in the course of his discussion, he no longer invoked the Great God Jehovah; he simply insisted that the achievement of freedom and equality always had been the sacred intention of both revealed religion and history.

By 1847, his account of the historical process, that he saw as necessarily culminating in social and political revolution, was delivered in basically economic terms.[74] With confidence, he spoke of the propertied classes. They were interested in industrial development and in attaining markets for their goods. They fostered the passage of legislation, tariff regulations, and tax measures to serve their ends. One of the direct consequences was the increasing emiseration of the working class. Tariffs and taxation resulted in a rapid decline in the living standards of urban workers. They were compelled to suffer subsistence wages, in order that entrepreneurs might exploit competitive advantage in "free" markets.

With the resulting profits, entrepreneurs would sustain and further increase their gains and market access. Hess spoke of that system as not only resulting in the exploitation of labor but also of reducing the survival potential of the entire middle class. He argued that under the extant system, wealth would necessarily concentrate in fewer and fewer hands, with monopolies determining both distribution and prices. The inevitable consequence would be deepening, and ultimately unsustainable, cycles of declining effective demand, with underconsumption precipitating crises of "overproduction," pandemic unemployment, the cessation of productive activity, and a catastrophic erosion of the quality of life.

Within that context, Hess argued, workers are constrained to endure a life of oppression, exploitation, precariousness, and absent opportunities. Living labor is compelled to sell itself to survive—to thereby "alienate" its very essence to others, those agents who would be instrumental in its stultification. The process Hess described was much like that found in Feuerbach's recitation of how human beings alienate themselves in traditional religion.[75]

Hess conceived this dialectical process irresistible, susceptible to neither good intentions nor political reform. The redemption of humankind could only follow a social and political revolution that would sweep away individual

---

[73] See Hess, "Kommunistisches Bekenntniss in Fragen und Antworten," in *Philosophische und sozialistische Schriften*, pp. 366–368.

[74] The following account follows that in Hess, "Die Folgen einer Revolution des Proletariats," ibid., pp. 427–444.

[75] See the discussion in the second part of the exposition ibid., pp. 433–436.

ownership of, and hereditary rights to, property. The abolition of private property would begin to resolve the offending "contradictions." Private industry would then be transferred to a "central workers' administration" that would oversee production and ensure the equitable satisfaction of needs. By the end of the decade, Hess had thus supplied an extended account of the historical process that he insisted would inevitably bring deliverance to the wretched and oppressed masses—in the form of a communist "Peoples' Republic"—in which authority, through law, would ensure the equality of material and spiritual satisfaction of all human needs.[76]

In his exposition, Hess spoke of authority, law, order, and centralization in the state as critical to the realization of freedom. Like Hegel, he conceived obedience to law and authority as freedom manifest—when that law and that authority represented the ultimate, best interests of collective humanity. Under such conditions, the interests of the individual were those of the community—and acting in conformity with law that represents one's own ultimate interests cannot be other than freedom.[77]

Under such revolutionary arrangements, the state has the obligation of educating the population to the realities of life in a "solidarist" community—a community in which the interests of the entire population would be the interests of each individual. The most elementary responsibility of that education would be devoted to the conveyance of an appreciation that law and authority provide a necessary defense against antisocial and selfish tendencies that would directly thwart everyone's interests.[78] At its more advanced levels, the state would be responsible to teach the truths of a general "science," devoted to the history of humanity and its redemption. In meeting those responsibilities, the organic state would be fostering human development.

"Centralization" in the organic state, Hess argued, was "not an enemy of individual freedom"—rather, it would serve to curtail the "arbitrary willfulness and selfishness of citizens," minimize "provincialism and caste prejudice, as well as all lawlessness." For Hess, like Hegel, the greatest freedom was possible only in circumstances of the greatest order.[79]

For Hess, like Hegel, the state is obliged to foster a spiritual consciousness that will ensure unity and well-being to the community. In that important sense, the activity of the state is "holy"; it is discharging its most fundamental

---

[76] Hess, "Rother Kathechismus für das deutsche Volk," ibid., pp. 453–455. Hess identifies his communist workers' regime as a "Volksrepublik." See ibid., p. 457.

[77] See the discussion in Hess, *Die europäische Triarchie*, in *Philosophische und sozialistische Schriften*, pp. 156–157.

[78] Ibid., p. 179.

[79] Ibid., pp. 156, 179.

responsibilities to that historic purpose that informs all of life. The state is the agency of that universal reason that governs the world—and it is from that fact that the state derives its legitimate power. For the younger Hess, reason was nothing less than the will of God—and the will of God was directly invoked by the state in order to marshal human beings to their true purpose.[80] Other than in terms of language chosen, the logic that vindicated the power of the state was not to change in Hess' accounts in the years that were to follow.

By 1845, the more mature Hess no longer made recourse to God by name— but argued that it was *history*, informed by reason, that directly demanded and guided conduct. By that time, God and reason were both united in history and revealed themselves in its passage. Hess maintained, for example, that the communism he advocated was neither a commandment of God, nor was it "a *theory* ... that one learned. Communism was the *conclusion of the evolutionary history* of society."[81] In effect, he argued that history had sacred and, by entailment, moral purpose. Hess had "sacralized" history.

In the early 1840s, when he spoke of God's direct supervision of the course of history, Hess informed his audience that it was God, himself, who provided the criteria for the distinction between right and wrong. "Good," Hess maintained at that time, "is anything that furthers the development of a godly consciousness; bad is anything that obstructs or impairs that development."[82]

For Hess, that prescriptive development of a godly consciousness involved the unity of all human beings in the state—a state in which "religion and life, church and state, were no longer *separated*"—in which "politics was holy and religion effective."[83] As his delivery changed over time, the criteria made available for making moral distinctions was no longer specifically attributed to God. History provided them.

What had been identified as a "godly consciousness" in his past was identified as a "mature consciousness" by 1845. However it was identified, its function remained essentially the same. A mature consciousness would sensitize human beings to prevalent social and economic "contradictions," inspiring them to their resolution. The process involved—whether requiring either a "godly consciousness" or one that was "mature"—remained remarkably similar. What had changed was that God had become less personal, less scriptural. History performed the same task—and the result would be the same: human salvation in freedom and equality.

Human salvation, originally the very purpose of God's will acting in history,

---

[80] Ibid., pp. 105, 126–127, 176.
[81] Hess, "Zei Reden über Kommunismus," ibid., p. 352.
[82] Ibid., p. 50.
[83] Ibid., pp. 105, 133.

remained the same—only by 1845, it was history, itself, that was addressing the task. By the time he wrote "Die Folgen einer Revolution des Proletariats"—just before Karl Marx and Friedrich Engels wrote the *Communist Manifesto*—Hess argued that as human beings mature in history, the salvific process is driven and sustained by their own rational discernment—their acknowledgment of the law-governed regularities of the entire procedure.

For Hess, the maturation of human consciousness was recorded in history. The first sign that the law-governed process was culminating in the full freedom and equality of all human beings had been supplied in the revelatory philosophy of Baruch Spinoza. Spinoza attested to the reality of the cosmic unity and equality of all of God's creatures, most specifically those that are not only sentient, but rational as well.[84]

Hess maintained that unity, freedom, and equality were recurrent themes in modern philosophy, as human thought ripened to the full awareness of its moral responsibilities. In his judgment, the then recent history of German philosophy signaled the imminent realization of human fulfillment.

That Hess was convinced that the processes involved in human fulfillment required contingent conditions for their continued actualization was clear in almost everything he wrote. To fulfill its destiny, humanity not only required the material production recently made available by machine industry, but was required to create a community in which collective interests were given priority. That was true not only because morality required it, but because community life was an essential condition for the full articulation of the individual self as well. "True humanity," Hess argued, "can live nothing other than the life of its own kind [*Gattung*]."[85] In the final analysis, to achieve the fullness of self, the individual, in some existential sense, must be the community.

Postkantian philosophy suggested that human beings can come to know their world only by interacting, by sharing their cognitive awareness, with their peers. Like Hegel, Hess argued, implicitly and explicitly, that we depend on others to supply the confirmation for those truth claims that afford scientific understanding of the world and everything in it. Humans appreciate art, literature, and music, only as members of a community that shares evaluative criteria. In fact, Hess was to argue that reason itself is a byproduct of life lived in common—outside of which it remains sterile and unreal. Outside of community life, humans would never attain fulfillment in reason, truth, or appreciation.[86]

---

[84] See the entire discussion in Hess, "Socialismus und Communismus," *Einundzwanzig Bogen aus der Schweiz* (1843), ibid., pp. 200–201.

[85] Hess, "Deutschland und Frankreich in Bezug auf die Centralisationsfrage," ibid., p. 176.

[86] See the discussion in Hess, "Vorwort" to *Die letzten Philosophen*, ibid., pp. 381–385; "It is in society that persons are rendered human, social." Hess, *Die europäische Triarchie*, ibid., p. 154.

Given such an account, one can understand the passion with which Hess criticized the social solipsism of Max Stirner—and Stirner's advocacy of the primacy of the self. Hess objected to the "alienated, . . . isolated, heart- and spiritless, soulless, lifeless thing" that the philosophical egoist, the advocate of radical individualism, made of the individual human being. For Hess, real, living human beings, in essence, were social, communal creatures (*Gattungswesen* or *Gemeinwesen*)—who, in common history, shared a common education, spoke a common language, and enjoyed common achievements.[87] The fulfillment of their humanity was the consequence of a life lived in community.

It was this sense of the fundamental importance of community, in the intellectual and moral life of the individual, that originally made of Moses Hess a socialist and communist. He held the very essence of humanity to be communal; human beings, in their very being, were "collective creatures."[88] Individuals could not survive, much less prosper, outside of a community of similars.[89] More than that, outside of a life lived in common, human beings would be devoid not only of art and science, but morality as well.

For Hess, life lived in community and history forever remained something of a sacred matter. In 1845, by that time very familiar with the work of Feuerbach, Hess could maintain that it was true that the "essence of God was the transcendent essence of humanity—and the true teaching concerning the essence of God saw it as the essence of humanity: *Theology is, in fact, anthropology.*" However true, Hess was to argue that Feuerbach had not carried the analysis far enough. Hess insisted that "the quintessence of humanity is *social* [*gesellschaftlich*]." To attain fulfillment, human beings are fated to work together, toward common goals, for what, ultimately, are identical interests. "True Feuerbachianism becomes the lore of life lived in community—it makes of Feuerbach's *anthropology, socialism.*"[90] All of which bears all the traits of the Hegelianism in which the thought of both Feuerbach and Hess found its source.

Philosophical individualism was dismissed by Hess as the product of a contemplative, self-satisfied, self-serving, and complacent bourgeoisie. Philosophical individualism was an intellectual commodity fabricated by, and employed in the service of, egotists and those advocates of economic competition who conceived of persons only in terms of material wealth. Hess saw in sociological libertarianism an inhumane conception of society in which every human being

---

[87] Ibid., pp. 389–391; see Hess, "Über die sozialistische Bewegung in Deutschland," ibid., pp. 284–287.

[88] Hess, "Die deutsche Philosophie," in *Neue Anekdota*, ibid., p. 287.

[89] Hess, "Über das Geldwesen," in *Rheinische Jahrbücher zur gesellschaftlichen Reform*, ibid., p. 330.

[90] Hess, "Philosophie und Sozialismus," *Neue Anekdota*, ibid., p. 293.

was potentially the enemy of every other—a conception that fosters a complete loss of humanity and a return to the feral world of animals. Only philosophical aberrancy, thought gone grievously awry, could produce such reactionary and unpersuasive reflections on life.[91] For Hess, such notions were not only grievously mistaken, they were irredeemably immoral.

This kind of analysis contributed to the rationale that subtended Hess' conception of the nature and role of the state in the life of individuals living in communion. Like Hegel, Hess saw the state as the moral linchpin of collective life. Like Hegel, he saw community sustained by organization and law. He saw institutionalization in the very origin of life—in the first impulses that resulted in family living. He saw organization evolving and expanding from family life into that of tribal and national life, to ultimately culminate in "one great and holy union [*Reich*]."[92] Like Hegel, Hess saw the state providing the ethical ligaments of that union.

Supporting all of this was a foundation made up of faith, sacred conviction, and inspired belief. History was infused with moral purpose, and moved in calculated measure to the achievement of that purpose. By the time of his full maturity, Hess was convinced that history mandated that humankind undertake social and political revolution precisely for that ethical end. It was a conviction that required sacrifice in its service—a commitment that featured all the properties of a religious calling. At the very height of his intellectual powers, Hess could write, with complete honesty, that "the social revolution is my religion."[93] In the course of time, he had given fulsome expression to what he had spoken of, in his youth, as his "political religion."[94]

The Religion of Revolution

With the passing of Hegel, philosophy in Germany underwent rapid development. Some of it found expression in the increasingly radical opposition to Hegel's own work. Some of it took on the form of a critique of traditional religion. By the time that criticism appeared in Feuerbach's *Essence of Christianity* it had assumed implicit political form. The political nature of posthegelian criticism became still more strident in the work of Hess.

However one assesses their similarities and differences, a set of themes can be isolated in the work of Feuerbach and Hess that is of significance for the present inquiry. First of all, both authors chose *materialism* as the foundation

---

[91] Ibid., pp. 389–393.
[92] Hess, *Die europäische Triarchie*, ibid., pp. 150–151.
[93] Hess, "Rother Kathechismus für das deutsche Volk," ibid., p. 448.
[94] Cf. Hess, *Die heilige Geschichte der Menschheit*, ibid., p. 71.

of their epistemological strategy. They held that only materialism—the concept that human beings live in, and know, reality as a consequence of its immediate impact—would render them actors, rather than observers, of their world. Certainly for Hess, rather than simply attempting to know the world, humanity should change it to conform to a normative ideal of justice and freedom. Hegel had left his followers a contemplative perspective on knowing and living. Feuerbach had not fully emerged from such a persuasion. For Hess, there was an urgency, an immediacy, in his advocacy.

By whatever route, both Feuerbach and Hess had abandoned epistemological and/or ontological idealism and sought to make sense of things by appealing to immediate perception—assigning consciousness a derivative function in cognition. Knowing required a winnowing and a formulation by the community—for knowing was necessary for effective doing. For both, human consciousness was history's agent.

It is clear that the materialism espoused by both Feuerbach and Hess was possessed of properties that one would not intuitively ascribe to matter—or history. For both Feuerbach and Hess, refined sensory perception somehow revealed the *moral* qualities in things—in the sense that the world and everything in it seemed to have a purpose. For them, all of science seems to have revealed a purpose. Both conceived history a science, an inclusive science whose scope encompassed all the subsidiary and constituent empirical inquiries. In their view, history, as a "science," was clearly teleological—pursuing a predetermined moral objective.

The particular features both Feuerbach and Hess attributed to "reality" led them to acknowledge, both indirectly and directly, its affinities with *religion*. For both, reality was understood to be governed by *reason*, in pursuit of *moral* ends—and because both rational and moral, *necessary*. Finally, because rational, moral, and necessary, reality, correctly understood, was the fountainhead of *truth*.

In effect, both Feuerbach and Hess imagined that history, as reality, could reveal the impeccable truth about the destiny of humanity. More than its destiny, history prescribed and proscribed behavior. It assigned the responsibilities that made heroes of some, and villains of others—all in the framework of anticipated futures. For both Feuerbach and Hess, coming to understand history displayed almost all the features attendant upon becoming an adept of a living faith.

Associated with a living faith often, if not invariably, one finds an insistence on a binding sense of community, a community of the elect. It is a sense that leaves members linked by bonds of commitment, mutual support, self-sacrifice, and a readiness to labor for collective purpose. In the last analysis, the issues that bind the community together are essentially moral. There is the conviction that the community has some fundamental priority vis-a-vis the individual—and that any exclusive preoccupation with self is particularly objectionable.

A great deal of this was explicit or implicit in the work of Hegel—and residues can be found in the work of both the conservative as well as radical revisionists that followed him. More important for present purposes is the fact that all these elements appear and reappear in the political prose of revolutionaries throughout the nineteenth century. All of them are to be found in the private papers and published works of both Friedrich Engels and Karl Marx. Their presence there is a testament to Hegel and the continuity of his thought among those who imagine themselves having left him behind.

CHAPTER THREE

Friedrich Engels and Karl Marx
History as Religion

> This is our calling, that we shall become the templars of this Grail, gird the sword round our loins for its sake and stake our lives joyfully in the last, holy war which will be followed by the thousand year reign of freedom. And such is the power of the Idea that he who has recognised it cannot cease to speak of its splendor or to proclaim its all conquering might.... He who has once beheld it, to whom in the nightly stillness of his little room it has once appeared in all its brightness, can never abandon it, he must follow where it leads, even to death.... And this belief in the all conquering might of the Idea, in the victory of eternal truth, this firm confidence that it can never waver or yield, even if the whole world were to rise against it, that is the true religion ... the basis of the true positive philosophy, the philosophy of world history.
> —Friedrich Engels[1]

To those young people born into the time of troubles that followed the turmoil of revolution, Napoleon, and reaction, the first half of the nineteenth century was a period of both challenge and promise. It was they who would be charged by history with the responsibility of providing a response to challenge and a rationale that might sustain the promise.

Many of the most important young thinkers of the period were Hegelians, or former Hegelians, and as such were inspired by the conviction that humanity was traversing a necessary and inevitable sequence that would finally conclude in a system in which human redemption would be achieved. The convictions were more faith than science, and were to result in belief systems that assumed the catechistic features of church doctrine. How those belief systems evolved, forever retaining the traits of their Hegelian origins, is the present concern.

---

[1] Friedrich Engels, *Schelling and Revelation: Critique of the Latest Attempt of Reaction Against the Free Philosophy,* in Karl Marx and Friedrich Engels, *Collected Works* (New York: International Publishers, 1976. Hereafter *MECW*, with volumes identified before page identification), vol. 2, p. 239.

However the young were to put together those systems, their origins in faith remained ever evident. The young, themselves, were alive with passionate opinion and the indefatigable energy of the true believer. One sees evidence of all that in the earliest years of the conscious life of Friedrich Engels.

Born to a prosperous commercial family in Barmen on the 28th of November, 1820, he was reared in relative comfort in an intensely pietistic, Protestant environment. At seventeen, his schoolmaster could still commend his "religious feeling, purity of heart, agreeable habits and other prepossessing qualities."

By the time the young Engels was twenty-two, however, his father began to entertain serious misgivings. He suspected a "lack of character" in the young Engels' "tendency to extremes," and that he seemed attracted by "vapid new systems" opposed to the "faith of his fathers."[2] The "vapid new systems" of which his father spoke were made up of the heterodox religious notions entertained by those who identified themselves as "Young Hegelians."

In his "Letters from Wuppertal," printed in March 1839, when he was nineteen years of age, Engels gave ample evidence of his distain for the "mysticism" of the local religionists that "corrupted" every aspect of life. The local rural population had been traumatized by their transfer to urban factories. The combination of the stress of factory work and mysticism on the lower classes resulted in pandemic despair and an addiction to a crude religiosity that destroyed for them all prospect of a life of humanity and virtue.[3]

Engels' revealing "Letters from Wuppertal" reflected the thought of Ludwig Börne and those who had risen, under his leadership, to articulate objections to the prevailing system. The ideas of David Friedrich Strauss were soon to follow. Börne and Strauss proceeded to exercise influence over the educated youth of Germany at the time. Both were critical of the extant socioeconomic arrangements, as well as prevailing religious beliefs.

Börne inspired a school of literary critics and poets who were convinced that art criticism should serve as an instrument for political evangelism. Through their art, they sought to awaken Germany to a new era and a new social and religious order. For his part, Strauss had published his *Life of Jesus* in 1835, and had awakened a storm of discussion around the historicity and literal credibility of the Gospels. By October 1839, Engels had not only read his book, but declared himself "an enthusiastic Straussian."[4]

For the Young Hegelians, religion's emphasis on authority, tradition, and po-

---

[2] "School-Leaving Reference for Prima Pupil Friedrich Engels," "Friedrich Engels Senior to his Wife Elise," and "Friedrich Engels Senior to Karl Snethlage," in *MECW*, vol. 2, pp. 582, 585, 586.

[3] Friedrich Engels, "Letters from Wuppertal," ibid., vol. 2, pp. 9, 17, and passim.

[4] Engels, "To Wilhelm Graeber," ibid., vol. 2, p. 471.

litical passivity was considered a critical support for the established semifeudal institutions that governed the restorationist Germany that emerged from the Congress of Vienna. Strauss' critical investigation into the origins of Christianity was very quickly seen as flanking the defenses of the prevailing regime—to open the path for reform.

Certainly by the time Engels wrote his "Letters from Wuppertal," he was already under the influence of the work of both Börne and Strauss. For the purposes of the present discussion, it is more important that as he spoke of his indebtedness to Börne and Strauss, he indicated, at the same time, his intellectual obligations to Hegel—a fact that most certainly was to prove of more lasting consequence.

By his early twenties—however little learned he may have been of the intricacies of the system—Engels spoke easily of concepts that were familiar to Hegelians of all persuasion. He spoke of "modern philosophy" as having made comprehensible the thesis that reason somehow pervaded all creation. He went on to argue that "what is reasonable is, of course, also necessary, and what is necessary must be, or at least become, real"[5]—all of which was Hegelianism of the most elementary sort.

It is not at all clear what those notions actually may have meant, but for Engels they did seem to carry important implications in their train. One was to convince him of the universal rationality of things—a rationality that might escape the awareness of the "subjective" reason of the individual. That, in turn, implied that individuals should acknowledge their "subordination" to that universal and impersonal rationality[6]—to trust in its efficacy and morality. The young Engels was convinced that individual interests, however emphatic, "can never operate in history as independent, guiding aims, but always, consciously or unconsciously, serve a principle which controls the threads of historical progress."[7] It was a "secular" rendering of putting one's trust in the Lord.

The young Engels was prepared to contend that history was all of a piece—intrinsically rational and moral. It was governed by the eminently rational "World Spirit"—to which the individual, in the last analysis, was subordinate. He went on to speak of "world history" as the bearer of "Germany's life blood," and of Germany "serving" that "Spirit," from whose judgment "there is no appeal."

In that service, Germany functioned as "the pointer on the scales of European history, to watch over the development of the neighboring nations." Engels spoke of all this in the context of the "new Hegelianism" that had articulated

---

[5] Engels, "Schelling and Revelation," ibid., vol. 2, p. 200.
[6] Engels, "Alexander Jung, 'Lectures on Modern German Literature,'" ibid., vol. 2, p. 287.
[7] Engels, "The Internal Crisis," ibid., vol. 2, pp. 370–371.

itself after the death of the Master.[8] For the modern reader, around all of this there clings an unmistakable air of religiosity.

By the time he was twenty, Engels had put together a collection of convictions, drawn from a number of contemporary influences, which laid the foundations for his subsequent intellectual development. In the next few years, he was to mature into his beliefs, and take on the properties with which he has come to be known in history. We are told that this was a passage from "idealism" and "petty bourgeois democratic opinion," to "materialism" and "communism."[9] In fact, the transit had something of a different character.

Friedrich Engels (1820–1895)

From 1839 to 1844, between the ages of nineteen and twenty-four, Friedrich Engels gave expression to the components of that belief system that would govern his political life. By the time he had written *Schelling and Revelation* in 1841–1842, in defense of Hegel, he was prepared to speak of history as "a consciously occurring process," animated by "a self knowing Spirit." More than that, he continued, "that which exists as a consciously occurring process," moved by an omniscient Spirit, could only be "divine."[10] It was in that sense that the pious Engels could speak of the "new philosophy" as a "true religion" to distinguish it from the semblance of religion that prevailed in the retrograde Germany of his time.

At that stage in his intellectual development, Engels was at ease in speaking of the "Absolute Spirit" actualizing itself as a "concrete reality" in the political state.[11] His readiness to speak in such fashion was probably the result of the fact that, at that time, he was especially intent on the study of Hegel's *Philosophy of History*. It was a work he characterized as "enormous"—a text that he felt was as though "written from his own heart." He reported that every evening he "dutifully" read in the book, letting the "tremendous thoughts grip [him] terribly." It was in that work that the young Engels discovered that it was "Hegel's principle that humanity and divinity are in essence identical."[12] Engels seemed prepared to recognize that the "new Hegelianism," toward which he was drawn, had some of the major features of a religion—just as had the "old Hegelianism"—none of which seemed to disturb him in the least.

[8] Engels, "Ernst Moritz Arndt," ibid., vol. 2, pp. 137, 141, 143, 149.
[9] See the introductory discussion in Hannes Skambraks, ed., *Zwischen 18 und 15: Jugendbriefe von Friedrich Engels* (Berlin: Dietz Verlag, 1965).
[10] Engels, "Schelling and Revelation," *MECW*, vol. 2, pp. 213, 222.
[11] Engels, "Alexander Jung, 'Lectures on Modern German Literature,'" ibid., vol. 2, p. 289.
[12] Engels, "To Friedrich Graeber," ibid., vol. 2, pp. 486, 490.

As part of his derivative conception of the world, Engels conceived "objective reality" as "rational"—and history as the mechanism by virtue of which "the concept of freedom" was to be realized. For Engels, history required being "listened to."[13] As a consequence, he was prepared to maintain that history was possessed of "the right to dispose of the life, the happiness, the freedom of the individual, for [history] is the activity of mankind as a whole, it is the life of the species, and as such it is sovereign; no one can revolt against it, for it is absolute right. No one can complain against history, for whatever it allots one, one lives and shares in the development of mankind, which is more than any enjoyment." In substance and effect, history, the ultimate arbiter of rational freedom, has the right "to sacrifice the individual for the general."[14] "History," for Engels, was characterized by very singular, preemptive, moral authority.

By the time he had barely reached maturity, Engels had persuaded himself that one could speak of world history as a scripted drama, governed by an abiding purpose in which human actors found themselves performing assigned roles. The young Engels seems very early to have been persuaded that history was a morality play, a cosmic human drama, animated by human purpose, and driven by collective human interests.[15] Together with all of that, in evident agreement with what he took to be "Hegelian doctrine," he anticipated the "moral perfection" of human beings through their "merging into the world soul."[16] Not only was the world governed by moral purpose, but human beings could themselves only attain moral fulfillment by subordinating themselves to that purpose. Engels saw Hegelianism not only as a key to understanding history, but as a program for human salvation as well. Hegelianism had taught him that "mankind is of divine origin," and must, "without respite," make itself "the equal of God in spiritual perfection." As a neohegelian, Engels seems to have always been convinced of both the "divinity of humanity" as well as the divinity of all "that which exists."[17]

For the young Engels, history, in its totality, shared manifestly religious properties. He had learned all that from the neohegelians who sought the establishment of a new creed. Engels was convinced that humanity sought evidence that reason constituted "the inner essence" of all reality—evidence that traditional religion failed to provide. With Feuerbach, he reminded his audience that the

---

[13] Engels, "Diary of a Guest Student," ibid., vol. 2, p. 272.

[14] Engels, "Centralization and Freedom" and "To Friedrich Graeber," ibid., 2, pp. 356, 357, 491.

[15] As early as 1840, Engels spoke of history as having a "course" and "rushing" from one set of human ideas to another. See Engels, "Retrograde Signs of the Times," ibid., vol. 2, pp. 47, 48.

[16] Engels, "To Friedrich Graeber," ibid., vol. 2, p. 477.

[17] Engels, "To Friedrich Graeber, July 12–27, 1839"; "To Friedrich Graeber, December 9, 1839– February 5, 1840," and *Schelling and Revelation*, ibid., vol. 2, pp. 222, 458, 459, 490.

contrived religion of the conventional churches had alienated humankind from its most precious attributes—reason and morality among them. Traditional religion had failed to see the reason behind the world, and in the process demeaned and diminished humankind. Humankind could expect nothing from established faith in their efforts to regain lost integrity.

Instead of attempting to refurbish the decadent religions of the time in a futile effort to meet human requirements, Engels instead urged making recourse to what he identified as the "Bible of Universal History"—a "Bible" that was "the eternal book of God in which every man, while his spirit and the light of his eyes are yet with him, may see God's finger write." Engels proposed that we see God in "universal history." For us, he continued, "history is all and everything ... and we hold it more highly than any other previous philosophical trend, more highly than Hegel even. ..." Engels saw in universal history the tracings of "God's finger"[18] and the salvation of humankind.

For Engels, it was clear that a studied account of world history provided all the spiritual benefits hitherto expected from traditional religion. World history was the impersonal vehicle of human salvation, the repository of moral substance, and the irresistible agency of universal freedom. More than it was for Hegel, world history was for Engels "all and everything." Like Hess and Feuerbach, Engels found in history the truth of religion.

The clearly religious character of Engels' thought at the time distinguished itself from any standard religion by its increasingly specific content. Like almost all educated youth in postnapoleonic Germany, Engels soon occupied himself with the specifics of political, social, and religious reform. In his earliest writings, one finds a preoccupation with the life conditions of those around him. As has been suggested, his "Letters from Wuppertal," in 1839, contained objections to factory labor, and the human degradation it fostered. Those objections were essentially moral in tone and expression—and finding them in an article written by someone of Engels' persuasion was only to be expected. Similar sentiments were found in the publications of "new Hegelians" and their like, and were frequently accompanied by reasonably sophisticated economic and political analyses.

As has been suggested, Moses Hess typified an entire class of similar critics. Motivated by essentially religious inspiration, as early as 1837, one finds him inveighing against the disparities of wealth and poverty to be found throughout the most developed parts of Europe. In his *Die europäische Triarchie* of 1841, however much moved by moral considerations, we find him advancing the sociotheoretical claim that the development of tools influenced, if not de-

---

[18] Engels, "The Condition of England: *Past and Present* by Carlyle," ibid., vol. 3, pp. 463, 464.

termined, the emergence of patterns of social behavior. He saw an important relationship between the availability of specific instruments of production, and the appearance of specific social institutions. He attempted to trace a nexus between instruments of production and the moral failings of modern society.

With whatever data were available, Hess attempted to make a case that technological change produced only want among the class of workers—and that the industrial revolution had created pandemic poverty in England—to bring the nation to the brink of social revolution. The British "moneyed aristocracy" subjected the poor to such exactions that no other outcome was conceivable.[19] History would prompt revolution in order to resolve the "contradictions."

All of these critical elements were relatively commonplace in the intellectual and political environment in which the young Engels chose to pursue his interests. The entire atmosphere was alive with religious inspiration—with a call for the moral deliverance of human beings. That redemption would be forthcoming in the working out of history, through the activity of human beings prompted to seek change because of the very real social, economic, and political issues with which they were confronted. Not only had Hess given prominence to such issues, but Wilhelm Weitling, who dealt with many of the same concerns, had precipitated a significant reaction with the appearance of his *Garantien der Harmonie und Freiheit* in 1842.

As early as 1835, Weitling had become a member of the conspiratorial "League of the Just" in order to foster the revolutionary organization of the workers of central and western Europe. By 1838, he was advocating the mobilization of the entire working class in the disciplined effort to overcome the "tyranny of wealth" that created and sustained an immoral system whose most singular property was the exploitation of man by man. Weitling had early settled on the conviction that the first germ of that exploitation was to be found in earliest antiquity, when human beings made the fateful decision to abandon common ownership for private property. Without the intercession of private ownership into the common life of humanity, human beings never would have known anything of compulsory labor, hunger, penury, oppression, or open conflict. Weitling told his followers that before the advent of property "human beings lived in full equality, satisfaction, and peace.... Humanity, in its childhood innocence, lived in freedom and independence."[20]

Once private property made its appearance, human beings no longer sought satisfaction in community enhancement. They sought individual gratification,

---

[19] Moses Hess, *Die heilige Geschichte der Menschheit: Von einem Jünger Spinoza's, Die europäische Triarchie*, "Über eine in England bevorstehende Katastrophe," in *Philosophische und sozialistische Schriften 1837–1850* (Berlin: Akademmie-Verlag, 1961), pp. 64, 91–92, 160, 183–185.

[20] Wilhelm Weitling, *Garantien der Harmonie und Freiheit* (Berlin: Akadamie-Verlag, 1955), p. 10, and passim.

the accumulation of material assets, and its protection. Soon there were *exchanges* of fixed assets and commodities between property owners—to exploit opportunity costs to enhance personal profit and secure well-being. In such exchanges the strong and the clever invariably managed to accumulate more, and could more effectively protect what they had accumulated. Weapons were produced, and laws fashioned, all in the service of the protection of private property. Soon *foreign trade* was systematized so that the wealthy could accumulate still more—and arms were employed to provide that the profane traffic could be protected. For Weitling, contemporary society was the unjust product of original theft—the making private of what, by nature, was common. All the poverty, violence, and wretchedness that afflicts humankind is a direct, or indirect, consequence of that "original sin."[21] Like the account in the Old Testament, that sin was to exact its toll until redemption.

All the apparent talk of economic issues was strung together on sentiments that were religious in essence and in origin. It was all very familiar in the intellectual environment in which Engels matured. By the time he was twenty he was familiar with at least the thought of Hess and Weitling, active as they all were in the same circles. By 1843, Engels cited both in his published works.

By the early 1840s, Engels had familiarized himself sufficiently with that kind of material to confidently discuss the conditions that afflicted the generic "proletariat" in the world of commerce and industry.[22] Barely twenty-two years of age, he very quickly identified himself with the argument, and spoke with assurance and unself-conscious confidence of the "contradictions" that beset entire economies. He was fully prepared to comment on economic issues with few reservations—with all the confidence of a graduate student.

In December 1843, Engels spoke ominously of the antinomies of industrial society. He warned that they were dilemmas for which, under prevailing conditions, there was no solution. He spoke of the enormous wealth the modern system was capable of generating while, simultaneously, it could not avert creating a class of paupers, "absolutely poor people, a class which lives from hand to mouth, which multiplies rapidly, and which cannot afterwards be abolished, because it can never acquire stable possession of property. ... The slightest stagnation in trade," he continued, "deprives a considerable part of this class of their bread, a large scale trade crisis leaves the whole class without bread. When such a situation occurs, what is there left for these people to do but to revolt?" He concluded, therefore, that "revolution is inevitable for England."[23]

---

[21] See the discussion ibid., particularly chaps. 7 and 8.
[22] Engels, "The End of the *Criminalistische Zeitung*," *MECW*, vol. 2, p. 303.
[23] Engels, "The Internal Crises," ibid., vol. 2, pp. 373, 374.

It is difficult not to appreciate the sense of outraged justice that might lead to such a conclusion on the part of so young a scholar. Justice required punishment of those who exploited others. There would be little moral satisfaction in reform.

By the time he was twenty years of age, Engels was rehearsing all the claims that were to be the stock and trade of Marxists for the next century and a half. By the middle of 1843, his sojourn in England, as a representative of his father's interests, gave him the opportunity to observe the conditions surrounding, and the behaviors typifying, nonfarm labor. He could then supplement his opinions with his own personal observations and facts he gleaned from reports provided by inquiries conducted in the factories and workshops of the period. He spoke with some eloquence of the socialism that he anticipated would follow the revolution he judged both inevitable and imminent.

At least part of the reason he entertained such a judgment turned on his conviction that those proletarians he had come to know during his tenure in Manchester displayed singular virtues. They deserved their delivery. He spoke of their abiding interest in studies that dealt with their lives, addressed their concerns, explained their circumstances, and provided a suitable strategy.[24] Together with that, Engels reported a rapid growth of specifically communist sympathy among them.[25] Unlike most of the factory workers studied in the time since, those with whom Engels was familiar displayed all the engaging traits of disciples of a new faith.

By the end of the year, Engels expanded on his judgment. He spoke of Hess' "Triarchy," the "three great and civilised countries of Europe"—Britain, France, and Germany—as having all come to the conclusion "that a thorough revolution of social arrangements, based on community of property," had "become an urgent and unavoidable necessity." The "general facts of modern civilization," he insisted, forced the principal nations of Europe to a "necessary conclusion": they must all seek recourse in communism. He had convinced himself that "all nations, all different paths, must meet at Communism," because communism was "not the consequence of the particular position of the English ... but ... a

---

[24] In 1844 or 1845, Engels spoke with eloquence of the intellectual superiority of the British working class. He reported that he "often heard workingmen, whose fustian jackets scarcely held together, speak upon geological, astronomical, and other subjects, with more knowledge than most 'cultivated' bourgeois.... [That] the English proletariat has succeeded in attaining independent education is shown especially by the fact that the epoch making products of modern philosophical, political, and poetical literature are read by workingmen almost exclusively." Engels, *The Conditions of the Working-Class in England*, ibid., vol. 3, p. 528. Both Engels and Marx frequently made reference to the special intellectual gifts of the generic working class.

[25] See Engels, "Letters from London," ibid., vol. 3, pp. 379, 385.

necessary conclusion, which cannot be avoided to be drawn from the premises given in the general facts of modern civilisation."[26]

International communist revolution would be forthcoming as the necessary consequence of history itself. Like Hegel, Engels saw history as the "dialectical" product of extant conditions. Each epoch was the derivative, necessary product of a given set of antecedents. Very early in his maturity, Engels had settled on a Hegelian "science" of society.[27] His accounts characteristically described events by attributing to them implicit intent. Thus, he spoke of "the eighteenth century" as the time for "the assembling, the gathering of mankind from ... fragmentation and isolation.... The eighteenth century collated the results of the past, which had previously been scattered and appeared to be fortuitous, and laid bare their necessity and inner connection," which, in his judgment, could only result in a "universal social revolution."[28] He had persuaded himself that history had a destined terminus—an end that "must and will come."[29] Although events might appear fortuitous, Engels was convinced that he understood history's moral imperatives. It was a conviction he would entertain, and an expository pattern he would employ, throughout his life.[30]

At almost twenty-three years of age, the young Engels had put together his vision of the world. He had taken Hegel's grand metaphysical conception, in which history was the story of a divine force shepherding humankind to that promised land of final fulfillment—and made of it a "science." Like Hegel, Engels saw his world as alive with electric "contradictions"—contradictions that would move events forward. He saw in England industrial modernity in all its full complexity—its shameless excesses, and its wretched poverty. He saw in that "contradictions"—but contradictions of a peculiar sort. They were not *logical*; they were *moral*. However moral, they were nonetheless contradictions that engaged material, observable factors—variables that could function as causes. What distinguished them was the fact that the consequences of such material causes involved not only measureable *effects*, but *justice* as well. Like many, before and after, Engels sought not only to make sense of history, but to imagine that it would render justice.

In that sense, and for our account, Engels' "Outlines of a Critique of Political

---

[26] Engels, "Progress of Social Reform on the Continent," ibid., vol. 3, pp. 392, 393.

[27] See his discussion in his letter "To Wilhelm Graeber, 13–20 November 1839," ibid., vol. 2, pp. 486–487.

[28] Engels, "The Condition of England: The Eighteenth Century," ibid., vol. 3, pp. 479, 480, 481.

[29] Engels, "Outlines of a Critique of Political Economy," ibid., vol. 3, p. 441.

[30] Engels insisted that "historical development" pursued an "unavoidable march" to the "point at which [communism] becomes both possible and necessary." Engels, *The Condition of the Working-Class in England*, ibid., vol. 3, p. 525.

Economy," published in 1844, is among his most interesting early publications. It conveys a great deal about the kind of science that would animate some of the most important revolutionary movements of the nineteenth century—and it provides an appreciation of the profoundly moral imperatives that would sustain them.

Engels' long essay is a formidable work, carefully written and intellectually focused. Perhaps its most important feature, for expository purposes, is its unmistakably Hegelian character. It pursues its subject matter from "contradiction" to "contradiction," from "antithesis" to "antithesis"—in a "context of antitheses" that awaits "transcendence," "sublation," "supersession."[31] The transcendence, in which Engels expected all contradictions to be *aufgehoben*, proceeded in typical Hegelian fashion.

Economists, Engels tells his readers, commit themselves, without reflective thought, to the "validity of private property." They argue that private property is a singularly positive feature of life's circumstances; it is the hope of humankind, an extension of self, an inalienable right. In fact, Engels argues, it is the very existence of that "inalienable right" that makes of the earth a cursed creation. Professional economists fail to understand any of that. Engels informs them that it is private property that condemns millions to penury, to be denied all hope of owning property as their inalienable right. For Engels, that was the central contradiction of the modern world.

Only because concealed by "sophistry" and "hypocrisy," does the pretense that private property serves the general interests of humanity persist. But all the sophistry and hypocrisy in the world cannot conceal reality from those who are enlightened. Engels perceives the contradiction; academic economists do not. And still, history will triumph. All the sophistry and hypocrisy of all the learned economists cannot stand against it. Engels informs his audience that the "economist does not know himself what cause he serves. He does not know that with all his egoistical reasoning he nevertheless forms but a link in the chain of mankind's universal progress."[32] The "cunning of history" shapes to its service even the hypocrisies of learned gentlemen. Somehow or other, the cunning of history works through them.

Given the character and structure of his argument, it is clear that Engels' account is manifestly and singularly Hegelian. "Contradictions," in the version made available by Engels, would seem to move events that apparently follow a "dialectical"—a necessary and quasideductive—sequence. The course of that

[31] See Engels, "Outlines of a Critique of Political Economy," ibid., vol. 3, pp. 439 and, for example, 419, 421, 423, 429.
[32] Ibid., p. 424.

sequence may remain unappreciated to the participants, but each, somehow, is required to discharge his or her responsibilities. Individuals, consciously or unconsciously, knowingly or unaware, contribute to the process destined to conclude with the moral salvation of humanity.[33]

What that seems to mean becomes apparent in the course of his delivery. There are "factors," he argues, that are operative in the environment under scrutiny that will transform it in the fashion "history" intends. Academic economists either do not, or choose not, to perceive that. They do not recognize, or conceal the fact, that the evolving industrial economy of Great Britain, presumably committed to the prosperity of its nation's citizens, in fact produces pauperism, infanticide, and degradation for the vast majority. Academic economists apparently do not appreciate that private property generates competition, with each individual seeking personal advantage at the expense of his or her neighbor. Professional economists do not observe, or refuse to acknowledge, that workers compete against each other for labor without which they, and their families, must starve. Professional economists do not observe, or refuse to draw implications from the fact, that capitalists compete in order to increase their profits—at the cost of driving their competitors into the ranks of the proletariat. The result of which is that the numbers opposed to the offending system accumulate. Academicians fail to recognize, or refuse to report, that at the same time, those entrepreneurs who survive the carnage are driven to higher and higher levels of productivity, only to find themselves without a consumer base sufficient to clear their inventories at a profit. Learned economists fail to appreciate that all of this results in a system that drives itself, with oppressive regularity, from productive expansion to recession, from economic boom to industrial contraction. At all times, with expansion or contraction of the economic system, workers are marginal to the system, living at subsistence wages in good times and under threat of pauperism and starvation when times are bad. All of creation was cursed.

Even in the best of times there are superfluous workers whom the authorities recommend to workhouses or prisons. Academics advocate restricting births and allowing the "excess" population to perish. As though totally oblivious to all that, professional economists fail to acknowledge or report that the entire system must necessarily lapse into just such a chronic state of moral degradation and material decay.[34] Money becomes the only surviving ligament between

---

[33] Ibid., p. 439.

[34] A great deal of this is reminiscent of the publications of Moses Hess as well. The very necessity of historical laws, fashioned and imposed by a world spirit, are found in the earliest of Hess' publications. The greed and selfishness attendant on the existence of private property, the degradation

isolated human beings[35]—in a world devoid of love, compassion, meaning, and humanity. According to Engels, all of this is unknown to those learned academicians who have made economy their professed interest.

Engels' response is eminently Hegelian. The system necessarily produces its own "sublation," while professionals understand none of it. Modern industrial society, for Engels, is a society in which the number of those subjects who are necessarily in opposition irresistibly grows over time into the vast majority.[36] Those who defend the system systematically decrease in number. As the system grows in time, the poor become poorer and their numbers increase while the rich become richer and their numbers diminish. The system becomes increasingly productive while effective demand decreases throughout. With dysfunctions increasing in frequency and severity, Engels insists that the outcome can be predicted with certainty; the inevitable result is social revolution.[37] All of that, Engels argued, escaped the attention of professionals.

What had changed in Engels' delivery between 1840 and 1844 was not its Hegelian construction—and all the implications that entailed. Engels continued to conceive history moving with metered pace from the uncertain and featureless human consciousness of the past to the immanent full and free human consciousness trembling on the brink of realization in the then present. He perceived morality animating the entire process, with reason rendering it comprehensible to the initiated. He saw history's passage as inevitable, displaying all the unmistakable features of the Hegelian "World Spirit."[38]

Given this account, Engels allowed himself to anticipate certain consequences. About the same time that he published his "Outlines of a Critique of Political Economy," he wrote that should there be those who failed to understand history's enterprise, to voice "disbelief" in reason, despair of the intellect,

---

of human beings as a consequence, the competition that renders them debased, the dysfunctions of an immoral community that follow, are all found in the writings of Hess, whom Engels identified as the "first communist of the party." Engels, "Progress of Social Reform on the Continent," ibid., vol. 3, p. 406.

[35] Elsewhere, Engels approvingly cites Carlyle, who insists that in industrial circumstances, "Cash payment is the only nexus between man and man." Engels, *The Condition of the Working-Class in England*, ibid., vol. 3, p. 563.

[36] At one point, a short while later, Engels argues that the process might see "the proletariat ... soon embrace the whole nation, with the exception of a few millionaires." Ibid., p. 580.

[37] In the *Condition of the Working-Class in England*, Engels informed his readers, "These are all inferences which may be drawn with the greatest certainty.... Prophecy is nowhere so easy as in England, where all the component elements of society are clearly defined and sharply separated. The revolution must come.... It is too late for a peaceful solution.... The only possible solution is a violent revolution, which cannot fail to take place." Ibid., vol. 3, pp. 547, 581, 583.

[38] Engels affirms that historical results "must and will come." Ibid., p. 441.

and the truth to be found "in the 'Bible of Universal History,'" they would be expressing a "disbelief like none other." It would be "a disbelief" one would be compelled to "punish, not by burning at the stake," but certainly "with the most imperative command to keep one's silence." Those who "disbelieved" would be the enemies of truth and goodness—and would be required to remain mute.[39]

None of this seems appropriate if one is dealing with *scientific* opinion. One does not *punish* a difference of opinion in science. One punishes moral infractions, or religious heresies, or apostasies. An appeal to evidence, not punishment, is expected to resolve scientific disagreements. Punishments—ostracism, shunning, excommunication, defrocking, the imposition of silence—attend religious disputes. In science, none of that is expected to take place. All of which leaves one with a sense that Engels conceives himself dealing with something other than science as science is understood in the contemporary world. His position would seem to be the product of those religious sentiments that made up so much of his thought during his young manhood. They seemed to have influenced his thought well into his maturity.

It was in delivering his "Outlines of a Critique of Political Economy," to the *Deutsch-Französische Jahrbücher*, that Engels engaged the serious interest of Karl Marx—with whom he thereafter was to enter into lifelong collaboration. Dismissed at their first meeting in 1842, Engels subsequently impressed Marx with his "Outlines." Marx read the essay and prepared an outline in summary for his subsequent use. For years Marx was to refer to the work, and repeatedly cited it in the course of his later publications. Much later, he still spoke of it as a "brilliant sketch." There is the unmistakable suggestion in the available evidence, that Engels' essay was of more than passing interest to Marx; in fact, some have suggested that it exercised a "decisive influence" on the development of his thought; and that is very likely the case.[40] All the sentiments and the argued vision with which Engels identified himself were to find a place in Marxism as a revolutionary ideology.

By their meeting in Paris in August 1844, it was evident to both Engels and Marx that each had found in the other an intellectual ally. They were kindred spirits who would collaborate for the remainder of their lives. Both were convinced that they stood on the threshold of a new epoch in world history. They not only agreed in their anticipations of the immediate future, but their

---

[39] Engels, "The Condition of England: *Past and Present* by Carlyle," ibid., vol. 3, p. 457.
[40] David McLellan, *Friedrich Engels* (New York: Penguin Books, 1977), p. 39. The editors of the English edition of the Marx-Engels works remarked that Engels' "'Outlines of a Critique of Political Economy' ... was one of the causes which led Marx to study political economy." "Preface," ibid., vol. 3, p. xx.

very agreements were phrased in Hegelianisms that were to remain common to them throughout their collaboration. Anyone familiar with their work can hardly fail to recognize how much Hegelianism molded both its form and content. Together, inspired by common sentiments, and armed with neohegelian enthusiasms, they were destined to shape revolutionary thought for more than a century.

Karl Marx (1818–1883)

In the years before his fateful meeting with Friedrich Engels, the young Marx was occupied with his own education. He was a gifted student. Born to a well established family, his early life was governed by literary and artistic interests. Whatever literary efforts survive from his youth provide evidence of his acute mind and aggressive intelligence. Even his earliest correspondence was well crafted and engaging. With the intellectual maturity that came with his university studies, his productivity became increasingly impressive. His doctoral dissertation was notable, tightly written, carefully researched, conceptually focused, and clearly satisfactory to his academic mentors.[41] Almost immediately upon the completion of his doctorate, he embarked upon a career of social criticism and, eventually, revolutionary activity.

Between the years of his higher education and 1844, Marx might be identified as a convinced democrat and a political liberal. Such postures were considered "radical" in the political climate of the time. However radical, Marx's truly revolutionary career began roughly about the time of his encounter with Engels. The features of his revolutionary commitment are best captured in essays he produced in 1844, *The Economic and Philosophic Manuscripts*.

Between April and August 1844, months after Engels wrote his "Outlines of a Critique of Political Economy," the young Marx composed those documents that have come down to us as *The Economic and Philosophic Manuscripts of 1844*. They are documents that were subsequently laid aside, to remain unavailable for almost one hundred years. Recovered and published in the 1920s and 1930s, they are, for the purposes of the present exposition, singularly important.[42] In those documents Marx takes the occasion, at their very commencement, to identify the principal sources from which, at the time, he drew inspiration, insight, and substance. He duly acknowledged his intellectual indebtedness

[41] Karl Marx, "Difference Between the Democritean and Epicurean Philosophy of Nature," ibid., vol. 1, pp. 25–106.

[42] Most of the substance of the subsequent discussion is to be found in the *Economic and Philosophic Manuscripts of 1844*, ibid., vol. 3, pp. 229–346.

to Hegel, to Ludwig Feuerbach, to Friedrich Engels, and to Moses Hess; and throughout the text, there is unmistakable evidence of their influence.[43] Each clearly contributed, in special fashion, to that surrogate for traditional religion that was to become known to history as "Marxism."

As early as his first years at university, the young Marx had become a Hegelian. He wrote to his father that it was his intention to fashion "a philosophical dialectical account of divinity, as it manifests itself as the idea in itself, as religion, as nature, and as history."[44] It was an eminently Hegelian enterprise. The immediate difficulty was that Hegel had already accomplished it. Nonetheless, it was the task upon which the young Marx had settled.

Marx soon found himself in association with others equally fascinated by Hegel and Hegelianism. Through the early 1840s, Marx remained a Hegelian, but committed to that Hegelianism that had been revised and reformed by Ludwig Feuerbach—to be informed by substance found in the first works of Hess and Engels.

In the manuscripts of 1844, Marx made all that apparent without the least hesitation—and for the first time, he sought to make clear what his notion of "dialectics" might mean in the new context. He held it necessary, at that point in his intellectual life, to settle accounts not only with "Hegelian dialectics," but German philosophy as a whole. He judged both to be the point of origin of all then-contemporary revolutionary thought.[45]

Of all those revisionists who influenced the young Marx at the time, it was initially Ludwig Feuerbach who most critically shaped his views.[46] Marx identified Feuerbach as the thinker who was to transform the Hegelianism left as an intellectual legacy by the Master.[47] One need only reflect on the substance of Feuerbach's *Principles of the Philosophy of the Future*[48] to appreciate the cogency of Marx's judgment.

[43] Ibid., p. 232.

[44] Marx, "Letter from Marx to His Father in Trier," ibid., vol. 1, p. 18.

[45] Ibid., p. 233.

[46] It was during the writing of the *Economic and Philosophic Manuscripts of 1844* that Marx directly wrote to Feuerbach to tell him that he, Feuerbach, had provided socialism and communism with their "philosophical foundation." As has been indicated, Marx felt so indebted to Feuerbach that he ventured so far as to tell him that he "loved" him. "Marx to Feuerbach, 11 August 1844," Ludwig Feuerbach, *Briefwechsel* (Leipzig: Verlag Philipp Reclam, 1963), pp. 183–184.

[47] "It is only with *Feuerbach* that *positive*, humanistic and naturalistic criticism begins." Ibid., vol. 3, p. 232. I have elsewhere provided a brief account of Feuerbach's influence on Marx in providing him with his "inversion" of the Hegelian dialectic. See A. James Gregor, "Marx, Feuerbach and the Reform of the Hegelian Dialectic," *Science & Society*, 29, no. 1 (Winter 1965), pp. 66–80.

[48] Ludwig Feuerbach, *Principles of the Philosophy of the Future* (New York: The Bobbs-Merrill Company, Inc., 1966).

According to Marx's assessment, it was Feuerbach who, "in principle," had "overthrown the old dialectic," to provide, in its stead, a Feuerbachian alternative.[49] What that can be taken to mean is important. Feuerbach, throughout his analysis, retains the quasideductive character of the Hegelian dialectic[50]—what he changed was its content. Hegel's philosophy was relentlessly idealistic; that of Feuerbach, materialistic, sensualistic, empirical.[51]

Throughout most of his intellectual life, Marx either alluded to, or employed, what he took to be the dialectic. It is clear that the dialectic employed was essentially that of Feuerbach—Hegelian in form, but host to an alternative content. For those unfamiliar with the critical formative years of Marx's intellectual development, it remained uncertain how the dialectic was to be understood. Direct or indirect allusions were made regularly to the dialectic in Marxist literature—and yet what the dialectic was, and what its role might be, remained obscure. For all the frequency of its use, it remains unclear what the dialectic might be taken to mean. The dialectic has been sometimes spoken of as a special methodological procedure; at other times it seems to have been conceived as referring to some unique content. A review of Marx's treatment in *The Economic and Philosophic Manuscripts of 1844* is helpful in providing some instructive insight.

The "new dialectic," to which the young Marx had been converted, did not reject the quasideductive processes involved in the traditional dialectic of Hegel (however those processes were understood). The revisionists retained dialectics as a kind of informal logic—as a quasideductive set of rules, essential to historical explanation and prediction. That seemed to correspond to the uses to which it was put by Marx.

It is clear that the new dialectic, conceived by Feuerbach and employed by Marx, differed from that of Hegel almost exclusively in terms of content. While Hegel's dialectic proceeded through thought categories, the new dialectic traced, in real time, what it conceived to be a historic path through "concrete," "real," stages—measured in terms of content that was almost exclusively religious for Feuerbach and social and economic for Marx.

---

[49] Marx speaks specifically of a "Feuerbachian dialectic" in identifying the variations on that of Hegel, *Economic and Philosophic Manuscripts of 1844, MECW*, vol. 3, pp. 327–328.

[50] The entire analysis of Feuerbach's *The Essence of Christianity*, and the exposition in *Principles of the Philosophy of the Future*, trade on contradictions, contraries, negations, and antinomies.

[51] I have elsewhere discussed the influence of Feuerbach's revision of the Hegelian dialectic. When Marx spoke of his "inversion" of the Hegelian dialectic, what he was alluding to was the abandonment of idealistic content for that which was materialistic. There was no objection to the quasideductive form of Hegel's dialectic. See Gregor, "Marx, Feuerbach, and the Reform of the Hegelian Dialectic," pp. 66–80.

For Marx, the content of the new dialectic no longer concerned itself with "abstract thinking," but with content furnished by a *"true materialism,"* itself recommended by Feuerbach. There would be far less *conceptual* talk of "contradictions" and "antitheses" in the new dialectic—and more reference to actual conflict in the empirical world. As a consequence, *history* would no longer be a story of the resolution, the "supersession," of "contradictions" in "abstract" and "speculative thought." Rather, the entire dynamic of Hegel's dialectic would be mapped over the tensions that activate human beings in circumstances of "real sensuousness"—in which humankind struggles to resolve all the "self-estrangements" and "alienations" with which it finds itself afflicted. Marx insisted that only by acknowledging that human beings are "real," "corporeal," and "natural beings"—rather than simply phantasms of "abstract logic and self-consciousness"—might one really be "capable of comprehending the action of world history."[52]

Notwithstanding its substitution of content, the new dialectic did not alter the scope and character of world history. In the context of the new dialectic—as it has been in traditional Hegelianism—history would remain the story of the deliverance of humanity. No longer abstract, it would no longer deal with thought categories, but with "the true natural history of man." It would no longer deal with those seeming resolutions of self-estrangements that take place in the abstract self-consciousness of equally abstract human beings. The new dialectic would recognize in the human being something more than self-consciousness. Human beings would be understood to live a "true human life"—with all the sufferings and passion that constitutes that life. That life would include the same "self-estrangements," their "alienations," and their resolution, that one found in Hegelianism. The difference was that all that would take place, not in abstract thinking, but in the real world, in economics, law, and politics.[53]

Moses Hess and Friedrich Engels had urged that recognition on Marx. In the years immediately prior to the composition of the manuscripts of 1844, Marx remained a "democratic liberal." The democratic liberalism of that early period rested on the implications of the philosophical humanism of Feuerbach, and on the revisionisms of the Hegelian dialectic that entailed.

In the early years of his political activity Marx, like Feuerbach, spoke of Hegel's fundamental mistake as not making "real subjects" the basis of social and political inquiry. Marx complained that Hegel dealt not with "actual subjects" but with "mystical ideas" that he somehow fashioned into imagined enti-

---

[52] Marx, *Economic and Philosophic Manuscripts of 1844*, MECW, vol. 3, pp. 328, 331, 335, 336
[53] See the entire discussion ibid., pp. 294–321, 337, 339.

ties. What Hegel had done was to write a "biography of abstract substance"; he had projected selected attributes of humanity into conjectural space, and made of them independent, if airy, objects.[54] Marx was fully committed to that feature of the Feuerbachian critique of Hegelianism.

That particular revision of Hegelianism was of Feuerbachian origin; and Marx recognized it as such. The task, as Marx conceived it in the early months of 1843—before commencing his economic and philosophic manuscripts—was a "reform of consciousness" that would effect an abandonment of that "mystical consciousness that is unintelligible to itself, whether it manifests itself in a religious or a political form." It would be a reform of consciousness that would result in the realization of human desires long awaited. It would produce the practical, empirical satisfaction of essential human needs.

At the time, Marx identified what he sought as "true humanism"—while its substance was clearly Feuerbachian, its modalities were Hegelian. All the discussions found in those documents written by Marx before he composed the manuscripts of 1844 proceed in Hegelian meter and Feuerbachian cadence. History moves as a consequence of the sublation of contradictions; and we are told of a history moved to seek the redemptive achievement of a life "devoid of contradictions," in which humans would enjoy a "real species life," a true fullness of emancipation—a moral consummation. All those contradictions that drove history forward through time would be resolved in a Feuerbachian humanism.[55]

Almost all of this is Feuerbach transliterated into the locutions of the political liberalism of 1843.[56] Marx's radicalism of the period is the radicalism of Feuerbachian humanism. Like Feuerbach, Marx saw humankind estranged from its "essence" by a social and economic order that severed all species ties and "dissolved the human world into a world of atomistic individuals who are inimically opposed to one another."[57] Only total human emancipation could restore the flawless unity of individuals.

By the first half of 1844, Marx's assessments would be significantly transformed. The dialectic would remain the "new dialectic" of Feuerbach, char-

---

[54] See Marx, "Contribution to the Critique of Hegel's Philosophy of Law," ibid., vol. 3, pp. 23, 29.

[55] Marx, "On the Jewish Question," ibid., vol. 3, pp. 151, 153–154, 159–160, 162, 167.

[56] Only when real, sensuous human beings reabsorb into themselves "the abstract citizen, and as an individual human being has become a *species being* in ... everyday life ... and no longer separates social power ... from political power, only then will human emancipation have been accomplished." Only then would "the conflict between man's individual sensuous existence and his species existence" be abolished. Human beings would then be fully redeemed. Ibid., pp. 168, 174.

[57] Ibid., p. 173.

acterized by its rhetoric of liberation. That was to change as Moses Hess and Friedrich Engels were to fully exercise their influence on the increasingly radicalized Marx.

Both Hess and Engels were neohegelians, perfectly comfortable with the quaint "logic" and the religious locutions of the Hegelianism of the period. They conceived the movement of history a consequence of the "overcoming," the "resolution," of contradiction, antitheses, and antinomies. They structured their delivery in those terms. The differences in content became increasingly important, and, almost immediately, recast the thought of the young Marx.

Moses Hess had early addressed some of the empirical issues that increasingly would occupy the thought of Marx. As early as 1841, Hess had discussed some of the factors that he imagined negatively impacted the lives of human beings. While they were "real," rather than "abstract," factors, they were only marginally discussed by Feuerbach. By 1844, they were to become increasingly central to discussion among radicals—and Marx, by inclusion.

What was to remain constant were the neohegelian formulations common to all those who considered themselves "Young Hegelians."

Like most of the neohegelians, Hess was to address himself to the "estrangements of self," those "self-externalizations" that helped configure the lives of human beings in the modern era. The terms, and the informal logic, were those of Hegel, but, over time, the applications became increasingly "empirical." Together with Feuerbach, Hess insisted that the estrangements and alienations of which he spoke took place not in thought, as with Hegel, but in real flesh and blood circumstances. Unlike Feuerbach, Hess framed those "estrangements" and "alienations" not in psychological terms, but in terms of economic factors. Hess saw workers "externalize" themselves in labor—only to have the objects created by that labor serve in their own exploitation. The goods produced by workers would be employed by the regnant "masters of wealth" to dehumanize those who had produced them. Labor created commodities that became the private property of those who sold them for profit—a profit that was employed against the well-being of workers.

Hess provided the neohegelian dialectic of Feuerbach with an entirely different content. The concepts he invoked were economic rather than religious. He spoke of capitalists and not clerics. He spoke of real workers "projecting themselves" through labor into things that became the possessions of others—to then find themselves subject to alien and hostile powers they had themselves created. He spoke of the "contradictions" that resulted, destined to be "sublated," "superseded," in social revolution.[58] Hess employed the specifically reli-

---

[58] See his discussion of the imminent social revolution that awaited England because of the

gious references of Feuerbach to address fundamental economic concerns—always couched in the logic of Hegel.

Preserving the apparent logic of the Hegelian dialectic, Hess substituted talk of economic conflict and class tension for that of a clash of concepts. In supplying the Hegelian dialectic with alternative content, he did essentially that done by Feuerbach in his *Essence of Christianity*. The self-estrangements that Feuerbach analyzed in the religious life of human beings, Hess traced in the concrete life of living labor. For Feuerbach, individuals made compensatory projections of some of their own properties into a transcendent realm peopled by imaginary spirits. Those fictive spirits came to dominate and exploit, through church dogma and church institutions, the very human beings who were their source. For Feuerbach, that dialectical process was the central contradiction of religious life. "Externalizations" of themselves, entities of their own creation—deities and angelic spirits—came to warp and diminish human life. The contradictions were sublated in a change of consciousness—in which human beings recognized what had generated the prevailing antitheses.

Hess conceived the dialectical process in essentially the same manner; only Hess saw *workers* projecting themselves into things made—only to see those things arrayed against them. Workers who had "externalized" themselves in commodities, found themselves pauperized by those who made those commodities their own. For Hess, that was the central *contradiction* of modern life; it generated all the *antitheses* that provided the energy that activated the real history of the contemporary world.[59] Workers pauperized and threatened with starvation resolved the contradiction through social revolution.

By the time Engels began to occupy himself with these problems, he could only profit from the antecedent work of Feuerbach and Hess. They had already provided an analytic strategy made up of a quasideductive form containing empirical content.[60] What distinguished Engels' essays from theirs was the greater specificity in terms of substance. Engels, for example, concentrated on economic variables to an extent absent in the work of Hess. Following the same

---

"contradiction" involving "pauperism" in the midst of wealth. Hess, "Über eine in England bevorstehende Katastrophe," and *Die europäische Triarchie* in *Philosophische und sozialisisce Schriften 1837–1850*, pp. 162, 183.

[59] See some illustrative instances of the use of the Hegelian dialectic, contradictions, antitheses, and sublation. Ibid., pp. 94, 95, 96.

[60] As early as 1841, in his *Schelling and Revelation*, Engels cited his indebtedness to Hegel and to the works of Feuerbach. See particularly *MECW*, vol. 2, pp. 192, 195–197, 199, 201, 202, 209. Engels speaks of the Hegelian dialectic as "that inner motive force which constantly drives" human behavior. Ibid., p. 206. He accepts Feuerbach's revisions and has the dialectic refer to nature, empirical reality, as the foundation of mind. See ibid., pp. 216–217.

dialectical logic, he provided Marx a much more topically grounded rendition of the same themes. However the substance changed, what remained constant through all the varied depictions was the salvific logic of the Hegelian dialectic. More important for the present concerns is the fact that the familiar logic, together with its "new" and "concrete" substance, moved predictably through time with history as its medium. Engels spoke of the entire procedure as a manifestation of the "spirit," "the crown of which" he understood to be "world history."[61] In fact, for neohegelians, for Hess as it was for Feuerbach, *history* remained the agency that served the moral purposes of the world spirit—and human beings, responding to the contradictions that confronted them, moved world history forward to its redemptive ends.

When Engels wrote his "The Condition of England" in early 1844, he gave expression to all those themes. He spoke of the contradictions that provided substance to the times. He spoke of the "goal" of history—the "self-understanding" and "self-liberation" of humankind—through revolutions rendered inevitable by prevailing "antitheses." And he spoke of the history that would bring deliverance to humankind as "true science."[62] Those were all the elements that were to make their appearance in Marx's manuscripts of 1844. They are all elements of a secular religion.

In the pages of those manuscripts, Marx speaks of labor's estrangements. Like Hess and Engels before him, he speaks of the contradictions that result when the worker "externalizes" himself or herself in labor. He tells us that "the worker becomes all the poorer the more wealth he produces. . . . The *devaluation* of the world of men is in direct proportion to the *increasing value* of the world of things." That which "labor produces," he continued, "confronts it as something hostile and alien."[63] It is the kind of contradiction familiar to the "logic" of the dialectic. It is Feuerbach's new dialectic, peopled by the concrete, economic notions of Hess and Engels.[64]

Marx continues his exposition with the same logic and substance. "Objectified labor" becomes the "essence" of private property, of capital, of wealth.[65]

---

[61] Ibid., p. 213.

[62] Engels, "The Condition of England," ibid., vol. 3, pp. 469–470.

[63] Marx, *Economic and Philosophic Manuscripts of 1844*, ibid., vol. 3, pp. 271–272.

[64] Immediately before putting together the manuscripts of 1844, Marx reviewed an economic study published two decades before by James Mill. It seems perfectly obvious that Marx's interest in economic theory, and the literature surrounding the subject, found its inspiration in the recent work of Engels. Given form by the Feuerbachian revision of Hegel's dialectics, Engels supplied economic theory as the conceptual substance. See Karl Marx, "Comments on James Mill," ibid., vol. 3, pp. 212, 213.

[65] Engels refers to capital as "stored up labor." Engels, "Outlines of a Critique of Political Economy," ibid., vol. 3, p. 427.

So objectified, labor, as the private property of others, becomes hostile and exploitative to its creators—thereby giving rise to the central "antithesis" of the modern world. It is the supersession of that contradiction that will propel history. For Marx, recognition of that central contradiction—that private property is the manifest form of the estrangement of man—supplies an answer to the "riddle of history."[66]

For Marx, only "the positive transcendence of private property as human self-estrangement, and therefore as the real appropriation of the human essence by and for man" would solve history's central contradiction, and hence its abiding riddle. Only the abolition of private property would allow the "reintegration or return of man to himself." Only that would constitute the "genuine resolution" of all antitheses that separate "man and nature and man and man." It would end the "strife between existence and essence, between objectification and self-confirmation, between freedom and necessity, between the individual and the species."[67] It would bring to a moral conclusion the travails of created humanity. Humankind would be delivered.

How Marx chose to explain why that should be the case is instructive. He was always comfortable conceiving history as being charged with "tasks."[68] One of its apparent tasks was to oversee the gradual evolution of a free humanity—and that evolution was held to involve a protracted period, "a carrying into effect [of] old work."[69]

Marx, like Feuerbach, held that "man is the highest being for man." Convinced of that, Marx was prepared to argue that those who are righteous could only be bound by "the categorical imperative to overthrow all relations in which man is a debased, enslaved, forsaken, despicable being."[70] History, charged with being the demiurge of humankind's fulfillment, is understood to be not only teleologically directed, but animated by moral imperatives as well. Human beings are obliged to resist anything that diminishes humanity, that obstructs the full consummation of history's task.

In order to begin the progression that would conclude with the emancipation of humanity, we are informed that "*human* life required *private property* for

---

[66] "Political economy conceals the estrangement inherent in the nature of labor by not considering the direct relationship between the worker (labor) and production.... Labor produces wonderful things for the rich—but for the worker, hovels. It produces beauty—but for the worker, deformity." Marx, *Economic and Philosophic Manuscripts of 1844*, ibid., vol. 3, p. 273. Marx's allusion to the "riddle of history" appears ibid., p. 297.

[67] Ibid., p. 296.

[68] See, for example, Marx, "Contribution to the Critique of Hegel's Philosophy of Law," ibid., vol. 3, p. 176.

[69] Marx, "Letters from *Deutsch-Französische Jahrbücher*," ibid., vol. 3, p. 144.

[70] Marx, "Contribution to the Critique of Hegel's Philosophy of Law," ibid., vol. 3, p. 182.

its realization." To achieve its purposes, history would have to compel humanity to suffer the purgatory of original sin. The intrinsic logic of history *required* the emergence of private property—for it was to be private property that would generate all the contradictions that would bring history to its millennial resolution. Those contradictions included pauperism amidst wealth, private satisfactions versus public good, general utility versus private gain.[71] Like original sin, private property became the temporal cause of the degradation of humankind as well as the imperative behind its final redemption.

Given the initial script, the players, and their interrelationships, the drama of human deliverance unfolds in the fashion outlined in the works of Hess and Engels. The entire piece plays itself out against the background of industrial production, price, profit, subsistence wages, distribution, unemployment, capital accumulation and centralization, the diminution of the middle classes, and economic dislocation. Given the existence of private property, human beings are driven to unbridled egoism, competition, the indifference to larger concerns, and the exploitation of members of their communities. In the anarchy of self-seeking and personal aggrandizement, driven by the existence of private property, workers are denied the benefits of their labor. They are reduced to a marginal existence, and driven to compete with their fellows for the little available. Workers no longer create themselves through labor; they are degraded, impoverished morally and materially. The elements of all this are found in the earliest writings of Wilhelm Weitling, Moses Hess, and Friedrich Engels—they are the transliteration of the Christian doctrine of salvation. By the time he wrote the manuscripts of 1844, Marx had systematized it all, and delivered himself of what his followers were to thereafter call the "new social science."

For Marx, the "task of history ... is to establish the truth of this world" once all the obfuscations of abstract thinking and of professional economists and social theorists have been overcome. Once established, the truth demands the "positive transcendence of private property," and the consequent "return of man to himself"—the fulfillment of humanity through that perfect union in which the individual would become one with the universal.

History, as "the science of man," will come "to incorporate into itself natural science," to ultimately produce the *one*, *true* science. That science, in the service of humanity, would make evident the path human agents were to follow. It is that science which informs one that the positive transcendence of private property can be "accomplished solely by bringing about Communism." Between the years 1843 and 1844, Marx had moved beyond liberalism and representative

---

[71] Marx, *Economic and Philosophic Manuscripts of 1844*, *MECW*, ibid., vol. 3, p. 321.

democracy. By the beginning of 1844, he had discovered that Weitling's communism was no longer "abstract." He decided that it was a constituent part of that science that would deliver itself of the "Truth" that governed created life. History would show humankind the way to the attainment of that "total unity," the realization of the promise of human emancipation.[72] Communism was no longer a dogmatism to be dismissed. It was to be the culmination of secular history and the fulfillment of the moral aspirations of all humankind.

Almost immediately after he concluded work on the manuscripts of 1844, Marx invited Engels to coauthor, with him, a manuscript in which they would settle their accounts with the Young Hegelians—Hegelian revisionists who, Marx insisted, had betrayed their former radicalism. In the course of writing *The Holy Family or Critique of Critical Criticism*, Marx and Engels took the occasion to sharpen and systematize some of the concepts they would carry forward into their subsequent life's work.[73] In doing so, they would hardly modify the thrust of their argument. What would change would be the specificities of its content. Their claims would become more emphatic, and they would employ various forms of evidence in order to make more persuasive their case.

In the pages of *The Holy Family*, we are told that "the proletariat" not only *can*, but *must*, emancipate itself. The authors insisted, with all the authority at their disposal, that "it is not a question of what this or that proletarian, or even the whole proletariat, at the moment *regards* as its aim. It is a question of *what the proletariat is*, and what, in accordance with this *being*, it will historically be compelled to do."[74] What had been implicit was rendered explicit. History would not be denied. The meaning of the world was human fulfillment.

Hegel had said much the same. Hegel, however, understood history to be the history of thought—and the resolutions of contradictions and antitheses that drove thought to be conceptual. History found its most appropriate representation in the history of philosophy—in which all of life's contradictions and antitheses are sublated in dialectical analyses. For Marx and Engels history cannot be "an ethereal subject" separate from its subject matter—however Hegelian in form and expression—but material human beings in material circumstances.[75]

---

[72] Ibid., pp. 304, 305, 312, 313.

[73] *The Holy Family* was essentially the work of Marx, Engels having written one small section. Engels attempted to have Marx remove his name as coauthor because he felt he had contributed so little. Nonetheless, it seems clear that Engels had contributed to the general development of Marx's views.

[74] Marx and Engels, *The Holy Family*, MECW, vol. 4, p. 37.

[75] Marx was careful to remind us, "*History* does *nothing*, it 'possesses no immense wealth,' it 'wages no battles.' It is man, real, living man who does all that.... History is *nothing but* the activity of man pursuing his aims." Ibid., pp. 53, 79–80, 86, 93.

Marx and Engels tell us that it was Feuerbach "who annihilated the dialectics of concepts" and made man the essence, the basis of all historical activity.[76]

Out of this, an image emerges that will remain with Marxism throughout its development in the nineteenth century: human beings make their own history; but it is not made *arbitrarily, willfully*. History is made by human beings in particular circumstances—in circumstances structured by "real contradictions" and "empirical antitheses." Human beings, being what they are, are *compelled* to respond—and being what they are, one can predict those responses with scientific accuracy. In *The Condition of the Working Class in England*, Engels had written of "historic development" proceeding in an "unavoidable march," through a transition "both possible and necessary" to the attainment of human ends. Human history was the story of man's redemption.[77] That would be "the necessary consequences of ... historical development."[78] Marx and Engels were to remain true to those notions throughout their intellectual lives.

Marxism

The preparatory phases of the body of thought that was to become Marxism concluded with the composition, between November 1845 and August 1846, of *The German Ideology*. It was in that text that what was to be called the "materialist conception of history" was first formulated as a reasonably coherent doctrine. Thereafter, in 1847, Marx published his *The Poverty of Philosophy*, to be shortly followed, in 1848, by *The Communist Manifesto*—written by both revolutionaries—the version of their canon from which they would not depart and which would carry revolution forward into the twentieth century.

In all those works, one finds repeated all those claims tendered in the early works of Moses Hess and Friedrich Engels. There was the insistence that private property was the ultimate source, in time and circumstance, of human alienation;[79] that labor was the unique basis of wealth;[80] that those who arrogated to

---

[76] "Feuerbach ... completed and criticised Hegel ... by resolving the metaphysical Absolute Spirit into 'real man on the basis of nature.'" Ibid., p. 139.

[77] See ibid., pp. 150, 158.

[78] Engels, *Conditions of the Working-Class in England*, ibid., vol. 4, pp. 525, 582.

[79] Marx and Engels insisted that wage labor did not create property for the laborer; "it creates capital, i.e., that kind of property which exploits wage labor." The existence of private property ensured that labor would "alienate" itself in its activity. "Modern bourgeois private property is the final and most complete expression of ... the exploitation of the many by the few. In this sense, the theory of the Communists may be summed up in the single sentence: Abolition of private property." Marx and Engels, *Manifesto of the Communist Party*, ibid., vol. 6, p. 498.

[80] "Everyone knows that when supply and demand are evenly balanced, the relative value of any product is accurately determined by the quantity of labor embodied in it." Marx, *The Poverty of Philosophy*, ibid., vol. 6, p. 131.

themselves the wealth created by the labor of others set off a chain of inevitable consequences that would lead to a social revolution—by virtue of which humanity would achieve its ultimate redemption.[81]

The revolution in which humanity, in its entirety, secures its liberation, is the consequence of all the history that preceded it. It will be the inevitable "result of the whole of historical development."[82]

Like most neohegelians of the period, both Marx and Engels were convinced that human emancipation was the responsibility of history. Marx regularly spoke unself-consciously of "history" as "preparing" all the "practical elements for the emancipation of mankind."[83]

In the first draft of *The German Ideology* Marx wrote, "We know only a single science, the science of history."[84] Like many of the neohegelians, Marx and Engels both conceived history as a unifying science, absorbing all the natural sciences, characterized by all the rigorously lawlike properties of science.[85]

For Marx and Engels, history was a deterministic, predictive, unifying science. Consciousness, thought, ideals, were all "nothing else than the material world reflected." The passage of history was determined by "the material production of life itself.... All the different theoretical products and forms of consciousness, religion, philosophy, morality, etc., etc., arise from it, and tracing the process of their formation from that basis [is] ... the real ground of history."[86]

There was nothing particularly unique in this "dialectical" conception of history. It was shared by many scientistic materialists and philosophical realists in the nineteenth century. The features that made the notions of Marx and Engels

---

[81] See Marx and Engels, *Manifesto of the Communist Party*, ibid., vol. 6, p. 495.

[82] Both Marx and Engels consistently spoke of the "historical movement" that resulted in present circumstances. In this instance, Engels, "Draft of a Communist Confession of Faith," ibid., vol. 6, p. 96.

[83] Marx to Ludwig Feuerbach, ibid., vol. 3, p. 355.

[84] Marx and Engels, *The German Ideology*, ibid., vol. 5, p. 38, n.

[85] About two decades after he wrote the *Manifesto of the Communist Party*, Marx, with approval, quoted a Russian reviewer of his work who maintained that "Marx only troubles himself about one thing; to show, by rigid scientific investigation, the necessity of successive determinate orders.... He proves ... both the necessity of the present order of things, and the necessity of another order into which the first must inevitably pass over; and this all the same, whether men believe or do not believe it, whether they are conscious or unconscious of it. Marx treats the social movement as a process of natural history, governed by laws not only independent of human will, consciousness and intelligence, but rather, on the contrary determining that will, consciousness and intelligence." As quoted by Marx, *Capital: A Critical Analysis of Capitalist Production* (Moscow: Foreign Languages Publishing House, 1954), vol. 1, p. 18.

[86] Ibid., p. 19; and Marx and Engels, *The German Ideology*, MECW, vol. 5, pp. 53–54.

important for the present account turn on their apparent conviction that history is essentially both *teleological* and *moral*—having human emancipation as its purpose. Like Hegel, Marx and Engels conceived history as laboring to solve the "riddle" of human existence.[87] For neither was history ever understood to be a simple record of events and behaviors. Animated by human purpose, both saw in history unmistakable moral dimensions. Events, sequences of events, and the outcome of events, together with the behavior of participants, were to be identified as moral or immoral, good or evil—never simply as events and behaviors. Whatever their disclaimers, neither Marx nor Engels ever hesitated in displaying moral outrage at the infamies of the industrial system. They identified the behaviors of its agents as "vile," involving "callous egoism," "naked self-interest," "shameless exploitation," "profanations," and "brutal indifference" to the pain and wretchedness they caused.[88]

Like Moses Hess and Ludwig Feuerbach before them, Marx and Engels understood history as sharing some of the most prominent features of traditional religion. It had a moral purpose, and humanity was its preoccupation. Like Feuerbach, it seems evident that Marx and Engels, as neohegelians, understood the supersession, the transcendence, of religion to be something other than its simple denial. Marx understood that in Hegel's dialectics "the act of superseding" consisted in both "denial and preservation, i.e., affirmation." Thus, the supersession of religion was something other than its unadorned repudiation. Marx explained that "atheism, being the supersession of God, is the advent of theoretical humanism," which Feuerbach identified as a belief system that "takes the place of religion and has the essence of religion within itself."[89]

Both Marx and Engels certainly should have been aware that their "historical materialism" shared properties with conventional religion. It traced, with all the passion of the Old and New Testament, the purpose and meaning of life through time and in the behavior of mere mortals. It spoke of the introduction of private property as an original failing that warped creation—to initiate a cursed course of conduct. And it spoke of an ultimate redemption in that total unity in which humankind would once again find itself healed. At the end of his

---

[87] Marx spoke easily of "the complete return of man to himself" as the "solution" to "the riddle of history." Marx, *The Economic and Philosophical Manuscripts of 1844*, ibid., vol. 3, pp. 296–297.

[88] Marx insisted that however immoral the behavior of individuals, that behavior was to be understood as the result of circumstances over which individuals have no more control than they have over "natural history." Marx, *Capital*, p. 10.

[89] Marx, *MECW*, vol. 3, pp. 340–341; see the discussion of "supersession" on p. 341; and Feuerbach, *Principles of the Philosophy of the Future*, para. 64, p. 73.

life Marx, as he had in his youth, might well have written in truth, "I wrote ... a philosophical dialectical account of divinity, as it manifests itself as the idea in itself, as religion, as nature, and as history."[90]

What all that was to mean for the twentieth century only gradually became clear. Marxism was the first full, practicing exemplar of what we today identify as a political religion. The costs it would exact are now part of the unhappy history of our time.

[90] Karl Marx, "Letter from Marx to His Father," *MECW*, vol. 1, p. 18. For a convenient summary of the arguments surrounding the "religiosity" of early Marxism, see Heinz Röhr, *Pseudoreligiöse Motive in den frühschriften von Karl Marx* (Tübingen: J. C. B. Mohr, 1962).

CHAPTER FOUR

Leninism

Revolution as Religion

> [In the nineteenth and early twentieth centuries] socialism . . . announced its intention of becoming the religion for the new humanity, and its intrinsic link to religion cannot be doubted. . . . It is a complete dogma, a solution to the question of the meaning of life, the purpose of history. It is the preaching of socialist morality [as well as a] religion of self-deification. . . . The heart of Marxist socialism . . . is neither science nor philosophy but religion.
> —Nikolai Berdiaev[1]

After the appearance of *The Communist Manifesto* in 1848, the socialism of Karl Marx and Friedrich Engels developed in irregular and spasmodic fashion until the death of Engels almost a half-century later in 1895—twelve years after the passing of Marx. In the course of that development, the fundamental outline found in the *Manifesto* was given more substantive and detailed content.

Almost immediately following the appearance of the *Manifesto*, Engels urged the young Marx to quickly write a "thick book" that would provide compelling arguments to support the many broad claims—descriptive as well as predictive—to be found in the text. Engels was convinced that the deductive pattern of "inevitable" historical development—to which both young revolutionaries had become dedicated—required more than simple affirmation to be persuasive.

By the time they had authored the *Manifesto*, the founders of "scientific socialism" had persuaded themselves of the irrefutability of their convictions. Notwithstanding the vagueness and ambiguity of most of their central concepts, both imagined that they had managed to discover definitive "laws of social development." Schooled in the temporal "dialecticism" of Hegel, Marx and

---

[1] Nikolai Berdiaev, "Socialism as Religion," in Bernice Glatzer Rosenthal and Martha Bohachevski-Chomialk, *A Revolution of the Spirit* (New York: Fordham University Press, 1990), pp. 108, 109, 113.

Engels imagined themselves capable of taking the measure of history's sweep—the essentials of its past and the fullness of its future—all in terms of "lawlike regularities." They spoke of their eschatological expectations with the kind of conviction more typical of Old Testament prophets than scientists.

Like the prophets of old, they were less than tolerant of their critics. They were unaccommodating, rude, unjust, opinionated, dismissive, and disdainful of those who failed to fully accept their notions. Their works were peppered with the most abusive characterizations of those who did not agree with them. By nature, Marx seems to have been irascible, ill disposed to accept any kind of criticism. He rarely, if ever, took counsel graciously. Engels was no less dismissive of criticism—however uncertain it may be that his behavior could be ascribed to a natural disposition. Rather than attributing their conduct to a shared character flaw, what seems more plausible is that both Marx and Engels understood themselves possessed of *truths* against which no criticism could be legitimately advanced.

By the time of their full maturity, the system they finally delivered to their followers was far more complex and sophisticated than that to be found in the *Manifesto*. After 1848, Marx devoted much, if not all, of his time and energy to the study of economic theory—providing dense theoretical substance to the barebones notions found in relatively primitive simplicity in the *Manifesto*. The "thick book" that Engels urged him to write in the late 1840s resulted in the publication, in 1867, of the first volume of the multivolume "critical analysis of capitalist production": *Capital*.[2] Within its thousands of pages there was a studied effort to provide the rationale for claims advanced in the *Manifesto* a generation earlier. In Marx's judgment, that required the exhaustive analyses of commodity production in modern economy, an analytic account of use and exchange value, the provision of a "labor theory of value," of "theories" of surplus value, predictions concerning the concentration and centralization of capital, and speculation devoted to the establishment of wages and prices—all of which was supplied to give substance to the meager conceptual framework of the revolutionary creed of 1848.

While Marx was devoted to what were his economic studies, Engels produced texts that were conceived explicative of some of the critical philosophical and sociological issues both had engaged in writing the *Manifesto*. Some of Engels' works expanded upon themes only alluded to in the more youthful writings. His *Anti-Dühring*, portions of which were used to educate generations of

---

[2] Marx had published his *Contribution to the Critique of Political Economy* in 1859, but decided it was inadequate to his purpose. He chose to begin again, and the result was the first volume of *Capital*.

Marxists, and his *Ludwig Feuerbach and the End of Classical German Philosophy*, together with his *Origins of the Family, Private Property, and the State*, were to become staples of the final system.

For all that, the account Marx and Engels left as an intellectual legacy to their followers was sufficiently imprecise to permit, over the years, a variety of interpretations, formulated by "Marxists" both well disposed and talented. Each of them claimed, with some justification, to represent the original intent of the founders. Josef Dietzgen, Ludwig Woltmann, Jules Guesde, Georges Sorel, Otto Bauer, Max Adler, Rosa Luxemburg, Sergio Panunzio, Angelo O. Olivetti, and Eduard Bernstein, among others, all considered themselves true to the world vision of Marx and Engels[3]—and yet all delivered variants sufficiently different to cause other Marxists to identify them as deviant.

The fact is that there never was *one* Marxism. Rather, there was a family of belief systems, all related to the doctrinal legacy left by the founders—not one of which could convincingly claim unqualified "authenticity." Marx and Engels had left their intellectual heirs a collection of conjectures, convictions, opinions, surmises, moral sentiments, together with some empirically supported claims, all of which could be interpreted in a multiplicity of fashions. As a consequence, by the end of the nineteenth century, there was a diverse collection of individuals, political parties, groupuscules, conspiratorial sects, and reformist factions, that all advertised themselves, in some determinate sense or other, as "Marxist." What they all shared was an enduring faith in the inevitabilities of the system.

In Wilhelmine Germany, by the time of Engels' death, Marxists enjoyed impressive organizing and electoral success. In due time, their Social Democratic Party attracted dedicated leadership and a serious following—so that in the period before the First World War, the party represented the largest collection of organized Marxist revolutionaries in the world. Correspondingly, of all the delegations in the German parliament, the representatives of the party were among the most numerous. Under the circumstances, standardization of the party's belief system recommended itself—and a number of major theoreticians emerged to satisfy the demand, with Karl Kautsky the first among equals.

Before his death in 1895, Engels had been mentor to Kautsky. In 1891, under the influence of both, the German Social Democrats were provided a "standard" interpretation of Marxism in the Erfurt program.[4] Given his authorship,

---

[3] A discussion of the belief systems of some of the Marxists of the nineteenth century can be found in A. James Gregor, *Marxism, Fascism, and Totalitarianism: Chapters in the Intellectual History of Radicalism* (Stanford: Stanford University Press, 2009).

[4] See Karl Kautsky and Bruno Schönlank, *Grundsätze und Forderungen der Sozialdemokratie: Erläuterungen zum Erfurter Programm* (Berlin: Buchhandlung Vorwärts, 1905); Karl Kautsky, *The Class Struggle (Erfurt Program)* (New York: W. W. Norton & Co., Inc., 1971).

his party function, and his long relationship with Engels, Kautsky was to remain a major expositor of Marxist "orthodoxy" well into the twentieth century.[5]

Over the same period of time—the second half of the nineteenth century—social and political change was to destabilize the vast empire of the tsars thousands of kilometers in the East. The dynamism imparted to Russia by Peter the Great had spent itself by the middle of the century—and the empire had settled into a stolid unresponsiveness. The Crimean War at mid century demonstrated the intrinsic weakness of the system, however, and by the beginning of the 1860s, there was a sense that the entire sociopolitical structure required substantial, if uncertain, reform. Serfdom was abolished; institutions of local self-government (the *zemstva*), were established; censorship was relaxed; and efforts were made to liberalize traditionally autocratic institutions. None of this satisfied all the critics, and in 1866, an attempt was made on the life of the erstwhile "Tsar Liberator." The result was a reactive retrenchment on the part of the autocracy.

Adding to the strained circumstances, labor unrest impacted some of the major industrial centers, while restiveness simmered in the countryside. In industry, some of the earliest labor disturbances occurred during the first years of the 1870s. Concurrently, Russia produced an increasing number of educated young people, profiting from more liberal access to institutions that had been forthcoming during the first years of liberalization under Alexander II.

In that, there were the first intimations of the emergence of a pattern of unrest frequently observed elsewhere in unsettled environments. There was a measureable displacement of population from the rural, agricultural region to some of the major urban centers. Disengaged from traditional roles, and traditional moral constraints, such population elements became available for mobilization. Young people, trained in communication, more and more frequently showed themselves prepared to serve as mentors to those whose behavior was no longer governed by traditional patterns of conduct. Georgy Valentinovich Plekhanov, born the 29th of November (Old Style) in 1856, was among those prepared to serve as intellectual leaders of the dissidents.

Georgy Plekhanov (1856–1918)

Plekhanov was to play a major role in the introduction of Marxism into Russia, in the founding of the Russian Social Democratic Party, and in serving as inspiration to Vladimir Ilyich Ulyanov—Lenin. Plekhanov was to remain a

---

[5] Kautsky's *Die materialistische Geschichtsauffassung* (Berlin: J. H. W. Dietz, 1929) remains one of the better expositions available of the "Historical Materialism" of Marx and Engels.

revolutionary intellectual throughout his entire life, first as a *Narodnik* in his early manhood, to ultimately become the "father of Russian Marxism"—and, as such, leave an indelible imprint on the history of his country.

As a student in the Voronezh Military Academy, the young Plekhanov was introduced to the liberal thought of the period. He read the influential works of liberal thinkers such as Nikolai Chernyshevsky and Vissarion Belinsky. From them he developed his preoccupation with the underprivileged and oppressed. At the same time, and from the same sources, he also became skeptical of organized religion. When he left the Academy at seventeen, he was a religious skeptic committed to the service of "the people's interests."

When he arrived in St. Petersburg in 1873, revolutionary populism had begun to give evidence of its antiestablishment presence. In the summer of 1874, hundreds of educated youths left the cities as *Narodniki* ("populists"), to bring enlightenment and inspiration to the agrarians of the countryside. The *Narodniki* had convinced themselves that through all the changes of the nineteenth century, Russia's rural population retained a communitarian way of life, rooted in the property collectivism of the *mir* or *obshichina*. To the urban intellectuals, that made peasants natural agents of socialist change. The *Narodniki* saw in the remnants of collective ownership of land the potential for a uniquely socialist order. Urban youth was committed to the abandonment of their privileges in the effort to mobilize the peasantry, the "lowest strata of the people," to their purpose—in the course of which they would assist the agrarians in their struggle to ensure their rights in an environment in which scant material or spiritual sustenance was forthcoming. In the course of their efforts, the committed young people were prepared to pay with their freedom and well-being.

It was in 1875 that the young Plekhanov joined the *Narodnik* revolutionaries as a member of "*Zemlia i Volia* (Land and Liberty)." It was a memorable moment in his life. More than marking his entry into a revolutionary youth group, it was the year, at the end of which he read, for the first time, Marx's *Capital*.

For some years thereafter, Plekhanov remained in the ranks of the *Narodniki*. In 1878, he found himself involved in labor strikes in the urban areas. In the industrializing cities, instances of unrest had begun to increase in number and frequency. At about the same time, activities in the countryside gradually abated—and Plekhanov began to entertain doubts about the revolutionary potential of the peasantry. That judgment soon became general among revolutionary intellectuals, and seemed to feed a growing desperation among them. In their frustration, some members embarked upon individual acts of violence against government offices and government personnel.

By 1879, many, perhaps the majority, of the members of the revolutionary organization of which Plekhanov was member were alienated by just those actions. Few in *Zemlia i Volia* imagined that terrorism could unseat the monarchy and ensure liberty and security to the exploited subjects they sought to rescue. That, together with the realization that the peasantry was ill disposed to revolutionary enterprise, produced a sense of collective frustration among the youthful revolutionaries.

In April 1879, an attempt was made on the life of the Tsar. With its failure, against the objections of many, the members of *Zemlia i Volia* organized yet another venture in regicide. Together with others, Plekhanov objected. The result was the disintegration of the organization. The faction to which Plekhanov gave his allegiance survived a short time, but then, by the end of 1880, itself dissolved. At about that time, Plekhanov left Russia for Geneva. In Switzerland between 1880 and 1882—disillusioned by his experience among the advocates of peasant revolution in Russia—Plekhanov immersed himself in the primary literature of Marxism. It offered him an entirely different conception of social and political change.

Nikolai Berdiaev described something of the psychology of the Russian revolutionaries of the period. He emphasized their predilection for grand revelatory depictions of the world—accounts that explained and justified all the seemingly arbitrary, painful, and irrational events that constituted the substance of their lives.[6] Of those revolutionary intellectuals, Plekhanov was among the first to make evident his fascination with Marxism's "objective laws of history"— sweeping, all encompassing laws that assured him of the rational orderliness of humankind's social and political life[7]—irrespective of what that life might seem to be. It was a sentiment more akin to religion than social science.

In 1883, in his first specifically Marxist publication, Plekhanov made ready appeal to the notion that human history was governed by "inner, inevitable dialectics"—first revealed in the philosophical idealism of Hegel—to be subsequently embodied in the "dialectical and historical materialism" of Marx and Engels. As a new Marxist, admonishing those he sought to influence, Plekhanov could aver that "history," proceeding in conformity with the inevitable laws of the "dialectic," would pay "as little attention to the fears of revolutionaries as to the jeremiads of reaction."[8] Russian life was the overt result of a "process . . .

---

[6] Nikolai Berdiaev, *The Origins of Russian Communism* (London: 1937), chap. 1.

[7] Years later, with complete conviction, Plekhanov wrote that Marxism's "dialectical materialism . . . was the first to supply a method competent to solve the problem of the rational character of all that exists." Plekhanov, *Fundamental Problems of Marxism* (New York: International Publishers, n.d.), p. 31.

[8] G. V. Plekhanov, "Socialism and the Present Struggle," in *Selected Philosophical Works* (Moscow: Foreign Languages Publishing House, n.d. Hereafter *SPW*), vol. 1, pp. 66, 69.

taking place according to definite laws" that "do not depend upon the human will."⁹

The process, as Plekhanov understood it, involved human participation—but participation in the process entailed little that could pass as choice. Participation was law governed and indifferent to human preference. In speaking of Engels' dedication to the cause of proletarian emancipation, for example, Plekhanov argued that the behavior of Engels, himself, was not independently chosen—"free will" had precious little to do with it. Engels' "ideal was reality itself," Plekhanov tells us, but it was "the reality of tomorrow, a reality which will be fulfilled, not because Engels was a man of an ideal, but because the properties of the present reality are such that out of it, by its own interior laws, there must develop that reality of tomorrow. . . . From the objective standpoint the position of Engels appears as follows: in the process of transition from one form to another, reality seized on him as on one of the necessary instruments of the impending revolution. From the subjective standpoint it turns out it was pleasant for Engels to partake in that historical movement, that he considered it his duty and the great task of his life."¹⁰ Engels was a tool in the service of history's redemption of humankind.

Clearly a curious formulation, but one with which Plekhanov sought to explain the entirely law governed processes he imagined shaped individual and collective life. History, for Plekhanov, was eminently predictable because it was governed by inner "dialectical" laws. Lawlike regularities shaped the complex sequence of events that constitute its trajectory over time. In the process, human participation, whether unconscious or conscious, could only conform to the intrinsic requirements of immanent developmental laws.

"Scientific socialism," Plekhanov maintained, "explains the whole course of human cultural development." It explains "the spiritual history of humanity by the development of social relations"—with the "principal cause of this or that makeup of social relations . . . the condition of the productive forces, and the economic structure of society corresponding to them." Social relations and corresponding social structures emerge "indispensable and independent of the will" of human beings. Plekhanov maintained that Marx, "like Hegel, saw human history as a process conforming to laws and independent of man's arbitrariness." Until human beings understood those laws, they could only unconsciously participate in their operation. Once they became privy to their role and function, they could conform and contribute to the process—or they

⁹ Plekhanov, "Our Differences," ibid., vol. 1, p. 184, and *Fundamental Problems of Marxism*, p. 58.
¹⁰ Plekhanov, "Notes to Engels's Book *L. Feuerbach*," ibid., vol. 1, p. 525.

could lapse into actions that could only be quixotic. "We are free," Plekhanov contended, "only insofar as we know the laws of nature and sociohistorical development and insofar as we, submitting to them, rely upon them."[11]

In fact, Plekhanov's rendering of Marxism is arresting in terms of the strength of conviction with which it is expressed. He was convinced not only of its generic truth but also of its ability to predict the future with absolute assurance.[12] Plekhanov was not only convinced that Marx and Engels had discovered the truths governing natural and social life, he also attributed to the founders of Marxism an appreciation of the fact that the reality they understood so well "was striving to the great historical goal, a striving which nothing can stop."[13]

Together with everything else of which he was convinced, Plekhanov understood the very essence of that "great historical goal" to be *moral*. Like the founders of Marxism, Plekhanov believed that all of existence was infused with moral purpose. He described the "new morality" that must inevitably grow out of history as the product of the life circumstances of the proletariat. It was a morality—the harvest of the very conditions of life lived by industrial laborers—that would ensure the creation, growth, and prevalence of a new social order in which humanity would find material and spiritual fulfillment.[14]

None of this, of course, was original with Plekhanov. The founders of Marxism had said as much in works with which Plekhanov was both familiar as well as in those he may never have read. In his defense of Hegel, for example, the young Engels early delivered an impassioned argument for the *intrinsic rationality* of the "objective" world.[15] That rationality was embodied in the omnibus laws governing reality. The Marxist conviction that historical materialism provides the predictive "laws" that govern the entire history of humankind attests to the belief that existence—natural and historical—was inherently rational, and law governed. In full maturity, Marx had written that social events "result from the

---

[11] Plekhanov, *Fundamental Problems of Marxism*, pp. 76, 77, "For the Sixtieth Anniversary of Hegel's Death," ibid., vol. 1, pp. 477, 478. Plekhanov quotes Marx: "The sum total of these relations of production constitutes the economic structure of society, the real foundation on which rises a legal and political superstructure and to which correspond definite forms of social consciousness." "Notes to Engels's Book *L. Feuerbach*," ibid., vol. 1, pp. 77–78.

[12] He declares that "for us, what is coming into being is the necessary result of what is becoming obsolete. If we know that such a thing, and no other is coming into being, we are indebted for this to the objective process of social development." Plekhanov, "For the Sixtieth Anniversary of Hegel's Death," ibid., vol. 1, p. 475.

[13] Ibid., pp. 478, 483.

[14] Plekhanov, "Notes to Engels's Book *L. Feuerbach*," ibid., vol. 1, p. 530.

[15] Friedrich Engels, "Alexander Jung, 'Lectures on Modern German Literature,'" in Karl Marx and Friedrich Engels, *Collected Works* (New York: International Publishers, 1976. Hereafter *MECW*), vol. 2, p. 187; see his discussion in "Schelling and Revelation," *MECW*, vol. 2, pp. 202–203.

natural laws of capitalist production. It is a question of those laws themselves, of those tendencies working with iron necessity towards inevitable results."[16] History, for the founders of Marxism, was a rational, because law-governed, process. Plekhanov was only to repeat, with some regularity, what had become a doctrinal belief of the faithful. Because of the vocabulary chosen, Marxism was understood to be rigorously "scientific." It was held to possess the potentiality to explain everything.[17] It was a very singular conception of science.

Equally clear to the founders of Marxism was the fundamentally moral character of the entire process. The Young Hegelians, in their time, had rejected religion only to discover divinity in the history of humanity itself. The institutional God was abandoned at the same time that humanity was declared divine.

In 1844, Engels had written that "God is man." "Man," he continued, "has only to understand himself, to take himself as the measure of all aspects of life, to judge according to his being, to organize the world in a truly human manner according to the demands of his own nature, and he will have solved the riddle of our time."[18] The young Engels saw reality pursuing a fully predictable course—governed entirely by moral purpose.

Engels was clear. He insisted that communist revolutionaries sought to "give back to man the substance he [had] lost through religion." That would be accomplished by acknowledging that "history is all and everything to us and we hold it more highly than any other previous philosophical trend, more highly even than Hegel." In fact, Engels laid claim "to the meaning of history." We see in history, he went on, "not the revelation of 'God' but of man and only of man." He saw in history "its irresistible progress, its ever certain victory over the unreason of the individual," in the service of a new world aborning. It would be a world "based on purely human and moral social relationships."[19] History would provide the substance of a secular faith.

As early as 1839, Engels wrote to Friedrich Graeber that for him "moral perfection can be achieved only with the perfection of all other spiritual powers, with a merging into the world soul, and there I am with the Hegelian doc-

---

[16] Marx, *Capital* (Moscow: Foreign Languages Publishing House, 1954), pp. 8–9. Marx approved of the description of his system as having discovered "the special laws that regulate the origin, existence, development, death of a given social organism, and its replacement by another and higher one." Ibid., p. 19.

[17] See the entire discussion in Engels, "Socialism: Utopian and Scientific," in Marx and Engels, *Selected Works* (Moscow: Foreign Languages Publishing House, 1955. Hereafter *SW*), vol. 2, pp. 128–136.

[18] See Engels, "Progress of Social Reform on the Continent," *MECW*, vol. 3, p. 404, "The Condition of England: *Past and Present* by Carlyle," ibid., pp. 464.

[19] Engels, "The Condition of England," ibid., pp. 463, 464.

trine."²⁰ The connection is perfectly clear, and there is no suggestion that Engels ever changed his mind.²¹ History for Engels, as it was for Marx, was the story of humanity's redemption from the first fall from grace—the introduction of private property—into the communal circumstances of what was later identified as "primitive communism." All of this was found in the very first things written by both Marx and Engels. In their later renderings there was an enhancement of detail and a proliferation of subjects, but little changed with respect to those elements that made of their doctrine nothing less than a secular surrogate for religion. All of history was the story of the preparation of humanity for its ultimate redemption. Human salvation would be effected through proletarian revolution: the "emancipation of the workers contains," the young Marx insisted, "universal human emancipation."²²

All of this was to surface in the very first publications of Plekhanov as Marxist. However much, or little, of the early writings of the founders of Marxism he may or may not have read, he clearly captured the enduring sentiment that animated the Marxism of the early twentieth century. That is evident in Plekhanov's exchange of letters with Pavel Axelrod, his cofounder of the Russian Social Democratic Party. Plekhanov raised no objections to Axelrod's characterization of their mutual belief system. In a letter to Plekhanov, Axelrod spoke of the flawed properties of contemporary humanity, and the expectation of its perfection as the predictable consequence of the course of history—as though human perfection, somehow, was history's responsibility. Axelrod spoke, without hesitation, of this shared sentiment as "a kind of religious feeling" that gave rise to "a consciousness of spirit" that reaches "the stage of fanaticism or enthusiasm. . . . If there is no God who has created the universe," Axelrod continued, "then we are preparing for the appearance upon earth of divine men, possessed of the essence of all powerful reason and will, appealing to consciousness and self-consciousness, capable through wisdom of changing the world and directing it—that is the psychological basis of all my spiritual and social striving, ideas and actions."²³

Plekhanov voiced no objection to any of that. This seems to have been what both he and Axelrod imagined to be the psychological foundation of their mutual revolutionary aspirations. Knowing this, it is perfectly understandable why, by the time he wrote his last major exposition of dialectical materialism in 1908,

---

²⁰ Engels to Friedrich Graeber, 29 October 1839, ibid., vol. 2, p. 477.

²¹ Compare Engels' sentiments near the end of his life: Engels, "Ludwig Feuerbach and the End of Classical German Philosophy," *SW*, vol. 2, pp. 392–394.

²² Marx, *Economic and Philosophic Manuscripts of 1844*, *MECW*, vol. 3, pp. 280, 303.

²³ As cited in Samuel H. Baron, *Plekhanov: The Father of Russian Marxism* (Stanford: Stanford University Press, 1963), p. 173.

Plekhanov delivered himself of formulations that displayed all the properties of a secular surrogate of religion.

Plekhanov fully appreciated the history of the movement to which he gave allegiance. In his commentary on Engels' *Ludwig Feuerbach and the End of Classical German Philosophy*,[24] he acknowledged the renunciation of religion that was part of the system of convictions of the founders of Marxism—tracing that renunciation back to the Young Hegelians, and to Feuerbach. He also understood that religion had been "sublated" by Hegel and Feuerbach, and that "sublation," "supersession," "transcendence," did not mean a literal annihilation of religion. Religious feeling was not to be expunged, it had been *sublated*. Plekhanov was prepared to accept the Hegelian conviction that "every phenomenon" in the course of its development, is first negated, turned into its own opposite, only to have the "negation negated," with "the third phase of development [bearing] a formal resemblance to the first."[25] All of which was in the Hegelian tradition of the first Marxism.

What appears evident is Plekhanov's readiness to accept, as his own, a sublated, superseded political and secular belief system—the negation of the negation of institutional religion. It was a belief system innocent of any of the orthodox notions of theology: the personal creator, the promised immortality, and the worship of Jesus, the "theanthropos." The elements shared by his new secular faith included the conviction that reason governed all of existence, that only impeccable truth could serve as an inspiration for human commitment, and that moral purpose was the motive energy with which everything was infilled.

We have seen that Feuerbach had made a similar case in his own time. His "philosophical anthropology" was effectively a "new religion," in which all those human perfections that had been lost to transcendental beings could, once again, be restored to their empirical counterparts. No longer alienated, human kind would achieve the perfection promised by the fancies of theological orthodoxies. The proper restoration of those alienated attributes would produce the salvific results long advertised in orthodox theology. Like Axelrod after him, Feuerbach foresaw the redemption of flawed humanity by anticipating salvation in a religion not distorted by theological orthodoxy—in a religion predicated on a philosophical anthropology.[26]

For Feuerbach, not only was philosophical anthropology to become the sur-

---

[24] Plekhanov, "Notes to Engels's Book *L. Feuerbach*," *SPW*, vol. 1, pp. 484–538.

[25] Plekhanov, *The Development of the Monist View of History*, ibid., vol. 1, p. 612.

[26] See the entire discussion in William B. Chamberlain, *Heaven Wasn't His Destination: The Philosophy of Ludwig Feuerbach* (London: George Allen & Unwin, 1941), chap. 2; C. N. Starcke, *Ludwig Feuerbach* (Stuttgart: Ferdinand Enke, 1885), pp. 168–230.

rogate of religion, but politics itself was to become a worldview sharing the properties of sublated orthodoxy. He wrote to a correspondent, "We must once more become religious; politics must become our religion, but it can only do this if we have something ultimate in outlook, something which will make politics into a religion."[27] It was a sentiment that one could follow, like a red thread, through the revolutionary politics of the twentieth century.

In the nineteenth century, the young Karl Marx, himself, had argued the essence of the case—clearly of Feuerbachian inspiration—in his *Economic and Philosophic Manuscripts of 1844*. In the manuscripts, Marx spoke of religion as something to be negated; something to be sublated, superseded. But he also understood that "a peculiar role ... is played by the act of superseding in which denial and preservation, i.e., affirmation, are bound together." Thus, "atheism, being the supersession of God, is the advent of theoretical humanism." Humankind rejecting a belief in God, reconstituted its faith in humanism, with man, himself, serving as "the quintessence of all truth,"[28] and his redemption, history's ultimate purpose. As early as there was anything like Marxism, neohegelianism, as Feuerbachianism, had transformed religion into a secular creed.

None of this is remarkable. Years before, Moses Hess had written that although the young men of his time found themselves iconoclasts, and deemed the institutional churches objectionable, that did not mean that they sought an unqualified renunciation of religion. Hess maintained that what they sought instead was "a noninstitutional religion, because their religion was more than that of organized sects. [Their new religion] would be a truly universal religion that would permeate their lives." It would reflect the necessary progression of history; it would combine science and salvation; it would give expression to that human liberation that was implicit in the faith that history was the self-affirmation of the World Spirit. One could trace the passage of the World Spirit through time—through the great world cultures of antiquity to modernity—and perceive its contemporary promise in the imminent proletarian revolutions in England, France, and Germany.[29] Hess spoke of belief in all that as exemplifying the faith of a secular religion—one fundamentally concerned with the ultimate destiny of humankind. It was a secular religion infused with human relevant purpose, that imagined history possessed of moral concerns, and a goal that would find humanity liberated from all the burdens that ac-

[27] As cited in Karl Loewith, *From Hegel to Nietzsche: The Revolution in Nineteenth-Century Thought* (Garden City, N.Y.: Doubleday & Company, Inc., 1967), pp. 78–79.

[28] Marx, *Economic and Philosophic Manuscripts of 1844*, *MECW*, vol. 3, pp. 339, 340, *The Holy Family*, ibid., vol. 4, p. 79.

[29] Moses Hess, *Die europäische Triarchie*, in *Philosophische und sozialistische Schriften 1837–1850* (Berlin: Akademie-Verlag, 1961), pp. 109–112.

cumulated after the loss of primitive innocence at the very commencement of organized society.

Plekhanov's revolutionary creed shared all the constituents of just that kind of secular religion. It imagined life given structure by reason, a reason characterized by moral preoccupation. History, itself, served as the embodiment of all that. Plekhanov spoke of history conducting activities, employing human beings as its instruments—activities always molded to moral purpose. History was conceived the demiurge, the overarching executive of a predetermined and inevitable program—a program fashioned, somehow, in the mists of primordial time. The "new religion," as both Hess and Feuerbach foresaw, would make its appearance as a movement of political liberation. Its creed would be a social gospel that found expression in what was conceived to be exclusively "scientific" terms. It was to find expression in a scientism that typified the positivism of the late nineteenth, and early twentieth, centuries.

By the end of the nineteenth century, Plekhanov had given himself over completely to that creed. He was to inspire others with his conviction and his moral courage. What is equally clear, although not frequently addressed,[30] was a fateful continuity between the Feuerbachianism that inspired Marx and Engels and the belief system of the *Narodniki*—who were to shape, in the minds of those Russian revolutionaries who were to follow, the first rudiments of what was to become known as Bolshevism. Among those revolutionaries who were to follow was one Vladimir Ilyich Ulyanov—V. I. Lenin.

V. I. Lenin (1870–1924) and the Intelligentsia of Romanov Russia

On 22 April 1870, Lenin was born Vladimir Ilyich Ulyanov, in Simbirsk on the Volga. His father, a deeply religious man, was a schoolteacher who, by dint of competence and dedication, rose to the rank of director of public education of Simbirsk province, to become the bearer of the Order of Stanislav First Class—a distinction that made him a member of the petty nobility. Lenin, in effect, was born to privilege.

Throughout the second half of the nineteenth century, together with seminarians and those of religious calling in general, the Russian nobility contributed disproportionately to the ranks of the revolutionary intelligentsia. Vladimir Ilyich, scion of the petty nobility, a member of that revolutionary fraternity, was to transform the history of half the world. Raised in the sheltering embrace of

---

[30] A discursive treatment of the relationship was early made available by a confidant of Lenin—in Nikolai Valentinov, *The Early Years of Lenin* (Ann Arbor: University of Michigan Press, 1969).

a loving and supportive family, Vladimir Ilyich proved to be a perfectly normal adolescent, an exemplary student who excelled in sports, history, geography, and literature. Under the direct and indirect influence of Russia's revolutionary intelligentsia, all that was to quickly change.

In 1887, Vladimir Ilyich's brother, Alexander, decided to join in a terrorist plot against the reigning Tsar. In the course of planning the assassination, Alexander was betrayed and captured—and in April was sentenced to death for his part in the conspiracy. On the morning of the 8th of May, despite the desperate pleadings of his widowed mother, the young Alexander was executed.

We are told that with that, the youthful Vladimir Ilyich was transformed. His profound grief at his brother's death made him grim and taciturn. His biographers tell us that at the age of seventeen, Vladimir Ilyich Ulyanov had begun his transformation into Lenin.

In reconstructing the history of that transformation, we have convincing evidence of the influence of Nikolai Chernyshevsky on the emerging belief system of the young Vladimir Ilyich. Early in 1887, the young Lenin reread Chernyshevsky's novel *Chto Delat? (What Is to Be Done?)*. His first reading, when he was about fourteen, had been perfunctory, undertaken without application or reflection. The second reading was the consequence of his recognition that the novel had been the favorite of his martyred brother—and had provided much of the revolutionary substance that induced him to undertake an attempt on the life of the Tsar. The young Vladimir Ilyich read *What Is to Be Done?* with singular intensity. Years later, Lenin recounted that he read the work attentively, with pen in hand, making notes and analyzing passages in order to extract their full meaning and significance.

Even with the passage of time, Lenin continued to insist upon the impact on him of Chernyshevsky's novel. He duly reported that before his "acquaintance with the works of Marx, Engels and Plekhanov, it was Chernyshevsky who exerted the main overwhelming revolutionary influence on me—an influence which began with *What Is to Be Done?*" In effect, Lenin acknowledged that Chernyshevsky had "plowed him over," transforming him.[31] Before there was Marxism, there was the secular religious thought of Nikolai Chernyshevsky.

Lenin's enthusiasm for Chernyshevsky's work was never to diminish. Years later, he was to rise in defense of Chernyshevsky whenever the importance of his work was questioned. In effect, in 1887 the future V. I. Lenin made his first

---

[31] N. K. Krupskaya, *Lenin* (Moscow: Foreign Languages Press, 1959), pp. 40, 53; see A. James Gregor, *The Fascist Persuasion in Radical Politics* (Princeton: Princeton University Press, 1974), pp. 199–200; and Valentinov, *The Early Years of Lenin*, pp. 132–136.

appearance with Vladimir Ilyich's rereading of Chernyshevsky's novel. Thereafter, Vladimir Ilyich was to be no more.

Nikolai Chernyshevsky (1828–1889) was to exercise major influence over Russia's revolutionary intelligentsia throughout the end of the nineteenth century. His journal, *Sovremennik (The Contemporary)*, was among the most important of those publications advocating elemental change in autocratic Russia.

Chernyshevsky had grown up in a household of profound Orthodox conviction. In his youth he had been a sheltered and devoted seminarian—and there had been talk of the priesthood in his future. Even as he began to abandon his formal religious convictions, Chernyshevsky remained pious in many ways. He even continued to perform some of the standard rituals of Orthodoxy long after he no longer considered himself a believer—and he left us some evidence that, in the first stages of his alienation from the Russian Orthodox Church, he missed the security of his traditional faith.[32]

More important for the present account is the fact that Russian Orthodoxy had accustomed Chernyshevsky to a comprehensive and totalistic view of the world, accounting for the place of man in nature, together with a conviction that all of being was suffused with morality. In the years that followed his initial reservations concerning the Orthodox faith, Chernyshevsky sought the reconstruction of a surrogate system of beliefs that would provide the lost satisfactions of Orthodoxy. He ultimately put together an intense vision of humanity as consuming and inflexible as that of his former Orthodoxy. During his university years, between 1848 and 1850, Chernyshevsky sought to satisfactorily reorder his convictions.

While his institutional religious faith was unraveling, Chernyshevsky recognized the need for a sustaining system of beliefs. For a time he toyed with the pantheism of Hegel, but from all indications, his appreciation of the Hegelian system was indifferent at best. Ultimately, it was Feuerbach who managed to serve the purpose of reordering his vision of the world.

By September 1850, he had been won over entirely to the sacralized humanism of Feuerbach. Beside the *Essence of Christianity*, he had read *The Preliminary Theses for the Reform of Philosophy*, and the *Principles of the Philosophy of the Future*. In those texts he found the materialistic monism that provided the arguments with which he sought to counter the institutionalized patterns of thought that, in his judgment, compromised the freedom of human beings—being consistently used throughout the past to exploit the weakest and most vulnerable among them. Like Feuerbach, Chernyshevsky came to conceive

---

[32] See the discussion in William F. Woehrlin, *Chernyshevskii: The Man and the Journalist* (Cambridge, Mass.: Harvard University Press, 1971), chap. 2.

traditional religion as designed to lead human beings to accept and reconcile themselves to their lot in life, however unsatisfactory that lot might be.[33]

Chernyshevsky found in Feuerbach a philosophical humanist, prepared to deal with the destiny of humankind with integrity and compassion. He found there an effort to restore to humanity its lost virtues—virtues that had been alienated over historic time by institutionalized religion—to be assigned to those creatures of fancy that tenanted realms transcendental. Chernyshevsky agreed with Feuerbach that as celestial beings were enhanced in virtue, human beings were correspondingly diminished. Chernyshevsky saw in Feuerbachianism an effort to change all that, to make life on earth credible and morally satisfying. He saw in Feuerbachianism an anthropological and naturalistic doctrine that made the enhancement of humankind its purpose, and community the center of life.[34] He articulated a set of beliefs that united individuals in a community of ends that, in his judgment, made the entire enterprise fundamentally rational and moral.

In Feuerbach, Chernyshevsky found an argument that made the case for the negation of theology—and the apotheosis of man. Shorn of theological fancy, religious sentiment could be conscripted to the struggle for human deliverance. Only then, without the dream of heavenly hosts and transcendental divinities, might human perfection, fully rational and eminently moral, become a goal to which humankind might aspire with every expectation of success. Human beings could anticipate perfection as a consequence of humanity's reconciliation with itself. Once accomplished, life would find its fullness in love and community—all the alienated properties of humankind would be restored. Humanity, in essence, would become divine.

It was in these conceptions that Chernyshevsky found his "one vision of truth." He saw in these formulations the echo of the achievements of empirical science, so prominent in the middle of the nineteenth century. He understood Feuerbachianism to be the philosophical expression of the scientism of his time. In Feuerbachianism he saw the "laws of development" that governed the real world of nature and society—and promised moral and spiritual fulfillment to all of humankind.[35]

It is perfectly clear that the Feuerbachianism with which Chernyshevsky

[33] Ibid., pp. 48–61.

[34] "Man is not a particular being, like the animals, but a universal being. . . . The single man for himself possesses the essence of man neither in himself as a moral being nor in himself as a thinking being. The essence of man is contained only in the community and unity of man with man." Feuerbach, *Principles of the Philosophy of the Future* (New York: Bobbs-Merrill Company, Inc., 1966), paras. 53, 59, pp. 69, 71; see para. 63, p. 72.

[35] See Woehrlin, *Chernyshevskii*, pp. 69, 125, 127.

chose to identify was a deification of generic humanity.[36] Chernyshevsky had thus managed to reconstruct a system of beliefs animated by all the deeply felt sentiments that had sustained him as a seminarian. The major differences turned on his epistemologically uncertain *materialism*, and a moralism that was singularly *utilitarian*—all of which he had accepted from Feuerbach.

Inspired by his new beliefs, Chernyshevsky anticipated a "new world," created by the energies of evangelical "new men." They would bring a new consciousness to humankind. "New men," "austere, practical, and cold," would make their appearance among the "antediluvians" of nineteenth century Russia. Those of the "old stamp" would recognize in the "new men" their saviors— come to rescue them from the suffocating inconveniences of the modern world. "Intellectually impotent," the antediluvians would cry out, "Save us!" and fall in behind the "new men"—whom they would apprize "the best among the best, the movers of the movers, the salt of the salt of the earth." In their desperate search for redemption, the antediluvians would follow the "new men" with discipline and self-sacrifice.[37]

For Chernyshevsky, the "new men" would be alive with irrepressible determination and obdurate will—assets that would make the difference between victory and defeat in the impending revolutionary contest between the vanguard "new generation" and the denizens of the old creation. The determination and will of the "new men" would ensure the allegiance of the masses. The process was eminently simple. "Men," Chernyshevsky insisted, "drag themselves along in a beaten track simply because they have been told to do so; but tell them in a very loud voice to take another road, and, though they will not hear you at first, they will soon throw themselves in the new path with the same spirit."[38]

The "new people" would constitute a vanguard that would make history— infusing it with redemptive meaning. With and through the masses, the "new people" would make life flourish. Without their intervention, the masses would languish as prisoners of a life that would remain sterile and unedifying.

All of this found its inspiration, if not its substance, in the work of Feuerbach. He had argued that it was the empirical individual human being that was the foundation of objective reality. Individuals, sensing the impact of external objects, feeling sensory needs, provided the first elements of our knowledge of the world. Such individuals, organized in communities, had formulated those

---

[36] Feuerbach, *Principles of the Philosophy of the Future*, paras. 1, 29, 52, 53, 60, pp. 5, 46–48, 68, 69, 71.

[37] N. G. Chernyshevsky, *What Is to Be Done?* (New York: Random House, 1961), pp. 11–13, 24, 81, 86, 174–175, 241.

[38] Ibid., pp. 41, 229, 292–293, 302.

scientific truths that would govern life to human purpose. Humanity, lodged in communities of similars, had discovered truth in "species consciousness."[39]

Feuerbach had argued that human life had traversed a path from primitive religious belief, through the transcendental idealism of Hegel, to the "new philosophy" of empirical science he represented. Somehow, history had guided human sensibilities to that point in time when human kind was destined to find fulfillment. The old idealism, theologically inspired, had demonstrated its inadequacies. It was no longer an inspiration. Only the new philosophic surrogate for all the old beliefs could uniquely serve instrumental purpose in the final, moral, and material transformation of human life.

These ideas, fully articulated by Chernyshevsky, were shared by a unique cultural category of Russians—the intelligentsia. In fact, they distinguished themselves from the traditional educated classes by a belief system that inspired virtually all of them.

Collectively, the Russian intelligentsia was largely the product of the liberalization effected by the Russian autocracy around the mid nineteenth century. By the 1850s, with the first acknowledgements that change was necessary if the empire was to survive, the authorities fostered enrollment in the universities. For the first time in Russian history, for example, women and minorities were allowed to enter institutions of advanced learning. Fees were often waived or reduced for those unable to pay standard tuitions. Within a decade, the student body of St. Petersburg University trebled. All these candidates could not be readily assimilated in state bureaucracies or in the professional ranks that were growing less rapidly than the number of students being made available.

Many of the students, so rapidly produced, had been trained to deal with ideas rather than provided with special skills that might serve them in the state bureaucracies or the professions. Many of the graduates so characterized gave themselves over to whatever activities promised them a living. Many undertook literary pursuits, to earn a straitened and tenuous livelihood by indulging themselves in social criticism, tutoring, and translating the work of others. As an unhappy literary "proletariat," the intelligentsia succeeded in becoming more and more detached from conventional society. In their detachment, they were influenced by the latter-day enlightenment that had given Europe that secular faith in the universal life of reason, in scientism, meliorism, and socialism. It was an enlightenment that found its paradigmatic exponent in Feuerbach.

---

[39] "That is true in which another agrees with me—agreement is the first criterion of truth... the species is the ultimate measure of truth." Feuerbach, *The Essence of Christianity* (New York: Harper & Brothers, 1957), p. 158.

It was Feuerbach's "new faith" that inspired Chernyshevsky—and it was Chernyshevsky who was the unmistakable prototype of the Russian *intelligent*. By 1905, at the time of the first revolution that was to shake the imperial Romanovs, Russian political analysts charged the intelligentsia with responsibility for the political uprising and its signal failure. By the first years of the new century, members of the intelligentsia, as an identifiable cultural category, could be classified as sectarian revolutionaries, possessed of a kind of conscious or unconscious religiosity.[40] Critical analysts argued that it was that secularized religiosity that shaped their behaviors and derailed their efforts.

It was argued that the creed of Russia's intelligentsia was a "detheologized" religiosity that shared some of the traits of traditional Orthodoxy. Its vision was apocalyptic and chiliastic. It imagined itself possessed of an infallible method for saving humankind, an ability to faultlessly divine the laws of universal life, and enlist them in the service of man's redemption. According to their convictions, history provided the record of humanity's fateful and inevitable progression to a time and a place where the reign of reason would ensure everyone material and spiritual fulfillment.[41]

Typical of the belief system was the faith that history would produce the "saviors" who, through the workings of infallible "laws," would redeem humanity. Those saviors, individually and collectively, would arise as a fraternity of "heroes." As individuals, or as a fraternity, the role discharged would be "providential." The masses to be enlisted in their enterprise would be passive until summoned. In the guise of savior, the individual hero presents himself as "superman," with the entire social stratum "a special kind of aristocratic class," agents of a "benign" dictatorship charged by history with the unique responsibility of saving humanity.[42]

In the passion of their convictions, as humanity's saviors, Russia's revolutionary intelligentsia were dogmatic and militant. In everything said and done, it seemed clear that in their judgment there could be no ecumenical truth or universal norms. There was but one truth, sacred and exclusive—to which only they were privy. So certain were they of that truth, they shared a fanatical intol-

[40] "The nature of the Russian intelligentsia is religious." Sergei Bulgakov, "Heroism and Asceticism," in *Vekhi (Landmarks)* (Armonk, N.Y.: M. E. Sharpe, 1994), p. 49. The revolutionary faith of the intelligentsia "is psychologically analogous to religious faith." Semen Frank, "The Ethic of Nihilism," in *Vekhi (Landmarks)*, p. 142; see the discussion by Marshall S. Shatz and Judith E. Zimmerman, eds., in the Introduction to *Vekhi (Landmarks)* p. xxxviii; and Nikolai Berdiaev, "Philosophical Verity and Intelligentsia Truth," ibid., pp. 5, 8, 14.

[41] See Bulgakov, "Heroism and Asceticism," ibid., p. 21; Mikhail Gershenzon, "Creative Self-Consciousness," ibid., pp. 59–60; Frank, "Ethic of Nihilism," ibid., pp. 142–143.

[42] See the entire discussion in Bulgakov, "Heroism and Asceticism," ibid., especially pp. 28–29.

erance of any other claims. Any pretence that there could be alternative truths was met with derision and self-righteous opposition. The convinced revolutionary comports himself or herself as a "militant monk, a monk revolutionary. For the intelligentsia the political goal was not so much the introduction of some objectively useful reform, in the worldly sense, as the destruction of the enemies of its faith and the forcible conversion of the world. This monastically religious spirit was responsible for the intelligentsia's entire approach to politics—its fanaticism and intolerance."[43]

Nikolai Berdiaev identified all this with the peculiar mindset of Russia's revolutionary intelligentsia, "artificially isolated from national life." They distanced themselves, in his judgment, from all those national thinkers they deemed "hostile." They denied the independent significance of philosophy "and instead subordinated it to utilitarian social goals"—and as a consequence, were "dominated, wholly and despotically, by a utilitarian moral standard . . . wholly and oppressively governed by love for the people and the proletariat."[44]

So convinced were they that they had been charged by history with the redemption of humankind, the revolutionary intelligentsia imagined that they had fathomed all the truths of the world. They imagined themselves possessed of certain and irrefutable science. They had learned from Western Europe—and under the influence of Europe's "little enlightenment" of the nineteenth century, they had become *materialists*, and gave themselves over, without reservation, to the *scientism* of positivism—the notion that the solution to all problems, empirical, logical, or moral, was to be found in standard science. Chernyshevsky's *Anthropological Principle in Philosophy* gave full expression to that "new philosophy," to inspire Russia's intelligentsia with a kind of unsophisticated, if committed, materialism that looked, for all the world, like a surrogate for religion lost.

Before the advent of Marxism, it was Russia's revolutionary intelligentsia that conceived science, philosophy, education, and art exclusively as instrumentalities enlisted in the service of humanity's social and spiritual fulfillment. For such revolutionaries, science was "merely an instrument for affirming the reign of social justice and for utterly destroying those metaphysical and religious ideas which, [they] dogmatically assumed, support the reign of evil." It was they

---

[43] Frank, "Ethic of Nihilism," ibid., p. 151. Also, "[If] by religiosity we mean *fanaticism*, then, of course, the Russian intelligentsia is religious to the highest degree: that is, it is possessed of a passionate devotion to a favorite idea that verges on an *idee fixe*; it leads a person to self-sacrifice and great achievement on the one hand, and, on the other, to an abnormal distortion of his whole perspective on life and the intolerant annihilation of everything that does not agree with his idea." Ibid., p. 134; see Gershenzon, "Creative Self-Consciousness," ibid., p. 61.

[44] Berdiaev, "Philosophical Verity and Intelligentsia Truth," ibid., p. l.

who first maintained that those who advocate the independence of science and knowledge as transcending everyday political and/or moral concerns, could only be reactionary counterrevolutionaries. The political and moral beliefs of Russia's revolutionaries became unmistakably and unalterably *utilitarian*. The revolutionary intelligentsia elevated their beliefs into *dogma*, accepting almost any claim as incontrovertibly true that they imagined might contribute to their social purpose. They came to judge the truth of philosophical and scientific claims almost exclusively in terms of social and political criteria serving utilitarian ends. In their beliefs, only that could be deemed true that might serve as a weapon in the arsenal of revolution.[45] A dogmatic scientism and a commitment to utilitarian moral principles came to characterize the secular religiosity of Russia's revolutionaries at the beginning of the twentieth century. Initially a byproduct of the nation's radical intelligentsia, it was reinforced by an infusion of Marxism. Together, the belief system of the intelligentsia, inspired by Chernyshevsky, combined with Marxism to produce the thought of Plekhanov. It was that heady combination of elements that ultimately gave rise to the revolutionary doctrines of V. I. Lenin.

V. I. Lenin as Marxist

Lenin attested to the fact that it was the thought of Chernyshevsky that inspired him to revolutionary purpose. Before Marx, there had been Chernyshevsky.

In fact, it can be argued that Chernyshevsky continued to influence the revolutionary reflections of Lenin long after Lenin ceased to refer to him with any regularity. Like Marx and Engels in their treatment of Feuerbach, a case can be made that Lenin forever owed some critical part of his ideology to Chernyshevsky.

Marx and Engels maintained that, after their initial enthusiasm, they had left Feuerbachianism behind. They insisted that Feuerbachianism was flawed in many ways—and was unsuitable for their purposes. And yet, a persuasive case can be made that a central part of Feuerbach's intellectual, and specifically analytic, strategy continued to inform the ideological formulations of Marx throughout the remainder of his life.[46]

Much the same can be said of Chernyshevsky's influence on Lenin. Although Lenin sometimes spoke dismissively of Chernyshevsky's political thought as

---

[45] Ibid., p. 9; see the entire discussion ibid., pp. 1–8.
[46] See A. James Gregor, "Marx, Feuerbach and the Reform of the Hegelian Dialectic," *Science & Society*, 39, no. 1 (Winter 1965), pp. 66–80.

containing irreducibly utopian elements, it seems reasonably certain that much of that thought continued, forever, to be of importance in the articulation of Lenin's views. It can be argued that, like Marx and Engels, Lenin's political convictions were shaped by the sublated religiosity of Feuerbach—as that religiosity reached him, and Russia's intelligentsia of the period, through the revolutionary thought of Chernyshevsky.

When Lenin published the first doctrinal statement of what legitimately can be called "Leninism," he entitled his work *What Is to Be Done?*[47] Not only does the title bring us back to Chernyshevsky, but it was an essay in which Lenin made a forthright case for the special revolutionary role to be discharged by an elite—an elite meeting all the fundamental criteria described by Chernyshevsky for those "new men," those "saviors," on whom the future depended.

That the "professional revolutionaries" to whom Lenin made appeal were more like Chernyshevsky's "new men" than anything found in the writings of Marx and Engels seems evident. As early as the *Manifesto*, both Marx and Engels had spoken of a time when a "small section of the ruling class cuts itself adrift, and joins the revolutionary class." They spoke, as well, of that elite as that "portion of the bourgeois ideologists, who have raised themselves to the level of comprehending theoretically the historical movement as a whole."[48] Granted that, it is equally clear that they never attributed to that anticipated elite anything like the responsibilities Lenin assigned to his revolutionary vanguard.

It remains uncertain what the founders of Marxism understood the specific revolutionary function might be of the intellectual elite to which they made reference. At the time the founders of Marxism were putting together the *Manifesto*, Engels had written that "revolutions are not made deliberately and arbitrarily, but that everywhere and at all times they have been the necessary outcome of circumstances entirely independent of the will and the leadership of particular parties and entire classes."[49] There was no suggestion that either the requisite proletarian consciousness or successful revolution required the intervention of a small coterie of professional revolutionaries.

It seems clear enough that the founders of Marxism did not seem disposed to assign a special, and nonsubstitutable, revolutionary role to any intellectual elite. While, in one place, Engels granted that "Marxism" would be something obviously different without the thought of Marx, he went on, nonetheless, to

---

[47] V. I. Lenin, *What Is to Be Done? Burning Questions of Our Movement*, in Lenin, *Collected Works* (Moscow: Foreign Languages Publishing House, 1961. Hereafter *LCW*), vol. 5, pp. 347–567. Adam Ulam spoke of *What Is to Be Done?* as "the bible of Bolshevism." *Lenin and the Bolsheviks* (London: Secker and Warburg, 1965), p. 167.

[48] Marx and Engels, "Manifesto of the Communist Party," in *Collected Works*, vol. 6, p. 494.

[49] Engels, "Principles of Communism," ibid., p. 349.

argue that "Marxism" would have been discovered with or without Marx—to restore, once again, the "inevitability" of events, with or without, any "vanguard elite."

In fact, in the abundant materials left to followers by Marx and Engels, the entire discussion involving the role of individuals, and intellectual elites, in the making of the "revolutionary consciousness" of the proletariat, remains tortured and indecisive.[50] What was never in dispute was the conviction among the founders that, with or without the participation of select individuals or specific intellectual elites, the revolution was the necessary result of an intersecting set of inevitabilities.

It can be argued, on the other hand, that for Lenin, the revolution was not a simple inevitability; it required the necessary intercession of a declassed elite of bourgeois intellectuals—"new men"—without whom the proletariat would achieve nothing more than a "narrow trade union consciousness."[51] Lenin argued that if there was ever to be a Marxist consciousness among workers, "it would have to be bought to them from without. The history of all countries shows that the working class, exclusively by its own effort, is able to develop only trade union consciousness.... The theory of socialism ... grew out of the philosophic, historical, and economic theories elaborated by educated representatives of the propertied classes, by intellectuals." According to Lenin's thesis, without the leadership of that intellectual elite, the working class would forever remain captive of "bourgeois ideology" and a prisoner of capitalist exploitation.[52]

The "professional revolutionaries," of whom Lenin spoke, were nowhere to be found in the works of Marx or Engels. He, on the other hand, knew them very well. He understood them to be "few in number, tried, reliable, hardened, experienced, sparkling with energy, self-sacrificial, boundlessly devoted, immensely talented, and exclusively guided by genuine revolutionary theory."[53] They constituted an elite to which neither Marx nor Engels ever had made recourse. And while Karl Kautsky, before the turn of the twentieth century, had made allusion to a cohort of theoreticians who would bring "revolutionary consciousness" to the proletariat from "without"—they were but a poor anticipation of the

[50] See the entire discussion in A. James Gregor, *A Survey of Marxism: Problems in Philosophy and the Theory of History* (New York: Random House, 1965), pp. 175–185.

[51] "The proletariat can, and inevitably will, become an invincible force *only* through its ideological unification on the principles of Marxism being reinforced by the material unity of organisation." Emphasis supplied. Lenin, *One Step Forward, Two Steps Back: The Crisis in Our Party*, in *LCW*, vol. 7, p. 415.

[52] Lenin, "What *Is to* Be Done?" ibid., vol. 5, pp. 365, 370–371, 375, 383, 384, 422.

[53] Ibid., pp. 433, 444, 447, 448, 450, 454, 459, 461, 467, 473, 508, 515.

"professional revolutionaries" to whom Lenin appealed. Lenin's professional revolutionaries look more like Chernyshevsky's "saviors" than anything found in the expository literature of classical Marxism.

Lenin's professional revolutionaries embody in themselves the "conscious element" of revolution. It is their presence that ensures the functional availability of a "military organization" of effective agents. It is they whose thought represents true science—that true science that would ensure orthodoxy among the faithful. Lenin's professional revolutionaries would defend the truth of revolutionary doctrine against "amateurish, wretched, diluted, flabby, shaky, and vulgar theory"—harbored by "organizations of ordinary people" that could only lead the proletariat into "opportunism," political vacillation, and ultimate defeat.[54]

Lenin and his professional revolutionaries imagined themselves armed with unequivocal truths, against which any "freedom to criticize," any political or revolutionary "spontaneity" among the "masses," could only result in betrayal, opportunism, confusion, error, and signal failure. In that sense, Lenin admitted he was open to the charge of being "doctrinaire"—and that he was prepared to acknowledge the merit of periodic purges in the revolutionary ranks in order to defend the integrity of "theory."[55]

Lenin argued that Marxism was an impeccable science that delivered itself of revolutionary truths—truths that required faithful commitment for their effective discharge. Lenin understood Marxism to require a discipline and loyalty much like that of a religious order. By the time of the appearance of *What Is to Be Done?* Lenin spoke with "the sure instinct of a theologian . . . proclaiming *his* revisionism [to be] Marxist orthodoxy."[56] He became increasingly intolerant of those who would modify his strictures concerning revolution or the part to be played by the "new men" of his revolutionary vanguard. That provided insight into how doctrinal truth and implied policy might be determined in any particular instance.

Rosa Luxemburg spoke of an evident move on the part of the emerging Leninism toward "ultracentralization" of the Russian Social Democratic Party of the period—a move that "led logically to the emergence of one supreme leader," who would serve as the ultimate authority in terms of ideological interpretation of the revolutionary faith, and authoritative arbiter in terms of policy.[57]

---

[54] Ibid., pp. 354, 356, 360, 443, 466, 468, 511, 515n., 519, 523, 526.

[55] Ibid., pp. 320, 355, 412, 510, 519, 526.

[56] Ulam, *Lenin and the Bolsheviks*, p. 178.

[57] Ibid., p. 197; see the discussion in Rosa Luxemburg, *The Russian Revolution and Marxism or Leninism?* (Ann Arbor: University of Michigan Press, 1961), p. 64.

What that implied was a binding and unequivocal interpretation of what conduct was to be allowed true revolutionaries. Doctrine, policy, and behavior in the party were required to be consistent with revealed truth—all of which, in turn, necessitated a single and impeccable authority for the issuance of suitable prescriptions and proscriptions. What reveals itself is what Luxemburg identified as the peculiarity of Leninism—a call for the inflexible central control over all the constituent elements of the revolutionary organization. It was a circumstance unusual enough to engage her concerns. Given Lenin's interpretation, she anticipated Marxism devolving into what was nothing less than quasireligious dogma.[58]

In many respects, Lenin's revision of Marxism shared more affinities with the thought of Chernyshevsky and the Russian intelligentsia of the end of the nineteenth century than with that of Marx and Engels. His professional revolutionaries were more akin to Chernyshevsky's "saviors," "the best among the best, the movers of the movers, the salt of the salt of the earth." Without them there would be no redemptive revolution. If they relaxed their diligence, the "opportunism" and the frailties of the "antediluvians" would prevail—and the liberating revolution fail. For Lenin, the future inextricably depended on the disciplined and faithful commitment of "new men" as professional revolutionaries. While the enemy of Russia's intelligentsia—whom he considered undependable and vacillating, Lenin consciously or unconsciously retained many of their convictions—for many of those convictions found their original source in the thought of Nikolai Chernyshevsky.

When, in 1903, the Social Democratic Party assembled in congress, at what was essentially its founding meeting, Lenin proceeded to impose his vision on the party of Marx, Engels, and Plekhanov. Thereafter, he was to be titular head and principal ideologue of the faction of Social Democracy identified as Bolshevist. He had put together a variant of Marxism he imagined to be not one interpretation among many, but a flawless interpretation of the thought of Marx and Engels. Like Chernyshevsky before him, and many of the intelligentsia of the period, Lenin imagined himself speaking with the voice of history. It inspired his intractability as the leader of Bolshevism. It was an implacability that was to become legendary. It was at that time, and with that confidence, that he settled on the conviction that, after the anticipated revolution, there would be "no softness" in dealing with those who failed the doctrine. It was then that

[58] "Here we have the ... peculiarity of [Lenin's] conspiratorial centralism—the absolute and blind submission of the party sections to the will of the center: ... The blind subordination, in the smallest detail, of all party organs to the party center, which alone thinks, guides and decides for all." Luxemburg, *The Russian Revolution and Marxism or Leninism?*, pp. 87, 88.

he first formed the resolution that those who could not, or would not, conform to doctrine, would "be stood up against the wall and shot."[59]

Through the years between the Second Congress of the party and the November Revolution, Lenin remained steadfast in both his convictions and his attitudes. His possession of doctrinal truth made him the implacable enemy of what he understood to be the machinations of the *petite bourgeoisie*, of the political liberals, and of the advocates of parliamentarianism. While prepared, for pragmatic reasons, to work with nonbolsheviks, it was clear that strict orthodoxy in the party, as he understood orthodoxy, was his imperative. He was, and was to remain, the advocate of the strictest party discipline as defined by doctrinal orthodoxy.

Lenin suffered all the tribulations and reverses of the uprisings of 1905 without surrendering any of his convictions. He remained forever steadfast.

Throughout those years, to those Russian intellectuals caught up in a crisis of faith, Lenin conveyed a sense of political conviction nothing short of religious in intensity. During the time of trials after the failure of the uprisings of 1905, he demonstrated his absolute inflexibility in dealing with anyone who pretended to question his interpretation of Marxist thought.

Around the time of trials that attended the unrest of 1905, Lenin's attention was drawn to the publications of a number of party comrades in which they sought to discuss epistemological, ontological, and moral questions. The issues engaged did not touch on policy matters; they were concerned with the most abstract of philosophical deliberations involving the meaning of critical terms and the nature and credibility of the criteria governing truth determination in epistemological, ontological, and ethical deliberation.

Lenin interpreted it all as not only "incredibly muddled, and confused," but as a bourgeois, conscious, malicious, reactionary, and counterrevolutionary conspiracy against Marxism. Philosophical idealism, epistemological relativism, phenomenological agnosticism, pragmatic realism, are all dismissed as components of a vast plot on the part of "bourgeois intellectuals," no matter that they are members of the "party of the proletariat." Unless they intone the kind of "dialectical materialism" Lenin had made his own, they were all identified as real or potential enemies of the party.[60]

Between 1904 and 1906, A. A. Bogdanov had been a theoretician comparable to Lenin in terms of importance within the ranks of Social Democracy. A. V. Lunacharsky had been a favored intellectual spokesman for its cause. But both

---

[59] Ulam, *Lenin and the Bolsheviks*, p. 194.

[60] See Lenin, *Materialism and Empirio-Criticism: Critical Comments on a Reactionary Philosophy*, in *LCW*, 14, pp. 19–21.

had made the mistake of discussing the impact of the work of modern thinkers like Ernst Mach and Richard Avenarius on the philosophical interpretation of modern physical science—and how that interpretation might impact the philosophical speculations of some of the earliest Marxists.[61] That earned them Lenin's enmity. His response, the product of a year's devoted intellectual labor, was his unfortunate *Materialism and Empirio-Criticism*, a work that has been called "the most lamentable of his literary productions."[62]

The work was largely a political polemic against those thinkers who dared question anything about Marxism that Lenin was not prepared to countenance. In itself, it was essentially devoid of philosophical substance.[63] What it did accomplish was to provide insight into what the future had in store.

Before he achieved power in revolutionary Russia, Lenin could only berate, vilify, and verbally abuse his real, or fancied, political opponents. After the November revolution, he expressed his distain and intolerance in far more harrowing fashion. Marxists without number were to pay the price of Lenin's conviction that he possessed the exclusive and infrangible truth about history, revolution, and the future redemption of humankind.

The implications of all that were evident. The atmosphere of prerevolutionary Russia was alive with the sense of impending transformation. The intelligentsia discerned something of the transcendental in the doings of revolutionaries possessed of a truth they would allow no one to question. Even some of the intellectual leaders of the party spoke of putting together a kind of secular religion calculated to satisfy the common man's longing for a lost God. They formally advocated a surrogate religion for the proletariat. They were the "God builders" and the "God seekers" in the ranks of the revolutionary party. They unself-consciously acknowledged what the revolution required; making explicit what everyone knew to be implicit.

Outside the party there were others, originally Marxists themselves, who divined in the emerging pattern of behavior a dreadful foreshadowing of a fright-

---

[61] Most of what passes as the epistemology and ontology of Marxism is the work of Engels. Marx actually left very little that might be subject to systematic philosophical analysis. The intellectuals of the Social Democratic Party were attempting to understand what epistemological and ontological issues had been raised by the emergence of a new philosophy of science at the end of the nineteenth century. Most of Engels' philosophical speculations are found in Engels, *Anti-Dühring: Herr Eugen Dühring's Revolution in Science* (Moscow: Foreign Languages Publishing House, 1962), Engels, "Ludwig Feuerbach and the End of Classical German Philosophy," in *SW*, vol. 2, pp. 357–401, and Engels, *Dialectics of Nature* (Moscow: Foreign Languages Publishing House, 1954). The *Dialectics of Nature* was not available to Lenin.

[62] Ulam, *Lenin and the Bolsheviks*, p. 273.

[63] For a more extensive discussion of Lenin's philosophical argument, see A. James Gregor, "Lenin on the Nature of Sensations," *Studies on the Left*, 3, no. 2 (Winter 1963), pp. 34–42.

ening future. In 1906, Nikolai Berdiaev, himself initially a Marxist, spoke of the socialism of Lenin and his followers as a surrogate religion, as a belief system "that lays claims to replacing religion." Lenin's Social Democracy, Berdiaev insisted, was "the most perfect and finished form of ... religious socialism." It found itself in conflict with all forms of religion, he went on, because it was in direct and implacable competition with them.[64]

Berdiaev identified Lenin's Social Democracy as a "religion of human self-deification," recognizing in its political affirmations traces of the thought of Feuerbach and Chernyshevsky. He spoke of Social Democracy's chiliastic beliefs as anticipating a redemptive "millennial kingdom"; of its conviction that in the Day of Judgment, the "first shall be last and the last first." He spoke of Lenin's Social Democracy as having faith in a kind of "Hegelian Panlogism" that renders the material development of earthly "productive forces" not only fully rational but purposive as well. And he spoke of its attendant morality as narrowly utilitarian, enlisted in the transformative labors of the revolution.[65]

More than a decade before the revolution that would bring Lenin to power, Berdiaev spoke of the revolutionary instauration of a secular socialist state in Russia. He described that state as the product of "positivist socialist religion"—a state that would "be sovereign, unrestricted, and deified." It would be a "deification of earthly statehood ... a kind of false collectivity [*sobornost'*] in which the individual finally drowns and vanishes." In such circumstances, "neither freedom of conscience nor freedom of speech, nor any other freedom [would be] recognized as absolute according to the value system. Rather these freedoms will be valued according to the utilitarian considerations of the social power." The "religious socialist state," he went on, would be "a new form of absolute state, unrestricted by any unconditional values or ideas, by any inalienable rights."[66]

Berdiaev had drawn together all the threads that led from Hegel, through Feuerbach, through Chernyshevsky, to the Social Democratic Party of Lenin—and knit together the first image of the totalitarian state, and the political religion, that would make of the twentieth century a very special time in the history of humankind. Leninism was the first fully modern political religion that was to come to power. Stalinism was to follow. And they were not to be the last.

[64] Berdiaev, "Socialism as Religion," pp. 108, 109, 110.
[65] Ibid., pp. 113, 116, 117, 118, 120, 124.
[66] Ibid., pp. 118, 127.

CHAPTER FIVE

Fascism

The Antecedents

We want to form a nation; how can we succeed in this, unless we believe in a common purpose, in a common duty . . . a common faith? Your Country should be your Temple. God at the summit, a People of equals at the base. . . . Through you Italy will have, with one only God in the heavens, one only truth, one only faith, one only rule of political life upon earth . . . Authoritative Truth alone can give us salvation. . . . These thoughts contain the germ of the Religion of the Future. . . . [For our] Party is not a political party; it is an essentially religious party. It has its faith, its doctrine, its martyrs . . . and it must have doctrine inviolable, authority infallible, the martyr's spirit, and call to self-sacrifice.

—Giuseppe Mazzini[1]

Mazzini's politics were moral—more than that, religious. . . . One must comprehend his religion, the source of his moral teaching, which rendered effective his political action, providing the leavening of the Risorgimento. . . . Mazzini did not intend to found a new institutional religion, but to make appeal to that religion which is at the heart of us all . . . that inspires us to sacrifice in the service of our life's mission.

—Giovanni Gentile[2]

During the years in which Marxism drew itself together amid the turmoil of postnapoleonic Europe, developments on the Italian peninsula cast their shadow across the future. Like Marxism, the revolutionary ideologies of the peninsula were to impact history for almost one hundred years. That impact was to be as fateful as the growth of Marxism-Leninism on Europe's eastern periphery.

[1] Giuseppe Mazzini, "The Duties of Man," *The Duties of Man and Other Essays* (London: J. M. Dent and Sons, 1912), pp. 25, 57, 59, 73; "Faith and the Future," ibid., p. 150.

[2] Giovanni Gentile, "Mazzini e la nuova italia," *Memorie italiane e problemi della filosofia e della vita* (Florence: G. C. Sansoni, 1936), pp. 25, 38.

Italy, at the beginning of the nineteenth century, was a congeries of unsettled papal territories, diminished city states, foreign holdings, and ill defined enclaves, riven by differences of speech and style. Having defeated the Austrians at Marengo, Napoleon had swept over Italy to divide whole tracts of the peninsula, as spoils of war, among his relatives and faithful retainers—to reduce entire populations to a kind of fawning dependency on foreigners. The remaining territory of the peninsula was divided into relatively large geographic parcels: the Kingdom of Piedmont and Savoy, the Grand Duchy of Tuscany, the Duchy of Parma, the republics of Genoa and of Venice, together with the residual Papal States—with their residents clothed, in the words of Giuseppe Mazzini, in "the livery of wretchedness and political subjection." All the ills of government by the indifferent, greedy, and incompetent afflicted most of Italy. In the course of time, tens of thousands of Italians were lured, compelled, and entrapped into the military service of foreigners, to fall, under alien flags, in Spain and in Russia.

Finally, Napoleon was defeated, and the diplomats of the Congress of Vienna sought to restore to the peninsula the "legitimacy" he had undone. There was hope among Italians that the victors would be responsive to the demands of nationality—awakened by the Napoleonic enterprise. Instead, Klemens von Metternich, superintendant of the peace conference, was rather disposed to compensate the members of the antinapoleonic alliance for their respective efforts—and Austria was correspondingly rewarded for its role in Napoleon's ultimate defeat. Peninsular Italy once again was parceled out among alien kings and reactionary clerics. The Bourbons were restored to the Kingdom of Naples, and the Pope once again assumed his temporal powers in the central part of the peninsula. In the north, Austria annexed Lombardy, while Tuscany, Modena, and Parma, reorganized into duchies, became dependencies.

The other principle governing the behavior of the Congress of Vienna was the restoration of "legitimacy" on the peninsula. With the blessings of the Congress, the House of Savoy extended its control over Nice and the former Republic of Genoa. The Spanish Bourbon king, Ferdinand I, resumed the throne in Naples—and entered into alliance with Austria to ensure his own security.

The peninsula was so fractured that it depended, in large part, on Austria for the maintenance of its security and stability. The result of all of that was that reaction settled down on the peninsula, with the diplomats of the Congress of Vienna acknowledging Italy as little more than a "geographic expression" over which, for half a century, a cloud of repression and ill use would prevail.

The Risorgimento

The term "Risorgimento"—referring to Italy's perimodern "resurgence" in the nineteenth century—serves as a historical category into which an indeterminate set of behaviors might plausibly be accommodated. It is a concept designed to trace the course of a collective project that brought conationals together to "build the fatherland of Italians." Its terminus came with the announcement of the nation's reunification in 1861. When the Risorgimento is understood to have begun remains conjectural.

By the commencement of the nineteenth century, the conviction that political sovereignty resided with each nation's people had already been reasonably well established. The entire sequence of events, commencing with the French revolution, and in the conduct of Napoleon himself, made operative the principle of popular sovereignty—even among some established monarchies. During the first decades of the century, England had accepted the notion in principle—prepared for the coming changes in its own system of popular representation. With its appeal to national sovereignty, Ireland struggled for emancipation from the control of foreigners, and the Danubian principalities were convulsed by efforts to escape the dominance of the Turks—all in the pursuit of popular sovereignty—that political aspiration that was the legacy of the French revolution.

Germany, as has been suggested, found itself embroiled in political conflict and beset by intellectual iconoclasms at the very conclusion of the Congress of Vienna. In effect, all of Europe gave increasing evidence of immanent systemic change. No less might be said of Italy. As early as 1819, popular uprisings and conspiratorial rebellion shook Naples, Sicily, and Piedmont—to provoke a regime of stultifying responses on the part of the authorities.

On the Italian peninsula, many elements were drawn into the flow of events. Intellectuals and political leaders searched for useable symbols from their collective past that might be effective in mobilizing populations to the then contemporary task of making Italy—or marshal them to the defense of tradition. Among some, all the imagery of ancient Rome was recalled. Guidance was sought from the experience of an empire that once ruled the known world from Hibernia in Northwestern Europe to the Indus River in the east—and from the Danube in the north to the African littoral in the south. The Rome of memory had been a durable experiment in political rule, introducing law, order, social peace, and religious tolerance over seventy-five million inhabitants of heterogeneous cultural and ethnic provenience. There were those who imagined that the memory of all that might have engendered some sense of historic entitlement among Italians—they were expected to reject rule by others less accomplished—or at least arm themselves with Rome's lessons learned. Italians were expected to react to the fact that they, as a community that had once ruled the world, were denied a presence among the dominant powers of their time.

The centuries following the dissolution of the Roman Empire had seen the peninsula dissolve into a tissue of city states—localisms that rendered allegiance circumscribed. Venice, Genoa, Florence, Milan, and Pisa, for example, attracted populations that provided the foundation for the communes and city republics that defined an entire period of Italian history. The result was a sense of local allegiance that remained entrenched among Italians for hundreds of years, making reunification difficult. Localism militated against any sense of national fraternity.

In all of this, and throughout the sweep of time, the Roman Catholic Church influenced events in a complex and curious fashion. Since Roman times, the Church advanced a claim to the legacy of empire. The Church saw itself as *universal,* as had the empire. As a result, emperors and popes often found themselves in competition. As the legitimate political heir of the Caesars, popes often characterized their powers as both secular and divine—as well as universal. Even as late as the end of the thirteenth century, Pope Boniface VIII often varied his dress between imperial garb and papal vestments—holding himself to be both Pope and Caesar of a Rome Universal. All of which was to produce an issue that was not to be resolved even with the reunification of Italy.

The question generated by the competing claims of Pope and politicians turned on who was understood to be vested with ultimate control in a Catholic environment. What precisely was to be "rendered unto Caesar" by the faithful? The issue was certainly not one that might easily be settled. There were those who conceived the influence of the "Church Universal" as a necessary, if not sufficient, condition for once again uniting all the disaggregated parts of Italy. They were prepared to extend primacy to the Church in its contest with secular rule. In the conflict between those divided on the issue of ultimate, functional control of political circumstances, those prepared to acknowledge the primacy of the Church came to be identified as Guelphs. Those prepared to identify secular figures as charged with the primary responsibilities of rule were denominated Ghibelline. The distinction was to persist until, and through, the Fascist period in the twentieth century.

Through time, the issue was complicated by changes in the intellectual atmosphere. With the Italian Renaissance, the first suggestions of the modern world made their appearance. With the return to the cultural memories of antiquity, a form of humanism introduced a degree of dissatisfaction concerning the authority of the Church.

The Renaissance is generally considered a discernible period in the history of Europe in which the traditional register of medieval doctrines were, in part, abandoned and, in part, revised. The humanists of the age sought meaning in life, rather than in the afterlife; everything became increasingly earthy. Life was understood to possess autonomous importance in itself, independent of religion. It was the individual, through his or her own resources, who sought to establish and confirm that importance. Little recourse, in terms of sentiment or intellect, was made to the Church or its doctrines. Christology gradually faded into the background of individual and collective consciousness. The profane emerged at the expense of religiosity, and individual consciousness proceeded to displace authority. By the fourteenth century, it was evident that Europe was making transit from one epoch to another.

Attendant upon the transition was increasing scrutiny of the Church, its representatives, its doctrines, and its practices. An increasing number of articulate critics made their appearance as Amalricians, Jansenists, and Waldensians—among others. By the sixteenth century, in the northern reaches of Europe, Protestantism formalized the criticism—and in 1517, Martin Luther posted the "97 Theses" that signaled the disintegration of the Universal Church.

In 1519, the results were already evident. Charles V, invoking antipapal and antiroman argument, declared the primacy of imperial power. With the Church of Rome rendered subordinate to secular authority, *national* churches made their predictable appearance—and Luther, himself, committed the faithful to the "Christian Nobility of the German Nation."

In the evolving struggle, southern Europe occupied itself with the Counterreformation, correcting many of the most patent ecclesiastical abuses, both doctrinal and behavioral. In the Latin countries, the Roman Church reassumed an uneasy dominance, supported by censorship, threats of excommunication, and for periods of time, simple suppression. With the advent of the Enlightenment, inspired in part by the revival of the learning of antiquity that typified the Renaissance, and in part by the increasingly standardized conception of the experiential nature of science—traditional religion, with its concept of the *Corpus mysticum* as an explanatory account of life and its meaning, became increasingly unconvincing.

In northern and western Europe, particularly, all of this congealed into a form of scientism, a doctrine that held that all the questions of life could find definitive answers in experimental inquiry, in methodological empiricism. The disposition was to achieve its fullest expression by the end of the nineteenth century in "monism" and "positivism"—animated by a set of convictions, some of which hung over academic institutions throughout the nineteenth century.

In Italy, generic scientism gave rise to philosophical schools that were to feed on the dispute between secular and religious authority.

By the time of the Risorgimento, all the threads that were to fashion Italian Marxism, monism, and positivism were already influential on the peninsula. Together with the effects of the Reformation and its reaction in Italy, those of Renaissance and Enlightenment humanism rendered the effort to unite Catholic Italy enormously complicated.

It was into just that mix of unfortunate circumstances that those who sought the reunification of Italy were born. Their lives were to bear witness to the difficulty of the task.

Giuseppe Mazzini (1805–1872): Apostle of Reunification

Among those who labored for the reunification of the Italian fatherland, few became more celebrated than Giuseppe Mazzini and Giuseppe Garibaldi. Mazzini was born in Genoa on the 22nd of June in 1805, to be followed on the 4th of July, 1807, by Giuseppe Garibaldi, who first saw the light of day in the cramped quarters of a house in the then French city of Nice.

Both Mazzini and Garibaldi were to devote their lives, each in his own fashion, to the reunification of the broken peninsula and to the creation of a common fatherland. In fact, both were to live to see Italy united, with Rome as its capital. When the French suffered defeat at Sedan in the Franco-Prussian War of 1870, French troops were withdrawn from Rome in the forlorn hope of relieving Paris. With their withdrawal, Italy's King Victor Emmanuel seized the opportunity and directed his troops to enter Roma on the 3rd of November 1870, to finally satisfy the political longings of the Risorgimento and declare the city, in July 1871, the capital of a united nation. Shortly thereafter, in 1872, Mazzini—having given so much of himself to the making of a united Italy—died, to be followed, a decade later, by Garibaldi.

In the course of their political lives both Mazzini and Garibaldi harbored deep and persistent reservations concerning the role that the Roman Catholic Church might, or ought, to play in the reunification of the peninsula. From his earliest youth, Garibaldi held himself a foe of priests, whom he spoke of as "pestilential," and "enemies of the entire human race." By the time he could form his own judgments, he found himself attracted to the socialism of the Saint-Simonians, whom he conceived "apostles" of a "new" and secularized "faith." For the rest of his life, Garibaldi continued his venomous hatred of the

Roman Church and his half-articulated commitment to the unsure socialism of Saint-Simon's *Nouveau Christianisme*.[3]

It was Mazzini, ever the more reflective, who was more specific concerning his religious disposition. He forever insisted on the importance of religion to an Italy that aspired to viable nationhood. In February 1840, in a long letter to a friend, Mazzini spoke of Italy's need of "a faith, and a church"—clearly a faith and a church other than Roman Catholicism—that would animate an association that could mature into nationhood. The required church, according to Mazzini, was to be political,[4] inflexibly unitary, with an indefeasible faith in its secular mission. It was to be a faith and a church for which he would serve as "apostle."

Mazzini had convinced himself that the church he advocated could not be the Church of Rome. Mazzini held that the Roman Catholic Church had betrayed every principle of effective governance by corrupting individuals with promises of personal salvation and individual immortality—to the neglect of those strengths of character necessary to meet one's responsibilities. The Roman Church offered a conception of life innocent of any notion of what "*collective* Humanity" might demand of persons. Instead, Roman Christianity called up only "the feeble, unequal, isolated, fruitless powers" of solitary and selfish individuals.[5]

Mazzini spoke of a "regeneration" of Italy possible only by means of "a great religious principle" that marshaled masses to common tasks, that united individuals in common purpose. He spoke of apostles whose "insurrection" would "announce with its awful voice the decrees of God" concerning the nation's future.[6]

Religion remained a constant among Mazzini's political convictions and tactical maneuvers. It remained the foundation of all his efforts, capable of making them meaningful, not only inspiring his proposed reforms, but giving him heart to continue, against all odds, in their service. Only a faith, he

---

[3] See the account in Christopher Hibbert, *Garibaldi and His Enemies: The Clash of Arms and Personalities in the Making of Italy* (New York: New American Library, 1966), chap. 1.

[4] There were occasions in which Mazzini sought to draw a distinction between political and religious thought, but they were never successful. Ultimately the differences disappeared in his appeals for a "new religion" and a "new faith." See, for example, his appeal to "a new heaven ... represented by a new earth" with a "new dogma" and a "new moral code." Mazzini, "From the Council to God," in *The Duties of Man*, p. 314.

[5] Mazzini, "Thoughts on the French Revolution of 1789," ibid., p. 264.

[6] Mazzini, "Faith and the Future," ibid., pp. 148, 149. Mazzini wrote voluminously. His edited and unedited *Scritti politici editi e inediti* (Imola: TDS, 1941) runs many, many volumes. For the purposes of the present discussion, the materials readily available in English are sufficient.

insisted, could induce the kinds of sacrifice required by his personal mission, a mission with which he sought to inspire a nation. He spoke of obedience to God and a commitment to duty as religious obligations—and of a faith that he could neither silence nor renounce. He spoke of that sustaining faith "as neither Catholic, nor Protestant, nor Christian"—but nonetheless as "sincerely and profoundly religious."[7]

Mazzini thus gave form and content to a political surrogate for the established, traditional faith that he was convinced humanity had "transcended." Like many of the German revolutionaries of the same period, Mazzini opposed himself to traditional religion while continuing to believe that religious faith was an intrinsic component of human consciousness. While opposed to the Roman Church, he nonetheless conceived that those duties, political and social, that were the responsibilities of humankind, found their imperative origin in the will of the Creator. For Mazzini, religion was eternal, a forever element in human reality.[8] He held that while "religions die ... religion remains."[9] He was convinced that humanity had an irrepressible need of religion—to satisfy both deeply felt longings as well as pragmatic, psychological, and organizational imperatives.

The demanding struggle for nationhood, in an environment beset by egotism—narrow interest and self-serving disposition—had need of an offset in terms of an enduring faith in the morality of self-sacrifice necessary to accomplish a collective political mission. For Mazzini, it was religion and faith that ever provided the moral incentives for revolution.[10]

Mazzini was convinced that faith was needed by those charged with the task of fashioning a new nation out of the aftermath of the Napoleonic wars and the reactionary tangle left by the Congress of Vienna. Italy was to be a nation restored—to "rise again, great and honored"—by the will of God. It would be a "Third Rome," successor to the Rome of antiquity, and the Rome of the Universal Church. Its grandeur would be restored by awakening the greatness that slumbered in its potential. Revolutionary success would become manifest when

---

[7] Giovanni Gentile, *Albori della nuova Italia: Varietà e documenti* (Lanciano: R. Carabba editore, n.d.), part 1, pp. 203–204.

[8] "Religion is immortal ... ; it is born with the world, and 'will endure as long as the world shall endure' [Dante].... Remember that religion is a want, a necessity of the People; that all changes of form that have been in the world have never succeeded in extinguishing the religious sentiment." Mazzini, "The Patriots and the Clergy," in *The Duties of Man*, pp. 209, 214. See also Mazzini, "From the Council to God," ibid., p. 294.

[9] Mazzini, "The Duties of Man," and "Faith in the Future," ibid., pp. 21, 22, 29, 31, 161.

[10] "A Religion or a philosophy lies at the base of every Revolution." Mazzini, "Thoughts on the French Revolution of 1789," ibid., p. 266. Elsewhere he says, "Every Revolution is the work of a *principle* which has been accepted as a basis of faith." Mazzini, "Interests and Principles," ibid., p. 128.

Italy experienced "one only God in the heavens, one only truth, one only faith, [and] one only rule of political life upon earth."[11]

To accomplish all that required the invocation of a "religious sentiment"[12]—a sentiment that he was convinced "sleeps in our people, waiting to be awakened. He who knows," he continued, "how to rouse it will do more for the nation than can be done by twenty political theories." In an Italy challenged by historic tasks, he anticipated that only the emergence of a new "holy creed,"[13] a "people's religion," whose advocates would be "apostles," delivering a "gospel" of "authoritative Truths,"[14] could fulfill the nation's destiny. Only truths predicated on sentiments that were *social* in essence and historic in consequence could so serve. They would be truths that rejected the egotism and individualism of the Renaissance and the Enlightenment that had rendered true community impossible.

Mazzini spoke of the coming of a "new age," inspired by the principles of *association*.[15] He preached a liberty that was not the exclusive boon of individuals. He spoke, instead, of the liberty of entire peoples. In the awakening age, a "new religion," based on a "principle of sociality," with the nation as its inspiration, would "regenerate" humanity—preparing each person for sacrifice, obedience, and selfless commitment—to serve in a "holy mission" destined to bring freedom not to individuals, per se, but to entire *peoples*, and liberty to *nations*.[16] It would be a dedicated response to humanity's desperate cry for fulfillment—a fulfillment that could only come to a "humanity" the substance of which was "European," and whose form was "nationality." Fulfillment would come only through "Nationality, Liberty, [and] a common Fatherland"—through the dedication to "one God, one Law, [and] one End."[17]

[11] Mazzini, "The Duties of Man," ibid., p. 59.

[12] "Religious sentiment is the foundation and bond of all social fellowship, the only pledge of security for the continuous and pacific progress of every people that desires to be a nation." Mazzini, "The Patriots and the Clergy," ibid., p. 210.

[13] See "From the Council to God," ibid., pp. 288, 294, 308, 311.

[14] Mazzini entertained a complex notion of truth. He realizes that there must be some intersubjective criteria of truth in order to avoid intellectual anarchy and the relativity of subjective truths. His first formulation is *agreement* between the *individual* and the *collective conscience*. (See "The Duties of Man," ibid., pp. 40, 67.) The final account seems to be an "incarnation" of such truths in "apostles," possessed of "genius" and "virtue," who establish their possession of the truth by successfully mobilizing masses to sacrifice and to conquest in its service. See Mazzini's initial allusion ibid., p. 57.

[15] "Now, we believe the time has arrived for the principle of *association* to be solemnly and universally proclaimed, and become the center of all study, theoretical and practical, which aims at the progressive organisation of human societies, to shine at the head of our constitutions, our codes of law, the articles of our faith, . . . to indicate a new Age." Mazzini, "Faith and the Future," ibid., p. 191.

[16] See the discussion in Mazzini, "The Duties of Man," ibid., pp. 56–59.

[17] "Faith and the Future," ibid., pp. 144, 146, 149, 150, 154, 155, 158, 161, 176, 180.

Everywhere, the redemptive mission would be led by a party that was not simply political, but profoundly and fundamentally *religious*.[18] Indestructible, it would be a party with a "faith ... with a doctrine inviolable, authority infallible," all animated by a "martyr's spirit and call to self-sacrifice." Religious parties, Mazzini continued, "never die, except when the victory is won, when their vital principle has attained its full development, and become identified with the progress of civilisation and of morals."[19]

On the Italic peninsula, the future could no longer be contained. For Italians, "misfortune, suffering, protests, individual sacrifice, [had] reached their extreme limits.... The cup [was] full."[20] Foreign despots reigned over people who had forgotten their heritage of glory; the Fatherland was dismembered; the corrupt, all too often, reigned; and whole populations knew nothing of nationality.

For Mazzini, revolution would sweep all that away. It would sweep away all those bloodless concepts of personal liberty, individual rights, and particular material benefits. It would provide that collective freedom without which individual liberty would be meaningless. It would ensure the discharge of duties that would make meaningful rights possible.[21] And it would realize that national accomplishment and glory without which material satisfactions could only be of little consequence.[22]

Mazzini's revolution would be bearer of a new dogma, composed of truths first captured in philosophy and science, then "incarnated in the life of one or more individuals," each "privileged" in genius and virtue, capable of inspiring multitudes to sacrifice and conquest.[23] Such "prophets" and "geniuses," "apos-

---

[18] "It is ... religious sentiment which allows the thoughts and actions of Man ... and gives him the consciousness of a mission to fulfill ... ; it is that which makes all of his life a scene of self-sacrifice and charity.... From it flow strength and constancy ... indifference to danger, noble resignation in persecution and misfortune." Mazzini, "The Patriots and the Clergy," ibid., p. 209.

[19] Ibid., p. 150. In "The Duties of Man," Mazzini provides the "criterion" of truth as "the agreement" of the individual "voice of conscience" with that of the "general opinion of ... fellow men." "The Duties of Man," ibid., p. 35. Mazzini was later to identify such truths as "dogmas" "incarnated" in the will of one or more "prophets." Such dogmas apparently correspond to the conscience of individuals as well as that of "fellow men"—and are so recognized.

[20] Ibid., p. 153.

[21] "You have no rights, save as the consequence of duties fulfilled." Mazzini, "From the Council to God," ibid., pp. 318–319. See Mazzini's early catalog of human rights, and the qualifications he invokes. He clearly rejects the exercise of those rights and that liberty which impair the achievement of "the collective purpose of the Nation." See ibid., pp. 79–82. He argues that one secures one's rights "by *deserving* them, through self-sacrifice, [and] industry." Ibid., p. 117.

[22] See the entire discussion in Mazzini, "The Duties of Man," ibid., pp. 8–20.

[23] Mazzini, "From the Council to God," ibid., p. 302, n. Mazzini regularly spoke of sacrifice as the "only true virtue." See ibid., p. 291.

tles" of the new gospel,[24] would represent the true will of all—a will that was sacred, embodying as it would, the moral law.[25]

Under those circumstances, the revolutionary government that would result would be "the *mind* of the Nation, the people its *arm*, and the educated and free individual its prophet of *future progress*." To ensure the anticipated progress, Mazzini spoke of public education as involving processes responsible for inculcating individual and collective morality. Children would be educated to "the ruling principles and beliefs which guide the ... moral, social and political programme of their nation." He went on to insist that "the education which shall give your children this sort of teaching can come only from the Nation." Without such an education, he continued, any talk of a meaningful existence for individuals alone or in association would be unconvincing. Duties and rights could only be established in a carefully crafted political arrangement.

Within such an arrangement, individuals would not be permitted the freedom to choose to do evil. They would not be permitted to respond to the enjoinments of an "arbitrary will." Only when moral instruction has achieved its purpose and individuals conform to the public will does "Liberty regain its rights" for all associated citizens.[26]

While Mazzini's primary concern for the new nation was stability and a predictable future, he devoted a not inconsiderable amount of thought to its material foundations. In that nation, its economic imperatives included the systematic increase of capital and an escalation of production—fostered and sustained through a system of workers' cooperatives.[27] The program was calculated to diminish class conflict and preclude the possibility of a socialist threat to private property. For Mazzini, property was an intrinsic human right that was "eternal in principle."[28] In the nation liberated and economically productive, persons would find that the establishment of protected rights included the right to the ownership of property.

Mazzini's nationalism was thus animated by principled objections to the emergent socialism of the period. He objected to "Sansimonism, Fourierism, and Communism"—including, it was clear, the Marxism of Karl Marx and Friedrich Engels. He identified all such socialisms as "false and tyrannic" in

---

[24] Ibid., p. 319; see Mazzini's earlier references to "apostles" blessed by God with "genius and more than common virtue," in "The Duties of Man," ibid., p. 74.

[25] While Mazzini speaks of rulers being elected by the people, he consistently speaks of rule by "men of virtuous genius," who correctly interpret the "moral law," as the "only form of legitimate governance." See ibid., p. 85.

[26] Mazzini, "The Duties of Man," ibid., pp. 86, 87, 88, 89.

[27] Ibid., p. 54 and sect. 11, "The Economic Question."

[28] Ibid., p. 103.

their "methods and application"—and erroneous in tactics and strategy. They all sought to correct whatever evils they identified by abolishing property, suppressing both wealth and the activity that produced it—actions Mazzini associated with that savagery that would "cut down the tree in order to gather fruit."[29]

Mazzini entered into maturity the spokesman of just such a set of convictions. His was a political creed with which he sought to inspire Italians to commit themselves to weaving together the scattered threads of a historic people.

Italy, in fact, was to be reunited in the years that were to follow—but it was to be reunited, not by that ideology, or by Mazzini alone. Between the political failure of the revolutionary year of 1848—and 1872—when the nation, once more, was united with Rome as its capital, it was armed conflict, political barter, and diplomacy, led by others, that together produced the desired result. How much of that was a consequence of Mazzini's efforts, and the efforts of his followers, is impossible to determine with any assurance.

What is clear is that the politics that dominated the reunification eventually took on the properties of classical liberalism crowded round with all the individualisms and cultivation of egoistic interests Mazzini had so much deplored. Italian politics began to take on the features of a parliamentarian liberalism in which Mazzini and his followers had so little confidence.

Nonetheless, in the minds and hearts of Italians, Mazzini left a doctrinal legacy that was to influence the politics of the nation through much of the twentieth century. Much of Mazzini's doctrine can be read as a response to tensions that had shaped Italian history for a thousand years. It was left to the future to determine which of the elements of that doctrine would continue to influence the history of the newly reunited nation.

Interpretations of the Risorgimento

By the time Italians celebrated the Jubilee year of reunification in 1911, much of the history of the Risorgimento had crystallized into distinctive interpretations. Its heroes had been identified and their deeds duly recorded. In the enthusiasm surrounding the success of the enterprise, little was made of the differences that distinguished those who were more secular from those who were identified as "neoguelph," disposed to assign a privileged role for the Roman Church in the evolving political affairs of the peninsula. The differences between the antimonarchists and monarchists, between those lay and those confessional, between those who favored association on the peninsula through

[29] Ibid., pp. 102, 104.

some kind of federal arrangement and those who advocated a more unitary union, tended to be papered over—or their importance diminished. The Jubilee celebrated fifty years of union and sought to overlook the confused and contested course of its accomplishment.

Nationalists like Alfredo Oriani (1852–1909) tended to see the entire Risorgimento as the product of the "mystical and religious" inspiration of Giuseppe Mazzini. However the period closed, with the machinations of the Savoyard monarchy and the intercession of foreign powers, Oriani portrayed the reunification as somehow the direct or indirect consequence of Mazzinism.[30]

While other interpretations competed for space and hearing, there was but one truth according to Oriani. By the first years of the century, he gave expression to an interpretation that he was convinced conveyed verities that time had tended to obscure. He spoke of Italy's reunification as taking place during a protracted period of crisis. It was a crisis spawned by the betrayal of Christianity—the consequence of that arid criticism identified as "higher" among the denizens of German universities.

Oriani spoke of David Strauss and the posthegelian polemicists—and the impact they exercised on the conventional faith of believers—not only in Germany, but in Italy as well. He spoke, without hesitation, of the passing of traditional belief systems—and the corrosive effects that all that had on an Italy in turmoil.

At the same time, Oriani mentioned the rise of alternative systems of belief that succeeded in filling the unoccupied space in the revolutionary consciousness of "new Italians." It was in that context that he spoke of the "modern" system of beliefs around which Mazzini had collected conationals. The new system was composed of beliefs somehow different from traditional religion, yet shared with them some of their defining traits.

By the end of the nineteenth century, Oriani had become convinced that Mazzini's was a belief system that found its ultimate rationale in the "pantheistic" thought of G. W. F. Hegel.[31]

It was Hegel who had argued that traditional religion was a "mythologized" precursor to a modern, emergent system. Hegel spoke of institutionalized religion as resting on a collection of vague sentiments and obscure feelings that captured only the first contours of the philosophical truth of spiritual life. He maintained that philosophy increasingly provided the understanding absent

[30] See particularly Alfredo Oriani, *La Lotta politica in Italia* (Rocca San Casciano: Cappelli, 1956), bk. 4, chap. 4, pp. 304–313.

[31] Oriani considered the revolutionary and "heretical" thought of Giordano Bruno as "prehegelian." Ibid., p. 127.

from the religion of the ordinary believer.³² It was only philosophy that revealed the full story of human spiritual evolution. Philosophy provided the account of history as the story of the evolution of the universal spirit, and the articulation of human liberty—of which religion was only part.

Granted that, Oriani was to argue that religion, the belief system of the ordinary person, might well be employed in their mobilization. They might, thereby, be marshaled to the full service of "the march of God on earth." Philosophy might well be the fully articulated rationale for the popular religion that was its preamble, but it also served national purpose.

Mazzini's new faith, making the nation the object of reverence, and the state the critical center of obligation, was a manifestation of that form of popular religion that was not only the antechamber to an entire philosophical system, but it was of practical necessity in making Italy a nation. Oriani saw Mazzinism as a faith that was not quite any recognized faith, as a religion that was not quite any recognized religion.³³ It was more a call to arms. It was an enjoinment, an invocation. It was calculated to conjure up "sacred battalions"—all afire with "religious fervor." It reached into the very being of human beings in association. It appealed to a sentiment as old as time.

For Oriani, whatever else it might have been conceived to be, Mazzinism gave every evidence of being a faith of politicoreligious character, absolutely necessary for the survival and persistence of the political state—the union of the living, the dead, and the unborn—and the necessary foundation of established morality.³⁴

One retraces all this in Oriani's prose. He speaks of life as a manifestation of "Spirit"—and the "State" as its principal agency. He attributes to the State the establishment of community—the family and of religion itself—without which individuals would never accede to the maturity of personhood.³⁵ In all of that Oriani makes evident that he conceived some form of Hegelianism a modern surrogate for traditional beliefs.³⁶ In fact, his entire conception of his-

---

³² That is the general sentiment of Hegel's lectures on the philosophy of religion. For a convenient summary, see G. W. F. Hegel, *Lectures on the Philosophy of Religion* (London: Routledge & Kegan Paul, 1962), vol. 3, pp. 360–367.

³³ In his last major work, Oriani chooses not to speak of a "faith," but of an "ideal." See Oriani's comments in *La Rivolta ideale* (Bologna: Cappelli, 1943), p. 5, but see pp. 254–256, where the distinction seems to disappear.

³⁴ Oriani, *Lotta politica in Italia*, pp. 306, 307, 308, 334, and *Rivolta ideale*, pp. 111, 255.

³⁵ Oriani, *Rivolta ideale*, pp. 10–19.

³⁶ Hegel is regularly identified as an inspiration for the thought of Oriani. See Alfredo Giorgi, *Alfredo Oriani* (Florence: R. Bemporad & F., 1935), p. 93; Adolfo Albertazzi, ed., Oriani, *Memorie inutili* (Bologna: L. Cappelli, 1927), vol. 1, p. vii; and Alberto Ghisalberti, Introduction to Oriani, *Lotta politica in Italia*, p. xviii. Oriani held that Hegelianism had "transcended" Roman Catholicism, but

tory was Hegelian in character, and the "spiritualism" that he saw in the "new Christianity" of Mazzini and his followers, no less so.[37]

By the first decade of the new century, the history of the Risorgimento was being parsed into interpretations that were to shape Italian thought. One such interpretation, that found idiom in the works of Oriani, saw Italy's reunification as a necessary stage in the evolution of humanity. Oriani understood Mazzinism to be inspired by the conviction that the reunification of the Italian peninsula was part of a necessary spiritual process. Mazzini was an "apostle" of faith in the process. In essence, Oriani conceived history as a Hegelian theodicy—a working out of humanity's spiritual destiny. Whatever else Oriani's interpretation of the Risorgimento was, it was a conception that was to have an echo in Italian thought long after the death of its advocate in 1906.

Giovanni Gentile (1875–1944) and the Risorgimento

Knowledgeable Italians spoke of Giovanni Gentile as "the last commanding voice of our Risorgimento." He was understood to have charged himself with the lifelong responsibility of fostering what he considered its unfinished philosophical, political, and religious tasks.[38] Such a depiction is supported by a collection of corroborative evidence.

From his youth, Gentile occupied himself with the events, and the protagonists, that made up the substance of the Risorgimento. We have his correspondence with his teachers and colleagues to confirm that, and his first full length scholarly study was devoted to the thought of Antonio Rosmini (1797–1855) and Vincenzo Gioberti (1801–1852), two major intellectuals of the movement committed to the political reunification of the peninsula.[39] In his account of the thought of both, Gentile outlined an interpretation—from which he was never to depart—of that critical period in Italian history.

Gentile conceived the Risorgimento the product of a shared, historic spirit,

---

a religion required another as its successor—and so Oriani anticipated the rise of a "third religion," inspired by Hegelianism, that would take the place of traditional Catholicism. See Oriani, *Rivolta ideale*, pp. 249–250, 254–255.

[37] See Oriani, *Rivolta ideale*, pp. 243–257.

[38] See Armando Carlini, *Studi Gentiliani* in *Giovanni Gentile: La vita e il pensiero* (Florence: G. C. Sansoni editore, 1958), vol. 8, p. 103; and Augusto Del Noce, *Giovanni Gentile: Per una interpretazione filosofica della storia contemporanea* (Bologna: Il Mulino, 1990), p. 59.

[39] Giovanni Gentile, *Rosmini e Gioberti: Saggio storico sulla filosofia italiana del Risorgimento* (Florence: Sansoni, 1958). The original edition appeared in 1898. The subtitle to the volume was added years later as though to make clear its emphases. See Giovanni Gentile, *Lettere a Benedetto Croce* (Florence: Sansoni, 1972), vol. 1; and Gentile-Donato Jaja, *Carteggio* (Florence: Sansoni, 1967), vol. 1.

which found expression in two conjoined popular movements: one expressed in *ideal* (literary, philosophical, and religious) *locutions*; and the other embodied in *political events*. At times, individual convictions and political events appeared to move in opposing directions, but eventually everything merged into a willed sentiment manifest in phenomena that, in the final analysis, created a nation. Only in retrospect, Gentile argued, does the "cunning of history," the "meaning" of it all, become evident.[40]

Gentile's interpretation turned on the conviction that, in the course of events, the contributions of individual thought and collective behavior were somehow fused in history—making manifest, thereby, a "divine energy," the cosmic "omnipotence" of an immanent "Spirit."[41] That such a Spirit was manifest in events was a metaphysical conviction—familiar to a contemporary subset of Italian students of philosophy—clearly Hegelian in origin and theological in spirit.

Throughout the remainder of his life, and certainly during the years here considered, Gentile held that human existence was defined by "Spirit." What that meant, for the purposes of the present account, was that existence, all of life, experience in all its forms, was "spiritual."[42] As has been suggested, what idealists meant by that, in general, was that human experience is captured exclusively in *consciousness*, and consciousness is identified in thought. We know "nature" captured in mathematical forms that are artifacts of thought. Idealists remind us that, as human beings, we do not confront, or simply observe, reality—we "construct" it through an interactive process acknowledged by philosophers since time immemorial.[43] The attempt to fully understand that creative process has led to a searching inquiry into ultimate questions of existence and meaning—into religious reflection—and inescapable acknowledgment of religious concerns as an intrinsic part of being human.

For Gentile, such convictions reinforced the confidence that religion would

---

[40] Decades later, in the service of Italian Fascism, Gentile provided a restatement of his interpretation in his *Origins and Doctrine of Fascism with Selections from Other Works* (New Brunswick, N.J.: Transaction Publishers, 2002), pp. 4–5.

[41] Gentile to his Professor, Donato Jaja, in a letter dated 7 October 1897, in Gentile-Jaja, *Carteggio*, vol. 1, p. 38. The substance of the discussion is derivative of chapter 1 of Gentile, *Rosmini e Gioberti*, pp. 3–42; see the preface to the first edition of 1898, pp. ix–xvi. The subtitle was added years later, by which time he was more confident of his interpretation.

[42] Gentile was careful to indicate that what philosophers meant by "spiritual" had nothing to do with the "spiritualism" that was made popular by theosophists and table rappings. See Gentile, "Il Regno dello spirito," *Il Modernismo e i rapporti fra religione e filosofia* (Florence: Sansoni, 1962), pp. 237–243. This brief essay, written in 1909, reflects Gentile's judgments of the period. The present account will depend on its content.

[43] One of the earliest of Gentile's expressions of this analysis is found in Gentile, "La Filosofia della prassi," in *La Filosofia di Marx*, reprinted in *I Fondamenti della filosofia del diritto* (Florence: Sansoni, 1955), pp. 297–298.

somehow contribute to the worldly process of political reunification on the Italian peninsula. Faith was a constituent part of life in all its forms. In the particular circumstances that attended the Risorgimento, it was evident that religion, and religious opinion, would serve critical purposes in the mobilizing of sentiment, and the shaping and direction of the collective will—so essential to political and human purpose. Gentile saw the working of "Spirit" in the faith and religious persuasion of the actors in the Risorgimento. Anyone who sought to diminish either, ill served the reunification of the nation.

Italy's history had provided the events, and Hegelianism had afforded the conceptual apparatus, to make such an interpretation persuasive to Gentile.[44] He applied it with considerable deftness in accounting for the behavior of the notables of the period. His treatment of the literary work of Alessandro Manzoni (1785–1873), for example, was characteristic of his discussion of the entire period.

Manzoni had become familiar with the work of Rosmini, an idealist critic of the kinds of empiricism that had found their way into Italian critical thought. Empiricism, the notion that sense perception was of primary, if not dominant, epistemological significance, had followed the French into the peninsula. British "naturalism," in its Gallic expression, had given rise to a form of "scientism" that tended to dominate Italian thought.

Scientism in Italy, as it did in all of Europe, held that empirical research could answer all questions. It was agnostic at best, and commonly atheistic. Its influence was evident in Italy at least through the first decades of the twentieth century.

Assisted by the reflections of Rosmini, Manzoni resisted what he took to be the entailments of that sort of "realism." Empiricism, with its emphasis on the epistemological importance of the senses, implied both materialism and secularism—at the expense of "spiritual" and religious thought. As an Italian, and as an intellectual, Manzoni was alienated by opinions that denied humankind's essential spirituality. Idealism had become central to Italian intellectual and political life.

What that did was to convince Gentile that impaired thought, a spiritually impoverished conception of life, succeeded only in confusing commitments and confounding mobilization among thinking Italians. In effect, religion and faith, in principle, were critical to the purposes of the makers of the Risorgimento.

[44] "The History of the World, with all the changing scenes with which its annals present, is the process of development and the realization of Spirit." G. W. F. Hegel, *The Philosophy of History* (New York: Dover Publications, 1956), p. 457.

Beyond that, it was clear that the religious conflicts that had given rise to Protestantism in the north, found expression in dissidence and doctrinal disputes in Italy within the institution of the Roman Church. Both right reason and practical considerations recommended that a form of religious expression be promoted that, while engaging Italians in the evolving political circumstances of the peninsula, would not precipitate confessional disputes. In such circumstances philosophical idealism, with its recognition of a generic religious sentiment, recommended itself. Such a faith would satisfy cognitive requirements, and serve practical political purpose as well. Except for the most committed fundamentalists, the religiosity of idealism would accommodate all.

The interaction of philosophical, religious, and nationalist motives, together had governed Italy's political history after the Renaissance. By the nineteenth century, the elements had become so intrinsic to the sequence of events on the peninsula, that one could hardly expect any account of the emergence of Italy as a nation without treating each in some detail.

In his earliest work, Gentile did nothing less. He traced developments from Giordano Bruno and Tommaso Campanella, through Giambattista Vico, to the shapers of the thought of the Risorgimento—acknowledging in every instance the difficulties with the Church. In all of that, he sketched the outlines of what he took to be the evolution of a popular will, both philosophical and religious in spirit, which was to re-create a nation.[45]

Gentile spoke of Bruno and Campanella as supplying the inspiration for major transalpine developments in philosophy. He saw British empiricism, utilitarianism, and individualism originally finding inspiration in the Italian Renaissance—returning to Italy in a form disadvantageous to its political and intellectual future. All of that was necessarily part of the "logic of history"—to the making of a national personality. It was a development that would not be complete until the imported empiricism, the epistemological emphasis on sense perception, was incorporated and subordinated to human purpose.

That would be the inspiration for an essentially "transcredal" belief system, a philosophicoreligious formulation, incorporating the results of empirical science, that would provide the grounds for self-sacrifice and a readiness to serve in the demanding atmosphere of a nation in formation. It would be a faith that, in principle, would appeal to all thinking Italians because, as a product of

---

[45] All of that, as has been suggested, was Hegelian in origin, and in substance. The immediate source of that Hegelianism was in the instruction of Donato Jaja (1839–1914), a major influence on Gentile as a student. See Gentile's eulogy at the time of Jaja's death, "Donato Jaja," in Gentile-Jaja, *Carteggio*, vol. 1, pp. ix–xviii.

shared right reason, it would satisfy intellectual demands as well as common religious and political impulse.

The reasoned faith to which Gentile appealed, was one rooted in Italian philosophical tradition, involving thinkers on the peninsula, at least since the time of Vico, through Rosmini and Gioberti, to become increasingly explicit in the works of Bertrando Spaventa (1817–1883).[46] It was a form of epistemological and ontological idealism that took shape throughout the Risorgimento that, in Gentile's judgment, was compatible with the spiritual and religious sentiments of both those like Manzoni, who sought to make Catholicism part of the movement to unite Italy, as well as those, like Mazzini, who anticipated what was essentially a nondenominational, national, religious faith.[47]

Gentile's interpretation, characteristic of Hegelian renderings in general, allows an author to deal directly with the complexities of history; to see in it all the constituents of "Spirit"—to ultimately see in one given outcome the notions, feelings, and intuitions that have given form, over time, to the legends, literature, art, religion, and philosophy of an entire people. It was an interpretation that was to typify Gentile's work for the remainder of his life.

Several contingencies contributed to the form, if not the content, of Gentile's retrospective on the Risorgimento. As an Italian, he was aggrieved that so much of the thought of his compatriots was dismissed or neglected by the international academic community. Once European scholars had exhausted all discussion of the thought of the Scholastics and the Renaissance, they showed no further interest in the philosophic reflections of Italians. It was as though Italians had entirely ceased philosophical inquiry after the late middle ages. Niggardly references to Italian philosophical thought were concealed in footnotes, and when there was reference to Italian scholars, not only were their analyses all too often misrepresented, but their names misspelled.

More than that, Gentile was clearly vexed by the fact that as a consequence of events across the Alps, French ideas, accompanied by French troops, too long had invested all of Italy. It seemed that he would have Italy free of both—if for no other reason than to mollify the attendant humiliation.

But there was more than that. As a young man, Gentile was unreservedly committed to an independent and united Italy. He was convinced that both foreign troops and foreign ideas militated against both. The interference of both

---

[46] Professor Jaja, Gentile's mentor, introduced him to the neohegelian idealism of Spaventa. See ibid., vol. 1, pp. ix–xviii.

[47] Traces of this account are found throughout Gentile's philosophical and historical writings. A convenient place for a summary account, written years later, is found in Gentile, "Bertando Spaventa nel primo cinquantenario della sua morte," *Memorie italiane*, particularly pp. 138–149.

in Italy's national integrity was to be countered. The political leaders of the reunification had managed the first; it was to the second that the young Gentile devoted his attention.

This is no better represented than by his work in philosophy itself. As early as his years as a graduate student, all those opinions gave distinctive form to his intellectual undertakings. He was opposed to empiricism and utilitarianism not only because they were of foreign origin, but because both contributed to secularism, hedonism, individualism, and subjectivism—the advocacy of which impaired public purpose and public institutions.

As a case in point, Gentile objected to the secularism that threatened the integrity of the Roman Church. That was because, in his judgment, the Church, whatever its failures, had fostered, sustained, and nurtured a sense of community and individual obligation among Italians for more than a thousand years. The nineteenth century required a reinvocation of just such virtues among the general population if the nation were to survive and prosper. His defense of traditional religion was a tactical recommendation. The "spiritless" empiricism and arrant selfishness explicit in Anglo-French philosophy threatened the political future of Italy.[48]

It was within that conception that one appreciates Gentile's emphasis on the religious character of Italian neohegelianism.[49] For one thing, as has been suggested, he was convinced that religion would be essential if Italians were to assume the grave responsibilities that followed national reunification. For Gentile, religion would constitute the necessary precondition for temporal virtues, secular sacrifice, and dutiful service. More than that, of course, was the fact that Gentile's philosophical convictions, like those of Hegel, were inextri-

---

[48] Gentile's objections to simple empiricism as an epistemological strategy was not generated by the fact that it was a foreign import. Hegelianism was itself of foreign origin; but its effects were not only benign, but, in his judgment, salubrious. Gentile argued that the Hegelianism he had inherited from Spaventa, had been fully assimilated to the Italian environment. Moreover, it incorporated the major sentiments of the dominant protagonists of the nation's reunification. His own Hegelianism was a "reformed Hegelianism," shaped by Italian genius and Italian interests. Those who introduced Hegelianism to the peninsula had given it a form, and supplied a content, prescribed by time and circumstances. See the discussion in Gentile, "I Neokantiani e gli Hegeliani," *Le Origini della filosofia contemporanea in Italia* (Messina: Casa editrice G. Principato, 1921), vol. 3, part 1. In the text, the exposition is shaped by Italian conditions, rendering neokantians and Hegelians in Italy peculiarly Italian. That British and French empiricism could not enjoy similar transformation seems to be the result, for Gentile, of the fact that they generated only negative results in a community struggling for political reunification.

[49] "Hegelian philosophy is an essentially religious philosophy in so far as it resolves religion into itself, and is religion: conceiving itself the revelation, indeed, the realization of God." Ibid., vol. 3, part 1, p. 380.

cably *theologizing* in character.⁵⁰ He was both philosophically convinced and politically persuaded that religion was an irreducibly essential part of the life of humankind, in general, and for Italians, in particular. For at least those reasons he welcomed the religious convictions—whatever form they assumed—that one finds in the thought of Bruno, Campanella, Vico, Rosmini, Gioberti, and Spaventa. He finds merit in the thought of all, irrespective of how they understood religious beliefs might function—as long as there was an overall defense of generic religiosity.

Given those parameters, Gentile's thought was unfettered by the demands of doctrinal orthodoxy. His expressed convictions were not those of a traditional Christian, having more in common with Catholic and Protestant philosophical dissidents than with the official doctrines of any church.⁵¹ As a consequence he could see worth, both in the neoguelph religiosity of Gioberti, the qualified orthodoxy of Manzoni, and the unorthodox faith, and the religious independence, of Giuseppe Mazzini and Giuseppe Garibaldi. For Gentile, all were makers of the Risorgimento, serving the nation and, thereby, all humanity.

As a consequence of all that, Gentile resisted every form of empiricism and materialism, the one because he found it manifestly implausible to conceive truth exclusively or primarily a function of observation, and the other because it dismissed, in principle, the possibilities of a reasoned religious faith. These judgments were to influence his thought throughout his professional life. They were evident in his youthful treatment of "classical" Marxism—the Marxism of Karl Marx and Friedrich Engels—that Gentile undertook at the same time that he was preparing his doctoral dissertation.

Gentile and Classical Marxism

Why the young Gentile undertook his rather detailed treatment of classical Marxism during the last years of the nineteenth century seems reasonably clear in retrospect. For one thing, Marxism was becoming of increasing interest to Italians at the time. The Italian Socialist Party had just recently been organized and there was much talk of the new philosophy that was its inspiration. While all that was transpiring, it seems that Gentile was actively interested in the defense, and in fostering a form, of antimaterialist, neohegelian idealism in which he had been schooled by Donato Jaja. The Marxism of Marx and Engels—the

---

⁵⁰ When his critics charged him with being a "theologian," Gentile responded: "A theologizing philosophy then? And why not?" Gentile, *Sistema di logica come teoria del conoscere* (Florence: Sansoni, 1940 [originally published in 1917 by Spoerri in Pisa]), vol. 2, p. 384.

⁵¹ See, for example, Del Noce, *Giovanni Gentile*, pp. 34–35, and n. 22.

rationale of the new socialist movement—was advertised as a "materialism" calculated to defeat the "retrograde" idealism of the establishment.

It was in those circumstances that Gentile chose to embark upon his analysis. At the same time, he sought to influence Benedetto Croce, already reasonably prominent, and seemingly well disposed toward some form of idealism.[52]

It seemed that Gentile judged Croce to be important to his efforts. Not only was Croce tendentially well disposed toward epistemological idealism, but he was so situated that he might have impact on socialist intellectuals. At that time—as circumstances would have it—Croce was impressed by the work of his Marxist colleague, Antonio Labriola. At the very least, that was an impediment to Gentile's initiatives. As a materialist, an epistemological empiricist, Labriola was an intellectual opponent of everything Gentile espoused.

What emerged from those circumstances was Gentile's decision to undertake a systematic critique of Marxism, using Labriola's recent publications on historical materialism as focus. Gentile chose those essays not only because they engaged the interest of Croce, but because they embodied what was perhaps the most competent exposition of Marxism available on the peninsula.[53] For at least those reasons, Gentile considered dealing with them to be of immediate importance. By 1897, Gentile had prepared and published the first part of his analysis.[54] It took on form and substance that was largely predictable.

One of the major implications of his idealist persuasion—with consciousness serving as the foundation of right reason—made moral imperatives subject to some kind of reasoned vindication. Gentile was convinced that the moral imperatives that inform human conduct require, in some ultimate sense, a metaethical basis. Human beings choose to behave in one rather than another fashion because convinced they have ethical grounds for so doing. If Marxists affirm that their choices are governed by the "highest morality, antiegoistic, selfless, and philanthropic," they are obliged to supply the subtending rationale that they imagine makes them binding. Unless that could be accomplished, their claims were idle.[55]

Labriola seemed very well aware of something like these conditions. In his essays on historical materialism, Labriola spoke of "moral consciousness" as "an empirical fact," and of the "ethical formation of each individual." He went

[52] See Gentile's letters to Croce from 1896 through 1898. Gentile, *Lettere a Benedetto Croce*.

[53] Labriola's major works have been translated into English: Antonio Labriola, *Essays on the Materialist Conception of History* (Chicago: Charles H. Kerr and Company, 1904) and *Socialism and Philosophy* (Chicago: Charles H. Kerr and Company, 1934).

[54] There were two parts to his critique that were ultimately published together as *La Filosofia di Marx: Studi critici*, reprinted in *I Fondamenti della filosofia del diritto*.

[55] Gentile, "Una critica del materialismo storico," in *La Filosofia del Marx*, ibid., pp. 183–185.

on to add that what "science" must do "is to understand how that conscience is formed."[56]

Labriola seemed to believe that once "science" could reconstruct the process through which moral consciousness was formed, the ethical issue would be resolved[57]—as though once it is known what *causes* one's moral consciousness, no questions of right and wrong would arise. Gentile simply dismissed the implied treatment as totally unresponsive to what was the real issue.[58] It was not a question of how moral consciousness arises, but what *justifies* moral choice. For Gentile, choices are made, not caused. Gentile's treatment of the issue is illustrative of his entire intellectual strategy. He saw choice as crucial, not only in dealing with moral questions, but in formulating and resolving cognitive dispute.

Like idealist epistemologists, in general, Gentile rejected the notion that one could come to know reality by simply observing it. Knowing did not simply happen. Consciousness, choice, individual and collective, was intrinsically involved in the process of coming to know the world. He argued that, in some sense, both Marx and Engels were aware of that. He argued, as well, that they ever remained uncomfortable with the notion that human beings somehow were little more that observers in coming to know the world. In his judgment, there was no intelligible way to account for cognition as the product of humans simply sensing an "objective," preexistent, "external" reality. For idealists, consciousness would have to be an intrinsic, constituent, and constructive factor in the entire process.[59]

---

[56] Labriola, *Essays*, p. 207.

[57] See the discussion ibid., pp. 110–111.

[58] Labriola seems to concede some of that. In his *Socialism and Philosophy*, pp. 72–73, he states that "human beings have never been exclusively theological or metaphysical, nor will they ever be exclusively scientific." It is not clear what that means, but it seems to suggest that "pure science" will never be able to adequately explain, much less vindicate, human behavior. Gentile characteristically analyzes human behavior in an entirely different fashion, distinguishing its empirical from its ethical dimensions. See the discussion in Gentile, "La Filosofia della prassi," pp. 203–224. A Marxist, the contemporary of Labriola, simply states that Labriola "like Marx and Engels, seems to have shelved the problems of cognition and moral consciousness, as concrete studies, after adopting historical materialism." Ernest Untermann, "Antonio Labriola and Joseph Dietzgen," an appendix to Labriola, *Socialism and Philosophy*, p. 227.

[59] There is a brief summary of Gentile's critique in A. James Gregor, *Giovanni Gentile: Philosopher of Fascism* (New Brunswick, N.J.: Transaction Publishers, 2006), chap. 5. Gentile addressed the issues involved in some detail. In some of his first works, the young Marx had spoken of the failure of materialists to deal with the dynamics involved in knowing, treating knowing subjects as passive recipients of sense perception. Marx subsequently became preoccupied with economic questions, and the epistemological issues involved were never seriously addressed. Engels, in his maturity, decided on a peculiar form of pragmatic realism—that effectively foreclosed the issue. Lenin simply confused all the issues. Many Marxists were aware of the problems to which Gentile alluded. There

Many Marxists at the turn of the century tended to agree, in principle, with Gentile's criticism. A typical Marxist comment was that "the first generation of Marxian theorists," including both Marx and Engels, never provided "the complete solution of the problems of cognition."[60] An appeal to Kantian epistemology by many Marxists of the period was only one of the consequences.[61]

Gentile argued that the young Marx was sufficiently astute to recognize the inadequacy of a materialist empiricism in satisfactorily analyzing the most fundamental questions of cognition, in general, and moral consciousness, in particular. He argued that for Marx's efforts to render a materialist epistemology more convincing, "matter" would have to be endowed with those properties intrinsic to Hegel's "Spirit." Spirit and matter would share dynamic properties that would allow their effective assimilation. In the process, Gentile reminded his audience, "matter would have to be furnished those traits that had been assigned exclusively to thought" by Hegel.[62]

In effect, Gentile argued that for the materialist epistemology many Marxists had attributed to Marx to have intelligibility, his "materialism" would have to have the idealist properties of Hegelian metaphysics. That, in turn, would carry in its train a notion of spirituality that would make "philosophy and religion" common in "content, however different in form."[63] Of philosophy and religion, one would be acknowledged as true as the other, however different in presentation. Both, directly or indirectly, would satisfy idealism's criteria of truth. Any analysis of the "reformed" Hegelianism of the young Marx could only reveal it to be in an unsteady state, neither materialist nor idealist.

For the young Gentile at the end of the nineteenth century, idealism was destined to prevail over the challenges of any form of materialism. Like most of the important leaders of the Risorgimento, Gentile was not only an idealist, but a nationalist and a statist as well. As he matured into his responsibilities, he proceeded beyond the uncertain idealism of Gioberti and Rosmini, to take the measure of Giuseppe Mazzini—harbinger of his politics during the *Ventennio*—the twenty years of Fascist rule in Italy.

---

is a more extended discussion of some of the epistemological issues involved in A. James Gregor, "Lenin on the Nature of Sensations," *Studies on the Left*, 3, 2 (Winter 1963), pp. 34–42.

[60] Untermann, "Antonio Labriola and Joseph Dietzgen," p. 232.

[61] See the contemporary discussion in Ludwig Woltmann, *Der Historische Materialismus: Darstellung und Kritik der marxistichen Weltanschauung* (Duesseldorf: Michels' Verlag, 1900).

[62] Gentile, "La Filosofia della prassi," p. 224. That is the central theme of Gentile's entire discussion of the philosophy of the young Marx. See A. James Gregor, "Giovanni Gentile and the Philosophy of the Young Karl Marx, *Journal of the History of Ideas*, 24, 2 (April–June 1963), pp. 213–230.

[63] Gentile, "La Filosofia della prassi."

Gentile and Mazzini

In the intensity of life on the Italian peninsula in the years between the turn of the twentieth century and the coming of the Great War, Gentile addressed himself to the complex question of Mazzini's role in the making of the nation.[64] In 1903, in a long review of a biography of the "apostle" of the Risorgimento, Gentile was more than slightly dismissive of Mazzini's theoretic and philosophic gifts. Gentile affirmed that Mazzini, as distinct from Gioberti, with whom he was initially associated, appealed more to sentiment than intellect during the first, "romantic" period of mobilization for the drive to reunite the peninsula.[65] It would seem that in Gentile's judgment, at the time, Gioberti, among others, served as the intellect, while Mazzini supplied the heart, of the revolution.

Gentile captured the distinction in his discussion of the religion advocated by Mazzini. The religion to which Mazzini appealed was neither Roman Catholic nor Protestant. It was evocative rather than deliberative; it was picturesque rather than specific; it was vague rather than coherent. Mazzini had held religion to be "the core of everything, guide, light, force, ... the eternal, essential, immanent element of life"—but seemed either loath or incapable of being more specific about its form or substance.

Mazzini, according to Gentile, held that religion was absolutely essential to life lived in community. Mazzini insisted that "a true society does not exist without a common system of beliefs and a common purpose." For Mazzini, Gentile continued, "religion is the principle and the condition of every true community; uniting participants, and providing morality" necessary to support and sustain collective energy.[66] That having been said, one is still left with a catalog of questions concerning substance.

Gentile reminded his readers that Mazzini regularly alluded to "political religion" as the adhesive that would bind together all Italians. He sought a form of "political catholicism" that would find expression in "one nation, one national association, one faith and one church." It would be a church through which he would pursue his purposes. It would be an expression of political faith, different from those institutional forms available. It would be a faith that would embody the call to collective mission—destined, in the judgment

---

[64] In general, the subsequent discussion will refer to the collection of essays devoted to Mazzini, written by Gentile during those years and collected in Gentile, *Albori della nuova Italia*, part 1, pp. 173–237.

[65] Gentile, "Una biographia critica di Mazzini," ibid., p. 178.

[66] Ibid., pp. 180–181.

of its leaders, to inevitable success. Mazzini had announced that "we do not have *opinions*; we *know* and *believe*." "Mine," he continued, "is certainty, not opinion."[67]

Part of that certainty was a function of Mazzini's conviction that spirituality was immanent in history, providing meaning to the entire complex sequence of events. There would be "a new heaven and a new earth, which would gather unto itself as one, in the love of God and of humanity, everyone in faith and common purpose." Such a faith would infuse humankind with ardor, with a sense of purpose necessary to collective achievement. It was a faith that was an integral part of a conception of life, Gentile argued, predicated on a conviction in life's spirituality. It was a rejection of material interests as sole determinants of conduct, and an acknowledgment of moral perfection as the sustaining purpose of a life fulfilled. All of which, Gentile insisted, "is, in a certain sense, true." But what all of that requires if it is to be convincing, he went on, "is philosophy, not faith."[68]

As the years passed, Gentile's opinions modified themselves sufficiently to permit him to rise to the defense of Mazzini's thought. When a new book made its appearance in 1912, insisting on the indeterminacy and lack of coherence of Mazzini's thought, Gentile was quick to respond that one might find within that vagueness and obscurity a "solid and vital core" if one were to look. Gentile went on to suggest that when one succeeds in mobilizing masses to a purpose, such a person engages more than sentiment by his appeal. As was the case with Jesus, Gentile proceeded, the appeal may initially touch the heart, but beyond that, there is content. For sentiment alone is fleeting—and historical purpose requires enduring commitment and sacrifice—something which Mazzini, and all those who succeeded to historic accomplishment, succeeded in engaging.[69]

By the time of the coming of the Great War, Gentile spoke of Mazzini's doctrine as "religiopolitical"—as incorporating components drawn from Vico and Gioberti—and capable of inspiring a readiness to sacrifice, and a commitment to duty, among millions. Gentile had become palpably aware of what was necessary to enlist humanity to vast enterprise. It is difficult not to relate that awareness to the electric atmosphere generated by nations preparing for war. As Europe descended into catastrophe, Gentile ventured on a more generous interpretation of the thought and political life of Mazzini.

By the fall of 1914, all of Europe stood on a precipice. In a short period of

[67] Gentile, "Il Pensiero di Mazzini," ibid., p. 203–205.
[68] Gentile, "Una biografia critica di Mazzini," ibid., pp. 181, 183, 192.
[69] Gentile, "Dopo dodici anni," ibid., pp. 195–196.

time, Italy would be drawn into one of the most sanguinary conflicts in human history. It was a conflict that would transform the life of Gentile and countless millions of others. In that time of troubles, Gentile would work to make his ideas relevant. He was to employ the thought of Giuseppe Mazzini as a means to that end.

CHAPTER SIX

Fascism

The State as Religion

> Religion is not properly something to be added to morality; it is immanent in it and without it there could be no morality. Nor could there be any State.
> —Giovanni Gentile[1]

> At the very roots of contemporary history... is the universal value and significance of Fascism.... [It] brings with it the exaltation, and what is essentially a religion, of the State.... The party State of Fascism is an ecclesiastical State, to distinguish it from the indifference of the atheistic and agnostic State.
> —Sergio Panunzio[2]

In that unfortunate summer of 1914, the assassination of the heir to the Austrian throne set off a chain of events that led to the outbreak of the Great War of 1914–1918. For four years thereafter the youth of Europe was consumed in an armed conflict in which there were to be no real victors. By the middle of 1915, Italy was drawn into the futile struggle, in the course of which it was to suffer the loss of six hundred thousand of its young men. The new nation was tried as few nations ever had been.

It was in those unhappy circumstances that Giovanni Gentile continued his studies. His interpretation of history and of philosophy became increasingly sophisticated, articulate, and specific. In 1912, he had already published his *I Fondamenti della filosofia del diritto*, to be followed by the first edition of his major work, *Teoria generale dello spirito come atto puro* (translated into English as *The Theory of Mind as Pure Act*).[3] As Italy was drawn into the Great War,

---

[1] Giovanni Gentile, *Genesis and Structure of Society* (Urbana: University of Illinois Press, 1960), p. 153.

[2] Sergio Panunzio, *Teoria generale dello stato fascista* (Perugia: CEDAM, 1939), pp. 5, 19.

[3] Gentile, *I Fondamenti della filosofia del diritto* (Pisa: Spoerri, 1911), to be followed in 1916 by *Teoria generale dello spirito come atto puro* (Bari: Gius. Laterza & figli, 1924. Fourth revised edition), translated as *The Theory of Mind as Pure Act* (New York: The Macmillan Company, 1922). This had

Gentile became more and more intensely involved in political activity. He published articles on contemporary events in a variety of journals and newspapers in which he spoke of the nation's spirit as the real agent of its history—and of leaders who embodied the will, and served the spirit, of an entire people.[4]

As the war drew to a close Gentile became more and more involved with nationalist organizations—with which he shared affinities, but with which he did not identify. Whatever his reservations, he agreed to publish a series of articles in the nationalist journal *Politica*,[5] articles that provide considerable insight into his evolving political commitments. They also provide collateral evidence of his changing interpretation of the work of Giuseppe Mazzini.

Gentile and His Postwar Assessment of Mazzini

In the article he published in the first issue of *Politica* immediately after the close of the Great War, Gentile outlined what he conceived to be the relationship between politics and philosophy. It was a relationship to which he had made allusions in the past, but his article "Politica e filosofia" provided the occasion for a direct statement of his political convictions.[6] In delineating the nature of the presumed relationship between politics and philosophy, all the elements that had made up the substance of his interpretation of the Risorgimento appeared once again. He spoke of politics as an extension of philosophy—without which, politics would be without foundation and politicians without guidance.

In his account, Gentile made a case for considering the relationship of philosophy to politics from two perspectives: one "classical," and the other "modern." "Classicists," he argued, conceived both philosophy and politics products of what was essentially the passive contemplation of externalities. Cognition was seen as the result of simple sensory perceptions of a "natural" world of things and causes. Human beings were but observers in a complex intersection of causal chains. He distinguished that perspective from one that was "modern"—an orientation that saw *thought* inextricably associated with coming to know the

---

been preceded by a stenographic monograph, *L'Atto del pensare come atto puro*, in 1912, republished in 1937 by Sansoni.

[4] These were subsequently collected and published as *Guerra e fede* (Naples: Ricciardi, 1919) and *Dopo la vittoria* (Rome: Editore La Voce, 1920).

[5] The editors of *Politica* were Francesco Coppola and Alfredo Rocco, members of the leadership of the Italian Nationalist Association—which ultimately merged with Fascism. For some discussion of the relationship of the organized Italian nationalism to Fascism, see Alexander J. DeGrand, *The Italian Nationalist Association and the Rise of Fascism in Italy* (Lincoln, Nebr.: University of Nebraska Press, 1978); A. James Gregor, *Young Mussolini and the Intellectual Origins of Fascism* (Berkeley: University of California Press, 1979), chap. 4.

[6] Gentile, "Politica e filosofia," *Politica*, 1, no. 1 (Dec. 1918), pp. 39–54.

world—and in coming to know the world, changing it. The relationship between human consciousness and the world was interactive, rather than passive. The consequence was that consciousness, thought, was inseparably associated with *action*—with philosophers and politicians charged with changing the world.

Gentile understood the classical view as one that imagined the world a place in which human beings were inextricably imprisoned in a concatenation of causes from which no escape was possible. Classicists conceived life structured by causalities. In that version, human beings were construed as nothing more than passive subjects of a causally linked chain of events. Whatever convictions they might entertain about influencing that sequence was illusory. Reality was a complex intersection of deterministic natural laws which human beings might come to know, but which they could not sway. For classicists, knowledge is understood as a vain reflection of an "external" fixed and finished reality. It was a notion about cognition that gave rise to the positivisms, and the scientisms, of the nineteenth century. The "mirror theory" of perception, that imagined knowledge growing out of sense perceptions that were, at their best, "true reflections" of a given reality, provided the grounds for the dismissal of things unseen, of religion and faith—which, in turn, led to an impairment of commitment[7]—and, by entailment, a betrayal of the meaning and reality of the Risorgimento.

It was into this context that Gentile was to assimilate the thought of Mazzini. Gentile maintained that what he identified as the classical conception of the world, and of the role of human beings in it, was incompatible with the views of Alessandro Manzoni and Vincenzo Gioberti, and all the leaders of the Risorgimento—who saw freedom in the behaviors of human beings, and spirit in their history. Scientism, and the materialism it fostered, not only failed the leaders of the movement that made Italy a nation, but jeopardized that nation's future.

For Gentile, positivism, scientism, materialism, and its associated atheism, were the defective products of a confused epistemology. Modern philosophy rejected the "abstract intellectualism" of the old philosophy. Modern philosophy conceived the world a function, in the last analysis, of human decisions to transform reality. "Other than a spectator of a world already fashioned," Gentile contended, "human beings can muster energy and, through their own initiative, intervene as effective actors in an ongoing process—to be the creators of good and evil."[8]

Gentile argued that human beings, possessed of free will, operate beyond

---

[7] See the discussion in A. James Gregor, *Giovanni Gentile: Philosopher of Fascism* (New Brunswick, N.J.: Transaction Publishers, 2006), chap. 5.

[8] Ibid., pp. 40–41. This is not the place to attempt to make a very complex epistemology comprehensible. There are some accounts in English that are helpful. See Roger W. Holmes, *The Idealism of Giovanni Gentile* (New York: The Macmillan Company, 1937); and Pasquale Romanelli, *The Philosophy of Giovanni Gentile: An Inquiry into Gentile's Conception of Experience* (New York: n.p., 1937).

the false dichotomies of knowledge as distinct from will—theory as distinct from practice—and thinking as distinct from doing. Life, Gentile insisted, is a seamless continuity of active thinking—a thinking which is, at the same time, a doing. It is a process in which "many are united in a superior spiritual individuality"—to produce that which manifests itself in "all of history, as well as in the life of the State."[9]

Thus, by the end of the Great War, Gentile rehearsed all the features of his "modern" political philosophy—and, almost immediately, related it to the political thought of Mazzini. In a subsequent issue of *Politica*,[10] he spoke of the political doctrines of Mazzini. At that juncture, he clearly was prepared to be much more generous in his appraisal. For Gentile, Mazzini's thought was "modern"—often misunderstood, or unappreciated, by classicists. When reviewers remarked on the "shallowness" of Mazzini's thought, Gentile would remind them of its effectiveness. If Mazzini had failed as an abstract thinker, Gentile reminded them that he had been intuitively correct in inextricably linking thought and action.

More than that, if a shallow thinker, Mazzini, nonetheless, had somehow succeeded in divining that history is fashioned not by individuals, but by individuals as they give voice to collectivities. History, Gentile insisted, is made by collectivities that are inspired by a sense of mission, that inform those States that, in turn, found nations. Peoples, infilled with a sense of mission, with duties to be discharged, animate States and found nations. It was Mazzini, Gentile reminded Italians, who perceived the nonsubstitutable role of faith in all of that—in the forging of futures. It was he who fostered the necessary religiosity that was to serve as the inspiration of renewal. And it was he who saw all of life as spirit, and materialism a fraud and a delusion.

By that time, it had become clear to Gentile that Mazzini's doctrine was essentially moral and pedagogical—unmistakably animated by what were religious values. He saw religion at the very heart of Mazzini's thought—and was quick to defend its presence. In an article devoted to Italy's political problems, "Il Problema politico," published in *Politica* a year later, Gentile reminded his readers that it was Mazzini who had made the life of the spirit the substance of his invocations—and had addressed the concrete issues of politics with what, in essence, was "the fire of religious faith."[11]

---

[9] Gentile, "Politica e filosofia," p. 50.

[10] Gentile, "Mazzini," *Politica*, 1, no. 2 (January 1919), pp. 184–205.

[11] Gentile, *Discorsi di religione* (Florence: G. C. Sansoni editore, 1955), p. 9. The article, originally published in *Politica*, was reprinted in *Discorsi di religione*. It was reprinted throughout the Fascist period because it provided an exposition of Gentile's political thought—by that time the rationale for the Fascist State.

In his treatment of political issues on that date, Gentile not only invoked the political thought of Mazzini, but he recalled all the major leaders of the Risorgimento with whom he identified. All of them he associated with deeply held religious opinions. They had all made recourse to "spirit" in their pursuit of solutions to concrete political problems. Gentile, in fact, was reaffirming his interpretation of the Risorgimento—in which the role of Mazzini, and his belief system, were decisive.

The spiritualism of which Mazzini spoke, Gentile saw as derivative of an intuitive epistemological and ontological idealism. Gentile conceived Mazzini one in a line of thinkers reaching back to Italian antiquity and, in the modern period, commencing with Hegel, and continuing through Spaventa. "Il Problema politico" was the last of the three related articles in *Politica*. Together they provide an outline of Gentile's own political convictions, as his philosophical idealism finds expression in political form.[12] They demonstrate how he conceived the thought of Mazzini as, in substance, an anticipation of his own.

What emerges out of the discussion in "Il Problema politico" is a vision of political life as the context in which individuals seek the moral fullness of self—to be achieved only in an ethical community—given form and substance by a well ordered State. That State is seen as a State already immanent in each individual's most intimate being.[13] It was a conception of the State as immanent in us—individually and severally. For Gentile, it was the immanence of the State that made a collective "we" of individuals. It was a philosophical conception of the State that was irreducibly collective, fundamentally "ethical," and preeminently religious—and Gentile associated it with Mazzini. It was a State that elicited sacrifice and to which was owed service. It was a State that armed itself against amorality and irreligion. It was a State opposed to all forms of political "neutrality," agnosticism, and egocentricity. It was a conception of the State that refused to allow it to be employed as an instrument in the service of isolated individuals or special interests.

It was Mazzini, Gentile wrote, who had intuited all of this. He saw individual life as religious, as a life lived in the spirit, moved to duty and sacrifice for an ideal, in and through which, true selves were to be found.[14] In that very clear

---

[12] In a variety of places Gentile outlines the connections between his epistemological idealism and his political convictions. The final statement is to be found in his *Genesis and Structure of Society*.

[13] "Liberal individualism makes the State a simple ... product of the will of individuals, failing to recognize its ethical substance, and the [fact that it is the] effective reality of that community that each individual finds at his very core, the living roots of his personality and the source of his rights." Gentile, "Il Problema politico," in *Discorsi di religione*, p. 21.

[14] Ibid., p. 7. Gentile spoke of the "life in the spirit" in just such fashion very early in his academic

sense, Gentile was forever to argue that Mazzini was a precursor of Fascism, and that Fascism was the culmination of the efforts of the major political leaders of the Risorgimento.

Gentile and the Politics of Postwar Italy

By 1919, Italy had survived the war and had emerged nominally victorious. However victorious, the nation was deeply divided. Italy's socialists, in general, had opposed the war, shunning those within its ranks who embraced the nation's intervention. The "national syndicalists" had opted for Italy's entry into the war because they conceived the war as intrinsically "revolutionary." They anticipated a nation transformed at its conclusion. There were nationalists who saw in Italy's involvement in the war an affirmation of its international significance. In general, it was expected that the war would transform Europe. By the end of 1914, Benito Mussolini (1883–1945), a national leader of Italian socialism, chose to lead the forces for intervention for many of the same reasons.

The conclusion of the Great War brought disillusion to many. Disillusionment did little to limit the competition for place in the struggle for political power. Many groups contended, for different reasons, for a role in the rehabilitative politics of the shattered nation. There were developmental nationalists, and traditionalists. There were liberals and reactionaries. Some Marxists, enthused by the Bolshevik revolution in Russia, embraced a Leninist variant of socialism. A revolutionary Communist Party made its appearance—alongside a more traditional reformist party that continued to decry the war's costs and denounce those who had been instrumental in fostering Italy's entry into the conflict. Roman Catholics organized themselves into a mass party, and on the periphery of the nation's politics, Mussolini founded an association of combat veterans—who soon came to be known collectively as *Fascisti*.

By that time, Gentile had increasingly established himself as a major political theorist.[15] Independent of official party affiliation, Gentile had occasion to engage the leaders of Italy's Nationalist Association on a number of topics that were to shape the political environment of the postwar period. Gentile was sufficiently confident of his own political views to engage Enrico Corradini, leader

---

career. See Gentile, "Il regno dello Spirito," republished in *Il Modernismo e i rapporti fra religione e filosofia* (Florence: Sansoni, 1962), pp. 237–243, originally published in 1909.

[15] In 1916, Gentile published a brief version of his *I Fondamenti della filosofia del diritto* (Pisa: Marioti, 1916). Years later, Gentile was to build on this foundation to address the issue of the essence and function of the State. See the Preface to *I Fondamenti* (Florence: G. C. Sansoni, 1955. Third edition), pp. vi–vii.

of the Nationalist Association, in an exchange concerning the political thought of the leaders of the Risorgimento.

Corradini, like many nationalists, was an advocate of a strong State and argued against what he took to be the individualistic, antistate liberalism of the thinkers of the Risorgimento.[16] Gentile, in response, held that in judging the significance of the political thought of the Risorgimento, one must recognize that within that flood of reflection at least two kinds of liberalism could be identified. One was all but fully compatible with the imperatives that inspired the State-centered, developmental nationalism of Corradini. That was the liberalism that rejected individualism in principle; it was a liberalism that conceived the nation and the State as essentially collectivistic in orientation; it was a liberalism that understood that the nation required productive development and economic sophistication. Gentile reminded Corradini that it was that original liberalism that sought the mobilization of individuals to the demanding purposes of the State. It was that liberalism that recognized that given the anticipated, arduous responsibilities of the new State, individuals must see in their respective lives a mission, and life a sacrifice. *That* liberalism argued that the political State was understood as servicing the needs of the individual only because the State was understood to be the "embodiment of the individual's will in its most profound rationality and legality." For *that* liberalism, Gentile continued, the State was the incarnation of the most fundamental rational will of individuals. Individuals obeyed the State because the State was the concrete manifestation of their rationality. In Gentile's analysis, that provided the ethical grounds for what appeared to those less enlightened as the "political subordination of the individual to the State."[17] It was the kind of liberalism that Gentile identified with Mazzini.

By the time of his exchange with Corradini, Gentile was prepared to acknowledge that the liberalism of Mazzini was something fundamentally other than the generically individualistic and implicitly permissive liberalism that characterized Italian politics at the close of the nineteenth century. He identified Mazzini as the "apostle of nationality and of the nation." He held that Mazzini "intuited, in the most profound manner" the fact that a nation is not composed simply of egocentric individuals, shared territory, or language. The nation was something other than a common political life, shared memories, traditions, or customs. Only when all those natural things become constituents

---

[16] See, for example, his discussion in Enrico Corradini, "Voci del passato," and "La nuova forza dello stato," *La Marcia dei produttori* (Rome: "L'Italiana," 1916), pp. 44–54, 90–100.

[17] Gentile, "L'ideale politico di un nazionalista," *Guerra e fede*, p. 56; see the entire account, pp. 53–59.

of a much more intense moral and spiritual union do they become part of the essence of a nation State. Gentile argued that it was that recognition that defined the relationship of individuals to the State. Individuals do not come together and contract in order to fabricate a State. Gentile maintained that Mazzini had intuited as much. The State was not put together by individuals—it was *immanent* in them, the spirit of their collective selves. Reason and analysis, Gentile argued, understood the State to be a reality that was not the consequence of action "*inter homines*, but rather *in interiore homine*"—not the product of some sort of contractual relationship between human beings, but as an immanence of a "we" that was shared.[18]

Mazzini understood, Gentile argued, that a people could be divided among themselves along the lines of dialect, custom, tradition, or religion, and still be a people, a nation. A nation, Gentile held, is informed by a collective consciousness of nationality. Gentile argued that Mazzini instinctively understood all that. And he recognized that, at its very foundation, the consciousness of nationality was religious in character. The sense of nationality was not the product of the impact of a concrete thing or set of natural things. Nationality was rather a sentiment and a consciousness that appreciated that the nation was a "grand spiritual reality," a "mission," a "purpose"—something in which people believed, in which they had faith, and for which they were prepared to sacrifice and, if necessary, die. Nationality was a sentiment religious in character and cognitive in expression.

Gentile held that "the nation, for Mazzini . . . was the common will of a people prepared to affirm itself . . . to realize its proper personality in the form of a State." He insisted that such was the exalted conception of the "nation as a State," held by Mazzini. He argued that Mazzini saw "the nation as a State . . . as a product of an active faith, an energized will, that shapes . . . a proper moral personality out of a collective consciousness." Gentile held that Mazzini understood the nation to be "our destiny," the very "substance of our personality," the product of our most "serious labor, sacrificing the individual to the collectivity . . . a struggle unto death . . . in the service of the ideal."[19] This, in Gentile's judgment, was Mazzini's "new religion."[20] Nationalism was to be measured both in sentiment and in terms of calculation in service.

By 1919, Gentile conceived Mazzini as the harbinger of a collectivistic, in-

---

[18] Gentile, *Discorsi di religione*, p. 23. Gentile had already made his case about the immanence of the State in the individual in 1916 in chap. 4 of his *Fondamenti della filosofia del diritto*.
[19] Ibid., pp. 11, 12, 13.
[20] See the discussion of Mazzini's views on self-sacrifice in Gentile, "Andrea Towianski," in *Il modernismo e i rapporti fra religone e filosofia*, pp. 256–257.

dustrializing, antisocialist, revolutionary State that would remake the nation.[21] Gentile, like Mazzini, was prepared to anticipate the emergence of a new State that would mobilize all the resources of an economically retrograde Italy so that it might, once more, assume its proper place among the most advanced nations of the world. That, Gentile insisted, would thereby successfully bring to a conclusion the unfinished struggle that began with Mazzini and the patriots of the Risorgimento.[22]

In 1920, all this found expression in Gentile's long essays *Discorsi di religione* and *La riforma dell'educazione*. Once again, he spoke of the thinkers of the Risorgimento and of Mazzini. He spoke of the State "conceived as a moral reality, a substance that was a manifestation of a free ethical will"—literally a conception of political life as fundamentally "religious" in character.[23]

All of this rested on a neohegelian conception of experience as fundamentally "spiritual," with "abstract" life finding "concrete" expression in a universal consciousness. It was a conception in which individuals appear only as transient "abstractions" within a transcendent "unity" that is life's ultimate, "concrete" reality. In the dialectical articulation of intervening categories between the abstraction of individuals and the reality of the spiritual Absolute, the political State plays a critical role as the ground of personality, the agency that provides the critical circumstances and the necessary occasions for the fulfillment of self.[24]

---

[21] Gentile was antisocialist in the same sense as Mazzini. He, like Mazzini, defended individual property rights and was an advocate of class collaboration in the service of rapid industrialization. See the discussion in "Lo spettro Bolscevico," "Ordine," and "La crisi morale," *Dopo la vittoria*, pp. 37–42, 43–48, 69–91.

[22] See the discussion in Gentile, "L'Epilogo, 11 November 1918," ibid., pp. 26–30.

[23] Gentile, *Discorsi di religione*, p. 9. One finds the full statement of Gentile's position in his *The Reform of Education* (New York: Harcourt, Brace & Co., 1922), available in authorized English translation by Dino Bigongiari.

[24] "This then is the world: an infinity of things all of which have however their root in us. Not in 'us' as we are represented ordinarily in the midst of things, not in the empirical and abstract 'us' which feeds the vanity of the empty headed egoist, of him who has not the faintest notion of what he really is, who can therefore think of himself only as enclosed within the tight husk of his own flesh.... No! they are rooted in that true 'us' by which we think, and agree in one same thought, while thinking all things, including ourselves as opposed to things.... The world ... is in us; it is our world, and it lives in the spirit.... The basis of every thinkable reality is our spiritual reality, one, infinite, universal—the reality which unites us all in one sole spiritual life.... In the political community by which individuals are united into a higher individuality historically distinct from other similar ones, we must see a form of universality.... The nation therefore is as intimately pertinent and native to our own being as the State, considered as Universal Will, is one with our concrete and actual ethical personality.... We realize it in every instant of our lives, by our feelings, and by our thoughts, by our speech and by our imagination, indeed by our whole life which concretely flows into that Will which is the State." Gentile, *The Reform of Education*, pp. 14, 31, 108, 116.

Together with this generic conception of nationality and politics, Gentile had put together a reasonably sophisticated historical notion of the political State, and the challenges any State might face in the postwar world of his time. In substantial part it was a conception, however more philosophically subtle, fully compatible, in Gentile's judgment, with Mazzini's convictions concerning political religion and its functions.

Through 1920, Gentile found no political party that seemed to give persuasive expression to these convictions. The appearance of Fascism in 1919 was as yet uncertain in form and intention. Mussolini, as its leader, had been a nationally acknowledged Marxist intellectual—originally entirely orthodox in his opinions—to only gradually gravitate toward other opinions. By 1919, following a route traversed by many Marxists during the first decades of the twentieth century, he had become a political nationalist, a developmental socialist, and a philosophical idealist of sorts[25]—the prefiguration of a fateful convergence.

None of that seemed certain. There were many factions among the men around Mussolini—sufficiently clouding the future so that any commitment by Gentile at the time might very well be more than ill advised. There was debate everywhere. Even among nationalists there was considerable dissention. Everywhere, there was discussion about the character of the anticipated postwar political system and the economy that would attend it.

Gentile failed to find a place in any of the organized political parties. He clearly rejected Marxism, particularly in the form it had assumed by the time of the Great War. He rejected Marxism and the materialism, agnosticism, and atheism it inevitably seemed to bring in its train. The liberalism of the industrialized State, with its individualism and hedonism, was intrinsically unattractive to him. He found no institutional home for his philosophical and political beliefs. None of the established political parties represented enough of his opinions to make themselves attractive to him.

By the time Fascism acceded to power at the end of October in 1922, that had changed. Gentile had become convinced that Mussolini's revolution was heir to a substantial part of Mazzini's doctrinal legacy.[26] Granted the emphatic differences that separated postwar Italy from the nation Mazzini struggled to

[25] An attempt has been made to try to summarize this complex process in Gregor, *Young Mussolini and the Intellectual Origins of Fascism*, and Gregor, *The Ideology of Fascism: The Rationale of Totalitarianism* (New York: The Free Press, 1969), chap. 3. For the many deviances in the Marxist ranks during this period, see Gregor, *Marxism, Fascism, and Totalitarianism: Chapters in the Intellectual History of Radicalism* (Stanford: Stanford University Press, 2009).

[26] See in this context, Giovanni Gentile, in "Origins and Doctrine of Fascism," and "What Is Fascism?" in *Origins and Doctrine of Fascism with Selections from Other Works* (New Brunswick, N.J.: Transaction Publishers, 2002), pp. 1–6, 20–24, 53–55, 57, 60. For a discussion of Gentile's influence on Mussolini's opinions, see Gregor, *Marxism, Fascism, and Totalitarianism*, pp. 283–293.

unite, Gentile argued that the echo of Mazzini's call to sacrifice and service had inspired the young men who fought in the trenches for years in the effort to finally achieve the dreams of the heroes of the Risorgimento.[27] With the advent of Fascism, Gentile made the Mazzinian liberalism he knew, part of the studied rationale for Mussolini's totalitarian State.

In retrospect it is difficult, at best, to determine with any conviction how much of such a conception was specifically Mazzinian and how much Gentilean. Given its unsystematic character, it will remain forever uncertain how much of Mazzini's thought objectively served as the potential philosophical grounds for Mussolini's Fascism. What seems clear enough is that Gentile had convinced himself that Mussolini's political thought was in the Mazzinian tradition. Gentile was prepared to argue that Fascist totalitarianism was a fulfillment of the promise of Mazzinism. He conceived a direct continuity between the political thought of Mazzini and what was to become the political doctrine of Fascism. What had been missing from Mazzini's political idealism was an articulated philosophical rationale. Gentile conceived his "actualism," as his formal philosophy came to be known, as supplying that missing component.

Political Religion in the Thought of Giovanni Gentile

In a very substantial sense, Gentile conceived his idealism as providing the cognitive base of Mazzinian thought. Like Mazzini, Gentile saw religious sentiment at the very foundation of politics. The difference between them was that Gentile understood religious sentiment, religion itself, as but a "moment," an expression, one form, of the "Absolute Spirit," the ultimate reality of existence as consciousness[28]—metaphysical notions entirely absent from the thought of Mazzini. In the more inclusive context of Gentile's idealism, one might speak of religion only as a constituent of a larger "Absolute"—possessed of the essential properties of consciousness—an epistemological and ontological formulation entirely absent from Mazzinian thought.

Gentile was fully prepared to acknowledge the reality of religion, but conceived its rationale as inescapably predicated on a more comprehensive understanding of "Being" as reality. Religion was but one aspect of the effort under-

---

[27] A summary statement in English of Gentile's position is available in his *Origins and Doctrine of Fascism*, sects. 1–4, pp. 1–14.

[28] "Being is . . . the world of consciousness. . . . Spirit is consciousness . . . [and] consciousness is a synthesis of subject and object. . . . The three essential moments correspond to the three absolute forms of the spirit: art, religion, and philosophy. . . . Art is the consciousness of the subject, religion the consciousness of the object, and philosophy the consciousness of the synthesis." See the account, written in 1909, in Gentile, "Le forme assolute dello spirito," *Il modernismo*, pp. 259, 260, 264.

taken by human consciousness to understand its own reality. None of that was to be found in the writings of Mazzini.

Gentile's radical idealism rested on the immediate conviction that the first and unimpeachable truth we entertain as thinking human beings arises out of the reality—and our immediate awareness of that reality—of thinking itself.[29] For Gentile's "actual idealism," there is at least one truth forever insulated from doubt: that there is thinking. We find ourselves at the center of that thinking—and out of current thinking we fabricate the subjective and objective reality of a universe of "internal" feeling and "external" things.[30] In the complex, if practical, sorting out of such components, we "dialectically" identify "subjective" feeling—emotive expression and sentiment—with art. The "objective" we associate with "things" beyond ourselves[31]—with the ordered, lawlike persistence of form and content—and with God, that "unknowable," "immutable" finality beyond all "external" things.[32]

In the dialectical process out of which all such distinctions arise, human beings establish binding criteria for truth ascription in the several categories of reality—subjective or objective as the case might be. Gentile characterized all that analytic activity as necessarily "abstract" in a meaningful sense—each category necessarily less than the "concrete" totality. Within the concrete reality of things, artistic, scientific, and religious truths are severally governed by different admissibility criteria—governed largely, if not exclusively, by pragmatic considerations. Philosophy instructs us that in the last analysis, all such distinctions made in thought must ultimately resolve themselves, once again, in the "concrete" unity of immediate thinking.[33]

Gentile's entire philosophical system was predicated on a rejection of what

[29] "There is no philosophical or scientific research, nor is there thought of any sort that is not an expression of faith in thinking itself." Gentile, *L'Atto del pensare come atto puro*, sect. 1, p. 11. It was in that long essay, in 1911, that Gentile made a first effort at systematically explicating his "absolute idealism."

[30] By 1916, Gentile had published his first full statement of his philosophical position as *Teoria generale dello spirito come atto puro*.

[31] Empirical science is one of the cognitive artefacts that results from these distinctions. See the account in *Discorsi di religione*, pp. 52–53.

[32] "Everything conceivable concerning reality (that which is conceivable, the concepts of experience) presupposes the very act of thinking. And in that, one perceives the source of everything.... Modern man senses God in himself, and in the power of the spirit celebrates the essential divinity of the world." Gentile, *La riforma della dialettica hegeliana* (Florence: Sansoni, 1954. Originally published in 1913), pp. 6–7. In this context see ibid., chaps. 2 and 3.

[33] See the distinction Gentile draws between his "actual idealism," his conception of "pure experience," and the "absolute idealism" of Hegel, ibid., pp. 229–230, 241–245. Philosophy, for Gentile, was "thinking in its maximum concreteness." Gentile, *Sistema di logica come teoria del conoscere* (Bari: Laterza, 1923), vol. 2, p. 323.

he called the classic notion of "reality" as an imagined arena in which congeries of "subjects" find themselves opposed by a preexisting "reality"—to which they must adapt. As has been suggested, he argued that modern philosophy had made the case for the identification of being and thought, of truth and humanity. Like the neohegelians of the mid nineteenth century, he saw those developments as nothing less than "the establishment of a *regnum hominis* ... the instauration of a true humanism."[34] None of this is found in Mazzinism.

For actual idealism, human beings were not simply prisoners of a preexistent reality that limited their freedom of action and rendered them passive objects of "causes" over which they had little, if any, control. Gentile argued that human beings, in fact, had existential control over their lives. Their decisions determined the features of their world, and their choices reflected an abiding moral perspective. He rejected the notion that the "real" world, the empirical world, had features forever free of the influence of human decision and choice.

For Gentile, the criteria governing truth ascription in any domain are always the consequence of deliberation and choice. For Gentile, human beings are responsible, in a deep philosophical sense, for the kind of world in which they live. They are never simply subject to externalities, to a "reality" over which they have no control.[35] At that point, actualism overlapped with the activist convictions of Mazzini.

These were the philosophical reflections with which Gentile faced the crisis of the First World War. They provided the scaffolding for the arguments he made in support of Italy's active involvement in the struggle, and for his advocacy of a postwar program. When he put together his postwar articles in *Politica*, they gave expression to what can only be identified as "political religion." By 1920, as has been suggested, Gentile had delivered himself of what he thought Mazzini had meant with his invocation of God in the pursuit of the new nation's political ends.

Gentile made the case that the advocates of the peninsula's political reunification were anticlerical because they saw Italy's prevailing institutionalized religion as divisive, serving to disunite those they would rather lead in unity to achieve that integral nationhood for which all struggled.

Like Gentile, Mazzini made it abundantly clear that he did not oppose religious sentiment. Again, like Gentile, he considered religiosity an intrinsic part

---

[34] Gentile, *La riforma della dialettica hegeliana*, p. 114.

[35] There is a conveniently accessible treatment of a substantial part of Gentile's professional philosophy in English in Gentile's *The Theory of Mind as Pure Act* and *Genesis and Structure of Society*.

of life lived as a human being. Religious sentiment provided the impetus for the formation of each human being's personality; it furnished the ethical direction governing moral behavior.

It was perfectly clear to Gentile, that Mazzini's social and political thought was inextricably rooted in religious sentiment. Like Gentile, Mazzini spoke of life as shaped by duties and responsibilities, themselves a function of moral imperatives. Gentile understood Mazzini as affirming that religious sentiment, and those ethical and moral imperatives that sentiment entailed, as being at the core of politics and the foundation of the State.[36]

Gentile argued that Mazzini's entire conception of life was profoundly religious. He reminded his audience that the very essence of religion was the pursuit of an ideal that transcended the individual—that found its inspiration and its power in a vision of something greater than self—that transcended the personal and immediate interests of the "abstract" individual.[37]

All of that required a philosophic rationale—which Gentile held to be his own actualism. Religious sentiment was but a moment in a much more comprehensive worldview. It was that larger worldview that rendered generic atheism, and thoughtless agnosticism, indefensible. Gentile held all that to be of singular importance. Irreligiosity and the attendant anticlericalism threatened the success of creating a nation and ensuring its viability. Both left citizens without a sense of obligation, a disposition to serve, and a readiness to sacrifice.

Gentile argued that the rejection of religious sentiment was an implicit rejection of any appeal to a sentiment that could unify a nation and inform a State. Instead, the agnostics, skeptics, and atheists imagined that society was nothing other than a contract between isolated and unreal individuals, who through the agency of an imagined contract, came together to become makers of a State whose sole function was to facilitate their satisfaction and well-being.

Gentile held that all that flew in the face of Mazzini's most fundamental political convictions. Mazzini's State was irreducibly ethical in substance. Its purpose was the fulfillment of collective moral ends. Not being part of a moral enterprise, individuals could not achieve the fullness of self. Mazzini insisted that for the ultimate achievement of true humanity, all citizens of the political State must be imbued with the fundamental principles of morality. For Mazzini, in effect, the political State must necessarily assume an ethical character.

Pursuing the same convictions, Gentile contended that the reality of its ethical and moral responsibilities of the State necessarily endowed it with that fun-

---

[36] See the discussion in Gentile, *Discorsi di religione*, pp. 6, 7, 18–23.
[37] Ibid., pp. 27; see pp. 73, 82.

damentally religious character unrecognized by political liberals and atheistic Marxists. To deny the religious character of the State was to deny a religious environment in which human beings might become something other than transient creatures, living in a meaningless world, to little if any purpose. It would be to deny the reality of a shared consciousness, to reject the common truths that make our world truly ours—the foundation of our lives as human beings.

For Gentile, without the affirmation of those binding truths there could be no ultimate grounds for all the relative truths advocated by agnostics. Those philosophical truths that saw true humanity in the shared consciousness that sustained reality, afforded the substructure of a moral life, the necessary condition for a common culture, the ground for a shared existence. For Gentile, and for Mazzini by implication, the State is the agency that protects and fosters art, science, and morals—and, in the final analysis, provides the conditions for a life possessed of meaning.[38]

Gentile proceeded to argue that those agnostic liberals who pretended to see in the State nothing more than the result of a contract between individuals, failed to appreciate the reality of the State as an "ethical substance," as giving expression to that immanent community that "individuals find at the very center of their being, the living essence of their personality."[39]

Given their intrinsic confusion, agnostic liberals make of the State an obstruction to individual purpose—when, in fact, the individual does not find the political State an obstruction to his or her most profound purpose. Rather the State is a necessary instrument in the service of individual moral fulfillment. Gentile insisted that the entire question of the relationship between politics and religion "is the same question of the religiosity of culture and thought in general." He argued that to pretend that the State might survive devoid of religiosity is to suppose that it might exist entirely without thought.

Upon the least reflection, Gentile maintained, we recognize in the State the very matrix of our humanity, the foundation of our moral selves, the potential necessary for the fulfillment that is the promise of humanity. For that reason, Gentile maintained, we find ourselves prepared to obey the State's enjoinments, sacrifice in its service, and deny ourselves selfish and fleeting gratifications in order to satisfy its prescriptions. It is the State that creates and sustains all the preconditions for a life fulfilled. It is the State that protects and administers; it provides public service and instruction; and it nourishes culture and fosters industry and agriculture. The State ensures the transcendence of the individual, the realization of an ideal morality beyond the immediate interests of the soli-

[38] See ibid., pp. 20–21.
[39] Ibid., p. 21.

tary self. In that explicit sense, the State is infused with religiosity. In its irreducible morality it reflects the "intrinsically religious character of life itself."[40]

In all of that, Gentile saw the fulfillment of Mazzini's most profound political convictions. In all those senses, Gentile's political and social philosophy was neohegelian as well as Mazzinian. It was a reformed Hegelianism, and the missing conceptual foundation of Mazzinism. It represented, in broad outline, the same ontologic, the same metaphysics of being, to be found in the thought of Hegel[41] and implied in the reflections of Mazzini. It was a neohegelian formulation of the political and social advocacies of Mazzini—and those leaders of the Risorgimento who thought as he.

By 1922, Gentile had become the advocate of an emphatic nationalism and a philosophic statism. Moved by the crises that befell Italy with the turn of the new century and its involvement in the Great War, Gentile acknowledged that philosophy was compelled to address eminently practical concerns. He spoke of the urgency involved in securing Italy a proper place in the world of developed nations. He spoke of creating a "greater Italy" through its "transformation" under the auspices of "new men who would bring to political life a system of new ideas in a new spirit, free of all those antique prejudices, petty manners, and behaviors of a time now long passed." Through the agency of the anticipated "new men," Italy would be "domestically transformed, employing all the national energies revealed by the war successfully fought, together with the discipline that renders the nation capable of a vast productive enterprise, of a pacification of social conflict, and a political reorganization of the State." Postwar Italy would experience a restoration of order, through the "imposition of an iron discipline," and a systematic collaboration of classes, that would serve "to preserve, guarantee, promote, and secure ... the public patrimony ... that now requires consolidation and expansion ... the necessary condition of future justice and well-being" in the "supreme interest of the nation—that interest which is in the interest of all." Economic development would not only ensure the nation a place in the modern world, it would facilitate the resolution of those subsidiary problems of overpopulation and oppressive domestic illiteracy.[42]

Gentile anticipated that all this would take place in the context of a "new and

---

[40] Ibid., p. 29; see the entire discussion in sect. VIII of the text, particularly pp. 36–37, 40–41. Compare Gentile's reflections with those of Mazzini, "The Duties of Man," "Thoughts on the French Revolution of 1789," and "From the Council to God," in *The Duties of Man and Other Essays* (London: J. M. Dent and Sons, 1912), pp. 7, 13, 21–22, 28–29, 32–35, 51, 64–65, 69, 81, 84, 90–92, 275, 303, 307, 314–317, 327.

[41] See Gentile, *Discorsi di religione*, part II.

[42] Gentile, *Dopo la vittoria*, pp. 34, 35, 46, 47–48, 51, 53, 64–65.

modern form of democracy"—the product of a fresh and innovative political philosophy—that found its origin in social theory that rejected the individualism of eighteenth and nineteenth century Anglo-French thought.

Given that analysis, Gentile was prepared to extend priority to the political community of the reunited and victorious nation. He conceived it enjoying a distinctive moral and legal precedence over those individuals of which it was composed. He had already made his case that individuals achieve their true humanity only as members of a community—in this case, the newly reunited and victorious nation. He maintained that all that imparted to the State "an interest and right superior to those of the individuals who are its constituent members." In effect, Gentile argued that the State had the moral right to demand sacrifice and service of its citizens. Neither classes, special interests, nor individuals, could demand rights from the State. Rights were always grants made by the State, contingent on the performance of duties.[43]

As has been indicated, Gentile conceived the State immanent in the individual. Like Aristotle and Hegel, Gentile understood the community—in a profound sense—prior to the individual. The State, on special occasions, and through the medium of gifted leaders, can speak for the collectivity.[44]

Gentile conceived the State the manifest expression of the community—and in the best circumstances the voice of its ethical and moral self. Since no political arrangement could exist without the express or tacit acquiescence of its people, its laws, and its customs, the expression of a collective will, fostered and protected by the State, defined liberty, and made freedom real. It was within that ordered environment that individuals became truly human. For Gentile, "the State was neither external to the individual nor was the individual conceivable as an abstract particularity outside the immanent ethical community of the State, in which individuals find their effective liberty."[45]

What emerges from Gentile's publications, before the rise of Fascism, is a conception of a revolutionary government, arising from the crisis of the postwar years in Italy, led by "new men," who would guide the nation into accelerated economic and industrial development. Through the medium of a "new,"

---

[43] See the entire discussion in Gentile, "Le due democrazie," ibid., pp. 107, 110–113.

[44] See Gentile's discussion in "Il significato della vittoria," ibid., p. 5. This notion is predicated on Gentile's conviction that there are only many persons if personhood is considered "abstractly." In the reality of consciousness, "there is but one concrete Person, universal and unique.... All persons are in reality one Person." Gentile, *La riforma dell'educazione: Discorsi ai maestri di Trieste* (Florence: Sansoni, 1955. Originally published in 1920), pp. 70, 77. That granted, in principle and under special conditions, one person can speak for multitudes.

[45] See the discussion in "L'Idea monarchica," and "Liberalismo e liberali (1),"in *Dopo la vittoria*, pp. 151–157, 172.

disciplined, collectivistic "democracy," the nation would create for itself a future that would challenge the dominance of the advanced, industrial, traditional democracies.

All of that would be predicated on a profoundly religious conception of collective life, clearly having its origins in Hegel, but making transit through the political advocacy of Giuseppe Mazzini. It was that conception of philosophic collectivism and renovative politics that found itself compatible with the first Fascism.

Gentile, Mussolini, and the First Fascism

In the years between the turn of the twentieth century and the end of the Great War, political thought in Europe took on the features that, through the coming decades, would shape events. Classical Marxism devolved into a number of variants, the most important of which was Bolshevism on the one hand, and Italian revolutionary syndicalism on the other.[46]

In Italy, within that turbulence, all the components of what was to become Fascism made their initial appearance. Out of the generic nationalism of the Risorgimento, a specific form of political nationalism began to assume uncertain form. By 1909, the young Mussolini had made the first provisional moves toward a nontraditional expression of revolutionary nationalism.[47] He made equally tentative association with the ideology of the Risorgimento by alluding to the work of Alfredo Oriani. He spoke of Oriani's *La Lotta politica in Italia*—a work that included the interpretation of the Risorgimento as the result of the "mystic and religious" nationalist efforts of Mazzini—as "magnificent."[48]

Not only did the young Mussolini express such sentiments with respect to Oriani, it was soon equally evident that he held Mazzini in regard. In his acrimonious disputes with the Mazzinian Republicans in the Romagna, Mussolini made very clear that whatever disagreements he had with them, he nonetheless respected the "prophet" of Italian reunification. Equally evident on those occasions was the fact that Mussolini fully understood what doctrinal Mazzinism entailed. In the course of his exchanges, Mussolini rehearsed all the properties Mazzini had broadcast throughout his revolutionary career.

Mussolini reminded his audiences that Mazzini was a nationalist—and, in principle, a statist. He was the advocate of a social morality that made duty and

---

[46] For a discussion of the entire process see Gregor, *Marxism, Fascism, and Totalitarianism*.
[47] See the discussion in Gregor, *Young Mussolini and the Intellectual Origins of Fascism*, chap. 4.
[48] Benito Mussolini, "La teoria sindacalista," in *Opera omnia* (Florence: La fenice, 1964. Hereafter *Oo*), vol. 2, p. 128.

service cardinal virtues. He supplied the rationale for those virtues by making an appeal to an unorthodox theology—a theology through whose agency he mobilized his followers. Philosophically, Mazzini was an antipositivist, the enemy of materialism and atheism—and he was an antimarxist foe of socialism, an opponent of class warfare, and defender of private property.[49]

In all his exchanges, Mussolini remained respectful of Mazzini, and reserved his barbs for those republicans who refused to read the works of the Apostle. It was evident that what separated him from Mazzini was the commitment Mussolini had made to Marxism and to socialism as it found expression in Italy.

It was during those years that the entire "subversive" movement on the peninsula began to disaggregate. The syndicalists, with whom Mussolini cultivated affinities, began to review what they took to be their commitments as revolutionaries.

Italy was entering into a singular time of troubles. By 1911, it became embroiled in a potential military conflict with the Turkish caliphate. At that juncture, some of Italy's revolutionary syndicalists began to reconsider their role when their nation found itself involved in international conflict. Syndicalist theorists began to argue that the well-being of the nation would impact the circumstances of workers whom they were obliged to defend. As such, syndicalists had to decide whether or not to support their nation should it find itself involved in armed conflict. Some of the major tacticians of revolutionary syndicalism advocated support.

It was in that setting that those same tacticians began to appreciate the merits of an appeal to nationalism in their efforts to mobilize workers to that nation's cause.[50] They attracted to themselves many in the ranks of traditional and antitraditional nationalists. At that point in time, Mussolini was not one of them. While sympathetic to syndicalists, he struggled to remain true to the orthodox Socialist Party.

Mussolini persisted in his orthodoxy—introducing some variations on that orthodoxy in an effort to better adapt to prevailing circumstances—while Gentile was framing those political convictions he claimed to have found in the political legacy left by Mazzini. Gentile and Mussolini seemed to be following different theoretical paths. Both continued on their respective course until the crisis of the Great War changed all parameters.

The major part of Mussolini's difficulties arose out of his very life circum-

[49] Mussolini, "Marx, Mazzini e ... Paoloni," "Andrea Costa in un libro di Paolo Orano," "Il Contradditorio di Voltre," "Note polemiche," "In Tema di santità," "In Tema 'funebre,'" "Profeti e profezie," *Oo*, vol. 3, pp. 67–68, 96–97, 136–137, 167, 197, 268–269, 314.

[50] See the discussion in A. James Gregor, *Mussolini's Intellectuals: Fascist Social and Political Thought* (Princeton: Princeton University Press, 2005), chaps. 2 and 4.

stances. A socialist from the time he was a schoolboy, he had enjoyed a rapid rise in the ranks of the Socialist Party of Italy. An acknowledged leader of Italian socialism, he read widely, and assiduously sought to exemplify Marxist consistency in his opinions.

Although committed to doctrinal Marxism, Mussolini read widely in the works of nonmarxist, and even antimarxist, authors. By the end of the first decade of the twentieth century, we know he had read at least something of the works of both Giovanni Gentile and Giuseppe Mazzini[51]—neither of whom qualified as a Marxist of any sort. For all their nonmarxism, their influence over his intellectual evolution can be reconstructed with considerable confidence.

Of more significance for the purposes of the present account is the fact that as early as the first decade of the century, Mussolini recognized the fundamentally religious character of Mazzini's political doctrine. He acknowledged that Mazzini's religiosity was neither clerical nor orthodox in any traditional sense. Mussolini recognized in Mazzini the advocate of a nontraditional, *political* religion.[52]

At the same time, Mussolini was aware of the fact that the revolutionary creed he, himself, favored, had begun to take on more and more features of the same kind of secular religiosity. Early in the first decade of the new century, Mussolini had come under the influence of Sorelian revolutionaries—and soon spoke of Georges Sorel's views as religious in character—and of human beings being moved to overt political action by *faith* no less than empirical conviction. More than that, he began to speak of revolutionary socialists, however much convinced of the scientific character of their belief system, as being sustained by faith—and their party as an *ecclesia*—a kind of church.[53]

In Italy, between the outbreak of the War in Tripoli and the advent of the Great War, all these notions swirled around those intellectuals who charged themselves with the leadership of revolutionary movements. By the end of 1914, Mussolini had broken with the official Socialist Party over the issue of Italy's neutrality in the burgeoning conflict[54]—and found himself attempting to chart a course between all the emerging factions—ranging from a developmental nationalism infused with Mazzinian religiosity, a form of syndicalist nationalism

---

[51] It is uncertain just how much of the works of Gentile Mussolini read during this early period, but we do know that by the time of the Great War, he was familiar with his ideas. We do know that he was very familiar with the work of Mazzini, giving ample evidence of having read some of his major publications by 1910–1911. See the comments in Gregor, *Marxism, Fascism, and Totalitarianism*, chap. 11.

[52] Mussolini, "Note polemiche," and "Profeti e profezie," *Oo*, vol. 3, pp. 167, 314.

[53] See Mussolini's discussion in "Da Guicciardini a Sorel," ibid., vol. 4, pp. 171–174.

[54] See the discussion in Gregor, *Marxism, Fascism, and Totalitarianism*, chaps. 6 and 11.

that featured some Sorelian fideistic traits, and a form of neohegelian socialism introduced into currency by the students of Giovanni Gentile.

Mussolini's choices did not become any easier with the passage of time. As the war drew in more and more of the major powers of Europe, more and more revolutionary radicals opted to support the war effort of their respective nations. French, British, Russian, and German socialists of all persuasions proceeded to overcome their ideological reservations. French and Italian syndicalists were particularly emphatic in the defense of their respective nations. They held it obvious, irrespective of whatever interpretation one might impose on what Marx had written so long ago, that workers still retained a sense of national consciousness. By 1915, syndicalist radicals like Filippo Corridoni had become convinced that the war demonstrated that the nation might very well serve as a revolutionary "community of destiny," around which workers, entrepreneurs, intellectuals, and lay persons might collect themselves, in the pursuit of revolutionary purpose.

By the beginning of 1915, Mussolini had committed himself to a kind of national socialism that saw the revolutionary future in terms of national and social values. At that same time, Mussolini began to speak of the political ideas of Mazzini with a new sense of appreciation. In the face of international armed conflict, he spoke plainly of seeing more relevance in the ideas of Mazzini than in those of Marx. It was the "truths" and "prophetic idealism" of Mazzini that called all Italians to duty in service of their threatened nation.[55]

As the crisis matured, Mussolini spoke of life as "varied, complex, multiform—rich in possibilities, filled with surprises, and prodigal in contradictions"—circumstances that recommended every effort to fashion a political strategy that might effectively guide his conduct. He urged that in that time of universal tribulation, revolutionaries must be free to abandon whatever political notions have shown themselves no longer viable—and search out others more functional—"to turn," for example, "to Mazzini, if he articulates concepts that lift our waiting spirit . . . and inspires us to action."[56]

Mussolini turned to Mazzini because he found an appeal to a sense of mission there that might inspire Italians in their time of challenge. He found, in the pages penned by Mazzini more than half a century before, an insistence that all Italians of conscience must assume their historic responsibilities, if the nation was to prevail. If Italians were to prove themselves moral agents, make of

---

[55] "We have the freedom to repudiate Marx, if Marx is superannuated and finished; we are free to turn to Mazzini if Mazzini speaks to our soul the word that lifts us to a superior sense of our humanity," Mussolini, "Dopo l'adunata," *Oo*, vol. 7, p. 153. See also Mussolini, "Il Dovere dell'Italia," "Sacrifici e vantaggi," "Mazzini e . . . Mussolini," ibid., pp. 101–102, 282, 436–439.

[56] Mussolini, "Dopo l'adunata," ibid., vol. 7, pp. 152–153.

their fatherland what it was destined to be, they were obliged to undertake their duty in united, collective, and sacrificial effort. Mussolini was convinced that Mazzini's "prophetic idealism" would bring the nation into the modern world where it would, once again, serve humanity as a creator of culture.[57]

By the time Mussolini found himself in the trenches facing the enemies of the fatherland, reading Mazzini's political prose had become part of whatever leisure he enjoyed. He reported that he found inspiration in those pages. In his judgment, Mazzini was "prophetic" in anticipating the future of the nation. He outlined a strategy of mass mobilization for a nation reunified, of masses guided by leadership inspired by faith—by those prepared to labor and sacrifice for a chosen future.[58]

After that, Mussolini's appeals to the thought of Mazzini became increasingly frequent and detailed. In April 1918, as the Great War was drawing to its conclusion, Mussolini spoke of Mazzini's appeal to the nation's workers—those who had sacrificed for victory. It was in that context that he spoke of a "national syndicalism"—of a political doctrine that would unite all productive workers in that program of rapid economic and industrial development advocated by Mazzini—to complete the work of the Risorgimento, lifting the nation to the rank of a major world power.[59]

At the same time, more and more of the ideas of Giovanni Gentile surfaced in Mussolini's prose. Many of Gentile's students had appealed to him in his struggles with the orthodox socialism that preached "absolute neutrality" in circumstances that had seen the entire civilized world drawn into a conflict that gave every evidence of having the potential to determine the future course of world history.[60]

All of that was to bring Mussolini to a juncture where he found himself embracing an epistemological and perhaps ontological posture indistinguishable from that of Gentile. In 1921, irrespective of the intensity of the political struggle in which he found himself, in a speech before the assembled representatives of the nation, Mussolini felt it was of sufficient importance to publicly affirm that he, and his party, had renounced "positivism," the empiricism so popular in Italy before the outbreak of the First World War, to commit themselves to a "spiritualism" into which all the antinomies of matter and consciousness resolved themselves. He argued that it was the "spirit" that alone remained—and into

[57] Mussolini, "Il monito di Oriani," and "Sacrifici e vantaggi," ibid., vol. 7, pp. 253–254, 282.
[58] Mussolini, *Diario di guerra*, ibid., 34, pp. 77–78.
[59] Mussolini, "Dopo l'adunata proletaria di Genova," "Politica estera: O con Meternich o con Mazzini," "Per il trionfo della Giustizia," and "È la grande ora!" ibid., 11, pp. 21–22, 281, 429–431, 458. See the discussion in Gregor, *Marxism, Fascism, and Totalitarianism*, chap. 11.
[60] See the discussion in Gregor, *Mussolini's Intellectuals*, chap. 5.

which all commonplace "realities" were absorbed. By the end of 1921, Mussolini was prepared to speak in Gentilean phrases—and by the time of the March on Rome in October 1922, he spoke of Giovanni Gentile as his "teacher."[61]

Almost immediately thereafter, Mussolini invited Gentile to join his cabinet as Minister of Public Education. In May 1923, Gentile made formal application for membership in the Partito nazionale fascista, and in November of that year he became Senator of the realm. He proceeded to found the journal *L'Educazione fascista*, as a vehicle for the public articulation of formal Fascist doctrine. In effect, by 1923, Gentile assumed the responsibilities of an official spokesman for the regime. Thereafter, he was to regularly publish essays in defense of its philosophical position.[62]

Gentile's first published works in defense of Fascism were directed against those who denied it substance. To make his case for its substantiality, Gentile traced some of Fascism's critical concepts into the intellectual legacy of the Risorgimento. Out of that legacy he sorted two distinct forms of "liberalism." One clearly was of foreign derivation. The other was a "liberalism" that was peculiarly Italian and Mazzinian. It was a liberalism that was demanding and centralizing—in which individuals were disciplined and responsive—in which they saw their own intrinsic development in the articulation of the State.[63] Gentile saw features of all that not only among the political thinkers of the Risorgimento in general, but specifically in the thought of Giuseppe Mazzini—who conceived the isolated individual of Anglo-Saxon liberalism an implausible "abstraction"—empty of both moral substance and significant personality. Mazzini understood the individual to be one in moral unity with the community—given character by participation in its historic mission.[64]

Gentile went on to characterize Fascist doctrine as a "total conception of life." He was to insist that, like that of Mazzini, Fascist doctrine was more than a political belief system; it was "a religion."[65]

By 1929, the discussion had matured into the publication of a major exposition of Fascist doctrine that specialists have identified as a "document of major

---

[61] Mussolini, "Per la vera pacificazione," *Oo*, 17, p. 298. In the beginning of 1924, Mussolini spoke of Fascism as a "spiritual revolution"—in much the same fashion as Gentile—as a solvent of that materialism that had dominated Italian philosophical thought for almost a century. See Mussolini, "Da chè parte va il mondo?" ibid., 18, p. 66.

[62] It seems that Mussolini had put together the fabric of the first Fascism with the threads of doctrine collected from a variety of sources. Equally certain is the fact that Mussolini found Gentile's sophisticated rationale for his political religion of singular use and applicability.

[63] Gentile, *Che cosa è il fascismo* (Florence: Vallecchi, 1925), pp. 47–49.

[64] Ibid., pp. 25, 26, 35.

[65] Ibid., p. 38.

importance," depicting the ideology of the regime in a fashion that not only served to rebut the contention of critics that Fascism was innocent of a reasoned foundation, but which wove its rationale into the history of Italian thought.[66] In fact, *Origins and Doctrine of Fascism* was a continuation of Gentile's general history of Italian contemporary thought—with emphasis on the intellectual relationship shared by the Fascist revolution and the Risorgimento.

The *Origins and Doctrine* drew upon a long essay that Gentile had published in April the year before. Given its more generous perspective, his essay on "Il pensiero italiano del secolo XIX" spoke of the thought of the intellectual leaders of the Risorgimento in terms of the then Italian revolutionary present. In that effort everything Gentile had written from the turn of the twentieth century, until his rendering of the rise and prevalence of Fascism, came together in a connected narrative.

In the *Origins and Doctrine*, Gentile spoke of Mazzini's thought as central to all the political developments in the late nineteenth, and the first quarter of the twentieth, century. Gentile held that it was Mazzini's doctrine, in faith and religiosity, that inspired Italians, throughout the entire period, to revolutionary purpose. His faith and religiosity made Mazzini perhaps "the most religious thinker of the nineteenth century. ... It was a religious conception ... that envisioned all reality governed by a willed consciousness, incarnated in humanity—not in individuals, but in peoples. The laws of that subtending spirituality revealed themselves in the consciousness of persons who, as dutiful human beings, divest themselves of their materialistic limitations and their egoism, giving themselves over to life as a mission requiring self-sacrifice for its realization."[67]

Gentile traced all those continuities into Fascism. He recognized their features in the multiple sources of Fascist doctrine. More than that, Gentile argued that the lines of argument that surfaced in Fascist thought, while Mazzinian in origin, were demonstrably more sophisticated.

In the course of his account, Gentile repeated the judgment he had made at the beginning of the century concerning Mazzini's political ideology. He did not hesitate to acknowledge that one does not find a systematic philosophical treatment of reality, as spirit, in the work of Mazzini. That would require the work of other contemporaries, like Antonio Rosmini, Vincenzo Gioberti, and

[66] Giovanni Gentile, *Origins and Doctrine of Fascism*. See the comments of Augusto Del Noce, *Giovanni Gentile: Per una interpretazione filosofica della storia contemporanea* (Bologna: Il Mulino, 1990), p. 300.

[67] Gentile, "Il pensiero italiano del secolo XIX," *Memorie italiane e problemi della filosofia e della vita* (Florence: G. C. Sansoni, 1936), p. 233.

Bertrado Spaventa, who took up the idealism of Kant and Hegel and created, for Italians, a modern philosophical interpretation of experience.[68]

All of this was drawn together by the time of the First World War and the advent of Fascism. Once again Italy was animated by an idealism that had clear affinities with that with which Mazzini identified. Gentile contended that, with the passage of time, "the thought of Mazzini had matured into the Fascist revolution." Mazzini had anticipated the rebirth of the renovative faith of Italians as a consequence of the intercession of a leadership sensitive to its proper invocation—a leadership capable of appealing to that "sentiment of religiosity that is at the heart of every human being." It was Mazzini who revealed the insubstantiality of that privative individualism that was at the core of that "mechanical liberalism of abstract classical economics"—that undermines the concreteness of the ethical State and the conscience of citizens. In Gentile's judgment, it was Mazzini who rejected that liberalism that failed to understand the nature of community—of true association. It was Mazzini who made the "fundamental spiritual unity of citizens the postulate of the totalitarian mode of understanding collective human life."[69]

By 1931, Gentile had traced all of this back to the nineteenth century political thought of Mazzini. Gentile maintained that Fascism represented a form of the "authoritarian liberalism" that was critical to Mazzini's political philosophy. That liberalism was the consequence of Mazzini's "comprehension of life in terms of an ethical and religious conception" that saw the individual indissolubly one with the State.[70]

In 1932, Gentile was commissioned by Mussolini to provide a formal statement of Fascist doctrine—and in that year the *Enciclopedia italiana* published *La dottrina del fascismo* as an insert over the name of Mussolini himself.[71] The essay was divided in two parts, "Fundamental Ideas," and "Political and Social Doctrine." The first part, the "Fundamental Ideas," was entirely written by Gentile, with very few cosmetic changes made by Mussolini. The entire insert appeared over Mussolini's name, making it an official rendering of Fascist doctrine.

The entire account is a stenographic restatement of themes that Gentile had already made familiar in his expositions for over a decade. The *Dottrina* made it all readily available.

In the pages of the *Dottrina*, Fascism was spoken of as a conception of life essentially "spiritual" in character, with the term meaning what it meant for Ger-

---

[68] Ibid., pp. 233–236. Here, Gentile repeated the same judgment he had tendered before, and immediately after, the rise of Fascism. See Gentile, *Che cosa è il fascismo*, p. 24.

[69] Gentile, "Mazzini e la nuova Italia," *Memorie italiane*, pp. 23, 32, 38, 41, 42.

[70] Gentile, "Risorgimento e fascismo," ibid., pp. 116, 117.

[71] Benito Mussolini, *La dottrina del fascismo*, Oo, 34, pp. 117–138.

man idealism. The world of human experience was a world of consciousness, of thinking. The "reality" of ordinary "abstractions" is parsed out of thinking and thought shared.

In the "Fundamental Ideas" individuals are not conceived as stand-alone entities that somehow find themselves in a deterministic, preestablished, law governed, empirical world, composed of discrete things and other persons. In the *Dottrina*, individuals are understood to be organic components of a larger consciousness. They are each an "individual who is both nation and fatherland," united in "a generational tradition and in a mission that overcomes that natural disposition to pursue life as limited to a brief span of pleasure—in order to awaken one to a superior life that transcends both time and space... in that entirely spiritual existence in which each finds value as a human being."

For all those reasons, the *Dottrina* argued, Fascism is philosophically antiindividualistic—in the sense that it was opposed to those nineteenth century materialists who imagined that single individuals were born into an empirical universe, there to contract relations and shape themselves. Like Aristotle and Plato, the *Dottrina* rather conceives the community prior to the individual. Rather than unique individuals coming together to fashion a community, it is the community that fashions individuals. Human beings achieve personhood, true individuality, in processes that are intellectually, morally, and empirically community fostered and sustained—and State informed. In all those essential processes, the political State serves central and imprescriptible purpose. In a determinate sense, the political State serves as "the true reality of the individual." The State informs the nation; making of it a reality where before it was only a potentiality. The State creates the circumstances in which the nation provides for the continuity and freedom of the community and the individuals of which it is composed. The State creates conditions by virtue of which the nation is both acknowledged and respected in the inclusive society of nations. The State provides that constant environment essential for education and security, and the growth of morality; it provides liberty and material well-being, as well as mediation between individual, corporate, and category interests. The Fascist State is, in that sense, *totalitarian*. "It is the synthesis and unity of every value; it interprets, develops and empowers, in its entirety, the life of a people." The Fascist State was understood to be an entity charged with ethical responsibilities—that "ethical entity" anticipated by Mazzini in his earliest doctrinal exhortations.

Correspondingly, the *Dottrina* announced that the rationale of the Fascist State constituted "a system of thought" that "served ethical purpose... and moral ends," prescribing a "life that was understood to be serious, austere, and religious." In fact, the *Dottrina* continued, all the central conceptions of Fascism were *religious* in character. They conceived life a struggle in which human beings attained the fullness of moral personhood in community through sacrifice, labor, obedience, and diligence—and, if necessary, sacrifice unto death.

By the time Fascism reached its maturity in the early 1930s, there could be no doubt that it was a form of political religion that had implications for individual and collective conduct that were to affect the life circumstances of millions. It shared features with other expressions of political religion as they manifested themselves throughout the century. What distinguished Fascism was its conscious recognition of its essential character.

By the late 1920s, Sergio Panunzio, one of Fascism's most authoritative spokesmen, described the Partito nazionale fascista as a "spiritual association . . . collected around a common faith and a common political creed." He went on to argue that "a political idea and a religious creed are phenomena sharing close affinities. One might better speak of a follower of a modern [revolutionary] political party not in terms of party affiliation, but as a member of a church, an *ecclesia*."[72]

Panunzio carried his analysis further, acknowledging that Fascism, while singular in many respects, shared its essentially religious features with other modern revolutionary parties. He argued that Lenin's Bolshevism, for a variety of very fundamental reasons, had abandoned much, by the end of the nineteenth century, of what had become traditional among many socialists. Bolshevism had taken on anew those properties that originally found expression in the work of the Left Hegelians—Moses Hess, Ludwig Feuerbach, and the young Engels and Marx. In its own fashion, Bolshevism had restored all of that. Everything that had been swallowed up in the academic Marxism that was German Social Democracy before the First World War resurfaced in Leninism.

Bolshevism had rekindled the fires that smoldered under the ashes of the nineteenth century. V. I. Lenin carried the political passion of Nikolai Chernyshevsky into the new century, to call upon a vanguard of "new men" who would charge themselves with the salvage of a cursed creation. Lenin, whose truths were impeccable, and whose moral principles were austere and exacting, imposed on revolutionary Russia a creed that was unmistakably religious in character.

Panunzio traced the history of Bolshevism to turn of the century Russia, from its first appearance as a faction in the ranks of revolutionary socialism, to its transmogrification into a unitary party State. In power, Bolshevism constructed a party State, having all the features of a political church: a catechism of infallible truths, a library of sacred texts, a roster of charismatic anteced-

---

[72] Sergio Panunzio, *Il sentimento dello stato* (Rome: Libreria del Littorio, 1929), pp. 228–229.

ents, a standard liturgy, missionary purpose, and a demanding ethic of sacrifice, dedication, and obedience. Its *totalitarianism* was a logical consequence of convictions held and the singularities of the institutions in which they were made manifest.[73]

Years later, at the close of the system, immediately before Fascism disappeared into history, Panunzio wrote his definitive *Teoria generale dello stato fascista* in which the same account was repeated in greater detail.[74] In that rendering, he recognized all the features of a political religion not only in Stalin's Soviet Union, but in Hitler's National Socialism, and in the Kuomintang of Chiang Kai-shek.[75]

In general, perhaps more so than in any other modern revolutionary movement, Fascist intellectuals well understood the system they fostered and sustained. More than most scholars in the West, they divined some of the essentials of what was entailed in predicating a political arrangement on a belief system conceived both salvific and morally impeccable. It was something the twentieth century was yet to learn. Only now, in retrospect, can something of the whole story be told.

[73] Ibid., pp. 235–240.
[74] Panunzio, *Teoria generale dello stato fascista*.
[75] Years after the end of the Second World War, Ugo Spirito, perhaps Gentile's most accomplished student, undertook an insightful comparative analysis of the forms of Marxism that had imposed themselves on the Soviet Union and Mao's People's Republic. He traced all the properties of political religion in both systems. See Ugo Spirito, *Comunismo russo e comunismo cinese* in *Il comunismo* (Florence: Sansoni, 1965).

CHAPTER SEVEN

The Religiopolitical Background of National Socialism

> Wagner was possessed of the sure conviction ... that "every genuine effort, and every enabling power, committed to the regeneration of humanity, can only arise out of the deep soil of a true religion"—a "return to nature." ... He maintained that "the making of regenerate humankind grows out of religion ... a new religion."
>
> —Houston Stewart Chamberlain[1]

Nineteenth century Germany proved to be the incubator for a variety of alternative political movements. The first Marxism grew out of posthegelianism and the decomposition of traditional religion. At the same time—and perhaps in part the result of a confluence of the same factors—an intense, xenophobic nationalism succeeded in bringing together some of the most talented and aggressive intellectuals of the period. Before Giuseppe Mazzini began to stoke the fires of nationalism in Italy, the volunteers of Friedrich Jahn took up arms against Napoleon at the Battle of Leipzig. German intellectuals began to speak of a "sacred mission" that was incumbent upon all Germans—to foster, sustain, and defend the imperishable rights of their specific "community of destiny." Napoleon had made Germans sensitive to their plight. Germany was not a nation. It required unification, empowerment, and definition.

Before all that could assume definitive form, Johann Gottfried Herder (1744–1803) had written of nations, their particular essence, and their singular significance. That took on importance in an environment in which the Enlightenment, in general, together with the influence of empiricism, had led many to abandon all notion of community. It had become increasingly commonplace among intellectuals to consider human beings first as individuals—and only subsequently as members of a natural fraternity. It was held that communities

---

[1] Houston Stewart Chamberlain, "Richard Wagners Regenerationslehre," in *Rasse und Persönlichkeit* (Munich: F. Bruckmann A.-G., 1925), pp. 137, 139.

were fabricated associations, of secondary importance in coming to understand the cognitive and moral life of persons.

Individualists argued that while politics might well impact lives, that impact was contrived and derivative, one of the consequences of the failure on the part of thinkers to understand the truths involved. The first priority urged was that individuals assume responsibilities for their own proper lives—not for "the Good Cause . . . God's Cause, the cause of mankind, of truth, of freedom, of humanity, of justice." The individual should make himself his cause—not to assume burdens in "the cause of his people, his prince, or his fatherland." All such causes are contrivances, calculated to ensnare the individual and diminish his sense of self.[2]

Herder was to mount objection to the entire conception of the preeminence of the individual. He emphasized the importance of the community in cognitive and cultural life. The individual was a yield of community life—a function of life lived in intimate alliance. Human life is pursued in association. Human beings are not created, nor do they survive, nor prosper, in isolation. Human beings are intrinsically social creatures—they are born to families, to collectivities. They did not come together at some time or another and decide to construct a society. Herder rather saw individuals as members of discrete historical and cultural communities—each such community a source out of which constituent members drew distinctive cognitive substance. Reasoning and understanding were inextricably related to membership in a historical confraternity.

Herder spoke of the influence of the community's language and myths on each person's thought processes—and understood language and myth part of the harvest of a people's unique history and environmental circumstances. He held that language was a special community product, giving voice to a people's soul—its inmost essence. He understood speech to be an organic development that encoded the common intellectual, moral, and artistic experience of countless generations in the historical life of a community. For Herder, a language, and the culture to which it gave expression, was the product of a *Volk*—of an organic union of persons—an uncommon association.[3]

Herder spoke of these "volkish" associations as communities united by in-group sentiment, natural bonding, mimetic behavior, common speech, a mutual history, and a shared goal culture—an unbroken concatenation of those living, those who had lived before, and those who would come after. The con-

---

[2] See the full account in the volume by Max Stirner, originally a "young Hegelian," *The Ego and His Own* (New York: E. C. Walter, 1913), with the quoted portions to be found on p. 3.

[3] See the discussion in J. G. Herder, *Ideen zur Philosophie der Geschichte der Menschheit* (Berlin: Aufbau Verlag, 1965), vol. 1, bk. 4, chaps. 4, 6, pp. 140–147, 154–157; and bk. 7, chap. 1, pp. 246–251.

sequence was a continuity that united, through time, all the members of the historical community.

The heroes and geniuses who arose out of such communities not only spoke its language, but expressed its deepest sentiments—giving tongue to its most profound aspirations. They shared with it something formative, and real, but transcendent. Herder argued that more than individual genius spoke in the creativity of Dante and Shakespeare. It was the organic, living, historical community that spoke through them.[4] Artists and thinkers, in however unique a form, give expression to the "soul" of the historical collectivity—the soul of the *Volk*.[5]

In the course of just such reflections, students and intellectuals began to speak of the *Volk* as a spiritual community somehow different from, and more fundamental than, the people who inhabited that culture region identified as Germany. The *Volk* was somehow more than the sum of contemporary Germans. The *Volk* had some ill defined, but "type forming" properties (*typenformende Kraft*), that rendered its many members, one.[6]

Because of his emphases, by the beginning of the nineteenth century, Herder's work precipitated a spate of philological and folkloristic inquiries into the origins of the German language. There was an increasingly intense search for the "original" Germans—creators of the primal language.

German scholars sought their specific linguistic forebears among all the peoples of history. Over time, more and more human resources were committed to the sustained search for the linguistic, psychological, and moral substance of the Teutonic *Urvolk*—the primordial Germans who provided then contemporary Germany its spiritual legacy.

It was not long before German, as a language, was traced to Sanskrit roots, and the connections that related all the Indoeuropean languages confirmed. The "Aryan," "Indoaryan," or "Indoeuropean" languages provided the ligaments that bound the peoples of nineteenth century Europe together through-

---

[4] One finds elements of these same sentiments in the poetry of Friedrich Gottlob Klopstock, a contemporary of Herder. He was given to the mythology of the early German tribes. He abandoned the Western gods for those of the German myths. Wotan spoke to his soul where Jehovah no longer could.

[5] See the discussion in Herder, *Ideen zur Philosophie der Geschichte der Menschheit*, vol. l, bk. 9, pp. 343–348.

[6] Similar sentiments were found among those attempting to fashion a nation out of Italians. "To one who sees in a Nation something more than an aggregation of individuals born to produce and consume corn, the foundations of its life are, fraternity of faith, consciousness of a common *ideal*, ... the body of religious, moral, and political principles in which the Italian people believes, ... the common ideal to which it is striving, [as well as] the *special* mission that distinguishes it from other peoples." Giuseppe Mazzini, "To the Italians," *The Duties of Man and Other Essays* (New York: E. P. Dutton & Co., 1912), pp. 234, 235. See Giovanni Gentile's comments on Vico's thoughts concerning the people of Italy. Giovanni Gentile, *Giambattista Vico* (Florence: G. C. Sansoni, 1936).

out time. More immediately relevant to our exposition, as early as mid century, German scholars were prepared to speculate on the anthropological properties of the carriers of those languages—and talk began of an Aryan "race" that was the supposed initial carrier of Indoeuropean language. Where Herder had hesitated to identify language with race, by mid century, many German academicians made ready connection. More than that, by mid century specialists were studying the morphological features of the various human "tribes" that had fallen under scrutiny—and had determined that cranial capacity, and the physical properties of the cerebral cortex, determined mental abilities, so that some "tribes," or "races," clearly suffered in comparison with others.[7]

By mid century, German intellectual life gave fulsome evidence of at least two distinct currents of thought. One—usually identified with the "left"—found its exclusive origins in the "reform" of Hegelianism. The other—energized by assertive nationalist sentiments—immersed itself in the social philosophy of nationhood. In both, religious residues were evident, to influence, directly and indirectly, both developments and outcome.

Ludwig Feuerbach was an emblematic figure for all of that. Among Marxists, Feuerbach was a transitional thinker who provided the link between Hegel and Marx. For nationalists, Feuerbach was the thinker who made social philosophy and theology, *anthropology*. In a time of Germany's spiritual crisis, it was he who refocused attention away from Christ, to humanity, as the theanthropos. It was he who insisted upon restoring divinity to humankind.

Among nationalists, there were those who were to conceive divinity unequally parsed among humanity's various "tribes"—and by 1854, Count Arthur de Gobineau could write of "Germanic peoples, so long misunderstood," as "one single family," responsible for "everything great, noble, and fruitful."[8] For those activists attempting to forge a nation out of the debris of an ancient empire, such conjectures served as inspiration.

Out of the reformed Hegelianism of Feuerbach, and the "scientific" racism of Gobineau, elements came together to give form to an exacerbated nationalism and an insistent statism that was to carry Germany into the twentieth century. One of the most important figures in that development was Richard Wagner—Germany's unmatched master of opera as folk drama.

[7] See, for example, Carl Gustav Carus, *Symbolik der menschlichen Gestalt: Ein Handbuch zur Menschenkenntniss* (Leipzig: Brockhaus, 1853), particularly pp. 366–371. Carus associated intellectual, emotional, artistic, and moral properties with the phenotype of individuals and groups of individuals.

[8] Arthur de Gobineau, *The Inequality of Human Races* (New York: G. P. Putnam's Sons, 1915), p. xv. Gobineau also insisted that "the racial question overshadows all other problems of history, that it holds the key to them all." Ibid., p. xiv.

Richard Wagner (1813–1883)

Participant in Germany's time of troubles, in the politics of the early 1840s, Friedrich Engels had written that the young people of his time were prepared to become "the new templars of the grail," to take up the sword in a holy war that would conclude in an apocalyptic reign of a thousand years—transforming a fragmented Germany from what was little more than a money making enterprise into a moral community.[9] It was not an uncommon sentiment found among the young and the not so young.

For all intents and purposes, by the end of the 1840s in Germany, political revolution had failed in its purposes—and most of the available collective energy was transferred to what was essentially the moral dispute captured in Engels' youthful prose. It was conscience that seemed to animate the most secular of radicals—with one of its major byproducts a sustained critique of traditional religion. Criticism of institutional religion had become a focus of attention for both left and right in posthegelian Germany.

Variants of all of this are to be found in the contemporaneous sentiments of Richard Wagner. Five years Marx's elder, Wagner was born in 1813. By the time of the failed revolution of 1848—like other disillusioned posthegelians—he fell under the influence of Feuerbach. Like them, he found much to criticize in the "unintelligible" and "abstract" idealism of academic thought—in whatever form it assumed;[10] and like them, he welcomed the "reality," the "concreteness," evidenced in Feuerbach's *Wesen des Christentums*.

In all of this, Wagner tended to dismiss orthodox Hegelianism as largely incomprehensible and politically irrelevant.[11] At best, Hegel's nationalism was diffuse and his notions of "Spirit," abstract. Wagner rather sought nationalism in the *Volk*, and Spirit in its creativity—in the kind of psychological "projections" of which Feuerbach had spoken. For Wagner, *Volk* was the very essence of a nation, and myth and legend gave voice to its soul.

After Feuerbach, it was Schopenhauer who provided some of the specifically philosophical components of Wagner's belief system. Those components were

---

[9] Friedrich Engels, *Schelling and Revelation: Critique of the Latest Attempt of Reaction Against the Free Philosophy*, in Karl Marx and Friedrich Engels, *Collected Works* (New York: International Publishers, 1976), vol. 2, p. 239.

[10] See the account in Houston Stewart Chamberlain, *Richard Wagner* (Munich: F. Bruckmann, 1904), pp. 185–188.

[11] It is important to recall that Wagner was a convinced German nationalist as early as the beginning of the 1840s. Hegel, while a statist, was not a nationalist as nationalism was understood at that time. See the entire discussion in Shlomo Avineri, "Hegel and Nationalism," in Walter Kaufman, ed., *Hegel's Political Philosophy* (New York: Atherton Press, 1970), pp. 109–136; and Avineri, *Hegel's Theory of the Modern State* (New York: Cambridge University Press, 1972), pp. 239–241.

largely, if not essentially, moral in substance. For Wagner, morality provided the real tissue of life and history. He seemed to believe that he found a similar emphasis in the philosophical anthropology of Feuerbach.

For Wagner, Feuerbach seemed to entertain a vision of life that was driven by purpose—a defense of human beings as group animals—a commitment that was indistinguishable from those of the most demanding religions. These were the features that were to characterize Wagner's conception of human life and human responsibility—even after he distanced himself from Feuerbach.

What clearly distinguished Wagner from most of the left Hegelians of his time was his unqualified German patriotism—which came together with the romantic suggestion of an intrinsically Germanic religion, a "realistic" religion that was a projection of the sentiments, the sensibilities, and the aspirations of the original Teutonic *Urvolk*, the *Volk* that he was convinced constituted the primeval source of all the German creativity he so much prized. For him, religion was a uniquely creative reflection of a people's soul—inextricably "volkish" in essence.

Almost immediately after the failure of domestic political revolution, on the 14th of June in 1848, Wagner delivered a political speech to the Fatherland Association (the *Vaterlandsverein*),[12] of which he was a member. It was to be one of the few public political addresses of his life. In the address, he sought to give expression to his mature, if politically conflicted, German patriotism. Delivered to an audience composed almost entirely of social radicals and antimonarchial activists, the speech, at best, was opaque, complex, and seemingly uncertain in delivery.[13] For years thereafter its intent was almost entirely misunderstood. Some thought it to have been "revolutionary" and "republican," while others, more surprising still, interpreted it "anarchic" and "communist."

On the occasion of the speech, Wagner commenced his remarks with seeming support for an "open republic, sans monarch"—a system that would entail the abolition of the traditional nobility, so that all Germans, however poor and however undistinguished, might once again enjoy all the rights and privileges that typified their tribal forebears—the *Urvolk*. He went on to champion the

---

[12] The delivery appears as "The *Vaterlandsverein* Speech, June 1848," in Richard Wagner, *Prose Works* (London: Kean, Paul, Trench, Trubner and Co., 1892–1899), 8 vols. All of Wagner's prose works alluded to in the summary that follows will be taken from this English translation. Chamberlain provided a careful exegesis of Wagner's speech in "Richard Wagner und die Politik," in *Rasse und Persönlichkeit*, pp. 144–170.

[13] Years later, Houston Stewart Chamberlain remarked on the special character of Wagner's address to the *Vaterlandsverein*. In that delivery, Wagner had called upon his audience to commit themselves to the "complete regeneration of human society"—an injunction entirely religious in inspiration. Chamberlain, "Richard Wagners Regenerationslehre," *Rasse und Persönlichkeit*, pp. 136–137.

liberation of all citizens from subservience to wealth or power in whatever form. All that was calculated to foster human regeneration—the restoration of German liberty and the rebirth of lost Teutonic virtues—among which the most cardinal was the willingness to sacrifice for the *Volk*, a product of the intrinsic sense of that loyalty characteristic of "true" Germans. For Wagner, *loyalty* and the defense of *freedom* were to forever remain defining German properties.

During this initial period, Wagner gave expression to two themes that were to occupy him in the years that were to follow. In his essays "Art and Revolution," and "The Art Work of the Future," both written in 1849, he attacked Roman Catholic Christianity as an internationalism that threatened the integrity of the German *Volksthum*. According to Wagner, Roman Catholicism, by virtue of its fundamentally Middle Eastern origins, had corrupted the rich North European heritage of Germans. They were left bereft of their mythology, their vital folk legends, and with that, their moral sensibilities. In Wagner's judgment, a religion defiled by Middle Eastern "Semitism" had "Judaized" the German *Volk*.

As early as his first political essays, Wagner had a reasonably well defined body of convictions that would regularly resurface throughout the remainder of his life, in both his public and private statements. None of those convictions were peculiarly his own. In fact, their components were fairly commonplace in the vexed intellectual environment of the period.

Views very much like those held by Wagner are readily found among authors of the period. Hegel, for example, had early affirmed that "every nation has its own imagery, its gods, angels, devils or saints, who live on in the nation's traditions"[14]—all of which, as far as Germany was concerned, had been swallowed up by traditional Christianity.

Hegel argued further that the Christianity that had replaced the religious life of Germans had been warped by those "Jewish intellectuals" who had collected around it at its inception. As a consequence, the "Christianity" that resulted was something other than that which might have been anticipated. Whatever else it was, it was a Christianity that was somehow "alien." It was, in his judgment, a "Jewish Christianity." Somehow or other, history had made Judaism "the Fatherland" of Germany's religion.[15]

It was clear that for Hegel, on occasion, nations adopted and adapted the imagery of aliens: their gods, angels, devils, or saints—their legendary heroes and figures of fancy. But in the case of Christianity, Jewish imagery, sentiments,

---

[14] Hegel, "Positivity of the Christian Religion," *Early Theological Writings* (Chicago: Chicago University Press, 1948), pp. 145.

[15] Ibid., pp. 145, 181.

and dispositions had smothered "true" German religiosity. At times in his life, it was evident that Hegel had grave reservations concerning the intrinsic character of the Judaized Christianity that resulted.

Hegel seems to have held that the threat to German life posed by Catholic Christianity was associated with the toxic influence of international Jewry itself. It was an opinion not uncommon among German intellectuals of the nineteenth century—and it was a judgment that was to regularly resurface in Wagnerian thought. Like many intellectuals of the period, Hegel saw the Jews, the products of a millennial history of rootless dispersion, as corrosive of the group integrity of a nation, any nation. Hegel had early spoken of "the mean, abject, wretched circumstances" in which the Jews found themselves in modern times. That seemed to contribute to their meanness of spirit. He spoke of contemporary Jews as possessed of a "universal enmity" toward others (an *odium generis humani*). Moreover, they were, in his judgment, intrinsically materialistic as well, devoid of a sense of beauty, and of humanity.[16]

Whether or not he had read those specific essays, Wagner's thought contained all the same sentiments. More than that, in his prose of the period, Wagner went on to suggest that the Jews, given their "ungerman" properties, in some sense, were responsible for the unbridled commercialism and materialism that undermined national solidarity and corrupted German artistic life. None of those notions, once again, was unique to Wagner—or peculiar to Hegel.

Some years before, as a case in point, in the autumn of 1843, Karl Marx had himself addressed the "Jewish Question." He spoke of the peculiar properties of Jews that rendered them incapable of meaningfully participating in national life. The Jews failed, Marx maintained, because they saw themselves not as Germans, but as members of "the Jewish people"—a people that imagined itself "chosen," alienated from all those not so distinguished. The Jews harbored, as Hegel had suggested, a disdain for the rest of humanity.

More than that, Marx spoke of the Judaism of "the everyday Jew" as nothing other than commercial "huckstering." He proceeded to inform his audience that the Jew's "worldly god" was nothing other than "*money*." Animated by their materialistic devotion to wealth, Jews made money "a world power" and the "Jewish spirit ... the practical spirit of the Christian nations." In fact, Marx proceeded, "Christianity is the sublime thought of Judaism.... Consequently, not only in the Pentateuch and the Talmud, but in present day society we find

---

[16] Hegel, "The Spirit of Christianity and Its Fate," ibid., pp. 190, 191, 196, 199, 201. 205. Max Stirner was to write, "Their *unspirituality* sets Jews forever apart from Christians; for the spiritual man is incomprehensible to the unspiritual, as the unspiritual is contemptible to the spiritual. But the Jews have only 'the spirit of this world.'" Stirner, *The Ego and His Own*, p. 24.

the nature of the modern Jew, and not as an abstract nature, but as one that is in the highest degree empirical, not merely as a narrowness of the Jew, but as the Jewish narrowness of society."[17] Christianity, according to Marx, had been Judaized—to make the Judaized "Christian" beliefs of contemporary Germans, the fatal source of their moral involution.

However demeaning, none of this was particularly original with either Hegel or Marx. That form of antisemitism had become a recurrent feature of the thought of politically active Germans early in the century.[18] There were suggestions of such sentiments in the writings of Goethe, Fichte, and Schopenhauer.[19] As a consequence, the fact that Wagner harbored such notions is not surprising—nor is it required that he be familiar with the early theological writings of Hegel, or those of the young Marx, in order to explain the presence of such views in his repertoire. Such opinions were not uncommon, even among those who could not be identified as dedicated nationalists or conscious antisemites.

In the period immediately following his speech before the *Vaterlandsverein*, Wagner went on to elaborate on those qualities he was to forever identify with "true Germanity." He spoke of the readiness of Germans to make free commitment to leadership, and to extend an abiding loyalty to that leadership, once chosen. Wagner held all that to be essential to the German national character. It became part of the rationale for the kind of polity he advocated in his political address of 1848. Formed of voluntary commitment and an inalienable loyalty, such a political arrangement—truly German—would be *regenerative*, restoring to the nation the essential properties of primordial *Germanenthum*.

Wagner argued that in their indefeasible loyalty and obedience, Germans would find freedom. His argument turned on the conviction that the "true German concept" of rulership involved the unqualified leadership of one who enjoyed the full and unrestricted loyalty of his people. The restoration of such rule to its "genuine German expression" would bring "true" freedom to those who were loyal. In their loyalty and obedience, Germans would be loyal and obedient to their truest selves.

Such a union of leaders and nation would render Germany invincible. With

---

[17] Karl Marx, "On the Jewish Question," in Marx and Engels, *Collected Works*, vol. 3, pp. 147, 169, 170, 172, 173, 174.

[18] None of these sentiments were universal. Herder, in his discussion of the *Volk*, had argued "the time will come, when no one in Europe will inquire whether one is a Jew or a Christian, for then Jews will live as equals under European law and contribute to the furtherance of the common State. Only a constitutional barbarism would hinder or impair their abilities." Herder, *Ideen zur Philosophie der Geschichte der Menschheit*, vol. 2, p. 287, but see Peter Pulzer, *The Rise of Political Anti-Semitism in Germany and Austria* (Cambridge: Harvard University Press, 1988).

[19] See the references in Ludwig Schemann, *Deutsche Klassiker über die Rassenfrage* (Munich: J. F. Lehmanns Verlag, 1934).

that invincibility, the leader could assure Germans the fullness of freedom. He would give expression to the true political, social, and cultural interests of the *Volk*. German freedom would thus find fulsome expression in the loyalty that was definitive of Germanic psychology. It would be the result of Germany's regeneration.

All of that was already implicit, if not fully explicit, in Wagner's first political speech in 1848. By 1849, when he delivered his "Art and Revolution," Wagner made increasingly clear what he meant by the "social revolution" he advocated. It became apparent that what he meant by revolutionary social and/or political change was manifestly different from any notions entertained by most revolutionaries of the period. Revolution for Wagner meant "rebirth" and "regeneration" for a world that, in his decided judgment, was suffering systemic moral decay.[20]

At the core of his notion of regeneration was a syndrome of interrelated beliefs. Revolutionary regeneration required a dedicated commitment to all and everything that was "truly German"—and there was the clear conviction that what was truly German was to be found in its purest expression among the *Urvolk*, the "original" Germans.

All of Wagner's creative works constitute evidence of that conviction. Virtually all the themes that provided the substance of his music dramas, for example, were those of Teutonic mythology and fable. He found in the myths and legends of the fabled past all that was truly German—unencumbered by the nongerman influences that afflicted the Germany of the mid nineteenth century.

Equally important is the fact that all the heroes in his works epitomized what he understood to be unalloyed Teutonic virtues. Influenced by the thought of Arthur Schopenhauer, Wagner saw true Germans possessed of tragic virtues—renunciation of the material world and unflagging loyalty to a transcendent, difficult cause—almost impossible of attainment.

Through "sweat, affliction, anxieties, and an abundance of pain and suffering," through sacrifice and loyalty, true Germans sought redemption in a world already decadent.[21] A fundamental weapon in the struggle for redemption involved the restoration of a truly Germanic religion—that would recapture those properties that were essentially those of the Teutonic *Urvolk*.

By recalling to life, in his dramas, the behaviors of the heroes of Teutonic legend, Wagner sought the restoration of a truly Germanic religion. He invoked

[20] See the discussion in Chamberlain, *Richard Wagner*, pp. 172–173.
[21] See Wagner's discussion in both renderings of his "Judaism in Music," that of 1850 and that of 1869.

art in order to captivate the collective imagination—inspiring Germans to their historic responsibilities. In the behavior of his heroes, Wagner sought to portray the reality of a Germanic Christ, thereby to work for a restoration of true virtue, and a viable faith for the *Volksthum*.[22] Whatever his Christianity was to be, it would be distinctly and imprescriptibly Germanic.

In a time in which traditional religion was subject to increasingly intense criticism, Wagner resolved his reservations by combining his nationalism and his profoundly religious disposition into an intensely personal surrogate for traditional Christianity. He found in his personal Christianity an expression of "true" Teutonic religiosity. As a consequence, throughout the remainder of his life, he sought to further what he held to be "the realization of a pure Christianity," freed of the encumbrances of a decadent world—and divested of that Semitic god of an alien people. He sought what he held to be a religion freed of the corruption of a world that knew little other than competition for material gain. For Wagner, "true Christianity" was to be found in the moral purity of the first Germans who, in their initial exposure to the message of Christ, perceived in it an alternative form of their most fundamental principled beliefs. They intuitively stripped the Christianity, to which they were introduced, of all the ungerman encumbrances that had accumulated around it after the passing of Christ—and, according to Wagner—proceeded to live their Christianity in Teutonic authenticity.

Wagner was convinced that religion, like art, constituted the very foundation of society, and that a "purified religion" was the indispensable ingredient of any proposed regeneration of fallen humanity. For any given society, the elements of that religion were to be found in the beliefs of its founders. For Germany, its substance was to be found in the faith of the original Germanic tribes that peopled the dawn of the nation's history.

In time, what that meant for Wagner became increasing evident. Gradually, the features that appeared in little more than embryonic form in 1848 became increasingly pronounced. By the time he produced the last revision of "Religion and Art" in 1880, Wagner held that Christianity had been ruined by insidious Judaic influences—and had impaired the integrity of the community. In "Know Thyself," written around the same time, he insisted that the alien influence of the Old Testament had rendered Christianity effectively ungerman—and had become a fateful source of corruption. All the disabilities alluded to in "Judaism and Music," first written in 1850, were rendered increasingly explicit in order to

---

[22] In that sense, Wagner was antihegelian. Hegel had insisted that "the project of restoring to a nation an imagery once lost is always doomed to failure." Hegel, "Positivity of the Christian Religion," p. 149. The central motive of Wagner's operas was the restoration of Germany's lost faith.

provide a systematic "examination of Jewish influence" in art and society. By the time of his death, Wagner was absolutely convinced that the anticipated regeneration of German life necessitated the availability of a "true religion"—a genuinely Teutonic faith—cleansed of Jewish adulteration. He identified much of the societal decline he lamented with that very adulteration. He spoke of it in the course of attempting to explain "the unconscious feeling of aversion towards the Jewish essence[23] on the part of the *Volk*." He saw the aversion, on the part of Germans, as an instinctive existential response on the occasion of mortal threat.

Wagner considered the Jew a danger to the very survival of the *Volk*. Not having shared in the history or the language of the *Volk* community, Wagner argued that Jews could not "participate in its maintenance and perpetuation." Not having been among the *Urvolk* at the creation, the Jew must remain forever a stranger among strangers. The Jew's participation in the *Volk* community must forever remain characterized by qualities that were "alien, cold, strange, indolent, unnatural, and distorted."[24]

Again, many such sentiments were to be found among thinking Germans of the period. Ludwig Feuerbach, in 1841, for example, had written that "the Israelitish religion is the religion of the most narrow hearted egoism. Even the later Israelites," he continued, "scattered throughout the world, persecuted and oppressed, adhered with immovable firmness to the egoistic faith of their forefathers." They believed, he contended, that "the world was created for the sake of the Israelites; they are the fruit, other nations are their husks."[25] Hegel had said no less. Marx had suggested that Jews had contributed to, if they, themselves, had not directly contrived, the worst features of oppressive capitalism. One finds similar judgments in the works of social progressives, socialists, and reactionaries alike.[26]

What distinguished Wagner's convictions from those of many of his contemporaries was their increasingly elaborate and intricate formulation and intractable hostility. While the convictions were clearly his own, by the time of his

---

[23] The German term is "*Wesen*," and can be rendered either "being" or "essence." "Essence" would seem better to capture Wagner's meaning. See Leon Stein, *The Racial Thinking of Richard Wagner* (New York: Philosophical Library, 1950), p. 107.

[24] See his "German Art and German Politics," written in l867, and his "Modern," written in 1878.

[25] Ludwig Feuerbach, *The Essence of Christianity* (New York: Harper & Brothers, 1957), p. 298.

[26] See the selected references in Schemann, *Deutsche Klassiker über die Rassenfrage*. For a more extensive treatment of similar sentiments authored by prominent Germans of the nineteenth century, see Schemann's *Die Rassenfragen im Schrifttum der Neuzeit* (Munich: J. F. Lehmanns Verlag, 1934). Reference to Werner Sombart's *The Jews and Capitalism* (London: T. Fisher Unwin, 1913. Originally published in 1911) is particularly relevant in this context.

death, they had been supplemented, and given more intricate form, by one of Europe's foremost racist thinkers.

Towards the end of his life, in 1876,[27] Wagner entered into a mutually influential relationship with Count Arthur de Gobineau—the best known of the racist theoreticians of the mid nineteenth century. By 1880, Gobineau and Wagner had become more than friends. They shared not only mutual respect, but a set of convictions that were to systematize Wagner's entire belief system—a belief system that was to survive Wagner and influence some of the most important political actors of the twentieth century.

Count Arthur de Gobineau (1816–1882)

Gobineau was to bring a fateful component to the social and political convictions of Richard Wagner. His study, *The Inequality of Human Races*,[28] first published in 1853–1854, was harbinger of what was to come. It was a multivolume work identified by the German anthropologist Eugen Fischer as the "great forerunner" of that "racial historical standpoint" that conceived the "Nordic race" the creator, the necessary hereditary artisan, of the products and values that came to distinguish the culture of Western civilization.[29] Gobineau's work was a publication that was to deliver both structure and the semblance of natural science to Wagner's thought. More than that, it was to make explicit some of the implications of Wagner's views.

Gobineau's thesis was simplicity itself—it was his contention that there "are real differences in the relative value of human races." He argued that there were entire human races that were intrinsically incapable of launching and/or sustaining civilization—that is to say, entire races incapable of arranging and fostering settled life, an abundant culture, and a complex, scientific existence. Nature had chosen to make others responsible for such accomplishments.

In the judgment of Gobineau, "whites, as distinct from the remaining races,"

---

[27] Wagner had met Gobineau earlier, but the relationship that developed during the last years of their lives was the consequence of the later encounter.

[28] Arthur de Gobineau, *Essai sur l'inégalite des races humaines*. An English translation of the first volume of the work was rendered in 1855 by H. Holz as *The Moral and Intellectual Diversity of Races*. The more easily available English translation of the first volume appeared early in the twentieth century as *The Inequality of Human Races* (New York: G. P. Putnam's Sons, 1915). While the original work covered four volumes, it is the first volume that delivers the central theses. The remaining volumes carry arguments in support of the theses—which, while interesting, are not critical to the present account. Citations will be made to the Putnam text. While the differences between the two translations of the first volume are interesting, they do not influence that analysis.

[29] See the discussion in Hans F. K. Günther, *Racial Elements of European History* (London: Methuen & Co., Ltd., 1927), chap. 12.

were understood to be singularly "gifted with reflective energy, or rather, with an energetic intelligence." He was convinced that given "the immense superiority of the white peoples in the whole field of the intellect ... all civilizations derive from the white race, and none can exist without its help." Among those of the white race, Gobineau was to identify subsets, "Aryans" and "Germanics,"[30] as particularly gifted branches—and he tended to assign special creativity to their members. They were the material sponsors of all great civilizations ranging from Asia to the New World. Once "Aryan" or "Germanic" blood was exhausted or corrupted, he warned, those civilizations and cultures would lapse into irretrievable decay.

He went on to contend that a society and a civilization would remain viable only so long as it "preserves the blood of the noble group that created it."[31] Such societies and civilizations persist as long as their founders survive with their initial hereditary potential intact. Critical to that intactness was resistance to reproducing with representatives of lesser races.[32]

At the conclusion of the first volume of his work, Gobineau reviewed the making of ten great civilizations, seven of which he attributed exclusively to the creativity of "Aryan" members of the white race. "Indian civilization" was attributed to "white men of Aryan stock." Egyptian civilization, in turn, owed its founding to an "Aryan colony from India." The civilizations of the Middle Eastern "fertile crescent" were similarly attributed to "branches of the Aryan family." Furthermore, he continued, "Aryan colonies" brought the "light of civilization" to China. No less could be said of the Greece and Rome of antiquity. Finally, he concluded with the judgment that "the tone and character" of modern civilization was provided essentially by the descendants of "the Germanic conquerors of the fifth century."[33] The less creative types alluded to by Gobineau included members of the yellow race, whom he judged "mediocre in everything." Members of that fraternity were understood to be capable of "appreciating and taking over what is useful," but unable to independently create "a civilized society."[34] He went on to assess "the negroid variety as the lowest"

---

[30] It is difficult to reconstruct a coherent classificatory scheme covering the components of Gobineau's account. There seems to be a comprehensive "white race," of which "Aryans" and "Germanics" constitute subsets. The classification "Aryan" seems to incorporate, among other constituents, "Germanics." For the purposes of exposition, it is important to note that there is an important distinction between *germanisch* ("Germanic") and *deutsch* ("German"). Unlike the latter, the former has a much broader reference—denoting a class of persons not defined by political identity. "Germanic," as we shall see, includes far more than Germans.

[31] Gobineau, *The Inequality of Human Races*, p. 210.

[32] Ibid., pp. 207, 210, 211.

[33] Ibid., pp. 211–212.

[34] Ibid., pp. 206, 207.

of existing types. Concerning them, he contended, they "always move within a very narrow circle.... [Their] mental faculties are dull or even nonexistent." As a consequence, he held that "negroids" are "father to no civilization or sophisticated society"—and by his very presence the black threatens humanity's cognitive and moral prospects.[35]

Such convictions inspired Gobineau to argue that civilizations are founded and furthered by select creators—and would degenerate when their productive talents diminished and/or disappeared. Such a misfortune was invariably the "consequence of the various admixtures of blood which they undergo" in the course of time. When a creative race permits "miscegenation" with those less endowed, creative and moral decline must inevitably follow. Conversely, Gobineau claimed that "a people will never die, if it remains eternally composed of the same national elements.... So long as the blood ... of a nation keeps to a sufficient degree the impress of the original race, that nation exists."[36]

As a consequence of those convictions, Gobineau maintained "that the racial question overshadows all other problems of history." He insisted that the issue "holds the key" to all problems, and that "the inequality of the races from whose fusion a people is formed is enough to explain the whole course of its destiny."[37]

Gobineau maintained that racial mixture of unlike types not only conduced to creative and moral decay, but undermined, as well, the common instinct and shared collective interests that unified a people. With the admixture of individuals of "vastly different racial type," there would be a loss of that sense of affinity essential to community life. As "alien" elements are added to the subject population, the vast difficulty of harmonizing the whole fosters a state of growing anarchy. At the same time as social tensions increase, talent diminishes proportionately. Given his convictions, Gobineau concluded that, as a result of miscegenation, societies "are led down to the abyss of nothingness, whence no power on earth can rescue them. Such," he affirmed, "is the lesson of history."[38]

Wagner found much of this convincing, and by the time of his death, had incorporated much of it into his own system of beliefs.[39] Gobineau pro-

[35] Ibid., p. 205.
[36] Ibid., pp. 33, 34, 35, 211.
[37] Gobineau, "From the Author's Dedication (1854)," ibid., p. xiv.
[38] "Artistic genius, which is equally foreign to each of the three great types, arose only after the intermarriage of white and black.... The world of art and great literature that comes from the mixture of blood, the improvement and ennoblement of inferior races—all these are wonders for which we must needs be thankful." Ibid., pp. 208, 209, 210. Compare ibid., p. 211.
[39] By the end of his life, Wagner had committed himself to convictions that clearly reflected the influence of Gobineau—who had, by that time, become a fast friend. By the end of his life Wagner

vided Wagner a broad context into which his convictions might be accommodated.

At about the time that Wagner incorporated critical components from the work of Gobineau into his thought, Gobineau, himself, was adding increasing complexity to his analysis. In the manuscript on which he was working at the time of his death, *The Significance of Race in the Life of Peoples*,[40] Gobineau addressed the role played by Jews in European history—in a manner unmistakably reminiscent of Wagner. Already present in his earlier work, in his last and unfinished manuscript, Gobineau proceeded to emphasize Jewish influence on Germanic Europe as a special confirming instance of the fact that race was a critical factor in understanding history. It was a contention fully compatible with Wagner's belief that the Jew would forever remain alien to *Germanenthum*.

In fact, employing his own craft, Gobineau provided substance to Wagner's conjectures. In his final work, Gobineau chose to focus on the Jews. He wrote of the "Semitic peoples"—yet another subset of the white race—who, at some time or another, he argued, had mingled their biological heritage with blacks. He alluded to the legacy of that mixture. He spoke of the resultant intellectual and moral impairments—and suggested that those disabilities explained the "instinctive" social tensions that characteristically arose between Semites, primarily Jews, and Germanics. Gobineau had expanded on notions found in the prose Wagner had produced in the years after his speech at the *Vaterlandsverein*.

Gobineau gave expression to mutually held views. Wagner acknowledged that Gobineau's affirmations appealed to him "with the most terrible force of conviction."[41] By the late 1870s, Gobineau had emphasized the role of the Jews in his panoramic view of history. He accomplished that by speaking of the "anarchic" mixture of peoples in the latter part of the history of Rome. He maintained that within that mixture, the Jews, as "hybrid Semites," exercised inordinate influence—little of it positive. When the Germanic tribes, in the fourth and fifth centuries of the common era, found their way into the disintegrating empire, they sought its political and cultural restabilization. According to Gobineau, the subsequent history of the Holy Roman Empire, and the gradual

---

accorded "special weight to the race issue" and to the fact that intermixture between a gifted and less gifted race could only result in the overall decline of civilized life. See Chamberlain, "Richard Wagners Regenerationslehre," particularly pp. 140–142.

[40] Gobineau, *Die Bedeutung der Rasse im Leben der Völker* (Munich: J. F. Lehmanns Verlag, 1926). What follows is largely a summary of Gobineau's thought. See particularly pp. 51–52, 61–67, 68, 103, 105–106.

[41] Wagner, "Herodom and Christiandom," in *Prose Works*, vol. 6, p. 282.

rebirth of culture in Europe, was the story of an existential conflict between Jews and Germanics.

For Gobineau, the Germanic tribes provided the fresh talents that fueled the rebirth of civilization in Europe. As those developments matured and creative communities emerged, the presence of Jews in their midst precipitated tensions of serious magnitude. As "aliens"—whatever their positive attributes may have been[42]—the Jews exercised ominous influence through their control of community finances—which allowed them to inordinately sway those who ruled, as well as unconscionably exploit artisan, industrial, and agrarian labor. In effect, in Gobineau's judgment, the influence of the Jews on European civilization and culture was largely negative. They were, in effect, harbingers of political, social, cultural, and economic devolution and decay.

By the time he had settled on those convictions in 1879, Gobineau pretended that his views were based on grounds that were essentially "scientific." Like the evolutionary biologists of the later nineteenth century, Gobineau sought to make relevant empirical distinctions within his domain of inquiry—something Wagner never felt disposed to undertake. As a consequence, Gobineau sought to distinguish "race," as a concept, from "nation" and "*Volk (peuple)*"—something Wagner never attempted.

In the pages of his *Significance of Race*, Gobineau specifically identified his "Germanics" as a *race*, characterized by defining physical traits: a given range of stature, for instance, together with general depigmentation. More than that, tall, slender, blond, and blue-, or grey-eyed Germanics, according to Gobineau, were gifted with relatively distinctive mental properties—that included not only singular cognitive endowments, but special behavioral dispositions as well.[43]

Conversely, Gobineau held a "people" to be a mixture of closely related races whose affinities allow them to share properties of soul: psychological, cultural, and moral. He spoke of *nations* as the political union of peoples who may or may not be composed of those closely related—in terms of racial origin.[44] Thus, the Scandinavian nations shared a common racial consanguinity—while the Hapsburg Empire of Austria Hungary did not.

---

[42] Gobineau was eloquent in his admiration of the Jews. "What did the Jews become [in a singularly] miserable corner of the earth? They became a people that succeeded in everything, . . . a free, strong, and intelligent people [who] . . . had given as many learned men to the world as it had merchants" (*The Inequality of Human Races*, p. 59). That admiration did not reduce his preoccupation with their negative impact on the Germanic world.

[43] See specifically, *Die Bedeutung der Rasse im Leben der Völker*, p. 49. Gobineau speaks of the Germanic preoccupation with "personal rights" and generic freedoms.

[44] Gobineau was not convinced that humankind had a monogenetic origin. He was at least half convinced that races of humankind were distinct species and were of polygenetic origin. See chaps. 10 through 12 of *The Inequality of Human Races*.

Unlike Gobineau, Wagner neither sought to couch his convictions in scientific jargon nor ever attempted so grand a schematization. Nonetheless, there is every evidence that he accepted the generic elements of Gobineau's account. What Wagner and Gobineau shared was manifest. What distinguished the two was Wagner's emphasis on political purpose, the need to mobilize resistance to those circumstances that fostered racial decline.

Wagner realized that in order to achieve his goal, mobilization would be required. Mobilization would require not science, but deep conviction—faith. For Wagner, a specifically Germanic Christianity, freed of "Semitic materialism," and characterized by the mythology and legendry of the "*Urvolk*," would be necessary. It would be a faith of the creators of Germanic civilization, culture, and tradition. Wagner was to insist that the only defense against advancing decadence was the invocation of a "true" Germanic religion. That would provide the necessary conditions of regeneration of the Germanic peoples.

In "Religion and Art" Wagner made clear that he imagined that his music might orchestrate the rekindling of Germanic faith. He conceived music conveying to Germans "the essence of religion free from all dogmatic fictions"—a "new religion" that would provide an increasingly decadent society with a therapeutic, regenerative faith.[45]

By the end of his life—through the direct and indirect influence of Gobineau—Wagner had settled on what he held to be the principal factors that had produced the social and political decline of Germany—the Germany that he was convinced held the promise of the rebirth of civilization. He was prepared to argue that behind the disintegration of morals, the coarsening of behavior, the erosion of artistic standards, and the almost extinction of the loyalty and heroism that once typified the German—there were two primary factors: racial miscegenation and the influence of the alien Jew.[46] It was Gobineau who had fully framed those articles of conviction in a "theory of history."

For Gobineau, and for Wagner as well, the Germanic peoples, Teutons and Aryans, as "prototeutons," were among those specially creative elements responsible for the major cultural achievements of all humanity. With their passing, the cultural creativity of peoples would fade, and modern civilization would lapse into irreversible decay.[47]

---

[45] See the comments in Michael Burleigh, *Earthly Powers: The Clash of Religion and Politics in Europe, from the French Revolution to the Great War* (New York: Harper Collins, 2005), p. 273.

[46] See account in "Herodom and Christiandom," the third supplement to "Religion and Art," in *Prose Works*; together with the description in Chamberlain, *Richard Wagner*, pp. 220–223.

[47] See Wagner's introduction to "Gobineau's Ethnological Resume" (1881), and Gobineau, *Die Bedeutung der Rasse im Leben der Völker*, the introduction to Gobineau's incomplete *Rassenkunde Frankreichs*.

Gobineau and Wagner shared those convictions. While Wagner's beliefs antedated the appearance of Gobineau's work, that work provided their systematization. When Gobineau's work was first brought to his attention, Wagner found the exposition familiar, composed of views he already entertained. The fact is that Gobineau's theses were essentially compatible with those that Wagner early had made his own—Gobineau had given them a remarkable range and scope. While the scaffolding was provided by Gobineau, much of the substance was Wagnerian.

By 1883, both Wagner and Gobineau were dead. As fate would have it, there already was a gifted spokesman prepared to propagate and defend their ideas. In fact, his work was to reveal just how compatible were their worldviews. Houston Stewart Chamberlain's works were to deliver the fullness of their belief systems—and render them popular.

It was Chamberlain, who, in the final years of the nineteenth century, gave finished form to the convictions of Richard Wagner. The major publications in which that exposition was contained were to effect important consequences in the future. It was to measurably influence the history of the twentieth century. It was destined to shape the convictions of an entire generation of Germans—and project the ideas of Wagner and Gobineau far into the twentieth century.

Houston Stewart Chamberlain (1855–1927)

Houston Stewart Chamberlain was an Englishman, born in Southsea, England, in 1855, the scion of a notable British military family. Foreclosed from pursuing a military career by fragile health, Chamberlain tentatively sought out an academic career—a decision that took him to the Continent. His studies in France and Germany were substantial, providing him generous instruction in biology, geology, astronomy, as well as human physiology and anatomy.

In the course of his studies, Chamberlain became increasingly enamored of Imperial Germany—the Prussian Germany of Otto von Bismarck. By the time of his first maturity, Chamberlain was impressed by virtually everything German, its intellectual achievements, its moral posture, its art, its military, and its emerging promise. In Dresden, he fell under the spell of Richard Wagner—his music as well as his emphatic German nationalism.

The remainder of Chamberlain's life was spent in the systematic study and defense of both Wagner's music and his nationalism. The result was literary production of impressive quantity and quality, including specialized studies ranging from a work on what he held to be the quintessential Germanic philosophy of Immanuel Kant, to detailed renderings of the life and work of Wagner—all of which had political implications.

Chamberlain's works would directly and indirectly influence the leadership of Germany through two world wars and half a century in time. The most important of them, *The Foundations of the Nineteenth Century*,[48] made its appearance in 1899, at the very close of the nineteenth century. By 1941, the popularity of the work required the publication, over the years, of twenty-seven successive German editions.

The Foundations was undertaken clearly to serve as an explication and defense of the political thought of Richard Wagner. Elements of every theme found in Chamberlain's *magnum opus* can be traced to sources in the scattered writings of "the Master."[49]

Chamberlain brought to his task a measure of erudition absent from the prose works of Wagner, and a subtlety not found in that of Gobineau. For all that, *The Foundations* was a well crafted synthesis of both.[50] What Chamberlain sought to accomplish with his work was an interpretation of Wagner's thought as he understood that thought.[51] While his task required he hew closely to the convictions embodied in the original,[52] it is evident that Chamberlain sought to supplement Wagner's thought where he felt it fragmentary or uncertain. That notwithstanding, he attempted to supply the requisite supplements without betraying any of Wagner's original intent. By that time, it had become evident to everyone seriously concerned that much of the Master's thought had found articulation in the work of Gobineau.

Similar to the effort of Gobineau, Chamberlain's *Foundations* succeeded in putting Wagner's beliefs into a broad historical context, lending them a special

---

[48] Houston Stewart Chamberlain, *Foundations of the Nineteenth Century* (New York: John Lane Company, 1911), in two volumes. References will be made to this translation. *Die Grundlagen des neunzenten Jahrhunderts* (Munich: F. Bruckmann K.-G, 1941) will be employed when there are questions concerning translation or interpretation.

[49] Chamberlain attempted a systematic exposition of Wagner's specific thought in his *Richard Wagner*. In that work, every theme that finds full expression in *The Foundations of the Nineteenth Century* is found in embryonic form.

[50] Chamberlain was critical of some of Gobineau's judgments, but they were marginal to his main theses. In one place, Chamberlain objected that Gobineau had identified Jewish influence on European civilization as *always* negative—a proposition with which he could not concur. In fact, as has been indicated, while Gobineau's views on the Jews were almost always negative, there were clear instances of his admiration. More important was Chamberlain's objections concerning Gobineau's conceptions concerning the nature of races and their origins. Chamberlain, *Foundations*, vol. 1, pp. 254, 263; see vol. 2, p. 246; cf. vol. 1, pp. 280, n.

[51] After the First World War, Chamberlain addressed Wagner's thought with great specificity. See "Richard Wagners Regenerationslehre," "Richard Wagner und die Politik," and "Vorwort zur vierzehnten Auflage der Grundlagen des XIX Jahrhunderts," in *Rasse und Persönlichkeit*, pp. 126–143, 144–170, and 189–200.

[52] Chamberlain hewed so closely to Wagner's ideas that a critic charged him with plagiarism! See the comments of Lord Redesdale in the Introduction to vol. 1 of the *Foundations*, p. vii.

scope and coherence. *The Foundations* was a history essentially composed of three parts: the first devoted to the anthroposociological nature of Grecoroman antiquity; the second sought to provide a history of the movement of the Germanic peoples into the "racial chaos" of the late Roman Empire; and, finally, an account of the specific role of Germanics[53] in the creation of modern Europe.

As did Gobineau, Chamberlain wove a historical tale of vast population migrations, beginning with the demographic expansion of migrants from the highlands of Asia into India and Persia. These *Arya*, as those migrating populations of herdsmen, shepherds, and warriors were called, were the makers of the civilization of India, its architects, its metaphysicians, and its poets. Other "Aryans" fared West, to found the civilization of Persian antiquity—to provide history a civilization given special character by the religiosity of the Zendavesta.

Chamberlain dutifully acknowledged that the history of these Aryans is uncertain, subject to scholarly dispute. He never pretended to possess convincing data concerning their itinerary; he granted the speculative character of that part of his exposition. He went on to recount that other peoples, perhaps related, found their way to the Mediterranean littoral—sharing impressive cultural affinities with the Aryans of Asia and the Middle East. Along the coasts of the inland sea, these peoples fashioned the Greece of fabled antiquity and the Rome that would ultimately overwhelm all of Europe from the Mediterranean to the limes of Scotland.

It is with the disintegration of the Roman Empire that Chamberlain embarks on his special history. It is a history that is devoted primarily to the centuries between the decline of the empire and the advent of the nineteenth century—commencing with the birth of Christ and concluding with the founding of a united Germany.

The principal protagonists of his story are variously identified as "Aryans,"[54] "Indoeuropeans," and then alternatively, as "*Homo europaeus*," "Teutons," and "Germanics." He acknowledges distinctions among and between these demographic categories, but the distinctions he entertains are never pursued very systematically. The reasons for that are not far to seek.

Chamberlain, as an informed student of natural science, had put together a conception of *race* that conceived it a dynamic constant, the result of a pro-

[53] Chamberlain typically used the term *Germanen* ("Germanics") to identify his principal protagonists. "Germanics" does not refer to Germans (*Deutschen*), but to an ethnic family that includes a variety of other groups.

[54] Chamberlain does not seem overly concerned with the actual existence of an "Aryan race." He tells his readers that even were it "proved that there never was an Aryan race in the past, yet we desire that in the future there may be one. That is the decisive point for men of action." *Foundations*, vol. 1, p. 266, n.

cess that, over time, took a biologically active community through expansion, selective outbreeding, protracted inbreeding, to a measure of uniformity of traits that made of it a "pure race."[55] Communities undergoing the process of raciation could appear as tribes, federations, or nations—any and all of which themselves could serve as "race cradles." Tribes, federations, or nations that had achieved the requisite measure of homogeneity might be identified as "races." "Purity" would be a measure of achieved physical and psychological uniformity.[56]

Thus, in the course of his account, Chamberlain speaks of various Aryan races, and they seem to range over a number of candidate peoples—who "differ very much from each other" revealing, for example, "the most different structure of skull, also different color of skin, eyes and hair"—something one would expect if race formation involved the processes he had outlined. "Indoeuropeans," in turn, appear to overlap, but are not necessarily coextensive with, the class of persons identified as "Aryans"—something one would expect, given, once again, Chamberlain's conception of raciation. Chamberlain finds an "Indoteutonic" or "Indogermanic race"—a race that could hardly have existed among the Aryans of Indian and Persian antiquity—but which might have emerged in the course of the changing history of Indoeuropeans.[57]

Given these notions, the Indoteutonic, or Indogermanic "race" appears in history as a compound entity. Chamberlain speaks of them as a "race" composed of "a number of races" including "the Alemanni, the Marcomanni, the Saxons, the Franks, the Burgundians, the Goths, the Vandals, the Slavs, the Huns and many others." These are all spoken of as both "races" and "genuine nations," and alternatively, as "pure bred races"—at different stages of raciation.[58] Similarly, Chamberlain mentions an ensemble of "Teutonic or Germanic races"[59] composed of "Celts, Teutons (*Germanen*) and Slavs, and from whom—mostly by indeterminable mingling—the peoples of modern Europe are de-

---

[55] All of this was fundamentally different from the notions advanced by Gobineau. Gobineau imagined that the "pure" races of antiquity could only decline as a consequence of their interaction with members of less gifted races. His views were unrelievedly pessimistic. See Chamberlain's comments, ibid., vol. 1, p. 263; Chamberlain refers to the implications of Gobineau's pessimism in vol. 1, p. 315. Chamberlain points out that in affirming a conception of static races Gobineau neither recognizes nor allows for the fact that noble races can be both created and restored "at any moment."

[56] See the entire discussion ibid., vol. 1, pp. 269–289.

[57] Ibid., vol. 1, pp. 114, 264.

[58] Ibid., vol. 1, pp. 320–321.

[59] Again, in the English translation, the translator renders Chamberlain's *Germanen* as "Teutons," in order to avoid any misunderstanding that the term refers to "Germans." As has been suggested, in German, the term *Germanen* has an unmistakably wider reference than *Deutschen*. See the discussion ibid., vol. 1, pp. 495–497.

scended." All these, he argues, appear to have "belonged originally to a single family"—probably as "Aryans" at the first stage of their evolution.

Of all the races, incipient or partially developed, Chamberlain selected a subset, the "Germanics (*Germanen*)," as the "soul of Western culture." More significant still, he understood Western civilization to have commenced only when "the Teuton [*Germane*] with his masterful hand [laid] his grip upon the legacy of antiquity."[60] Thereafter, in his judgment, history is the story of a conflict—cultural, social, political, and biological—between Teutonics (or *Germanen*) and "nonteutonics."

In general, Chamberlain conceived nonteutonics the "hybrid" flotsam of the "racial chaos" that disfigured the final decades of the Roman Empire. Within that residue were the Jews, who subsequently were to play a decisive role in the history of Europe—one that Chamberlain, in the final analysis, deems to have been "threateningly perilous" to the Germanic "spirit." In his assessment, Jews were to exercise "a large, and in many ways an undoubtedly fatal, influence upon the course of European history since the first century."[61] It was a pernicious influence that Chamberlain was to track through the history of fifteen hundred years.

For Chamberlain, in the Germanic world, religion proved to be the arena in which Jewish influence was both the most enduring as well as the most impactful. Born of the confluence of Indogermanic, Semitic, and obscure African elements, institutional Christianity insinuated racial tension into the very heart of emerging Europe.

The differences that resulted turned on "the most contradictory views, doctrines and instincts of Jew and Indoeuropean" as those differences made themselves felt at the very core of the Christian faith. The entire struggle—which continued unabated over the centuries—was the result of the fact that within the organized Roman Church "two radically different souls" sought expression, one "Germanic and the other nongermanic." The struggle that roiled European history for centuries was the consequence of an "antagonism of races, and the irreconcilability of the mutually exclusive religious ideals."[62]

For Chamberlain, religious differences, at bottom, were always fundamentally *racial*. In one place, he even allowed himself to speak of religious conflict as not only racial in essence, but a physiological question of "brain convolu-

[60] Ibid., vol. 1, pp. 256–257 and vol. 2, p. 5. Chamberlain speaks of "*Die Germanen*," the Germanics, as being members of the Aryan "family" or "group" in vol. 1, p. 542. See the German edition, *Die Grundlagen des neunzehnten Jahrhunderts*, vol. 1, pp. 304–305.

[61] Chamberlain, *Foundations*, vol. 1, pp. 250, 351.

[62] Ibid., vol. 1, p. 552; vol. 2, pp. 15, 22, 33, 69, 415; see pp. 10, 15 and 20, where Chamberlain speaks of religious conflict as a conflict between "racial instincts."

tions"—apparently a function of inherited anatomical differences. He argued that physiological brain differences would compel whatever entered the mind "to bend and yield." The consequence, he was to insist, was that whatever the stimuli, for Jews religion could only find expression in a form that was hierocratic, obdurate, egoistic, intolerant, materialistic, arbitrary, antimetaphysical, and anti-individualistic—a "politically colored, theocratic communism"[63]—and a continual affront to Germanic moral and political sensibilities.

Institutional Christianity, as it emerged from the "racial chaos" that was Rome in its final decades, was an unfortunate amalgam of Germanic and Jewish religious impulses, further confounded by the superstitions of Egyptian and Middle Eastern paganism. As fate would have it, Germanics, constitutionally independent, sublimely flexible, tolerant, idealistic, rational, metaphysical, and individualistic, were compelled, by the Christianity cobbled together by the heirs of Rome's disintegration, to submit to hierarchical and dogmatic constraints. They found adaptation extremely difficult. Submission to the demands that resulted from the unnatural coupling of racially incompatible elements created the stresses that found expression in episodic heresy, systemic disobedience, and schismatic activity. Germanics could never quite adapt to the organizational demands of Roman Catholicism.

In that parlous state, religious conflict in Europe was to persist for a thousand years, with Germanics attempting to define themselves within the contradictions of the prevailing organized faith. Chamberlain identified the struggle within Christianity, as it emerged from the crumbling empire, as one of Germanics struggling against the "Semitism" of the official church—seeking an outlet for their Indoteutonic religious, philosophical, and artistic sentiments. The episodic and recurrent religious "heresies" that organized themselves against the Roman Church were evidence of Germanic alienation and an aspiration to achieve a restoration of racial integrity—the necessary consequence of the "antagonism of races," that manifested itself as the "irreconcilability of the mutually exclusive religious ideals"—all selectively struggling for mastery within the organized Church.[64]

Chamberlain traced the conflict through the centuries, until it becomes overt in the protest movements of Wyclif, Calvin, and Luther. In the course of time, the European "North," primarily composed of Germanics, found itself opposed to the European "South," made up of the Jewish-dominated racial debris of the late Roman Empire. Beginning in the thirteenth, and by the fifteenth and sixteenth centuries, the fatal struggle between Germanics and the products

---

[63] Ibid., vol. 1, pp. 228, 238, 240, 242, 244, 235, 311, 404–405, 411, 420; vol. 2, pp. 50, 108, 109, 122.
[64] Ibid., vol. 2, pp. 69, 80, 100.

of "the racial chaos" of late Rome matured into what appeared as intolerable doctrinal disagreements—but which, in fact and fundamentally, were struggles that turned on irrepressible racial differences.[65]

The true nature of the racial conflict that stained the history of emerging Europe was obscured because cloaked in religious raiment. It was easier to identify Jewish influence when it was not buried in religious context. It was more obvious when it appeared as power wielded as early as "Western Gothic times" when Jews already were "slave dealers and financial agents." It was more evident when, from that early influence, their sway extended over all of Europe, to see Jews assuming responsibilities as ministers of state under the Spanish Moors, as well as bishops and archbishops of the Church in Catholic Spain—and to serve as financial agents of the Babenberg princes as early as the thirteenth century. With Pope Innocent III important Church posts became available to Jews—and the knights of France pledged their assets to them in order to take part in the Crusades.

Chamberlain recounts in detail the extent of Jewish influence in emerging and emergent Europe.[66] He concentrates on direct and indirect Jewish suasion in the doctrinal and institutional structure of Christianity for several reasons. He considered their influence in the Church symptomatic of their overall social impact. Chamberlain was convinced that for fifteen hundred years institutional Christianity was the unacknowledged instrument of Jewish aggression in emerging Germanic Europe. He held that aggression to be more insidious than direct and open assault, hidden as it was in the faith of peoples. Jewish influence, as it exercised its effect through established religion, entered unopposed into the most intimate life of Germanics. Chamberlain was convinced that "all that ... derived from the Jewish mind"—in whatever form, must surely "corrode and disintegrate what is best in us."[67] A "Judaized" religion, according to both Wagner and Chamberlain, had proved to be the most effective weapon of the "antiteuton" in the unending race war that was the history of Europe.

While Chamberlain held all that to be the case, he did not neglect instances of overt Jewish influence in collateral, secular spheres. He pursued that "antigermanic" influence in finance, politics, and culture. In the final analysis, what he sought was the full "emancipation" of Germanic civilization from "Judaism" in all its forms—direct or indirect—because that influence signaled the real possibility of an end to Western civilization as a culture and a political system.[68]

[65] Ibid., vol. 2, pp. 108–109.
[66] Ibid., vol. 1, pp. 340–350.
[67] Ibid., vol. 1, p. 483, n.
[68] Ibid., vol. 2, p. 495.

Against that threat, Chamberlain appealed to the remaining "great Northern brotherhood" of Germanics, who, however enfeebled by racial crossing, still preserved the qualities that held the promise of European regeneration.[69] Central to Wagner's belief system was the conviction that Germany, itself, as senior member of that brotherhood, might serve as the agent of rebirth. Germans might champion a rebirth of those qualities of intellect and character from which many Germanics had been estranged by the machinations and inducements of less noble races—races that might speak the same language as Indogermanics, and traffic within their space, but which were "as far removed from [them] as if they lived on another planet."[70]

Chamberlain reminded his audience that antigermanic types had infiltrated Germanic Europe since the commencement of the common era. It is they—incapable of grasping the elements of Germanic character, the sense of loyalty and the thirst for freedom—who were responsible for the decline of Western culture and its political preeminence. For Germanics to struggle back from the moral and intellectual corruption that characterized the nineteenth century required not only selfless commitment and unparalleled dedication, but a consistent and unremitting racial policy as well.

For both Wagner and Chamberlain, the effort to embark upon the racial regeneration of the West involved a fairly detailed strategy. It necessitated a reawakening of racial consciousness that would require an appeal not only to the intellect, but to intuitive sensibilities as well. That appeal would be best made via art and religion. Religion inspires art, and art the rehabilitation of spirit. Artists, animated by the vision of a "true" religion, become the soul of the struggle for regeneration.

Christianity, in its truest form—both Wagner and Chamberlain argued—promised humankind "redemption" and "regeneration." In that promise the first Christianity, as Christ intended, was true to "the Indoeuropean tendency of mind"—a tendency "which represented a sharp contrast" to "all Semitic and specially to all Jewish religion."[71] Chamberlain argued that the first Christianity was Germanic in inspiration—the product of the original thought of Christ—himself Germanic.

Chamberlain maintained that there was convincing evidence that Christ was anything but a Jew. Out of the research first generated by the analysis of institutional religion so prominent during the first half of the nineteenth cen-

[69] Ibid., vol. 1, pp. 516–517; and "Richard Wagners Regenerationslehre," pp. 126–143.
[70] Chamberlain, *Foundations*, vol. 1, pp. 558–564, 571.
[71] Chamberlain, "Richard Wagners Regenerationslehre," pp. 139, 140, *Foundations*, vol. 2, pp. 61, 62.

tury, the figure of Christ, himself, emerged as the focus of attention. The result, Chamberlain argued, was that the historical evidence collected in the course of the debate strongly suggested that whatever else he was, Christ was not a Jew.[72]

The Jews, themselves, spoke of Galilee, the birthplace of Christ, as "the district of the heathens," an area of scant concern. Only rarely did the region occupy the interest of the political leadership of Judea. Chamberlain reports that the indifference of the Jews was the result of marked differences in character and deportment that seemed to have distinguished the inhabitants of the province from the rest of the Jewish community. Hundreds of years before the common era, Galilee had been laid waste and depopulated by the Assyrians—thereafter to be restocked with nonjewish populations brought in from elsewhere. The suggestion was that, whatever the prevailing religion may have been at the time of Christ's birth, the population of the region was not biologically kin to the Jews. Chamberlain argued that the probability was that Christ was biologically Indogermanic. That was at least one of the reasons that he was rejected by the Jews.

All of this had been extremely important to Wagner. Religion was a critical component in his program of Germanic regeneration. He conceived religion not only the very foundation of his worldview—but a vehicle of Germanic palingenesis. All that, coupled with the fact he was a convinced antisemite, made the issue of Christ's ethnicity a matter of peculiar significance. If religion was to provide regenerative inspiration, it would have to be Germanic at its source. It could not have a Jew as its founder.

Wagner had insisted that regeneration, the revitalization of humanity, could only be the harvest of a soil that was religious in essence. Only religious inspiration, couched in metaphysical language, philosophical concepts, and framed in art,[73] might reawaken the life-giving passion of those who must assume the responsibilities requisite for regeneration. For Wagner, the agents of regeneration could only be Germanics—and the religion that would serve them as a tool could not possibly be one infected, in any way, by Jewish contaminants.[74]

It was within those parameters that Chamberlain wrote his *Foundations*. The anticipated inspiration for the Germanic renewal would be a "new" religion, and a "new" philosophy. However Christian in public expression, it would deliver itself of "a new idea of the Divine, and a new conception of a moral

---

[72] What follows is taken from Chamberlain, "The Galileans," in *Foundations*, vol. 1, pp. 200–213.

[73] Chamberlain speaks of "Germanic art" as essential to mobilizing the numbers required to achieve regeneration. That attained its most effective expression in the poetic dramas of Wagnerian opera. See ibid., vol. 2, p. 558 n.

[74] Chamberlain, *Richard Wagner*, pp. 239, 243, 246.

order of the world."⁷⁵ Its content would reflect the lawfulness and morality of nature.⁷⁶ It would be "Germanic," free of that toxicity that not only threatened the preeminence of the race upon which the civilization of the world depended, but its survival as well.⁷⁷

Chamberlain anticipated that to awaken Germany to its task, to discover and foster the truth of a purified Christianity, would involve a protracted struggle of historic scope and significance. The advent of the First World War convinced him that his judgment had been correct.

With the first battles of the Great War, Chamberlain reaffirmed, with particular emphasis, his conviction that Germany bore the responsibility for "healing" humanity. He held that the other "civilized" nations, however racially Germanic they might be, were incapable of politically governing the rehabilitation of humankind because possessed of a clutch of convictions that were fundamentally wrong—errant notions that had inspired the French revolution of 1789.

Chamberlain insisted that the invocation of the political ideals, "liberty, equality, and fraternity," served only to intellectually mislead, and politically confound, members of organized society. "Liberty" could not mean doing as one chose. Instead, he reminded his audience that German philosophy taught one that "liberty" could only be a function of a well-ordered state; "equality" meant a common responsibility to perform one's duties; and "fraternity" alluded to an intuitive sense of common biology.

Chamberlain unpacked those convictions by arguing that it was not man who made the State; it was the State that fashioned man. In so doing, a sound State administers laws that reflect those of nature—with nature's laws understood to be the embodiment of God's will, and in humanity's best interest. Those who dutifully conformed themselves to nature's laws were both obeying the will of God and serving their own interests—thereby being profoundly religious, fully rational, commendably loyal, and truly free.⁷⁸

---

⁷⁵ Chamberlain, *Foundations*, vol. 1, p. 480.

⁷⁶ See Chamberlain's discussion of "nature" as educator in "Die Natur als Lehrmeisterin," in *Rasse und Persönlichkeit*, pp. 102–111. Discussions of the role and nature of Germanic science surface in a variety of places in *Foundations*, where he speaks of "nature" to whom we may "entrust ourselves . . . with great confidence"; see vol. 1, pp. 267–268; see the discussion of "new philosophy" and "new religion" in *Foundations*, vol. 2, pp. 411–429.

⁷⁷ See *Foundations*, vol. 1, p. 542. Germanic science, although inspired by nature, would have to be governed by "intuition" and "common sense." Science, as it was understood by nongermanics, was often mistaken in emphasis and far too artificial in drawing conclusions. See ibid., p. 268.

⁷⁸ "Germany has been selected to undertake the leadership of the healing of itself and other nations of the world. . . . It is not man who makes the State, rather it is the State that makes men. . . . Given that reality, nature provides that the individual instinctively subordinates his interests to

All of that was idealist in inspiration and Hegelian in substance—and characterized the thought of many "racial nationalists" of the period. Chamberlain insisted that the nation's leaders must understand their responsibilities in just such fashion. Together with an appreciation of the nature of the State, they must also possess a profound comprehension of nature's laws—some of which addressed the shared psychological properties of racial cohorts. The leaders of a racially homogeneous community rule because everyone is animated by the same consciousness and obeys the same natural laws of community, survival, and prevalence. What results is an harmonious hierarchy of responsibilities and duties—a system of effortless conformity on the part of citizens that represents a morality of the highest order.[79]

In effect, by the time of the First World War, Chamberlain articulated an entire, distinctive, political system. It clearly incorporated the convictions shared by Gobineau and Wagner—but was more nuanced, literary, and expansive. It was to be projected beyond the Great War, to influence many who, in turn, were to influence Germany, impact all of Europe, and ultimately, savage the world.

---

those of the State—for nature is God's will, made natural law.... Nature, in its entirety, is willed by God." See the entire discussion in Chamberlain, *Politische Ideale* (Munich: Bruckmann A.-G., 1916), pp. 24, 28, 30–42, 46, 48, 49.

[79] Ibid., pp. 71–77, 88–89.

CHAPTER EIGHT

National Socialism

Race as Religion

The concept of religion is everywhere the same, and because religion performs a necessary function in our consciousness, it will never perish.... There is no question that, today, a new religion will emerge out of those elements provided by natural science.
—Ludwig Woltmann[1]

A German volkish church is today the desire of millions.... The so called Old Testament must be rejected once and for all—to finally renounce the failed efforts of the last fifteen hundred years to render us all spiritually Jews.... The longing to provide the soul of the Nordic race expression in the form of a German church is the foremost task of our century.
—Alfred Rosenberg[2]

The end of the First World War found Germany traumatized by its losses in the field as well as the dissipation of its hopes for the future. It was not only the lunatic destructiveness of the war itself, but Germany's loss of stature among the advanced industrial nations, that left Germans devastated.

Millions of combat veterans returned from the front without prospects, and often without the respect they felt they had earned. The defeated nation was in turmoil, its leadership broken by the threat of revolution, its population impoverished and uncertain. What remained of government attempted to stanch the tide of defections and disarm rebellion. Combat veterans organized paramilitary militias to defend the nation against "Red revolution," and nationalists sought to give political expression to their dream of a soon to be resurrected fatherland. It was in that environment that Adolf Hitler decided to embark on the political enterprise that would bring him to power.

[1] Ludwig Woltmann, *System des moralischen Bewusstseins mit besonderer Darlegung des Verhältnisses der kritischen Philosophie zu Darwinismus und Socialismus* (Duesseldorf: Hermann Michels Verlag, 1898), pp. 78, 82.

[2] Alfred Rosenberg, *Der Mythus des 20. Jahrhunderts: Eine Wertung der seelisch-geistigen Gestaltenkämpfe unserer Zeit* (Munich: Hoheneichen Verlag, 1933), pp. 599, 603, 614–615.

In retrospect, it seems clear that Hitler's activities, initially, were not inspired by anything that might qualify as a coherent ideology. There is no doubt that he was a nationalist, an antisemite, and probably a racist, when he assumed the responsibilities of leadership in the National Socialist German Workers Party (*Nationalsozialistische Deutsche Arbeiterpartei*, NSDAP). However true that may have been, the evidence we have suggests that his political opinions lacked articulation—a systematic rationale.

Throughout his life, in the course of his public pronouncements, Hitler was ill disposed to cite either books or their authors to whom he might have been indebted. His private library, in significant measure, has been lost to history. In his writings and speeches, he mentions only Arthur Schopenhauer and Houston Stewart Chamberlain by name. He alluded to Friedrich Nietzsche and Karl Marx on occasion, but we have little on which to judge the extent of his familiarity with their work.

It is known that by the first years of the 1920s, Hitler was sufficiently familiar with the works of the racist theoretician Hans F. K. Günther to recommend at least two of them to new recruits of the NSDAP.[3] What is not clear is whether the volumes were the choice of Hitler, himself, or of someone else.

By that time, there were several in his entourage who might have suggested the books. There were expatriate Russians among them who brought considerable intellectual baggage in tow—some who were well informed racists and antisemites. Alfred Rosenberg was perhaps foremost among them.

At the very founding of the NSDAP, it was Rosenberg who served as ideological counsel to Hitler—and at the close of the Second World War, it was evident to those who reviewed the political history of the party that it was Rosenberg who served as "father of the ideology of the Third Reich."[4] It was a paternity that had a history.

Alfred Rosenberg (1893–1946)

Apparently, Alfred Rosenberg was not particularly well liked among party members. Whatever his personal relations in the party, ultimately Alfred Rosenberg was to be identified as "the chief theoretician of the NSDAP," and

---

[3] See the list: "Books that Every Nationalsocialist Must Know"—provided every member of the NSDAP by the party leadership, reproduced in Timothy W. Ryback, *Hitler's Private Library: The Books That Shaped His Life* (New York: Alfred A. Knopf, 2008), p. 57. Specifically listed were Hans F. K. Günther, *Ritter, Tod und Teufel: Der heldische Gedanke* (Munich: J. F. Lehmanns Verlag, 1920), and *Rassenkunde des deutschen Volkes* (Munich: J. F. Lehmanns Verlag, 1929; first edition, 1922).

[4] Serge Lang and Ernst von Schenck, in *Memoirs of Alfred Rosenberg* (New York: Ziff-Davis Publishing Company, 1949), p. 1.

"the father of National Socialistic letters."[5] It was he who crafted the ideology of National Socialism, and it was he who argued for its indefeasible truth. The history of the making of the ideology of National Socialism is of interest, and merits the telling.

By birth an Estonian, born in the Russia of the Romanovs, Rosenberg early succeeded in making himself prominent among the cohorts of the infant National Socialist Party. He was an important member in the years 1919 and 1920—and by the mid 1930s, he was one of the oldest, in terms of service, of the "old fighters (*alte Kämpfer*)" of the movement. He had served as editor of both the party newspaper (the *Völkischen Beobachter* [*The People's Observer*]), and its theoretical journal (the *Nationalsozialistischen Monatshefte* [*National Socialist Monthly*])—and in 1927, Hitler charged him with the leadership of the National Socialist Society for Culture and Learning, and its successor, the Combat League for German Culture.

There has never been any question that Rosenberg was one of the best prepared intellectuals among the founders of the party,[6] and whatever his reservations, Hitler confided to a colleague that Rosenberg "is the only man I always listen to. He is a thinker."[7]

Dietrich Eckart, popular playwright and publicist, early mentor to both Hitler and Rosenberg, while himself making very few pretensions to academic learning, was impressed by Rosenberg's intellectual credentials. Hitler, an autodidact, disdained academic inquiry—characterized, as it was, by complex subtleties, detachment, and qualification—as entirely unsuited to political exploitation. That notwithstanding, Rosenberg managed to earn Hitler's confidence. So explicit and emphatic were Rosenberg's political convictions that he immediately ingratiated himself—irrespective of Hitler's initial doubts concerning those who pretended to formal learning.

---

[5] Robert Cecil, *The Myth of the Master Race: Alfred Rosenberg and Nazi Ideology* (New York: Dodd Mead & Company, 1972), p. ix; and the commentary of Lang and von Schenck in *Memoirs of Alfred Rosenberg*, p. 2.

[6] Although Rosenberg attended a technical high school and undertook architectural studies in Moscow as a young man, German antiquities—art, history, theology, and anthropology—early captured his attention, and by the time of his migration to Germany, before his encounter with Hitler, he had already formulated the basic outlines of his major work. See the brief account in Cecil, *The Myth of the Master Race*, chap. 1; and Alfred Baeumler, *Alfred Rosenberg und "Der Mythus des 20. Jahrhunderts"* (Munich: Hoheneichen Verlag, 1943), chap. 1, part 2.

[7] Karl Luedecke, *I Knew Hitler* (London: Unwin, 1938), p. 82. Years after the end of the Second World War, Ernst Hanfstaengl, an early intimate of Hitler, reported that Hitler "was deeply under the spell of Rosenberg, . . . and Hitler seemed to have a very high opinion of his abilities as a philosopher and writer." Hanfstaengl, *Hitler—The Missing Years* (London: Eyre & Spottiswoode, 1957), p. 41.

When circumstances saw Hitler incarcerated in Landsberg prison in 1924, Rosenberg was assigned the responsibility of managing the party in his absence. Thereafter, Rosenberg remained a fixture in the party hierarchy as *Reichsleiter*, a "national leader"—to ultimately die in its service.

Throughout the years, whatever Hitler's practical qualms, Rosenberg remained National Socialism's principal theoretician. His *Der Mythus des 20. Jahrhunderts* (*The Myth of the Twentieth Century*), begun in 1917, was substantially complete by the early 1920s, before the appearance of Hitler's *Mein Kampf*. Rosenberg continued to modify the text, and the final revision did not appear in print until 1930. By 1942, there were almost two million copies of the *Mythus* in circulation. Never identified as an official party document (for reasons that shall be considered), the *Mythus* nonetheless remains the most fully articulate statement of National Socialist ideology.

While the most impressive of the accounts provided by a National Socialist intellectual, the substance of the *Mythus* had engaged Rosenberg even before he heard of Adolf Hitler or his political ideas. In fact, most, if not all, of the ideas that constitute the content of *Mythus* can be traced back to Rosenberg's earliest essays, written while still a student in Russia.

There, with revolution swirling about him, far from the German political scene, Rosenberg already had addressed all the major themes that were to define National Socialism. Still a student, he wrote of the "historic significance" of the "race issue." By 1917, at twenty-four, he spoke with authority about the intensity of the conflict between "Indogermanics" and "Semites"—to cast the first outlines of a work to be entitled *The Philosophy of Germanic [germanischen] Art*—intimations of the later *Mythus*.[8] A year later, he addressed a student audience in Reval on the "Jewish Question."

At the same time, his situation in Russia was becoming increasingly precarious, and soon he elected to leave for Germany—where he anticipated a more accommodating political environment. Once there, he expanded on his student lecture, making of it a long essay which he presented to Dietrich Eckart in Munich—to begin his fateful encounter with National Socialism.

Eckart was sufficiently impressed to invite Rosenberg to join him as a major staff member of the nationalist periodical *Auf Gut Deutsch* (*In Good German*). Moreover, on the strength of his initial impression, Eckart was prepared to introduce Rosenberg to Hitler—who by that time had begun to take on the

---

[8] Alfred Rosenberg, "Nirwana und Persönlichkeit," and "Erste Entwürfe zu der Scrift 'Philosophie der germanischen Kunst.'" in *Schriften aus den Jahren 1917–1921* (Munich: Hoheneichen Verlag, 1944), pp. 12–14, and 24–25. As has been suggested, among race theorists the term "Germanic (*germanisch*)" had a much broader reference than "*deutsch* (German)." Much of the discussion found in these early essays reappears in the *Mythus*.

features of a person of significance among nationalists.[9] It was Eckart who subsequently brought both Hitler and Rosenberg to Bayreuth, where they were introduced to the widow of Richard Wagner, in whose home her son-in-law, Houston Stewart Chamberlain, resided.

By that time, Chamberlain was physically disabled and confined to a wheelchair. Irrespective of his circumstances, he was so impressed by Hitler that he extended him his unqualified support. There seems to have been an immediate rapport between the older and the younger man.[10] As far as Rosenberg was concerned, the meeting with Chamberlain was perhaps of still greater moment. Chamberlain had been Rosenberg's inspiration from the moment when, at fifteen years of age, he first read the older man's *Foundations of the Nineteenth Century*.[11]

The entire critical sequence of events that would determine his future had begun with Rosenberg's arrival in Munich. He had chosen Munich, of all the cities of Germany, because of the availability there of a community of "White Russians"—Baltic Germans, royalists, antisemites, antimarxists, and generic nationalists—persons with whom Rosenberg felt an affinity. They had settled there after the Bolshevik revolution. As a community, sharing many of his ideas, they offered him substantial psychological and material support.

The expatriate Russian community in Germany had already made preliminary contacts with the individuals who were to put together National Socialism. They were to prove increasingly influential as the party grew in membership and political importance. It was they who brought a great deal of racist, and specifically antisemitic, materials with them from Russia. And it was they who were to inspire much of the incendiary antimarxist rhetoric of German nationalism.

More than simple ideologues, many of the expatriates brought with them management skills and funds that were to be of importance to National Socialism in its infancy. Many of the members of the expatriate Russian community were to serve National Socialism in a variety of significant fashions during its early years, and many were to persist in their connection with Rosenberg and the NSDAP until, and through, the Second World War.[12]

[9] See Rosenberg, *Dietrich Eckhart: Vermächtnis* (Munich: Franz Eher Verlag, 1935).

[10] See Rosenberg's comments on the relationship. Rosenberg, "Deutschlands Zukunft: die nationalsozialistische Bewegung," *Kampf um die Macht: Aufsätze von 1921–1932)* (Munich: Franz Eher Nachf., 1939), p. 614.

[11] F. T. Hart, *Alfred Rosenberg: Der Mann und sein Werk* (Munich: J. F. Lehmanns Verlag, 1937), p. 36. The texts that will be used in citations will be H. S. Chamberlain, *Die Grundlagen des neunzehnten Jahrhunderts* (Munich: F. Bruckmann K.-G., 1941), in 2 volumes; the English language translation that will be cited is H. S. Chamberlain, *Foundations of the Nineteenth Century* (New York: John Lange Company, 1911), in 2 volumes.

[12] See the entire discussion in Michael Kellogg, *The Russian Roots of Nazism: White Emigres and the Making of National Socialism, 1917–1945* (New York: Cambridge University Press, 2005).

Intimations of Doctrine

In about fourteen years of political agitation, National Socialism, as a doctrine and mass mobilizing party, grew from a small, marginal collection of alienated individuals into a political organization of about a million members. In 1933, Field Marshal von Hindenburg called upon Hitler to form a government, and Germany began its descent into catastrophe.

All of this was fueled by a variable set of convictions—first loosely framed during the early years of party history. In February 1920, the new party published a programmatic "Twenty-five Points" that were advanced as a general representation of its political intentions. Hitler had charged Gottfried Feder with the responsibility of the document's formulation.[13] Assigned the task of putting together an outline of the party's beliefs, the work that resulted was very much a summary of Feder's peculiar politicoeconomic beliefs and the entailments that he believed must necessarily follow. For all that, by the early 1930s, few of the recommended economic strategies incorporated in the "Twenty-five Points" enjoyed the confidence of the party's leadership. By the mid 1920s, it seems to have become evident to the leadership of the party that the movement required a full and persuasive rationale for an ideology in which Feder's nonstandard monetary policies would play, if anything, only a peripheral role.

Rosenberg was eminently well equipped to provide the requisite body of argued beliefs that might serve as a more comprehensive and fitting rationale. As early as the founding of the party, Rosenberg had been recognized as a gifted theoretician, armed with a set of convictions that found their origins in the work of Houston Stewart Chamberlain and Richard Wagner.[14] Sustaining his opinions were insights found in the epistemological and moral philosophy of Immanuel Kant and Arthur Schopenhauer—both of whom were recommended by Chamberlain.[15] Hitler, himself, had identified the thought of just those notables in his own ideological development.

---

[13] An English translation of Feder's programmatic work is available as Gottfried Feder, *Hitler's Official Programme and Its Fundamental Ideas* (New York: Howard Fertig, 1971). Hitler was originally so impressed by Feder's thesis on the "thraldom of interest," and its constraints on "productive capital," that he devoted several pages to its exposition in *Mein Kampf*, characterizing it as "one of the most essential premises for the foundation of a new party." Hitler, in Ralph Mannheim's English translation of *Mein Kampf* (Boston: Houghton Mifflin, 1943), p. 210; see pp. 209–214. A fairly comprehensive account of Feder's economic convictions is available in Feder, *Kampf gegen die Hochfinanz* (Munich: Frz. Eher Nachf., 1934).

[14] See Rosenberg's comments in "Houston Stewart Chamberlain," *Blut und Ehre: Ein Kampf für deutsche Wiedergeburt* (Munich: Frz. Eher Nachf., 1934), pp. 217–218.

[15] See the discussion in Baeumler, *Alfred Rosenberg und "Der Mythus des 20. Jahrhunderts"*, pp. 5–7; Rosenberg's publications from the years 1917–1919, in Rosenberg, *Schriften aus den Jahren*

Even before his meeting with Eckart and Hitler, Rosenberg had drafted the first essentials of an intricate and complex ideology. Its core was a theory of history that conceived human events the result of a direct or indirect conflict of races—each race driven by a unique and disparate set of dispositions.[16]

As early as 1919, at the very commencement of his ideological maturation, in a world suffering an increasing tempo of crises, pandemic unemployment, alienation on a mass scale, and political unrest, Rosenberg foresaw a rising demand for spiritual succor. Religion, he argued, satisfied a catalog of essential human needs. It afforded answers to questions concerning the very meaning of existence.[17] It bound a community together, particularly in times of stress. More than that, Rosenberg spoke of religion as critical to each individual's fulfillment of self. Before he entered the circle out of which National Socialism was to emerge, Rosenberg had already argued that religion was indispensable to the formation of individual and collective personality—because religion, itself, was a manifestation of the spiritual essence of each racial confraternity.[18]

As early as 1918, he was to argue that religion uniquely represented the "soul" of a race. He spoke confidently of a Nordic race soul (*Rassenseele*)—and of souls appropriately identified with corresponding races. It was in that context that he early occupied himself with the religious sentiment of Jews. He spoke of the perennial enmity they harbored toward nonjews.[19] He was convinced

---

1917–1921, part one, pp. 1–124; and Rosenberg, "Houston Stewart Chamberlain," *Blut und Ehre*, pp. 217–218. We know that the young Hitler had been enormously impressed with the artistry and thought of Wagner. See the account in August Kubizek, *The Young Hitler I Knew* (New York: Tower Publications, 1954). Hitler speaks of having read Schopenhauer at some time during the Great War. The occasion of his familiarity with the writings of Chamberlain is more difficult to establish.

[16] As early as 1917, Rosenberg spoke of the particular characteristics of the races and peoples of Europe—and identified "loyalty," "freedom," and "duty" as the values that animated Germans. At the same time, he made invidious comparisons between "Indogermans" and "Semites." Among Semites, the Jews were identified as singularly and distinctively "materialistic." They were seen dominated by convictions of their own superiority and their right to dominate the world. Wagner had said as much, and acknowledged that "one could no more mix Jews and Aryans than one could mix fire and water." See "Einzelne Gedanken," "Nirwana und Persönlichkeit," "Gedanken über die Persönlichkeit," and "Eine ernste Frage," in *Schriften aus den Jahren 1917–1921*, pp. 6–7, 12–13, 15–16, and 78–79. In full maturity, Rosenberg identified those theses as at the very heart of National Socialism. See Rosenberg, *Das Wesensgefüge des Nationalsozialismus* (Munich: Eher Verlag, 1934), pp. 12–13.

[17] Rosenberg, "Über Arbeit," *Schriften aus den Jahren 1917–1921*, pp. 23–24.

[18] Rosenberg, "Gedanken zur Kunst," "Über Persönlichkeit," and "Die Spur des Juden im Wandel der Zeiten," ibid., pp. 70, 116–124, 166–168. See Rosenberg's allusion to the role of religion as an essential of a people's culture in "Eine ernste Frage," ibid., p. 76.

[19] One of Rosenberg's early discussions concerning Judaism, originally published in 1920, has been translated into English as Rosenberg, *Immorality in the Talmud* (Lincoln, NE: RJG Enterprises, Inc., 2007).

that their confidence in themselves as God's chosen rendered them intolerant of others. They forever would remain separate from their hosts in mixed society—a persistent threat to the integrity of communal life. Jews, Rosenberg was to argue, rendered impossible the organic unity of community—and, as such, imperiled its very survival.

In 1917, at twenty-five, and little more than a graduate student, Rosenberg spoke of the Jews, as a group, as being uniformly "materialistic," as being irretrievably selfish and irremediably opposed to those who were not Jewish, inflamed by an intrinsic disposition to conceive themselves as privileged by God, destined to rule lesser, i.e., nonjewish humankind.[20] Before his commitment to political struggle, Rosenberg already saw the Jews, individually and collectively, as inimical to the fostering of creative community life. With Wagner, the young Rosenberg held that in order for Jews to subsist among Gentiles, without being a threat to the community, they would have to cease being Jews.[21] These, and similar judgments, were to remain constant elements in his belief system throughout his subsequent service to Hitler's Reich.

As early as the first years of the 1920s, Rosenberg was convinced that history played itself out in religious modalities. By the nineteenth century, he went on to argue, the surface features, but not the nature of the conflict, had changed.

Traditional religion had been mortally wounded. Established religion was found less and less credible. According to Rosenberg, the Enlightenment, the quaint scientific monism that grew out of its radical empiricism, the "scientism" of the "higher criticism" that was one of its consequences, had together created the occasion for the abandonment of conventional religion. At the same time there arose the opportunity to regenerate the primordial, pristine faith of the Nordic race—the proper counter to the Jewish threat.[22] Rosenberg anticipated that the historic conflict of souls had entered into epochal crisis.

To effectively face the challenge, Nordics would have to understand that traditional Christianity, at its origins, had been corrupted by Jews to suit their ends. As it began to fail as an instrument, modern Jewry devised a secular surrogate to serve the same purpose. Jews made recourse to Bolshevism, as an alternative, in order to continue to dominate nonjews. By the time he had

[20] Whatever his intellectual debt to Chamberlain, Rosenberg could not allow his judgments concerning Jews as a community to be influenced. As opposed to Chamberlain, Rosenberg could hardly allow Sephardic Jews being spoken of as "noble," or as enjoying "purity of race." See the discussion of Jews and purity of race in Chamberlain, *Foundations*, vol. 1, pp. 253–255, 271–273.

[21] Rosenberg, "Gedanken über die Persönlichkeit," "Staat, Sozialismus und Persönlickkeit," and "Eine ernste Frage," *Schriften aus den Jahren 1917–1921*, pp. 15–16, pp. 77–79.

[22] See the discussion of Günther, *Ritter, Tod, und Teufel*, pp. 151–161, in which the author celebrates the recognition of the "eternal law of the race" in the Germanic religions of antiquity. We know that Rosenberg read *Ritter, Tod, und Teufel*, during the time he was writing *Mythus*.

reached first maturity, Rosenberg had already assembled the essentials of that belief system that he, in time, would identify as the "essence" of National Socialism.[23]

In one of the first expositions of what he understood to be National Socialism, Rosenberg simply reiterated all those themes that had found expression in his first essays. In fact and in effect, it will be argued that it was Rosenberg who first gave full voice to what was to become the worldview of Adolf Hitler.[24]

Religion in the *Mythus*

While Hitler was still serving in defense of the fatherland as a combat soldier on the Western front, Rosenberg was already knitting together the system of beliefs that would carry National Socialism to victory in Germany. By 1917, Rosenberg had already begun the work that would finally emerge as *Der Mythus des 20. Jahrhunderts*.

Throughout the *Mythus* one can find traces of Rosenberg's earliest thoughts—and the recurrence of themes first found in his student essays. By the mid 1920s, those thoughts achieved a fullness of expression that made them integral parts of his *Mythus*—the argued defense of the ideology of National Socialism. Rosenberg made those thoughts the essentials of National Socialist doctrine—identifying the racial issue as its critical center. He carefully enumerated the catalog of subsidiary themes that were collateral to, or derivative of, the race issue. What resulted was the best available exposition of what National Socialists held to be true—as well as the policies Rosenberg expected those truths to sponsor.

As for the content of the *Mythus* itself, there has never been much doubt concerning its primary intention. It sought to provide the rationale for the revival of an "old, new Germanic religion"—a religion pledged to the regeneration of the Nordic race and its dominion over lesser breeds.[25] The *Mythus* made

---

[23] See his summary accounts in Rosenberg, "Einführung zum Programm der N.S.D.A.P." (1922), *Blut und Ehre*, pp. 105–113; and *Das Wesensgefüge des Nationalsozialismus*, particularly the section entitled *Rassenphilosophie und Staatsaufbau*, pp. 11–18. As early as 1920, he made the case for Jewish enmity against nonjews, manifest in their corruption of religion and their employment of Bolshevism. See *Der Spur des Juden im Wandel der Zeiten*, in *Schriften und Reden auf den Jahren 1917–1921*, vol. 1, pp. 125–323.

[24] See Rosenberg, "Einführung zum Programm der N.S.D.A.P.," *Blut und Ehre*, pp. 105–113; originally published in 1922.

[25] Rosenberg speaks of every social form, every state, being the product of a "dominant race" (*Mythus*, p. 529), and Nordics the sole culture creators, his advocacy of Nordic dominance follows. The theme of Nordic culture creation and "type formation" surfaces throughout the text. To cite an illustrative instance, see Rosenberg, *Mythus*, pp. 55–56. Rosenberg's view of the historic role of Nordics is the same as that he attributes to the Jews.

an undisguised appeal to the Wagnerian "dream eternal" of Indoaryans.[26] It was a reiteration of the principal themes of Chamberlain's *Foundations of the Nineteenth Century*.

For Rosenberg, the final resolution of the religious controversies that had tormented Europe for fifteen hundred years was imminent. It would result in the final victory of "Germanism" over the "Romish church."

Since the thirteenth and fourteenth centuries, according to both Rosenberg and Chamberlain, the Germanic racial soul had struggled to liberate itself from the encumbrances of a slave religion and its attendant superstitions. From his earliest days as a secondary school student, Rosenberg was convinced that traditional Christianity was the warped expression of the "bastardized soul" of raceless people.[27]

As a result of such reasoning, Rosenberg was convinced that the history of Europe, since the decline of Rome, represented a titanic struggle between races—Nordics as opposed to the raceless residue of declining Rome. Behind the scenes, the Jews intervened to ensure their own ends. Only in the eighteenth and nineteenth centuries did German philosophy muster the capacity to strike at the vitals of "Judaized Christianity." And only in that final phase did the opportunity arise for the full emergence of a truly Germanic creed.

Rosenberg (like Chamberlain before him) argued that the thought of Immanuel Kant advanced the occasion for a settlement of the millennial conflict between Aryan beliefs and that corrupted faith, born in the "chaos of races," that defiled the final days of the Roman Empire. In his judgment, it was Kant who made clear the fundamental differences between the natural world, the world of science, of perception, of phenomena, and the inner world of noumena, the unknown, the "thing in itself." Rosenberg read this to mean that the phenomenal world was the stuff of science—while the noumenal provided the ingredients of religion—the "essence" of "soul." Rosenberg's reading of Kant's work conceived it providing space for a "noumenal race soul"—the essence of his new religion.[28]

Clear from everything he wrote, religion was, for Rosenberg, a, if not the,

---

[26] Rosenberg used the terms "Indoaryan," "Indogermanic," "Aryan," "Germanic," and "Nordic" as substitution instances of each other because convinced that all shared a common "race soul." While the more discriminating racists tendered distinctions, Rosenberg seems to have felt that all the terms shared a common referent—thus he speaks of the Nordic race, under whatever sobriquet, possessed of a consistent "race soul" for "thousands of years," and of "Germanic character value" as "eternal, according to which everything else has to adjust itself." Ibid., pp. 567, 636.

[27] See the discussion ibid., pp. 74–76, 235–236, 457–458, 480, 604–605.

[28] See ibid., bk. 1, chap. 3, sect. 4, and pp. 131, 223–224; for a critical discussion of Kant and the implications of his epistemology, see ibid., bk. 1, chap. l, sect. 6. Rosenberg's interpretation, to say the least, was idiosyncratic.

defining expression of "racial soul." Art gave idiom to the race soul; philosophy advanced a defense of its "becoming"; and politics afforded it overt protection, preservation, and propagation. Religion gave it form and unity.[29] It was the life force, the myth, of race.

Rosenberg argued that clear intimations of all that were to be found in the earliest belief systems of the primordial Aryans. It was to be perceived in the "sun myth" of the first Germanics—a myth that united the universal laws of nature, biology, and spirit—a religion in which humankind's reason and will were brought into harmony with "the spirit of the race."[30]

Rosenberg anticipated that the task of the twentieth century was the invocation of a "new Christianity," a "new Germanic faith." By the time the *Mythus* achieved final form, the envisioned new religion was spoken of as a "union of religious and public politics" in the form of a new and more relevant myth.[31] Its establishment would be "the goal of the racially influenced cultural ideal of our time."[32]

In the same place, Rosenberg went on to speak of the evocative symbols of the looming myth. He affirmed that "once, it was the crucifix that drew thousands to itself.... Now, a new symbol has appeared.... The indisputable symbol of today's organic Germanic truth is the black swastika."[33] National Socialism, with its "old, new symbol," would animate that regenerative "new German national church" already foreseen by Wagner and subsequently fostered by Chamberlain.

Rosenberg expected different elements to collect themselves around the central myth, providing inspiration to those then awakening to racial consciousness. The new church would be animated by the ancient values of the durable past. It would be a church for a new epoch in which world history would have to be rewritten, identifying race as its primary determinant. For the first time it would become clear that the failure of Christianity had been written in its origins in the racial chaos of the ancient world. Designed to recruit the "der-

---

[29] See the discussion ibid., bk. 3, chap. 4, sect. 3, particularly p. 575. Rosenberg regularly speaks of the myth of the Roman Catholic Church, and the myth of Judaism. See, for example, ibid., p. 466.

[30] See the entire discussion ibid., bk. 2, "The Essence of Germanic Art"; bk. 3, "The Coming Reich"; and pp. 133–144.

[31] Rosenberg never provided a lexical, dictionary definition of the term "myth." Otto Gros, *850 Worte "Mythus des XX. Jahrhunderts": Erläuterungen zu Begriffen und Problemen* (Munich: Hoheneichen Verlag, 1938), p. 57, suggests "belief in the divine together with heroic sagas; more applicable, the spiritual [*seelische*], moral, and ideological inner coherence of a race or a people." In such cases of ambiguity, readers are driven to defining terms *contextually*, in the course of an exposition. See A. James Gregor, *Metascience and Politics: An Inquiry into the Conceptual Language of Political Science* (London: Transaction Publishers, 2003), pp. 136–137.

[32] Rosenberg, *Mythus*, pp. 21–23.

[33] Ibid., pp. 458, 688, 689.

acinated debris" of late Rome, traditional Christianity had no function in the modern world.

These were the grounds of Rosenberg's conviction that the new German national church would share little with traditional Christianity. The new church would emerge out of the stirrings of an increasingly urgent racial awareness. It was an awareness that demanded doctrine and practices in which one would find "mirrored the eternal, primal spiritual powers of Nordic humanity, as much alive today as five thousand years ago."

The new church would be expected to reconstitute that mystic union that first appeared in allegory and symbol as the religion of Germanic antiquity—in the old Aryan religions of the Vedas, the Eddas, the Avesta, and that hoary creed of Odin. It would be the Indoaryan faith of heroes. The new, emergent system of beliefs, like that of the primeval Indogermans, would constitute the foundation of a church composed of those prepared to die for the preservation and perpetuation of their specific humanity.[34] Its eschaton would be a community of destiny in which Nordic humanity might live in an environment infused with its own eternal values.

Rosenberg insisted that within the new church, the imposing figure of Christ would remain prominent—but it would be of a Christ transfigured. The new church would feature an "Aryan Christ"—a Christ that, in historic and anthropological fact, was in all probability not Jewish—and conceivably Nordic.[35]

Rosenberg argued that Christianity, as it first took shape as a consequence of the machinations of Paul—the Jewish Pharisee—contained little, if anything, of the original message of Jesus. Rosenberg argued that in Paul's hands, Christianity became a religion of slaves, a promise of succorance to the ill conceived and misbegotten—a teaching of submission and humility. All of that, Rosenberg argued, allowed Paul to mobilize racial Alpines and Hitherasiatics to his Christianity, in order to ensure Jewish dominance, both direct and indirect, in the disintegrating ancient world.[36]

Rosenberg anticipated a new church, opposed to the Roman Catholicism of raceless people who had been called to the service of Jews and Hitherasiatics. It would be a church suffused with visions of a "real Christ," "blond and

[34] Ibid., pp. 21–23, 678–679.

[35] Ibid., p. 76, n., and pp. 616–617.

[36] Ibid., pp. 36, 71, 74–75; see pp. 47–48, 50, 60. Rosenberg tended to employ the practice found, in Günther's work, of referring to Jews as a mixture of "Hitherasiatics" and "Orientals" (among others)—not as a "race," but as a "nation, volk, or group of noneuropean origin." See Günther, *Rassenkunde des deutschen Volkes*, pp. 110–111; and *Racial Elements of European History* (London: Methuen & Co., 1924), pp. 74–75. For a later, more exhaustive treatment, see Günther, *Rassenkunde des jüdischen Volkes* (Munich: J. F. Lehmann's Verlag, 1931).

slender," who came not to bring peace, but a sword. For Rosenberg, the real Christ, the inspiration for the new church, was a Christ surrounded by armed angels, and armed saints, together with a heavenly host prepared to do battle against an eternal enemy. Such a Christ would not be the "dark, wounded, and tormented figure hanging broken on a cross"—the product of "Romish Syrian" fabrication. It would be the illuminated, resurrected Christ—straight and tall in beauty and strength—as bearer of light in a darkling world. It would be an Aryan Christ who would speak to the awakened consciousness of the emerging epoch with the "primordial wisdom" of the race.[37] The new magisterium of the German national church would not only be sacramental, but political, and legal as well. It would speak in the language of shared myth—in terms that would unite practical reason, sure instinct, and inflexible will.[38]

The core of the new church doctrine would be a "blood myth," predicated on an interpretation of history that made specific communities of human beings—forever distinguished by clearly discernible physical traits, and united in a single racial "soul"—its principal actors.[39] Composed of just such communities[40]—each racial fraternity, informed by a specific racial soul, and its corre-

[37] Rosenberg, *Mythus*, pp. 412–414, 571–572, 601–608. One of the changes made in Rosenberg's *Mythus* between its first and final editions involved reducing the emphasis on the racial provenience of Christ, but whatever the reduction in emphasis, he continued to suggest that Jesus was of "Aryan" ancestry—following the arguments of Chamberlain and Günther. In the last edition of his work, Rosenberg speaks of the Amorites, of prechristian times, as providing strong Nordic racial infusions into Galilee, the birthplace of Jesus. Ibid., p. 27. In all of this, Rosenberg follows Chamberlain, *Foundations*, vol. 1, pp. 202–213. At the time that Rosenberg was preparing the *Mythus*, Günther, like Chamberlain, spoke of Christ as the probable result of a mix of Nordic, Mediterranean, and Near Eastern racial elements. See Günther, *Rasse und Stil: Gedanken über ihre Beziehungen im Leben und in der Geistesgeschichte der europäischen Völker, insbesondere des deutschen Volkes* (Munich: J. F. Lehmanns Verlag, 1927), pp. 112–113. Both Chamberlain and Günther mention the intrusion of "Nordic" Amorites, during the prechristian period, into the regions that saw the birth of Christ. Both argued that they were the source of both Nordic physical and psychological traits to be observed among an otherwise "dark" population. See Günther, *Racial Elements of European History*, pp. 128–129. There is credible evidence that Chamberlain first heard the contention of an Aryan Christ from Wagnerians. Wagner seems to have been convinced that the Christ of his anticipated Germanic redemption was not Jewish. Whatever the case, it was clear that Rosenberg, as well as many others during the same period, was prepared to argue the merits of the case for an "Aryan Christ." See, for example, Richard Noll, *The Aryan Christ: The Secret Life of Carl Jung* (New York: Random House, 1997), particularly pp. 144–146.

[38] Rosenberg, *Mythus*, pp. 114–117, 139. Rosenberg regularly spoke of a politicoreligious myth in some such fashion. His notion of "myth" shared some affinities with that of Plato. See Günther, *Platon als Hüter des Lebens* (Munich: J. F. Lehmann's Verlag, 1928).

[39] See the discussion in Günther, *Rassenkunde des deutschen Volkes*, pp. 276–289; and *Racial Elements of European History*, chap. 7.

[40] The list varied, but was fairly consistent in the race literature of the period commencing with the turn of the twentieth century—although the nomenclature did vary over time. The Western

sponding myth, would engage in a relentless struggle for survival and dominance. "Soul," for Rosenberg, was the spiritual analog of "race" as an empirical phenomenon. He understood "every race as having its soul, and every soul, its race."[41] Much of Rosenberg's analysis turned on that conviction.[42] For Rosenberg, all allusions to Nordic rectitude—to "freedom," "loyalty," "duty," "honor," and individual responsibility—take on meaning only in the context in which physiological race is understood the empirical manifestation of a race specific soul.[43] Each soul expressed itself uniquely in religion, art, politics, and history. At its best, and in consenting circumstances, each race found voice in distinctive cultural expression—in and through which members found consummation. For Rosenberg, his discussion of racial "souls" supplied the empirical and moral components of National Socialism as ideology.[44]

In his racial interpretation of history, Rosenberg hypothesized that there once existed a primordial home—variously spoken of as "Thule" or "Atlantis"—from which Nordics migrated to create those historic cultures that left us monumental traces in the Far East, the fertile crescent, Egypt, Crete, Hellenic Greece, and classic Rome.[45] For Rosenberg, the process was eminently simple: the migration of

---

race, for example, was sometimes to become the Mediterranean, and the Eastern became the Alpine. Günther objected to the use of the terms "Aryan" and "Semitic" as unscientific, indicating that they had no sure reference. He instead recommended "Nordic," for that collection of individuals who were largely depigmented, with blond hair and blue eyes, of fair complexion, tall and slender of stature—who tended to be identified as Aryans. See Günther, *Rassenkunde des deutschen Volkes*, pp. 318–319, n. l, and *Racial Elements of European History*, p. 257, n. l. The races identified by Rosenberg in his work were adopted, essentially, from Günther's texts. Although he did employ the terms "Aryan" and "Indoaryan," proscribed by Günther, Rosenberg most consistently spoke of his privileged race as "Nordic."

[41] See the discussion in Rosenberg, *Mythus*, pp. 23, 116.

[42] Chamberlain had consistently argued that races, in some fundamental sense, were malleable—that races were formed and re-formed in historic time. He remained uncertain if there ever was an "Aryan" race, and if there was, its properties were not constant. Chamberlain addressed himself to the entire question of race formation—and argued that races were formed through mixture, isolation, and selection, a process that could take place in decades. He felt comfortable, for example, speaking of the formation of a "Prussian race"—a product of the recent past. Günther dismissed such suggestions. While he did speak of "new races" being formed by the processes identified by Chamberlain, he insisted that they would involve millennia. Rosenberg rejected all such qualifications.

[43] Rosenberg, like Chamberlain, found evidence for the existence of such racial souls in history. Historic evidence, of course, is invariably discursive, selective, and fragmentary. Most historians are not in the least persuaded that by reviewing the history of peoples, one might convincingly identify certain traits with certain peoples—"creativity" to name only one.

[44] Rosenberg appears much more emphatic than either Gobineau or Chamberlain in the ascription of specific traits to each respective race soul. Clearly discernible racial "spiritual" traits appear most insistently in the work of Günther.

[45] See the summary account in Rosenberg, *Mythus*, bk. 1, chaps. 1–2, particularly pp. 22–34.

Germanics, Aryans, or Nordics, however one wishes to identify them, resulted in the creation of culture. Nordics were history's culture creators—without whom the world would know little of high culture or produce the necessary conditions for the true realization of individual and collective self-fulfillment.

For Rosenberg, all this was palpably true. History, he insisted, allowed little latitude for any other interpretation. Together with his racial interpretation of history, there were discussions of collateral and subsidiary issues. One such issue was important to the individual moral training that characterized National Socialism. It was an issue that was addressed in the schools, in the youth corps, and in the training of the military.

Rosenberg and Morality

National Socialism was emphatically anti-individualistic in disposition.[46] Its emphases were communitarian, collectivistic—and it was that emphasis that generated one of the most critical philosophical questions that occupied its defenders.

If, as Chamberlain, Günther, and Rosenberg were to insist, an irrepressible thirst for liberty typified the Nordic, if self-fulfillment were the goal, and freedom of choice essential to a meaningful Germanic life, then it would seem counterintuitive that the party would show partiality to the community at the expense of the individual. The fact was that the social philosophy of National Socialism clearly favored the community in any contest with individualism.[47] Deploring the "anarchistic" preferences of liberalism, National Socialist ideologues, in general, recognized that their social philosophy ran counter the prevailing libertarian permissiveness of the Western world. They rehearsed the attendant difficulties—which they identified as among the most fundamental of contemporary philosophical and moral controversies.

Otto Dietrich, Director of National Socialist Germany's Press Bureau, reported that the enemies of Hitler were given to asking "how personal freedom might be made compatible with the obligations of the individual towards the community" under National Socialism—or how the "individual personality might develop in such an environment?"—given the communitarian biases of the party.[48] To which he responded that an individual might be free, dutiful, sacrificial, and

[46] See ibid., pp. 504–505.

[47] In the "Twenty-five Points" of the official program of National Socialism, the preference is expressed as "the common interest before self-interest," and the "individualist theory of society" is spoken of as "corrupting." Feder, "The 25 Points," in *Hitler's Official Programme*, pp. 44.

[48] Otto Dietrich was Director of the Government Press Bureau during the National Socialist Period. An English translation is available of his "A Revolution in Thought" (Arabi, Louisiana: Sons of Liberty Press, 1997), see pp. 10–11.

loyal without conflict in National Socialist Germany—because, in doing so, the individual was acting in his or her most fundamental interests.

It was maintained that in Hitler's Germany, an individual could be free in his choice to follow a leader, be dutiful in his performance, sacrificial in fact, and loyal in deportment, because all those behaviors were consonant with his "inner essence." They were variable expressions of the single soul he shared with the community. In choosing his leader, the Nordic individual chose to follow him because he saw in him his own "true essence." A common "soul" spoke to, and through, the "Leader." In being dutiful, sacrificial, and loyal, the individual was being dutiful, sacrificial, and loyal to his most fundamental interests.

Like Rosenberg, National Socialist intellectuals dismissed, as a transparent fiction, the notion that individuals might be persons of substance independent of their community.[49] For Rosenberg, and National Socialism, the individual was but a single facet of a collective race soul—each facet sharing in the essential properties of the whole. Individuals followed a political leader, not simply because of an electoral decision, but because they recognize in their obedience a common response to shared sentiment. No less a competent than Carl Schmitt had argued that the "true governance" of a community could only rest on some form of underlying "homogeneity"—in which a people, individually and collectively, might see itself reflected in a leader. Sharing an "essence" with the governed, the policies of such a leader could only be the policies of the community.

Later, Schmitt was to argue that the shared homogeneity that allowed for effective and coherent governance, resided in race—in effect, a people and its leader shared a common *Rassenseele*.[50] Loyalty and obedience simply would follow. One would choose a leader because that leader reflected one's "essence." Dutifulness, sacrifice, and loyalty would be dutifulness, sacrifice, and loyalty to one's truest self. Individuals, each making his or her own choice, would give free expression to Nordic virtues—autonomy, loyalty, dutifulness, and honor, in their truest sense—while, to external observers, community interests would appear to overwhelm and subordinate those of the individual.

---

[49] "The individualistic doctrine which conceived the individual as possessed of substance independent of his community has shown itself nonviable." Rosenberg, *Mythus*, p. 695. "Only in the service of the whole community, only as a useful and active member within the framework of the national community, does the individual awake to the higher life." Feder, "The Basic Ideas," *Hitler's Official Programme*, p. 54.

[50] See Carl Schmitt, *Verfassungslehre* (Munich: Duncker & Humblot Verlag, 1928), part 3, particularly pp. 234–238; and *Staat, Bewegung, Volk*, the second edition of which appeared in 1934, translated in *Principii politici del nazionalsocialismo* (Florence: G. C. Sansoni, 1935), parts 1 and 2, particularly pp. 224–231.

The notion of "souls" that were race specific—is the very essence of racism. Without the confidence that the physical appearance of persons was a predictor of their behavior, there could be no racism.[51] Gobineau's work was predicated on that conviction, and Chamberlain's account of European history would make no sense without it—nor would the "anthropological history of civilization" of Günther or Rosenberg.

By the time Günther published his *Rassenkunde*, so influential in the work of Rosenberg, and in the thought of the first National Socialists, the connection between physiology and psychology ("spirit") was held to have been well established. In his major texts, Günther devoted a specific expository chapter to each of the several races of humankind. He spoke with confidence of the observable and heritable behavioral traits of the various race souls. The spiritual traits of Nordics included all those advanced by Gobineau and Chamberlain. An almost compulsive desire for freedom, a sense of personal honor, a disposition to loyally discharge one's duties, inventiveness, a thirst for adventure, and a longing for unconfined space, were only some of the familiar characterological traits ascribed to Nordics by Günther, and accepted by Rosenberg.

These were the constituent beliefs that allowed Rosenberg to construct a notion of history alive with moral imperatives—capable of serving as a collectivistic doctrine for a truly revolutionary political movement. They were beliefs from which a catalog of entailments might easily be drawn.

Entire races, as well as the individuals of which they are composed, were seen responsible for world history—for its glories as well as its infamies. Nordics, and everyone who individually shares the features of the race, are responsible for the high culture of humankind—its philosophy, science, and art. It is they, through effort and achievement, who provide the environment for the fullness of life—for its meaningfulness, its virtue, and its productivity. As such, Nordics must fiercely protect their hereditary gifts from dilution. They must obey nature's "inflexible laws" and eschew miscegenation—a biological mingling of races that could only result in the diminution or loss of creativity.

Rosenberg maintained that there are others, Asiatics and Mediterraneans, perhaps, who have proven capable of sustaining high culture—at least for some given time—but whatever their merits, at best they are, and could only be, subordinates, not mates, of dominant Nordics. Some Eastern and Southeastern Eu-

---

[51] "If human races were unequal only in appearance and heritable physical features, observable racial differences would hardly engage one's interests.... That specific spiritual traits [*seelische Züge*] more frequently than not are associated with certain physical features has become a commonplace... the correlation between spiritual and physical traits well established." Günther, *Rassenkunde des deutschen Volkes*, p. 175.

ropean races were conceived possessed of marginal creativity, and might provide collateral support to Nordic creative talents. On the other hand, other races constituted direct threats to the integrity and the cultural future of humanity.

For the *Mythus*, Jews comprise an "antirace"[52]—and, as such, constitute a direct threat to the creation and maintenance of high culture. For Rosenberg, the Jews, as a biological community, instinctively antigermanic, animated by materialism and group selfishness, devoid of artistic sense, empathy, and community spirit, were enemies of life itself. In the last analysis, more than a threat to high culture, Rosenberg understood Jews to be a chronic threat to the very survival of humanity. It was they who introduced the flawed form of Christianity into Europe that thwarted its cultural development. It was they who undermined the humane and moral productive system of Germanics to introduce that form of capitalism that compromised its very integrity.[53] And finally, it was they who conspired to destroy European civilization by gathering together the racial inferiors of the continent to do the bidding of criminal Bolshevism.[54] Rosenberg, from his very youth, conceived Jews the mortal enemies of humankind.[55]

[52] The Jews as a community are frequently, if not consistently, spoken of as a "race" in National Socialist literature. Chamberlain spoke of a "pure Jewish race." Woltmann spoke of the Jews as an "alien race (*andersartigen Rasse*)." Ludwig Woltmann, *Politische Anthropologie: Eine Untersuchung über den Einfluss der Descendenztheorie auf die Lehre von der politischen Entwicklung der Völker* (Leipzig: Justus Doerner Verlag, 1936), p. 308. Günther, on the other hand, denies that Jews, as a group, meet the requirements that would qualify them as a "race." Günther, *Rassenkunde des jüdischen Volkes*, Introduction and chaps. 8 and 9.

[53] The conviction that the Jews had somehow corrupted Christianity at its birth was prevalent in the nineteenth century. Karl Marx subscribed to such a thought. In 1843, he wrote: "From the outset, the Christian was the theorising Jew, the Jew is therefore the practical Christian, and the practical Christian has become a Jew again. Christianity has only in semblance overcome real Judaism." Marx, "On the Jewish Question," *Collected Works* (New York: International Publishers, 1975), vol. 3, p. 173. Moreover, the notion that the Jews, in some sense, were responsible for at least some of the most objectionable features of the capitalist form of production was a notion not only entertained by Marx, but was fairly common among Germans throughout the nineteenth century. For his part, Marx described the modern economic world by insisting that "the god of the Jews has become secularised and has become the god of the world." See ibid., p. 172. As distinguished a scholar as Werner Sombart advanced something of the same thesis. Sombart writes, "The outer structure of the economic life of our day has been built up largely by Jewish hands. But the principles underlying economic life—that which may be termed the modern economic spirit, or the economic point of view—may also be traced to a Jewish origin." Werner Sombart, *The Jews and Modern Capitalism* (London: T. Fisher Unwin, 1913), p. 115.

[54] This thesis became the leitmotif of National Socialist propaganda. It was a theme that characterized Rosenberg's work since his time as a student. As early as 1918, Rosenberg had given full expression to the claim. See, for example, Rosenberg, "Staat, Sozialismus und Persönlichkeit," "Eine ernste Frage," *Schriften aus den Jahren 1917–1921*, pp. 73–79. These were claims that were common fare among White Russian emigres from the Bolshevik revolution.

[55] See, for example, Rosenberg, *Europa und sein Todfeind* (Munich: Frz. Eher Nachf., 1938).

Rosenberg had argued these theses before there was a National Socialism—and before Hitler had given final form to that doctrine that was to provide ideological content to his movement. As a student refugee from the revolution in Russia, Rosenberg had carried his beliefs in hand as a reasonably well articulated system—to gift them to those with whom he was destined to serve. All the elements of the general argument articulated in the *Mythus*, the theoretical vindication of National Socialism, are found in those early essays.

Like all ideologies, the belief system of the *Mythus* is composed of empirical claims and moral sentiments—all held together by an informal logic.[56] Like all ideologies, there is a hierarchy of values that gives ultimate structure to inherent moral sentiments. At the base of such structures one finds *primary* values that provide integrity to the entire system.

"Fulfillment of self" serves Rosenberg as such a primary, unproblematic value. It is *self-affirming*. It makes little sense to ask why one would want to fulfill oneself. To remain unfulfilled could hardly serve as a recommendation. Rosenberg's argument urges that to be fulfilled, to be free, honorable, dutiful, and loyal is to be true to one's essential Nordicity—one's racial soul, and one's fundamental humanity. For Rosenberg, that was to serve as the cardinal imperative of National Socialism.

Rosenberg's entire argument turns on the conviction that each person is fulfilled only by satisfying the demands of his intrinsic "racial soul." A Nordic is fulfilled by responding to the call of race—by satisfying the enjoinments of "blood." Following Günther, among others, Rosenberg argued that since every race has an integral, irreducible, and "primeval," character—a syndrome of behavioral traits that serve as its definition—every individual is fulfilled only in so far as his or her behavior conforms to just such a disposition to behave. Thus, a Nordic can be fulfilled only by pursuing the tasks of culture creation, to discharge duty with honor, sacrifice, autonomy, and courage. That can be achieved only in a community built upon, and protective of, just those Nordic values. As long as his race dominates the community, and its "soul" defines public morality, the Nordic is fulfilled as a person and provides others an environment conducive to self-realization.[57]

In other circumstances, when an unstructured heterogeneity of races disallows Nordic preeminence, not only is the potential for creativity radically reduced, but the moral sentiments of the community are confounded, and no

[56] See the general discussion in A. James Gregor, *The Ideology of Fascism: The Rationale of Totalitarianism* (New York: The Free Press, 1969), chap. 1.

[57] Rosenberg speaks of the intrinsic "longing for personhood" being satisfied by conforming to one's "racial type." *Mythus*, p. 529.

one prospers. Any community, not homogeneous, composed of "dissimilar (*artfremdig*)" races, is one in which individuals have reduced opportunity of fulfillment. The divergent dispositions of the members of such a community destroy its integral unity, its "organicity." Those who are denizens of communities composed of such disparate racial elements have significantly reduced opportunity to achieve fulfillment. One finds no set of coherent, mutually supportive values among them. Without Nordic dominance, such communities are devoid of a sustaining sociality. In such circumstances, individuals are left without guidance and structure—with scant potential for self-fulfillment.[58]

Convinced that only Nordics were "culture creators," Rosenberg was equally convinced that self-fulfillment for anyone could only be achieved under their superintendence. Other races, for a time, might continue a culture created by Nordics (as occurred in India and Egypt after the passing of Nordic "purity")—but history has demonstrated that without Nordics the prospects of continuity and development would radically diminish, with entire cultures suffering ultimate decay and extinction. Fulfillment would be unattainable for anyone.

Given the intrinsic value of self-fulfillment, the creation and furtherance of enabling culture becomes, itself, an unproblematic value—with those responsible for its creation and furtherance possessing singular value. Thus, of all possible social arrangements, Rosenberg recommends either an exclusively Nordic community, or alternatively, a community dominated by Nordics and supported by subordinates. In such instances, culture can be created, sustained, and fostered—to the ultimate benefit of all. The sacrifices demanded of other races in such circumstances would be justified, according to Rosenberg, by any rational and moral cost benefit analysis.

For their furtherance and maintenance, such Nordic, or Nordic dominated, communities required land—for only a community possessed of sufficient agricultural space can sustain a growing and active population. More than that, Rosenberg insisted that experience had established that Nordics can survive and prosper only in fundamentally rural environs; urban life threatens their survival.

In urban centers, birth rates decline, health is impaired, and morals are subverted. If Nordics are to attain selfhood as well as provide the opportunity for

[58] Part of Rosenberg's argument is that other, nonnordic, races are often possessed of "demonic," "telluric," and "chthonic" dispositions, producing not only a disintegration of "true" religion, but morally degenerate communities. There is measureable social and psychological deterioration correlative to the attenuation of Nordic social dominance. See ibid., pp. 35–43. The evidences of "racial bastardy," according to Rosenberg is manifest in a prevailing lack of clear goals, in individual and collective self-doubt, and in sexual depravity. Ibid., pp. 70–71. Rosenberg held that all that precluded the possibility of self-fulfillment on the part of individuals.

others to achieve fulfillment, they must first secure their own appropriate "living space (*Lebensraum*)."[59] A secure, resident agrarian base is an essential for the continuity of Nordic life. Rosenberg was to argue that the acquisition of sufficient space for some form of traditional agriculture was an instrumental necessity for the continuance and enhancement of Nordic—and by implication—world culture. These were central arguments of National Socialism—the rationale behind its foreign policy—and the inspiration for the new Germanic religion.

Adolf Hitler's *Mein Kampf*

There is persuasive evidence that, at the very founding of the political movement that brought Adolf Hitler to power, the ideas of Alfred Rosenberg contributed, in substantial measure, to the system of beliefs that provided the entire enterprise its rationale. It is as a consequence of that relationship that history has made Rosenberg complicit in those "crimes against humanity" attributed to National Socialism.

At the very foundation of National Socialism as a political movement, the ideas of Alfred Rosenberg served as rationale. As far as Hitler, himself, was concerned, he came to National Socialism already possessed of an unsystematic tissue of ideas—born of broad, if undisciplined, study.[60] Aware of that, some of the most knowledgeable of his biographers have also argued that his political convictions were anything but finalized before 1923.[61] What that suggests for the purposes of the present account, is that the articulation of Hitler's ideas profited from Rosenberg's direct intervention during the first years of their relationship. Rosenberg had arrived in Munich in 1919 already committed to a reasonably well framed set of convictions, that once incorporated in *Der Mythus*, resulted in a work that Hitler judged to be a "most tremendous achievement ... even greater than Chamberlain's" *Foundations of the Nineteenth Century*.[62]

There is conflicting evidence concerning Hitler's claim that he had already, in 1913, put together the "philosophy" and the "political views" that he thereaf-

---

[59] Ibid., bk. 3, chap. 3, sect. 3, particularly pp. 531–534.

[60] There is ample evidence of Hitler's bibliographic interests. Specialists have attested to that fact, and August Kubizek, friend of his youth, reports that Hitler "read prodigiously." See Ryback, *Hitler's Private Library*; and Kubicek, *The Young Hitler I Knew*, p. 168; cf. chap. 16. There is also suggestive evidence that his reading, however ample and enthusiastic, was not systematic.

[61] See the discussion in H. R. Trevor Roper's introductory essay, "The Mind of Adolf Hitler," in *Hitler's Secret Conversations 1941–1944* (New York: Signet Books, 1961), pp. xxv–xxvii; cf. Ryback, *Hitler's Private Library*, particularly pp. 114–117.

[62] As reported by Otto Strasser. There is every reason to believe that Strasser's account was accurate. See Norman H. Baynes, ed., *The Speeches of Adolf Hitler: April 1922–August 1939* (London: Oxford University Press,1942), vol. 2, pp. 988–989.

ter never had occasion to change. There is little question that he was, by that time, an antisemite and a nationalist—but that he had formulated a coherent "philosophy" seems, at best, implausible.[63] An argument can be made that apart from the unadorned antisemitism and nationalism—which Hitler had brought with him to Munich—the remaining content of *Mein Kampf* is a stenographic, bowdlerized version of that later to be found in Rosenberg's *Mythus*.[64] It is a version characterized by a different pattern of emphases, and a formulation that was unsophisticated, simple, and direct—but which, nonetheless, gave expression to all the elements of Rosenberg's account.

Much of the difference between the two narratives arises out of Hitler's insistence that a work whose primary intent is propagandistic, should be apodictic and uncomplicated—a catechism of a disciplined and unchanging faith.[65] Rosenberg's *Mythus* was hardly that.

Rosenberg sought to advance what he considered to be an academic case for the belief system of National Socialism. That required at least an effort to satisfy the truth requirements of complex cognitive claims. For Hitler, such subtleties could only diminish an argument's political usefulness. Hitler was dismissive of those efforts he took to be unduly "intellectualistic." He held that "academic" studies should be reserved for academic environments—where meeting practical demands was not an issue. For a revolutionary movement, such ventures, at best, were distractions. "All propaganda," Hitler insisted, "must be popular and its intellectual level must be adjusted to the most limited intelligence among those to whom it is addressed." He insisted that its message be simple, "with limited scientific ballast," and restricted to "very few points" which were to be repeated regularly without qualification.[66]

For at least those reasons, Hitler consistently held that Rosenberg's *Mythus* served poorly as a tool of propaganda. In his judgment, it was too opaque to appeal to a general audience, and too "abstract" to inspire unqualified confidence. As a consequence, he held that few would undertake to read the work in its entirety. He, himself, had only given it a "cursory reading"—and expected little more from his immediate entourage.[67]

---

[63] See the comments by Cecil, *The Myth of the Master Race*, p. 30.

[64] We are told that, during the early years of the movement, Hitler "was deeply under the spell of Rosenberg, who was far more the Party theoretician than the mere press agent.... Hitler seemed to have a very high opinion of his abilities as a philosopher." Hanfstaengl, *Hitler—The Missing Years*, p. 41.

[65] In this context, one should read Hitler's comments on the nature of propaganda and its relationship to the organization of a revolutionary movement. See Hitler, *Mein Kampf*, vol. 2, chap. 11.

[66] Ibid., p. 197; see vol. 1, chap. 6 in its entirety.

[67] See Hitler's comments in *Hitler's Secret Conversations*, sect. 190, 11 April 1942, p. 400; Henry Picker, ed., *Hitlers Tischgespräche* (Bonn: Athenaeum Verlag, 1951), sect. 132, 11 April 1942, p. 275; and

That does not speak to the arguments the work contained, which Hitler had received through discussions with Rosenberg at a time when the ideology of the movement, for the first time, was being crafted. Rosenberg's arguments unmistakably appear in *Mein Kampf*, in however abbreviated form. In general, those arguments turn on the role of race in history. More important than that evident reality, is the fact that the necessary philosophical and moral substratum presupposed by *Mein Kampf* is found, and defended, in *Der Mythus*.

At the time Hitler presented *Mein Kampf* to the public, he candidly admitted that it was not written for "strangers, but to those adherents of the movement who belong to it with their hearts."[68] It was neither intended to convince skeptics nor proselytize among opponents; it was calculated to reinforce the already established faith of the committed.

Hitler was not concerned with advancing convincing arguments. His delivery was unpretentious, expressed in the form of uncomplicated arguments that turned on notions about Darwinian competitive struggles and the survival of the fittest.[69] They were simple arguments expected to reinforce simple convictions already fully embraced.[70]

Rosenberg chose other responsibilities.[71] He intended his book to accomplish much more. He wished to advance a defensible *academic* argument for National Socialism as a belief system.[72] Thus, as has been suggested, while it is manifestly evident that for Rosenberg, *race* was the value that holds together his entire rendering, race, in and of itself, could not serve as a *primary* value in any

---

the comments of Max Domarus, *Hitler: Reden 1932 bis 1945* (Munich: Süddeutscher Verlag, 1965, four volumes.), vol. 1, p. 892, n. 353.

[68] Hitler, *Mein Kampf*, Preface.

[69] I have elsewhere attempted to summarize Hitler's arguments in *Mein Kampf*. See A. James Gregor, *Contemporary Radical Ideologies: Totalitarian Thought in the Twentieth Century* (New York: Random House, 1968), chap. 5.

[70] The core of Hitler's arguments in *Mein Kampf* is Darwinian. Neither Rosenberg nor Chamberlain was a strict Darwinist. The possible source of Hitler's Darwinist convictions was in the funded publications of Ludwig Woltmann, with which he was familiar, particularly Woltmann's *Die Darwinsche Theorie und der Sozialismus: Ein Beitrag zur Naturgeschichte der menschlichen Gesellschaft* (Düsseldorf: Hermann Michels Verlag, 1899), and *Politische Anthropologie*, originally published in 1903.

[71] That Rosenberg sought to discharge responsibilities other than to reinforce the faith of party members is probably the reason that the *Mythus* was never presented as an *official* publication of the party. It raised issues that Hitler was convinced should not be engaged.

[72] This is not the place to pursue an academic critique of an academic attempt. There is an abundance of literature that attempts just that. See, for example, Albert R. Chandler, *Rosenberg's Nazi Myth* (Ithaca, N.Y.: Cornell University Press, 1945). There is an abundance of critical literature in German. See, for example, Walter Künneth, *Antwort auf den Mythus: Die Entseheidung zwischen dem nordischen Mythus und dem biblischen Christus* (Berlin: Wichern Verlag, 1936). The critical literature concerning racism, in general, is very abundant. The concern here is with other issues.

coherent philosophical or moral argument. It is hard to imagine that anyone, even in the difficult circumstances that prevailed in the postwar Germany of the late 1920s, might assign *intrinsic* value to *race*. At best, *race* could only be of *contingent* value—in service to values that are considered in and of themselves of unproblematic, intrinsic worth.

As has been argued, Rosenberg's text makes reasonably clear that while race is his core value, his political and moral philosophy conceives *personality* of primary and intrinsic value. The same can be said of *Mein Kampf*, but only with supplementary argument. Without any of the intricacies of Rosenberg's argument, Hitler maintains that "true" selfhood can only emerge out of a racially coherent community. Without that coherence, individuals cannot mature intellectually, culturally, and morally. Communities that are "bastardized" impair the fullest development of self.

For Hitler only Nordics could supply the "truly human culture" necessary to the fullest development of self. Even in the physical sacrifice of self, the individual in such a culture enjoys, consciously or unconsciously, an existence infused with the "deepest knowledge," that gives a "deeper meaning" to it all. Without that profound wisdom, human beings "fall from heaven" into a base caricature of existence.[73] Rosenberg sought to make these pronouncements credible by advancing arguments in their support in the *Mythus*.

For Hitler, as for Rosenberg, "inner happiness" for human beings is possible only in a community in which the maintenance of "racial purity" is espoused as a moral responsibility. The difference lies in the fact that Rosenberg attempts to frame an argument in its support while Hitler simply insists that the imperative is ordained of "providence," and failure to obey could only result in inescapable "divine retribution."[74]

For Hitler, the fullness of self is a function of living a life shaped by one's invariant racial endowments. Whatever its fragmentary qualities, Hitler's argument rests on a notion of the unchanging character of "racial soul." It was understood to be a determinant influence on the character of the individual. Like Rosenberg, Hitler found the "scientific" support for those notions in the work of Hans Günther. Both turned to Günther for the support required for claims that were framed as though empirical.[75] Whatever in fact they were, the complex claims about the transtemporal character of racial souls and their relationship to the integrity of individual personality had overwhelming moral

[73] Hitler, *Mein Kampf*, pp. 298–300. This discussion parallels that found in Rosenberg's work in chap. 2 of the first book of *Mythus*, pp. 34–54.

[74] Hitler, *Mein Kampf*, pp. 327, 329.

[75] As we have seen, Rosenberg cites Günther at critical stages in his argument. We know from inspection of his private library that Hitler carefully studied Günther's arguments in order to support his own claims. See Ryback, *Hitler's Private Library*, pp. 110–111.

implication—and supply the emphatic affect one finds in both the *Mythus* and *Mein Kampf*—for both works have an unmistakable religious character. In the case of Rosenberg's work, its religiosity is explicit. With *Mein Kampf*, its religious features are unconfessed, but easily discerned.⁷⁶

When Hitler speaks of the "philosophy of life" that animates a political movement, he argues that in order to achieve success, such a general world view must be transformed into a catalog of dogmatic principles with which members are to be systematically inculcated. In the course of his exposition, Hitler does not hesitate to call upon "the Almighty," "Providence," and an "eternal will" as providing him guidance. He argues that while instruction is supplied by "science"—which discovers and codifies "nature's laws"—it is nature, itself, who "wills" them. He speaks of "nature" as "willing" life's rules—and any violation of its will renders one subject to a "deserved chastisement of eternal retribution."⁷⁷ For Hitler, nature displays all the traits of a jealous and vindictive divinity.

All of this is spoken of in the context of a "community of faith and struggle"—an association of believers infused with "apodictic" convictions that were taken to be "eternally true and ideal"—in service to a race that was the embodiment of a "higher ethics" representing an "eternal will" that governs the universe.⁷⁸ All of which constitutes an unmistakable rendering of what Rosenberg held to be the emergent "new religion of the blood" that, by its very intensity, would occupy all the energies of the twentieth century.

Both Hitler and Rosenberg spoke unequivocally of the advent of a *political religion*. The difference between their accounts turned on Rosenberg's clear acknowledgment that he was speaking of a new religion that rejected much of the substance of traditional Christian creeds. He spoke of a new Germanic national church—a posture that immediately made his *Mythus* the object of attack from both Roman Catholic and Protestant establishments. Rosenberg's proposed new church was immediately judged a competitive threat by traditional confessions. It was seen as a challenge emanating from the state—supported by the "arms of revolutionary masses."

Hitler sought to deflect all of that. He insisted on a hard distinction between religious and political associations—in the effort to allay Christian concerns. Hitler insisted on the distinction between church and state, and religion and revolution, in order not to divert political energy needed for achieving the im-

---

[76] The following account traffics on Hitler's discussion in *Mein Kampf*, pp. 377–385; in the German text, pp. 415–423.

[77] Ibid., pp. 284–289. In the "Table Talks," Hitler speaks of the "laws of nature" emanating from God, and of training persons to accept the notion that there is an identification of "Providence" with those same laws. He recommended obedience to the laws of nature on pain of "revolting against heaven." *Hitler's Secret Conversations*, pp. 140–141, 157.

[78] *Hitler's Secret Conversations*, pp. 380–383.

mediate goals of National Socialism.⁷⁹ It was at least for that reason that he did not allow Rosenberg's *Mythus* to appear as an official party publication.

Of course, Hitler never intended to respect the distinction between church and state as soon as he was free to act on his own convictions. He anticipated a general suppression of organized Christianity once he had defeated his foreign foes. With the end of the war, he planned to "solve the religious problem" in a fashion more radical than anticipated by either Chamberlain or Rosenberg. By making the state "the absolute master" of the issue, Hitler would solve the "religious problem" by eliminating religious leaders and suppressing all the features he found objectionable.⁸⁰

Hitler distinguished his convictions from those of Rosenberg on yet another ground. It appears that he had persuaded himself that *science*, per se, was the foundation of his system—although he allowed himself to characterize National Socialism as an alloy of both science and faith.⁸¹

On occasion, Hitler argued that he objected to Rosenberg because Rosenberg, unlike himself, seemed prepared to oppose science with *myth*. In fact, Rosenberg held a view that was much more complicated.

Rosenberg insisted that the Nordic worldview was "scientific." But if that were the case, its science clearly was a science with a difference. Science, for Rosenberg, was an undertaking that was anything but "objective" and "presuppositionless." He did not believe there could be any science that was either objective or innocent of presuppositions. He held such a conception of science to be little more than a fiction.

Given his views about the determinant character of race, Rosenberg was convinced that each race inevitably fashioned its own community-specific science. "Truth," for Rosenberg, was the organic union of racially conditioned, systematically collected regularities, and a synthesizing, directive, and autonomous will.⁸²

---

⁷⁹ See the discussion ibid., pp. 118–119.

⁸⁰ Like Rosenberg, and Chamberlain before him, Hitler spoke of an "Aryan Christ" and of the corrupt influence of the Jews on early Christianity, but unlike either, he did not anticipate a reformed national Christian church. He advocated the exclusion of Christianity from German political life. He explicitly objected to Chamberlain's Christian affinities. He anticipated that the dominance of priests, with their "humbug," would force Europe back into the dark ages. Whatever objections he may have entertained about Himmler's SS, Hitler seems to have considered it (at least episodically) a viable alternative to the traditional church. See the entire discussion in *Hitler's Secret Conversations*, sects. 148, 152, 163, 180, and 75, 17 February 1942, 19–20 February 1942, 27 February 1942, 4 April 1942, and 13 December 1941, pp. 304–305, 310, 329–330, 374–375, and 158–160.

⁸¹ Ibid., sect. 190, 11 April 1942, p. 400.

⁸² Rosenberg, *Mythus*, pp. 628, 682–683. In our own time, "post modern" epistemologists have argued a similar case for "Black science," "gender science," and "Native American science," all composed of community-specific truths. See Gregor, "Postscript" to *Metascience and Politics*, pp. 383–390.

What emerges from such a notion is instructive. As a matter of fact, it is almost always the case that the science marshaled to the service of political religion shares the pivotal properties of the science of Rosenberg's "myth." The fateful implication is that the science that inhabits a modern ideology is characteristically a science fashioned of irrefutable truths—against which standard science can make no appeal.

National Socialism

National Socialism's brief tenure demonstrated to the world the power of political religion. It was one of its most singular, and fateful, forms. Its costs, in human and material losses, have not yet been fully tabulated. Millions were consumed in its propagation and defense—and millions more scattered in its passage.

Everything that was to transpire was dutifully heralded in Hitler's *Mein Kampf*—and Alfred Rosenberg provided the rationale for the entire program. Like Marxism, National Socialism was born out of the religious debates of the nineteenth century. Unlike Marxists, Leninists, and Stalinists, the leaders of National Socialism were always aware of what they sought—the proper control of those religious sentiments that inspired obedience and sacrifice on the part of masses.

One can trace the full measure of understanding in the work of Wagner and Chamberlain—together with the collateral contributions of a host of social biologists and theorists. Ludwig Feuerbach had made theology anthropology, and Darwinists, like Ludwig Woltmann, made human beings, anthropological subjects, divine.

It was Ludwig Woltmann who, at the turn of the twentieth century, foresaw the coming of political religions.[83] They would be inspired by the natural and social sciences of a time of intellectual and confessional confusion. They were to be belief systems intensely moral, and rigorously disciplinarian, in which the state would undertake to make citizens piously conformist, socially responsible, and self-sacrificial. They would be religions that were indefatigably combative, serving "Truth," and given to forcibly converting or decimating the evil, ineducable, or irretrievable. Woltmann was never to know how correct his augury was to be.

---

[83] See the discussions in Ludwig Woltmann, *System des moralischen Bewusstseins*, chap. 6, *Politische Anthropologie*, chap. 10, and *Die Darwinsche Theorie und der Sozialismus*, sect. 7, chaps. 3–5.

CHAPTER NINE

Consolidation and Decay

> The sacralization of politics became an essential aspect of all the communist regimes that arose during the Cold War and copied the Soviet model.... All communist regimes established a compulsory system of beliefs, myths, rituals, and symbols that exalted the primacy of the party as the sole and unchallenged depository of power. They all dogmatized their ideology as an absolute and unquestionable truth. They all glorified the socialist homeland and imposed a code of commandments that affected every aspect of existence. They all safeguarded their monopoly of power and truth through a police state and hard line ideological orthodoxy backed by constant surveillance and persecution, which enormously increased the number of human lives sacrificed.
> —Emilio Gentile[1]

The 1930s saw the major powers moving relentlessly toward war. By the turn of the decade all the industrialized nations were involved in armed conflict. By its end, National Socialist Germany and Fascist Italy had been consumed, Europe, Japan, and much of continental China laid waste, and millions upon millions of lives sacrificed. Of those millions, millions had fallen in combat, and still more millions died at the hands of their own governments. They had died not because caught in the crossfire of international military operations, but had perished because of their real or fancied class membership, because of their "false consciousness," or because of their imagined racial origins.

The war saw the extinction of Fascism and National Socialism; but that signaled neither the disappearance of, nor a diminution of, the role to be played by secular religions in the lives of humankind. The conclusion of war initiated a new period in the history of secular religions. Whatever the forms assumed by members of the class thereafter, the most dramatic were those that identified themselves as Marxist in general, and Marxist-Leninist in particular. In Eastern and Southeastern Europe, the rulers of East Germany, Czechoslovakia, Hungary, Bulgaria, Yugoslavia, and Albania all characterized their systems as

---

[1] Emilio Gentile, *Politics as Religion* (Princeton: Princeton University Press, 2006), p. 112.

Marxist-Leninist. In Asia, in staggered succession, North Korea, Communist China, North Vietnam, and Laos took on the same attributes. The systems became increasingly standardized.

In Africa, Ethiopia, and Angola revolutionary leaders argued an ideological affinity. In Latin America, Fidel Castro announced that Cuba had become Marxist-Leninist in the very shadow of the United States. All shared identifiable features.

Immediately after the end of the war, a period of consolidation in Central and Southeastern Europe produced a constellation of states all tracing their origins to the nineteenth century intellectual labors of Karl Marx and Friedrich Engels. Sharing a common origin, they pretended to a common doctrine. That common doctrine took on the properties of a common faith, and the common faith fostered the commonalities of a church, with its hierarchical order of responsibilities, insistent orthodoxy, demonstrative piety, and eschatological certainties. Almost a third of the earth's population was inspired to revolution by a political religion that was the product of nineteenth century Europe in transition. Millions were gathered into the "proletarian dictatorships," to serve unsure purpose, at exorbitant cost.

Consolidation

In the Soviet Union, and throughout its satellite states, Marxism-Leninism was institutionalized, with V. I. Lenin its iconic founder, Josef Stalin its consecrated leader,[2] the unitary party its sanctified order of the virtuous, the texts of Marx and Engels its hallowed scripture, advanced manufacturing its foundation for a "workers' paradise," and the "creed of the builders of communism" its formulary—all surrounded about by ritual, incantation, and mass demonstration. Within that context, enhanced by his "victory over fascism," Stalin was not only the *Vozhd*, the "leader," "teacher," the "banner," and the "will" of the Soviet Union, but became "the hope of humankind" as well.[3]

Already the arbiter of truth in the interwar years,[4] after the Second World War, Stalin loomed ever larger over every aspect of life in the Soviet Union. Restoring the controls rendered lax by the effort to inspire the population to

---

[2] Stalin frequently made allusions to the New Testament in characterizing his "disciples." On one occasion in 1933, he explained to Mikhail Sholokhov that he had no choice in the matter. "The people need a god." Simon Sebag Monefiore, *Stalin: The Court of the Red Tsar* (New York: Vintage, 2005), p. 139 and n.

[3] For a documented account of this period, see ibid., parts 9 and 10.

[4] Josef Stalin, *Problems of Leninism* (Moscow: Foreign Languages Press, 1952) became the standard of orthodoxy in the Soviet Union. By the end of the Second World War, the volume had run through eleven editions.

the defense of the motherland in "The Great Patriotic War," the system became once again rigidly hierarchical. By the end of the 1940s, throughout the Soviet empire, power emanated exclusively from the top, and ritual obedience became a citizen requirement. The goal of the system was the creation of redeemed human beings—steadfast in loyalty, rigorous in commitment, faithful in execution, modest in demands, and sacrificial in service—denizens of a "new world" of Soviet industrial power and international responsibility.

Communist systems installed in Eastern and Central Europe after the end of the Second World War bore all, or substantially all, those features. Each with its own local variation, after the obligatory interval of "coalition" governments, they all shared hierocratic, credal, and liturgical properties with the Soviet model.

All the satellite nations indulged in a common faith that embodied itself in a "Leader" charged with defending and fostering orthodoxy. Maintaining the faith produced elaborate domestic security arrangements that involved secret police and intricate networks of citizen surveillance. Fostering the faith generated a system of supervision for education, publication, the transfer of information, and civilian communication. Attendant upon those efforts, a series of political trials decimated any whose heterodoxy might fuel dissent. In East Germany,[5] Poland, Czechoslovakia, Hungary, Bulgaria, and Romania, all opposition was foreclosed, employing suppression of varying degrees of severity. Supplemented by the expulsion of entire ethnic communities, Eastern and Southeastern Europe were "cleansed" of any real or fancied anticommunist opposition.[6]

What proved true in those regions under direct Soviet superintendence, was to be true in nations voluntarily associated with Moscow. In the Far East, the

[5] After the opening of the archives in Eastern and Southeastern Europe, the literature devoted to the political history of the single states associated with the "Soviet bloc" has become very large. One of the better works on the German Democratic Republic is that of Peter Sperlich, *Oppression and Scarcity: The History and Institutional Structure of the Marxist-Leninist Government of East Germany and Some Perspectives on Life in a Socialist System* (Westport, Conn.: Praeger, 2006), particularly chaps. 3 and 4.

[6] There is an entire library of books devoted to the history of demicide and suppression in the Soviet Union and its satellites. For the purposes of discussion, consult Stephane Courtois, Nicolas Werth, Jean-Louis Panne, Andrzej Paczkowski, Karel Bartosek, and Jean-Louis Margolin, *The Black Book of Communism: Crimes, Terror, Repression* (Cambridge, Mass.: Harvard University Press, 1999); Paul Hollander, ed., *From the Gulag to the Killing Fields: Personal Accounts of Political Violence and Repression in Communist States* (Wilmington, Del.: ISI Books, 2006); and Irving Louis Horowitz, *Taking Lives: Genocide and State Power* (New Brunswick, N.J.: Transaction Publishers, 1997). For an empirically based account of Soviet totalitarianism, see Michael Geyer and Sheila Fitzpatrick (eds.), *Beyond Totalitarianism: Stalinism and Nazism Compared* (New York: Cambridge University Press, 2009).

advent of Mao Zedong to power inaugurated a system sharing many of those overt traits with which we are here concerned. After 1949, a China in revolution was swept up in a recurrent phenomenon of religious frenzy, usually initiated by signals from superiors, but arising and sustained by spontaneous mass participation. For a quarter century, the intensity of the "collective effervescence," that characteristically accompanies secular religions, varied with time and place, but never disappeared. Mao became the "living sun," the "Greatest Genius" of all time, charged with the responsibility of keeping his Marxist-Leninist revolution "true"—to defeat the "ghosts" and "monsters" who forever seemed to threaten the promise of salvation.

To fulfill the salvific responsibilities of Marxist-Leninist revolution, Mao sought to swiftly industrialize agrarian China with uncertain plans and a peasant population. Obedience, dedication, and self-sacrifice became those essential martial virtues to be practiced by all. Ritual and chant attended the marshalling of energy. The "Thought of Mao Zedong" was harnessed to ensure miraculous success—and public confession conceived a certain path to personal redemption.[7]

In North Korea, an unlikely "greatest philosopher ever born in this world," Kim Il Sung, became the "Great Leader" of the Democratic People's Republic of Korea—prepared to lead his people, together with those of other "underdeveloped countries," to prepare "a path for their salvation." The Great Leader was acknowledged as "savior, a Messiah, a liberator of mankind who [had] been born in the world with a historic mission of showing [humanity] the path to a perfect happy life." Like Mao Zedong, Kim Il Sung, in the judgment of his followers, exemplified "the perfection of a saint, the wisdom of a great philosopher, the bravery and heroism of a great military leader, the administrative ability of the highest order, and above all, humanity."[8]

All of that was simply a hyperbolic rendering of similar formulations found in literally all the Marxist-Leninist polities that emerged in Europe, Asia, Latin America, and Africa after the termination of the Second World War—whether as satellites of the Soviet Union or as relatively independent entities. All the features of sacralization are found in the political liturgies of communist dictatorships in Ceausescu's Romania, Enver Hoxha's Albania, or that of Mengistu Haile Mariam's Socialist Republic of Ethiopia. Cuba's "Lider Maximo" shares sufficient traits with the "Never Setting Red Sun" of the People's Republic of

---

[7] For a more extended discussion, see A. James Gregor, *Marxism, China, and Development: Reflections on Theory and Reality* (New Brunswick, N.J.: Transaction Publishers, 1995), chaps. 3 and 4.

[8] See T. B. Mukherjee, *The Social, Economic, and Political Ideas of the Great President Kim Il Sung* (Pyongyang: Foreign Languages Publishing House, 1983), pp. 5, 291.

China, the "Great Leader" of the People's Democratic Republic of Korea, and the "Conducator" of Romania, to identify him as a member of a common subspecies of political actors. The differences among members are differences to be expected among a subspecies evolving under diverse circumstances and in different environments.

By the time all those political systems emerged in the farthest reaches of Asia and Africa, their common rationale had been significantly transformed.[9] Where traditional Marxism had predicted revolution in the advanced industrial nations—with the "assurance of a mathematical formula"[10]—Marxism-Leninism orchestrated revolution in the industrially least developed regions of the globe. Where the Marxism of Marx and Engels anticipated revolution undertaken by populations the "vast majorities" of which would be sophisticated, urban "proletarians," the revolutionaries of the twentieth century gathered illiterate peasants, in rural settings, to the cause.

Marxists, at the turn of the twentieth century, had all been convinced that the true liberation of humanity could only be achieved in advanced economies of scale. Industrialization was the necessary precondition of Marxist liberation. Only confident industrialization could ensure the success of social revolution by creating a society reduced to but two classes: a minuscule and increasingly vulnerable bourgeoisie opposed by a robust proletariat that constituted the numerical majority. Only advanced industrialization could create such circumstances, together with the material abundance that the envisioned liberation would require. Only a sophisticated and broad based economy would ensure both the productive capabilities for, and the availability of a politically mature and administratively competent population to staff, the forecast "socialist commonwealth."

Before the Great War, such convictions constituted the core of what was understood to be traditional Marxism. Proposed revolutionary tactics may have varied, but what was considered the necessary and sufficient conditions for the redemption of humankind was clear. Some imagined the revolutionary transformation attended by bloodshed; others expected the transition to be made through peaceful parliamentary means. Very few, if any, anticipated the pos-

---

[9] What follows is a summary of material I have treated at greater length in A. James Gregor, *A Survey of Marxism: Problems in Philosophy and the Theory of History* (New York: Random House, 1965), chaps. 5, 6, *Italian Fascism and Developmental Dictatorship* (Princeton: Princeton University Press, 1979), chap. 1, *A Place in the Sun: Marxism and Fascism in China's Long Revolution* (Boulder, Colo.: Westview Press, 2000), chap. 1, and *Marxism, Fascism, and Totalitarianism: Chapters in the Intellectual History of Radicalism* (Stanford: Stanford University Press, 2009), chaps. 5 and 10.

[10] Friedrich Engels, *The Condition of the Working Class in England in 1844* (London: George Allen & Unwin Ltd., 1950), pp. 296–297.

sibility of a measure of revolutionary violence that would consume millions and require the instauration of an enduring dictatorship. None conceived of a postrevolutionary government that would rule through regimentation and/or terror. All of that was to change with the appearance of V. I. Lenin.

The end of the First World War brought with it the rise of political systems animated by those secular religions with which the present discussion has occupied itself. In the empire of the tsars, a peculiar form of Marxism made its appearance—as revolutionary Bolshevism. It was almost immediately recognized as singular. Heir to all the normative qualities of traditional Marxism, it was provided a different content by its own version of the "dialectic of history."

Almost immediately upon Lenin's accession to power, what that meant became evident. Lenin intended to construct and sustain an inspired, ideocratic system—ruled by those in possession of indubitable truths and unfailing moral convictions. With Lenin's passing, Stalin was to become the system's unerring spokesman. Armed with its certainties, Stalin became master of the Soviet Union and ultimate arbiter of ideological orthodoxy.

By that time it was eminently clear that the entire structure of control depended on compulsory compliance defined in ideological terms. As a consequence, when the Soviet Union came to foster the construction of companion regimes after the conclusion of the Second World War, ideological issues were critical. Changes in doctrinal interpretation menaced the stability of established arrangements. Throughout the history of all these systems, ideological dissidents were conceived threats to tenure.[11] As Marxist-Leninist communism spread to Asia, Africa, and Latin America, doctrinal issues became increasingly portentous.

Where ideology, for Marx and Engels, was supposed derivative of the economic base of society, for Stalinists and poststalinists, ideology became an irreplaceable instrument of social control and policy vindication. Among the less sophisticated, a disarming candor typified treatment of the issue. Kim Il Sung affirmed, with absolute confidence, that "all human activity is determined by ideology." In fact, it was argued that rather than politics reflecting existing economic substructure, revolutionary ideology can engage the commitment of unschooled masses irrespective of "objective conditions." What is required is not the "maturation of objective conditions," but the inculcation of a suitable

[11] See Raymond Taras, ed., *The Road to Disillusion: From Critical Marxism to Postcommunism in Eastern Europe* (Armonk, N.Y.: M. E. Shape, Inc., 1992), where "critical Marxist thinking" is recognized as a guarded attempt to reform the Stalinist systems from within. The established incumbents were fully aware of the implications.

"ideological consciousness" among rural unsophisticates. "Ideological consciousness" was understood to be something "more important than anything else"—something that would sustain both revolution and subsequent social and industrial development. Both were functions of "making people fit" for their tasks by providing them a "proper ideological education"—proprieties that could only emanate from "the wise guidance of the leader."[12]

Disciplined loyalty is required in all such instances—a loyalty subtended by a familiar series of substitutions: "Loyalty to the leader is loyalty to the party, [and that] is loyalty to the ... interests of society." It is a loyalty that requires a measure of immediate personal sacrifice including "the cost of one's life in order to carry out the party's policies and decisions"—for "the life of a collective is always more valuable than that of an individual."[13] All of which captures the peculiar sacrificial cast of sacralized politics.

When one compares these formulations with those out of which they arose, their substantive poverty becomes evident. The cognitive qualities of the political faith born with Marx and Engels have declined appreciably over time. Whatever else happened to Marxism as a political religion from the occasion of its birth to its service as a rationale for the forced economic development of agrarian societies—its intellectual form and substantive content suffered irreversible impairments.

As Marxist-Leninist systems drew to a close at the end of the twentieth century, their pretended social science claims gave every evidence of decay. Their ideological rationale abandoned more and more of the scientific conceit of the work of Marx and Engels—and their normative elements became simplistic and increasingly unpersuasive. The implications of all that become manifest in the "Marxist-Leninist" revolution that overwhelmed the "gentle people" of Cambodia in the 1970s.

What it meant to be embroiled in Marxist-Leninist revolution in the late twentieth century is revealed in the ideology, and the behavior, of Cambodia's revolutionary leaders. To proceed with that requires a brief account of classical Marxism's own decay as a "scientific" theory of history.

[12] As cited in Mukherjee, *The Social, Economic, and Political Ideas of the Great President Kim Il Sung*, pp. 14, 56, 59, 64, 106, 108.

[13] Ibid., pp. 80, 108, 111. Of course, in the final analysis, the immediate surrender of one's life proves only a seeming sacrifice. In submitting to disciplined loyalty and self-sacrifice, the individual advances to what is identified as a "true political life," herald of "true freedom"—a freedom that becomes manifest in the realization that the "individual self" is really one with the "universal self," a unity with "humanity," forged "through love, truth, and sacrifice." Ibid., pp. 26, 82.

Decay

At the end of the twentieth century—despite the enormities of Stalinism—many thinkers in the advanced industrial democracies continued to find Marxism attractive. In retrospect, its appeal seems to have been the consequence of its insistent normative character. After a second world war in the space of half a century, Marxism inspired hope for the future. During the first years of the 1970s, many liberal academics and journalists appeared possessed of the notion that one or another variant of Marxism, or all of them together, heralded a future of peace, harmony, and abundance. For more than a century there had been those who discovered the prospect of human fulfillment in the works of Marx and Engels.

For Marx and Engels, and those who were to assume their mantle, history followed a fully predictable progression: from primitive communism, through slavery, to feudalism, to capitalism, and from thence to the humanity of socialism. For a century that had abandoned religion for science, a new science arose that provided a redemptive vision as morally satisfying as that once promised and lost by traditional faith. Through the first fifty years of the twentieth century, there were few intellectuals who were hermetically insulated from that gratifying expectation. And history seemed to continue to provide evidence in its support.

For many, the First World War confirmed the worst of Marx's prognostications. Capitalism had driven humanity into what could only be the Final Days. For a brief moment, redemption appeared imminent—only to have the interwar years confound expectation. Antibolshevik movements arose and swept across Europe. Inexplicably, the advance of saving revolution appeared to have stalled. Major industrial nations sank into economic depression, vast in scope and devastating in human cost—but none sought deliverance through a specifically Marxist revolution.

The Marxism of the founders predicted that revolution would come in circumstances that found industrial capitalism concentrated in monopolies of ownership and control, with the middle classes forced into the growing ranks of the proletariat. Those ranks would ultimately make up the vast bulk of the population of the advanced industrial communities. At the same time, the "organic composition" of industrial capitalism itself—the increasing investment in machinery and technology—would further and further depress the overall profit potential of enterprise, until the entire modern structure of market governed machine production would collapse, and the era of social property, collective control, and fraternal harmony would ensue.

Unhappily, none of that was to transpire. In the effort to account for reality's departure from theory, Marxists amended their expectations to allow a transitional time of troubles—an "imperialist epoch"—as a preamble to final resolution. The end culture would remain redemptive. What had changed was the "scientific" path to its attainment.

The Second World War brought fundamental changes. In the course of that war, Marxism, in its Stalinist idiom, extended itself into the very heart of Europe—and once again, there was the anticipation of a promised, universal, and resolutive socialism. None of that was to transpire.

Almost immediately after the end of the war, in 1949, Mao Zedong announced the victory of revolutionary Marxism in China—and following his own revolution in 1959, Fidel Castro brought Caribbean communism to Cuba. Thereafter, in the most unlikely places on the globe, pretended Marxist, or Marxist-Leninist, revolutionaries acceded to power. Vietnamese Marxists, for all their nationalist coloration, and the making of revolution in preindustrial, essentially agrarian, rather than "proletarian" environs, managed first to defeat French colonial power, and then survive American intervention.

After the success of Mao's revolution in China, there were few who chose to quibble any further about making revolution at the wrong stage in history,[14] in the wrong place, and with the wrong population base. It was decided that peasants, after all, might make "socialist" revolution any and everywhere—without the proletarian majority and without the advanced industrial base conceived necessary by the original theory.

By March 1975, the notion that peasants could undertake socialist revolution anywhere, and under any conditions, had become so prevalent that Fidel Castro felt comfortable opining that agrarian Africa, south of the Sahara, was the "weak link in the imperialist chain." There, semiliterate tribesmen might attain to "socialism" without making the tiresome transit through all those antecedent economic stages imagined necessary by nineteenth and early twentieth century Marxists.[15]

---

[14] Early in his career as a revolutionary theorist, Marx argued that "in general, people cannot be liberated as long as they are unable to obtain food and drink, housing and clothing in adequate quality and quantity. 'Liberation' is a historical and not a mental act, and is brought about by historical conditions, the [level] of industry, com[merce], [agri]culture." He went on to insist that revolution rested on "the development of productive forces" as "an absolutely necessary practical premise, because without it privation, *want* is merely made general, and with *want* the struggle for the necessities would begin again, and all the old filthy business would necessarily be restored." Karl Marx and Friedrich Engels, *The German Ideology* in *Collected Works* (New York: International Publishers, 1976), vol. 5, pp. 38, 49.

[15] As quoted in Yves Santamaria, "Afrocommunism: Ethiopia, Angola, and Mozambique," in Courtois et al., *The Black Book of Communism*, p. 697. Before his death, Ernesto "Che" Guevara

During the quarter century that followed the end of the Second World War, Marxist revolutionaries everywhere were imagined to be riding the crest of the future, destined to bring to suffering humankind the promise of a more just and humane order. Few among committed Western radicals gave credence to the increasingly prevalent accounts of Stalinist and Maoist inhumanity. More often than not, the stories of brutality, oppression, and mass murder in the Soviet Union and the People's Republic of China were summarily dismissed. Horrors of that order of magnitude could hardly obtain in a "socialist society." Such things could only be the consequence of fascist and/or "monopoly capitalist" rule. Only fascists or monopoly capitalists massacred innocents, forced them into slave labor, or "reeducated" them in concentration camps. Only capitalists destroyed millions of lives through aggressive war, economic exploitation, and reactionary suppression of the "people."

For an inordinately long time, just such a Manichean vision of the world dominated discourse among "progressives." Even after Josef Stalin's death, Nikita Khrushchev's revelations at the 20th Communist Party Congress did little to alter the thinking of most radical intellectuals. Most remained true to their political faith. For many, the disclosures concerning the bestialities of the system imposed on Soviet citizens by Lenin and Stalin only created temporary moral perplexity. Although disturbed, many refused to surrender their ideals when they discovered the horrors, unanticipated and initially perhaps unintended, that accompanied attempts at their realization in the Soviet Union. Horrified and outraged by the revelations, many, if not all, were prepared to break with Stalinism—but were loath to forsake Marxism. The result was that many, if not all, still sought the attainment of that unblemished society promised by "scientific socialism." They proceeded to transfer their enthusiasm to Maoism, or Castroism, or any number of other aspiring Marxisms in Africa, Latin America, or the Middle East—however little confidence they inspired.[16]

In 1975, the enthusiasm for liberation through Marxist revolution in other than industrialized settings had not abated. Castro's peasant guerrillas remained popular with Western intellectuals. Mao was still alive—having just shepherded preindustrial China through the "Great Proletarian Cultural Revolution"—and "socialist" Vietnam had emerged victorious from the conflict that had roiled largely peasant Southeast Asia for almost a quarter century. Many in the West continued to understand all that as evidence of the predicted liberation of hu-

---

announced that "socialist" revolution virtually could be made anywhere. "Objective conditions" played little role in the entire process.

[16] See the insightful discussion in Paul Hollander, *The End of Commitment: Intellectuals, Revolutionaries, and Political Morality* (Chicago: Ivan R. Dee, 2006).

manity. The proletarian world order, promised by Marx and Engels so long ago, appeared to be taking shape on the agrarian periphery of, and not within, the industrialized nations.[17]

In fact, what had transpired over time, and in response to circumstances, was the transmutation of the social science claims of classical Marxism: socialism no longer required the inheritance of an advanced industrial base—it could be constructed by peasant masses. Socialism no longer required urban sophisticates to administer a collectivistic productive and distributive system—that could be undertaken by peasant enthusiasts. What remained essentially the same was Marxism's qualities as a normative political religion.

The Marxism of Peasant Revolutions

Long before Lenin, Mao, or Castro, both Karl Marx and Friedrich Engels made clear their theoretical perspective on peasant revolution. Scattered throughout their works were commentaries on peasant struggles against oppression and exploitation.

Early in their collaboration, both Marx and Engels described what they imagined the role of peasants might be in the social, political, and economic revolution they predicted. Although peasants might serve as uncertain allies in the struggles of the urban proletariat, they saw them not only as basically conservative, but as essentially reactionary. They argued that, as a necessary consequence of their life circumstances, peasants were disposed to resist the forward movement of history.[18]

Both Marx and Engels held that the abolition of private property was the single most important prerequisite necessary for the advent of communism. Given that, the peasantry—with its irrepressible craving for personal ownership of land—could only be conservative at best, and reactionary at worst. Beyond that,

---

[17] Marx had clearly argued that "proletarian" revolution required some nonsubstitutable preconditions. He held that "if [the] material elements of a complete revolution are not present—namely, on the one hand the existing productive forces, on the other the formation of a revolutionary mass . . . then it is absolutely immaterial for practical development whether the *idea* of the revolution has been expressed a hundred times already, as the history of communism proves." Marx and Engels, *The German Ideology*, p. 54. The preexistent, fully developed "productive forces" were clearly a necessary precondition.

[18] "Of all the classes that stand face to face with the bourgeoisie today, the proletariat alone is a really revolutionary class. The other classes decay and finally disappear in the face of modern industry. . . . The lower middle class, the small manufacturer, the shopkeeper, the artisan, the peasant . . . are not revolutionary, but conservative. Nay more, they are reactionary, for they try to roll back the wheel of history." Karl Marx and Friedrich Engels, *The Communist Manifesto*, in Marx and Engels, *Collected Works*, vol. 6, p. 494.

Marx consistently argued that the "liberating" revolution he anticipated would be, of necessity, a *proletarian*, not a peasant, revolution. It was the proletariat that was the unique byproduct of the capitalist mode of production—and it was that mode, and that mode alone, that created the material and psychological conditions for the complete liberation of the individual from those oppressive constraints to which humanity had been subject throughout history. For Marx, "liberation" was a complex "historical" act undertaken by a psychologically "mature" proletariat, involving the abolition of private property, and predicated on the full flowering of society's material forces of production.

Throughout history, privative social and political relations between individuals and groups had always been a consequence of the absence of just such conditions. The first prerequisite to liberation would be the ripening of material productive forces. Human beings can be liberated, Marx insisted, only when "food and drink, housing and clothing in adequate quality and quantity" become available for all—for it is "the aggregate of productive forces accessible to men [that] determines the condition of society." Hence, he insisted, "the 'history of humanity' must always be studied and treated in relation to the history of industry and exchange."[19]

What is both implicit and explicit in Marx's account of the processes involved in human liberation, is the presupposition that the material productive forces available to humanity would have achieved, by the time of the anticipated revolution, their full articulation. For Marx, the "development of productive forces . . . is an absolutely necessary practical premise" for human liberation because, he went on, "without it privation, *want*, is merely made general, and with *want* the struggle for necessities would begin again, and all the old filthy business would necessarily be restored."[20]

The psychological maturation of urban factory workers—required to service the administrative needs of distributive socialism—would be a collateral of the full development of the material means of production. The abolition of humanity's oppression by human beings can only be accomplished if humankind achieves both that level of productivity capable of satisfying all human needs and the psychological maturity that would ensure the appropriate administration of a developed industrial system.

A society that attains that level of material productivity necessary for human liberation produces, at the same time, a system functional proletarian majority. Proletarians, as a class, fully capable of administering the new industrial

---

[19] Karl Marx and Friedrich Engels, *The German Ideology*, pp. 32, 33, 38, 43; see the entire discussion between pp. 32 and 38.

[20] Ibid., p. 43.

order, would usher in the promised freedom. They, and they alone, could be the "gravediggers" of human oppression. According to the first Marxists, peasants were the products of an earlier stage in the development of the forces of production, and were scheduled for extinction.[21] They were deemed incapable of serving as agents of human liberation.

Immediately before his death, on the occasion of considering the possibility that a peasant based popular revolution in Russia might usher in some form of Marxist "socialism," Marx maintained that the "materialist conception of history" conceived such an eventuality possible only if "socialist" revolutions simultaneously took place in advanced industrial environs—to provide the material abundance, and human agents, required.[22] Peasant revolutions, in and of themselves, would be incapable of lifting the burden of oppression from the shoulders of humankind. There is no evidence that Marx ever changed his opinions on the matter.

For his part, Engels very carefully considered the relationship of peasant rebellions to socialist revolution. In his extensive account of the late fifteenth and sixteenth century peasant uprisings in Germany, Engels' convictions were made abundantly clear.

In his treatment of Germany's peasant wars, Engels dealt with social evolution in the manner that typified Marxism throughout the lifetime of its founders.[23] Peasant wars, which have been recurrent everywhere in the world throughout history, were invariably the consequence of emotional, political, and economic oppression—but, whatever the intentions of their leaders, they never succeeded in liberating even a portion of humanity.

Of necessity, peasant wars were conducted in economic circumstances of limited productivity. They were conflicts between competing oppressors—each attempting to secure for themselves as much as possible of restricted yield. Until

---

[21] "[The] development of...large industry...causes an increase in the number of proletarians. ...In comparison with the nonproletarian classes, the small peasants and lower middle classes... the proletariat increases more rapidly than any other class in the state." Karl Kautsky, *The Dictatorship of the Proletariat* (Ann Arbor: University of Michigan Press, 1964), p. 14.

[22] See the entire discussion in Teodor Shanin, *Late Marx and the Russian Road: Marx and "The Peripheries of Capitalism"* (New York: Monthly Review Press, 1983). In response to the query whether an essentially peasant revolution in Russia might be able to "skip stages" and inaugurate a true socialist revolution, Marx wrote, "If the Russian revolution becomes the signal for proletarian revolution in the West, so that the two complement each other, then Russia's peasant communal land ownership may serve as the point of departure for a communist development." Ibid., p. 139.

[23] In the first volume of *Capital* (Moscow: Foreign Languages Publishing House, 1954), p. 764, fn. 1, Marx repeats the same judgment he made in 1848: the peasantry seeks to save itself from extinction—essentially by retaining its grip on private, landed property. As a consequence, the peasantry is inescapably "reactionary."

the productive base of the entire system expanded, nothing else would change—merely that peasants would suffer different masters. Engels argued that only when revolution reflected some fundamental changes at the productive base of society might one expect changes in the social relations that determine the quality of life. Only with the appearance of the proletariat—the class produced in the course of industrial growth—might the real promise of liberation be forthcoming. The peasantry, representatives of a preindustrial manner of production, could not be expected to supply the impetus for socialist transformation.

Until the new productive system fully emerged, Engels insisted, fundamental class relationships could only remain the same. The sound and fury of peasant uprisings could have no durable consequence. A preindustrial agrarian economy could barely sustain a given population at subsistence levels, much less satisfy all the real and fancied needs of a liberated humanity.

As long as human beings did not transcend agrarian productivity constraints, Marxists argued that class relationships could hardly be expected to change.[24] Even if peasant revolutionaries were to advocate the most radical of changes—the community of property and the corresponding abolition of class distinctions—there could be little in terms of real or sustained effect. Marx consistently maintained, as a case in point, that "only with large scale industry" would the "abolition of private property," and a true socialist order, become a real possibility.[25] Whatever their stated intention, peasant revolutionaries, at best, must forever remain unsuccessful in terms of human liberation.

At the time of the peasant wars, Germany was only just commencing its modern development. Local village industry was being everywhere replaced by the broader based guild system that produced commodities for larger and more remote markets. Trade introduced a remarkable opulence in towns that had begun rapid development. To protect that increasing material wealth, *burghers*, town dwellers, sought defense of political and property rights. Marx and Engels insisted that the true struggle for *proletarian* rights—that would liberate humanity—would have to await the requisite developments in the productive system.

Engels reminded his readers that peasant uprisings might very well prove antithetical to the progressive movement of history. Peasant revolutionaries sometimes found themselves led by urbanized, or semiurbanized, "plebians" who, however well intentioned, were fanciful in their aspirations and incompetent in practice. At such a stage of economic development, the growing townships were host to the social debris of systemic change—members of moribund

---

[24] See Engels' discussion in "The Peasant War in Germany," Marx and Engels, *Collected Works*, vol. 10, pp. 480–481.

[25] Marx and Engels, *The German Ideology*, p. 64.

classes, those without established occupations, and the intellectually indigent. Some of them—the scholars without profession, clerics without stipends, and craftsmen without markets—could only serve as uncertain leaders of revolution. Outside the settled townships, in the countryside, the vast majority of the population labored as peasants. They supplied the comestibles for the emerging population centers, together with the corvée labor necessary for whatever infrastructural development and maintenance there was. As serfs, the members of the peasantry served as beasts of burden for the privileged landed aristocracy. Levies on their labor obligated bondsmen to serve their "superiors." All were compelled to pay tithes, tributes, road tolls, and taxes. Failure to satisfy any of those obligations would bring abject ruin and brutal punishments upon them. Those were the conditions that rendered peasants mobilizable for rebellious purpose. They were the only population resources available to the revolutionary leadership of the time.

By the beginning of the sixteenth century it was clear that the entire economic and political system of feudalism was in transition. In the towns the burghers found themselves in constant conflict with the patriciate, the traditional princely, knightly, and clerical castes. With the changes that attended the growing guild industries—expanding trade, population movements, and the influx of new ideas—even the superordinate castes found themselves in uneasy comity. Conflicts emerged between the "honorables" and the clergy—and between the lesser nobility and the princes. Together with all that, rural clerics created tensions between themselves, their peasant charges, and the landed gentry.

Germany's peasant wars were a function of all this. The plebeians of the townships, the alienated lower clergy of the countryside, and the restive majorities of the rural areas, together made up the revolutionary tinder that fueled the sanguinary class conflicts of the fifteenth and sixteenth centuries—none of it, according to Marxist theory, destined to produce any real measure of human liberation. They constituted the necessary preamble to the advent of an industrial economy—which itself would require the systematic exploitation of labor to satisfy its capital needs.

Engels went on to argue that peasant revolts were invariably sustained by ideologies formulated by the declassed intellectuals of the growing urban centers and the restive countryside. Minor clergy, impoverished tutors, unemployed school teachers, displaced craftsmen, however marginal, were all ready and anxious to provide the rationale for the revolutionary reform of the established order.[26]

Given the basic realities, the revolutionary changes sought by the dispossessed, the displaced, and the morally outraged, manifested themselves as furi-

[26] Engels, "The Peasant War in Germany," part 1.

ous demands and uncertain enjoinments. There was pursuit of a utopian order as yet only dimly perceived. Their outlook tended to be "fantastic"—reminiscent of the lamentations of the prophets of old. In such circumstances, peasant revolution, whatever its animating ideology, could produce only farce or tragedy. Given the prevailing realities, the revolutionary leadership of the peasantry could not, and cannot, serve the pretended ends of the movement.[27]

According to classical Marxist theory, peasants, together with their tormentors, were destined to disappear with the rise of industrialized farming. They were but transients in the course of the inevitable march to victory by the *proletarian* representatives of modern industry. Under the best circumstances, peasant revolutions might serve as preamble to industrialization—a process that would redirect energy to the "primitive accumulation of capital" without which machine industry could not be established. That would inevitably require the compulsory "extraction" of "surpluses" from the rural sector—with all its associated violence and institutional threats of violence. Whatever the immediate results of peasant revolution, they would not include the liberation either of the peasants or of humankind.[28]

Granted the plausibility of the analysis, some time profitably might be employed in considering the sort of rationale peasant revolutionaries might put together to sustain their project. Engels has left us his thoughts.

Because of the primitive life conditions of agrarians, one would expect their rebellious outrage to find outlet in equally primitive expression—in "chiliastic dream visions," in "communism in fantasy," all caught up in the violence of "mystically minded sects."[29] All of their projects would be contrived, unreal. They would be undertaken at great cost to little consequence.

Engels suggests that because of their arduous life conditions at the hands of their oppressors, one would expect peasant revolutionaries to be hard, unforgiving, relentless, and prepared to "kill at the first opportunity" with unimaginable brutality. Accustomed to a life of "ascetic austerity," they would descend on their opponents with murderous ferocity.

Led by fevered charismatics, peasant revolutionaries would demand that everyone assume the obligation to work, to share, to sacrifice, and, if necessary, to die for the community. They would expect their millenarians to be paragons of virtue, "godlike."[30] Their political and social ideals would be those of peasant primitives from time immemorial.

[27] Marx simply recounted that "the great risings of the Middle Ages all radiated from the country, but equally remained totally ineffective." Marx and Engels, *The German Ideology*, p. 66.
[28] Engels, "The Peasant War in Germany," pp. 469–471.
[29] Ibid., pp. 414–415.
[30] Ibid., pp. 422, 428.

Characteristically, the ideology of peasant revolutionaries would take on the iconoclastic features of religious dissent. But theological disputes would soon lose their abstract and detached character; they would take on the properties of political and social demand. In effect, in his history of the peasant wars in Germany, Engels was describing the modern advent of political religion.[31]

Another socialist theoretician advanced very much the same analysis about six decades later. In 1913, Benito Mussolini, then a leader among socialist intellectuals, wrote a long essay devoted to the peasant wars associated with the martyrdom of the charismatic Jan Huss (1369–1415). He reported that in the sweep of violence that consumed city and countryside, the peasant revolutionaries of the period exacted brutal recompense from their opponents. Inspired by a sentiment both puritanical and ultraorthodox, the various sects of Hussites, Taborites, and Adamites brutalized and murdered in both defense and offense in the effort to realize their nationalist and communist apocalypse. Animated by a vision that was "both religious and nationalist," attended by "socialist" impulse, the Hussites, particularly the Taborites, were "fanatical" advocates of imposed orthodoxy in the service of "a movement more politicosocial than religious."[32] Like Engels, Mussolini identified the ideology of modern peasant revolution with a rudimentary form of political religion.

Such an account could only have inescapable implications for all those Marxists who chose to make revolution in primitive economic circumstances. In the twentieth century Lenin, Mao, Kim Il Sung, Ho Chi Minh, and Castro all made revolution in economically retrograde environments, peopled largely by peasants. Revolutions were not undertaken in advanced industrial economies, featuring material abundance and peopled by urban sophisticates.

Faced with the prospect of making a revolution in a marginally industrialized environment—or not making revolution at all—modern Marxists, characteristically, chose revolution. In order to vindicate that choice, Marxists, as Leninists, "creatively developed" inherited doctrine. They argued that "capitalism" had transformed itself so radically since the passing of Marx and Engels, that much of their "science" of revolution was no longer applicable.

At the turn of the twentieth century, Lenin argued that "imperialism" had transformed reality. Neither Marx nor Engels had foreseen any of that. Lenin maintained that by the end of the nineteenth century, industrial capitalism dis-

---

[31] Peasants seem to have forever used religious justifications for their uprisings. Modern peasant revolutions are distinctive in so far as their brutality is supplemented by modern technology. They are fully capable of consuming millions in their wrath.

[32] Benito Mussolini, "Giovanni Huss il Veridico," *Opera omnia* (Florence: La fenice, 1964), vol. 33, pp. 303, 306–307, 311.

tinguished itself from its immediate past by its "superexploitation" of outlying, less developed economies. The exploitation extended capitalism's life span but, at the same time, precipitated revolution in backward, essentially peasant, regions. Imperialism had realigned the historic "parallelogram of forces."[33]

All of that transformed revolutionary Marxism. Lenin died awaiting the proletarian revolutions in the advanced industrial nations that would salvage his revolution. He died unrequited. Stalin, unburdened by any felt need for Marxist coherence or intellectual integrity, took up leadership in what was to be the century's "first socialist society"—a society that would be driven, at the expense of peasants and workers alike, to full industrialization by the sacralized imperatives of an omnicompetent and omniscient leader.[34] "Socialism" would come to mean the forced industrialization of a politically defined space.

By the end of the Second World War, the decay of Marxism as a theory of human liberation was made manifest in the increasing insistence that the liberation of humankind could only be achieved by peasant revolutionaries. Instead of proletarian revolution in industrialized environs, it was the agrarian "third world," suffering medieval exploitation, which would defeat capitalism.

That would be accomplished by special violence—the peasant violence invoked by Mao Zedong in China, and that of Che Guevara in Latin America and Africa. It would be the consequence not of maturing economic conditions, but of the violence of peasants who had been taught to be "killing machines."[35] Marxism was no longer what it had been. It had been intellectually and morally transformed.

It was no longer necessary to await those material conditions so carefully cataloged by Marx and Engels, in order to embark on revolutionary violence. Revolution can be undertaken anywhere, but preferably in the countryside of the industrially backward regions of the globe where "the conditions of exploitation are indistinguishable from those of the Middle Ages"—where the peasantry, because of its "ignorance," requires the "revolutionary and political

[33] See the discussion in Gregor, *A Survey of Marxism*, chap. 6.

[34] A summary, informative description of the process is available in Geoffrey Hosking, *The First Socialist Society: A History of the Soviet Union from Within* (Cambridge, Mass.: Harvard University Press, 1985); an instructive rendering is found in Stephen Kotkin, *Magnetic Mountain: Stalinism as a Civilization* (Berkeley: University of California Press, 1995).

[35] Che Guevara went on to affirm, "Wherever death may surprise us, let it be welcomed, provided that this, our battle cry, may have reached some receptive ear and another hand may be extended to wield our weapons and other men be ready to intone the funeral dirge with the staccato singing of ... machine guns." Che Guevara, "Message to the Tricontinental: 'Create two, three ... many Vietnams,'" in John Gerassi, ed., *Venceremos! The Speeches and Writings of Che Guevara* (New York: The Macmillan Company, 1968), pp. 422, 424.

leadership" of those called "plebians" by Engels a hundred years before.[36] Revolutionaries sought to replicate the peasant wars that savaged central Europe at the dawn of the modern era. The difference was that the peasant revolutionaries of the twentieth century were expected to erect, out of their impoverishment, at staggering human and material costs, a modern industrial economy.

All of the retrograde cognitive and moral features of peasant revolution were welcomed by untutored Marxists like Mao and Che Guevara. Revolutionaries sought to undertake redemptive revolution to entirely unpredictable effect. Ideological "truths" became increasingly determinant, with faith a compulsory accompaniment. In those environments all the distracted fantasies we now associate with political religions surface. In their course, revolutionary virtue must be fostered, heresies suppressed, apostates punished, and enemies dispatched with exemplary violence and no remorse—in anticipatory payment for the promised apocalypse.

In his time, Engels knew enough of the homicidal fanaticism that attends armed rebellion in the peasant countryside to leave behind admonitions that might well serve contemporary revolutionaries. "The worst thing," he said, "that can befall the leader of an extreme party is to be compelled to assume power at a time when the movement is not yet ripe for the domination of the class he represents and for the measures this domination implies. What he can do depends ... on the level of development of the material means of existence. ... The social changes of his fancy [would have] little root in the then existing economic conditions."[37]

For Marx and Engels, the revolutionary manumission of humankind was possible only within a reasonably specific constellation of material preconditions. Attempts made in primitive economic circumstances in which there were hardly any of the requisites, could only prove abortive. The costs exacted in such attempts would be appalling. The evidence of history has been persuasive. The twentieth century has witnessed examples from a roster of peasant revolutions. It has been possible to follow their course and measure something of their human toll. Within that history, the peasant revolution in Cambodia is particularly tragic.

---

[36] See the discussion concerning the low intellectual qualities of the peasants in the countryside. Ernesto Che Guevara, "Guerrilla Warfare: A Method," *Che Guevara Speaks: Selected Speeches and Writings* (New York: Merit Publishers, 1967), pp. 75, 76, 77.

[37] Engels, "The Peasant War in Germany," pp. 469, 470.

The Background of the Cambodian Revolution

There is every indication that the declassed intellectuals, the "plebians," who made revolution in Cambodia appreciated very little of all this. Like peasant revolutionaries, in general, they had little, if any, systematic exposure to Marxist theory. In another place and another time, the Cambodian revolutionaries would have been identified not as Marxists, but as ultranationalists, irredentists, xenophobes, or archaists. None of that, of course, made them any less revolutionary.

Those were the background circumstances that prevailed when the world first heard that the capital city of faraway Cambodia had fallen to peasant revolutionaries on the 17th of April 1975. On that date, after a protracted conflict that devastated an entire nation, a tattered army of stern faced young boys, armed with instruments of death, occupied the streets of Phnom Penh. The day before, the clandestine radio of the Red Khmer announced the impending "liberation" of the nation. The announcement sent a thrill of anticipation through many intellectuals in the advanced industrial nations. The victory of the Khmer Rouge was taken to be new evidence of the impending deliverance of humankind promised by the Marxist theoreticians of long ago.

Of all the forces that conspired to produce Democratic Kampuchea, Saloth Sar, who was to become known to history as Pol Pot, was perhaps the most important.[38] Sar, who was to be the catalyst of peasant revolution in Cambodia, was born in 1925,[39] to a well to do peasant family in the village of Prek Sbauv near the town of Kompong Thom. It was a settlement probably more economically backward than any found in Engels' peasant Germany of the sixteenth century.

Together with that, we also know that Sar was raised in circumstances that would have awakened in him an emphatic sense of national humiliation and an associated feeling of outrage at the treatment of his people. Those around him would have communicated the fact that Cambodia had once been a great empire—and that less than a century before, the French had reduced it to a colony—supine and dependent.

---

[38] One of the better biographies is found in Philip Short, *Pol Pot: Anatomy of a Nightmare* (New York: Henry Holt, 2004). Cambodians refer to individuals by their given name, so that Saloth Sar is normally referred to as "Mr. Sar," or simply "Sar"—even though Cambodians follow the Chinese custom of providing the family name first—thus "Saloth" is the family name, and "Sar" the given name. In the following account, Saloth Sar will be referred to as "Sar."

[39] See the discussion concerning the date in David P. Chandler, *Brother Number One: A Political Biography of Pol Pot* (Boulder, Colo.: Westview, 1999. Revised edition), pp. 7–8.

Ample evidence survives that throughout his life, Sar harbored hatred, in equal measure, of both colonialists and his Vietnamese neighbors, both of whom he forever saw as a threat to the sovereignty and territorial integrity of Cambodia. In the course of his political evolution—whatever his real or imputed ideological commitments—that never was to change. It can be argued that by the time he reached early maturity, Sar—whatever else he was—was a political and cultural nationalist. Before their disappearance into history, the Red Khmer, the revolutionaries led by Sar as Pol Pot, maintained that their purpose had always been to "defend and forever maintain their nation, people, and race."[40] Whatever else they claimed to be, the Khmers Rouges gave ample testimony of being reactive nationalists—with all that the notion implies.

With early manhood, Saloth Sar was awarded a scholarship to study in France. In 1949, at twenty-four, colonial officials awarded him one of three student bursaries available to young Cambodians, in order that he might pursue his studies in Paris. It was an experience that was to shape his ideological convictions.

In the fifty years since the beginning of the twentieth century, Marxism, in all its variants, had infiltrated French intellectual life—and by the time of Sar's arrival, France was host to one of the largest communist parties outside the Soviet Union and Maoist China. Marxism—in its Stalinist variant—had become a staple of French intellectual life. All of which helps to explain the peculiarities of the intellectual beliefs Sar was to make his own.

By the time Sar found himself in Paris, classical Marxism had been transmogrified by Leninism, Stalinism, and Maoism—into a doctrine that imagined "socialist" revolutions transpiring in backward, essentially agrarian, economic environments. The socialist revolution itself would deliver the advanced industrial base of which Marx had so eloquently spoken. It came to be argued that revolutionary Marxism no longer required a mature, urban proletarian demographic to make its revolution; agrarian "proletarians" might serve equally well.[41] All that

---

[40] As cited by Ben Kiernan, *The Pol Pot Regime: Race, Power, and Genocide in Cambodia under the Khmer Rouge, 1975–79* (Second edition. New Haven: Yale University Press, 1996), p. ix. As will be argued, Kiernan made a case for a strong "racial" or "ethnic" component to the ideology of the Red Khmer.

[41] Both Marx and Engels left a confusion of speculations concerning the role of peasants in modern revolution. Both argued that peasants, incessantly desirous of land, were intrinsically "counterrevolutionary." On the other hand, peasants might serve as temporary "allies" in revolution. Given the speculations, it is hard to specify what the ideal ratio of peasants to proletarians might be in any revolutionary circumstance. It was eminently clear that Marx and Engels conceived *proletarians*, alone, to be "truly" revolutionary. What all that meant for any particular revolutionary strategy, at any particular time, has never been convincingly determined.

seemed to be necessary was that such agrarian "proletarians" be angry, armed, "class conscious,"[42] and available.[43]

By the time Mao Zedong wrote his "Report on an Investigation of the Peasant Movement in Hunan," in 1927, he no longer thought it necessary to provide a specific rationale for agrarian revolution as "Marxist." Marxists in China no longer looked to traditional Marxism for justification of their policies. After what had been an essentially peasant revolution in Russia, it was difficult to argue that proletarians would be the necessary, if not the sufficient, condition for making Marxist revolution. All that seemed necessary was the proclamation of one's revolutionary faith. "Marxist" revolution in China might equally well be made by peasants. In fact, by the time Mao succeeded to power, no one seemed to feel it necessary to deny him Marxist cachet simply because his revolution was essentially agrarian based.[44]

By the early 1930s, thanks to the efforts of Stalin, Lenin's peasant revolution in Russia, led by declassed bourgeois intellectuals, had been identified, without qualification, as an entirely "Marxist" enterprise. Stalin's "socialism in one country" had become the thinly veiled nationalist purpose of revolution—and rapid industrialization, the immediate imperative. By that time, all the objections of orthodox Marxists, like Karl Kautsky, had been swept away by purges and propaganda.

Kautsky had argued that a revolution such as that envisioned and carried out by Lenin, could only result in a total betrayal of Marxism.[45] Repeating the admonitions of both Marx and Engels, he held that lacking a mature proletariat, revolution in backward economic environs could hardly deliver the politi-

---

[42] It has never been made clear how "class consciousness" was to be defined. "Class consciousness" does not seem to be directly related to class membership or class interests. Peasants who lent their support to revolution were considered to have a suitable class consciousness; those that did not, were afflicted with a "bourgeois," or "counterrevolutionary," consciousness.

[43] Lenin had argued that revolutions on the periphery of capitalism would succeed in denying industry market outlets and businesses investment capital. Later Marxist-Leninists were to make these conditions preamble to the final collapse of machine capitalism—and the triumph of worldwide proletarian revolution. See the discussion in Lenin's *Imperialism: The Highest Stage of Capitalism* in *Collected Works* (Moscow: Progress Publishers, 1964), vol. 22, together with that found in Stalin, *Problems of Leninism*.

[44] Stalin's Comintern had considerable difficulty deciding that Maoism was Marxist. There is a long history of attempts to understand the Chinese revolution through the lens of Marxism—none of them particularly persuasive. When China entered in conflict with the Soviet Union in the 1960s, Moscow rekindled the charge that Maoism was never Marxist. See the account in Gregor, *A Place in the Sun*, chaps. 2, 4, and 5.

[45] See the classic statement of his position in Kautsky, *The Dictatorship of the Proletariat*, written while the First World War was still in course. It was followed by his *Terrorismus und Kommunismus: Ein Beitrag zur Naturgeschichte der Revolution* (Berlin: E. Berger, 1919).

cal, social, and economic democracy implicit and explicit in traditional Marxism—and necessary for true human emancipation.[46] Without democracy, in a primitive economic environment, with the majority of the population peasants, Kautsky anticipated widespread violence directed not only against primitive peasants, and ill defined "class enemies," but against those Marxists who found objectionable all the implications of revolution in retrograde economic circumstances. Kautsky argued that under such conditions pandemic violence would be required to secure minoritarian rule of the pretended "proletariat"—and terrorism to sustain it.[47]

By the 1930s, the essentials of all that had become less than a memory. Within the Soviet Union, Stalin had extirpated those orthodox Marxists who had survived the winnowing that accompanied and followed the civil war. Foreign intellectuals were often prepared to extend to him the benefit of the doubt. Stalin had "creatively developed" Marxism so that it might serve as the rationale for a singularly unmarxist developmental "socialism."[48] The world was to learn that meant not human liberation, but a forced march from an agrarian, to an industrial, economy.

The pursuit of autonomous industrial development in circumstances of technological backwardness and general poverty required that vast sums of investment capital be generated domestically. That was to be accomplished by imposing mandated quotas on every segment of the productive population. The draconian "proletarian state" exacted "surpluses" from the working population, producing particular hardship in the agrarian sector. Where such quotas could not be voluntarily met, they were extracted by force—leaving little for sustenance and still less for planting. The costs incurred involved massive violence and widespread famine in the rural regions.

Where industrial output quotas could not be met for whatever reason, entire populations were convicted of "counterrevolutionary" conspiracy, "hooliganism," or "sabotage," to be purged or spirited away to forced labor camps. How many perished during this period remains uncertain to this day. That they numbered in the millions is certain. Peasant revolution had exacted its toll.

With the Allied victory at the end of the Second World War, Stalin proceeded to declare that the Soviet Union's conquest of National Socialist Ger-

[46] Kautsky had made his case before the turn of the century in the first edition (1893) of his *Parlamentarismus und Demokratie* (Stuttgart: J. H. W. Dietz, 1911).

[47] In this context, see Rosa Luxemburg, *The Russian Revolution and Leninism or Marxism?* (Ann Arbor: University of Michigan Press, 1961), pp. 28, 48, 62, passim.

[48] See, for example, Stalin's comments on constructing "complete socialism" in one country, in "On the Problems of Leninism," in Stalin, *Problems of Leninism*, pp. 188–200.

many confirmed that his variant of Marxism was the only form that remained credible. In his judgment, those who opposed him had not only betrayed their fatherland, but Marxism and revolution as well.

The Making of the Cambodian Revolution

This was the Marxism to which Saloth Sar was introduced during his sojourn in Paris. By the time he became a Marxist, Stalinism was literally the only form of Marxism with which he had direct and immediate familiarity.[49] The Maoism he encountered at the same time was little more than its Asian variant.

Reassured by Stalin's "success" in industrializing Russia, Mao had embarked on the forced industrialization of a China more backward than the Russia Lenin had captured more than three decades before. Almost immediately after assuming total control, Mao sought to industrialize China, initially employing programs borrowed from the Soviet Union. At first an unimaginative mimicry, Mao's programs subsequently sought to expedite the entire process by introducing labor-intensive variations at ever increasing cost.[50]

What this was to mean for the people of Cambodia soon became clear. Sar would be armed with convictions that originated with Stalin and were further debased by Mao. When he left France in 1953, Sar was already a member of the French Communist Party, and, by 1962 when he assumed responsibilities as acting secretary of what was then identified as the "Workers' Party of Kampuchea," he carried with him a hopelessly corrupt form of Marxism.

In 1963, increasing pressure from the government, and his own restlessness,

---

[49] Sar later confessed that at the time of his sojourn in Paris, he had attempted to read some of Marx's "thick books," but understood nothing. He did profit from his reading of Stalin's *History of the Communist Party*. He took away from his reading a critical appreciation of the "primary revolutionary role of leadership"; of the necessity of regularly purging the ranks of the party and party leadership; of the necessary elitist character of the revolutionary party; and finally, of the importance of acknowledging that a revolutionary society need not traverse the "bourgeois" epoch, but could immediately make its way into socialism. See the discussion in Short, *Pol Pot*, pp. 65–68. In retrospect, it is evident that Sar's comprehension of Marxist theory was never anything but tenuous at best. His political postures reflected those of the French Communist Party of the period: Stalinism, antiamericanism, anticolonialism, and revolution. Members of Sar's circle admitted that they did not attempt to fully understand the "thick books" written by Marx and Engels. Most of their readings were restricted to pamphlets and articles. Among revolutionary Marxists, that generally has not been considered a special disability. Mao himself admitted he had never read more than part of the *Communist Manifesto*. There is no evidence that he ever read any further. Fidel Castro is said to have read only the introductory chapters of Marx's *Capital*—and, rather than reading any further, allowed "life to make him a revolutionary." See the discussion in Short, *Pol Pot*, chap. 2.

[50] See the discussion in Gregor, *Marxism, China, and Development*, chaps. 3 and 4.

moved Sar to abandon Cambodia's capital city and to assume the obligations of a rural revolutionary—mobilizing peasants to "Marxist" purpose. There is some persuasive evidence that it was after 1963, and before 1970, that Sar developed his final views about revolution, and the society he expected that revolution would produce.[51]

It was during this critical interval in his intellectual development that Sar visited China. As circumstances would have it, it was about the time of China's "Great Proletarian Cultural Revolution." It was a time of intensified "class struggle," shaped by the largely inscrutable distinctions advanced by party leaders. Class enemies were found and pursued everywhere, including in the innermost recesses of the Chinese Communist Party itself.

Maoist China had only shortly before emerged from the devastation of the "Great Leap Forward," in which millions of Chinese had been mobilized for "storming attacks" on complex economic problems—and the entire countryside mustered to service what was intended to be a program of "autonomous" agricultural and industrial development.

In the course of Mao's Great Leap, millions of peasants had been displaced, families disbanded, education disrupted, and impossible projects contrived. The Great Leap was the consequence of Mao's decision that socialist China should surpass Great Britain in the production of steel. Since China lacked the first prerequisites of heavy industry, "backyard furnaces" were jerry built everywhere—cobbled together as substitutes for required mills and foundries. To forge the requisite iron and steel, millions, skilled in little other than paddy farming, were charged with the production of the basic components necessary for the task.

Not enough that they were conscripted to attend crude furnaces that required constant supervision—millions were made responsible for harvesting the fuel necessary for the entire improbable enterprise. In the process, entire regions were stripped of trees and ground cover. Worse still, peasants were called upon to increase rice production at a time that saw them so employed.

The capital costs attendant on the production of iron and steel required that China radically increase its rice output. Exports would underwrite the capital expenditures involved. Mao insisted that if the nation were to carry weight in the world, it would have to field a military worthy of respect. And steel was critical to the construction of sophisticated weapons platforms—and rice exports necessary to pay for it all.

Unhappily, the burdens imposed on the peasantry were too great. In the

[51] There is persuasive treatment of this period in Chandler, *Brother Number One*, chaps. 4–5.

course of attempting to produce iron and steel in the countryside, peasants neglected their rice paddies, which fell into disrepair—and seasonal plantings were deferred. The consequence was a catastrophic decline in paddy yield.

As a result of that surreal effort, "the chiliastic dream vision" of a peasant revolutionary, Maoist China lapsed into one of the most devastating famines in history. Perhaps as many as thirty millions perished. Starvation was everywhere and malnutrition pandemic. Cannibalism was not unknown in the most devastated areas.

The failure was not only measured in lives. Whatever metals were forged in the primitive furnaces of the Great Leap Forward were so debased that they proved unsuitable for industrial use. The entire massive effort proved a failure of biblical proportions—in both lives and treasure.[52]

Sar could hardly have known any of that in 1966. At the time, even Sinologists in the West knew very little of the dimensions of the calamity. Sar, as visitor to China, would hardly have received any information about the magnitude of the failures from the state controlled media. Whatever he heard about the effort could only have been positive. Like many others, who should have known better, Sar was convinced of the merits of Mao's developmental delusions.

In 1966, Sar could have only been impressed by the instances of social mobilization, and presumed project successes, that characterized Maoist China during the Great Leap Forward and the then current Great Proletarian Cultural Revolution. For the revolutionary Khmers, Maoism became the truth of Stalinism, and both were seen as the embodiment of one single strategy of triumphant agricultural modernization and rapid industrialization.

Sar's visit transpired at a time when Maoists were arguing that Lin Biao's "Long Live the Victory of People's War" made the case that true revolution was destined to arise in the world's rural regions—from which revolutionaries would overwhelm the decadent "metropoles" of industrial capitalism. In a radical departure from traditional Marxism, industrial urban centers, with their proletarian denizens, were perceived intrinsically counterrevolutionary—and the world's underdeveloped periphery, with its preliterate peasantry, the source of Marxist redemption.

In effect, Sar returned from his visit to China with experiences that were to shape his revolution—a shaping that was to have fateful consequences for the people of Cambodia.

[52] There are now many accounts of Mao's "Great Leap Forward." An easily available rendering is to be found in Jung Chang and Jon Halliday, *Mao: The Unknown Story* (London: Vintage Books, 2006), chap. 40.

The Khmer Rouge Revolution

By 1970, Saloth Sar found himself leader of an armed peasant revolution. By that time political and military circumstances had entirely altered the disposition of forces with which he had to contend. He managed to have his meager forces armed and trained by Vietnamese "compatriots"—now all allied in a "liberation front" that was both antiamerican and "anti-imperialist." The "proletarian" revolutionaries of Hanoi and Beijing were prepared to extend support to Sar who, by that time, officially identified himself as "Pol Pot." As such, he entered into an international alliance of revolutionaries.

By the early 1970s, "true revolutionaries" were artless peasants, inspired by animal outrage, animated by an "indomitable will," and sustained by the clatter of automatic weapons fire.[53] By that time, it was no longer expected that urban proletarians would make Marxist revolution. "Proletarian *nations*" were expected to assume that responsibility. Languishing in economic backwardness, proletarian nations would undertake their own liberation. Their rural revolutionaries, as Mao and Pol Pot would have it, were "blank slates" upon which all manner of things might be inscribed. Peasant revolutionaries would be carriers of revolutionary intentions, loyal, steadfast, and committed—and inspired by a "love for their homeland"—a fulsome patriotism.[54] In the evolving neomarxism that resulted, nationalism and the language of internationalism, dictatorship and the talk of democracy, the making of war and the pretense of peace, patent inhumanity and pretended humanity, all subsisted in uneasy combination.

In those circumstances, the peasant revolutionaries of Cambodia won their war. On the day of their victory, they undertook to empty the cities of Cambodia of their inhabitants—to divest decadent urban dwellers of their "bourgeois" affectations—to have their virtue restored by living peasant lives.[55] In April 1975, in a grotesque replay of Mao's treatment of restless urban youth, more than two million Cambodians were driven into the countryside—in the course of which countless numbers were executed, and still more perished from starvation, exertion, and/or neglect. The Khmer Rouge expected that those who

---

[53] Guevara, "Message to the Tricontinental: 'Create two, three ... many Vietnams," in Gerassi, ed. *Venceremos!* pp. 421, 422, 423, 424.

[54] Guevara told revolutionaries that they could not expect that the "struggle for liberation" be undertaken by those nations already afflicted with the "contradictions of capitalism." There could be no hope of liberation from the advanced industrial nations. The revolution of "proletarian nations" would take place in the context of "love for one's homeland" and the "patriotism" of Marxist revolutionaries. Ibid., pp. 414, 416, 418.

[55] See the discussion in Margolin, "Cambodia: The Country of Disconcerting Crimes," in Courtois et al., *The Black Book of Communism*, pp. 584–585.

survived the forced migration would assist in increasing rice yields, the profits from which were to purchase essential material and technological imports[56]—for the Khmers Rouges, like the Maoists, fully expected to rapidly industrialize their agrarian economy.[57]

By August, the Khmer Rouge had settled on the developmental program that was at the core of its revolutionary intent. It was identified as a "Super Great Leap Forward"—expected to exceed the "successes" of Mao's own Great Leap.[58] Recognizing that Cambodia lacked the most elemental requirements for industrialization—capital, skills, and resources—the leadership of the Khmer Rouge invoked the mobilizing, organizational, and leadership tactics of Stalinism and Maoism as offset. "Proletarian consciousness" was expected to overcome prevailing material handicaps. "Objective conditions" were to be transcended by willed commitment. Employing the revolutionary strategies that had become part of the armarium of neosocialist developmentalism, the Khmer Rouge expected peasant Cambodia to be industrialized within a decade. The party, as the "proletarian vanguard"—both "absolute" and "paramount"—would "encompass everything." An unlettered peasantry would be inculcated with an appropriate "political consciousness," shaping them to their responsibilities. The discipline would be both "total" and military in character.

Under such administration, rice production was expected to escalate from one million tons per hectare to three million tons, and finally, to ten million tons per hectare. That would be accomplished by imposing a pattern of strict conformity on all Cambodians, cultivating selected virtues governing work habits, sex, and personal comportment. To create the required work environment, the leadership, composed of "a dour, puritanical group of people," forbade "unauthorized romance under the penalty of death,"[59] [and] considered makeup and colored, tailored clothing for women, a sign of Western decadence." "Pure" leaders hectored Cambodians to forsake "individualism, vanity, rank, boastful-

[56] Pol Pot's "objective was to increase production massively by increasing capital through the export of agricultural products." Ibid., p. 599.

[57] "The party has thus ordered that the national construction efforts to be carried out from now should be fulfilled rapidly so that ours will rapidly become a prosperous country with an advanced agriculture and industry." Pol Pot, victory address, July 1975, as cited in Elizabeth Becker, *When the War Was Over: Cambodia and the Khmer Rouge Revolution* (New York: Public Affairs, 1998), p. 161.

[58] See David P. Chandler, Ben Kiernan, and Chanthou Boua, eds., *Pol Pot Plans the Future: Confidential Leadership Documents from Democratic Kampuchea 1976–1977* (New Haven: Yale University Southeast Asia Studies, 1988), pp. 3, 5, 12, 14, 20, 29, 42, 110, 169, 171.

[59] "The atmosphere was extremely puritan; men and women talking to each other were expected to stand at least three meters apart.... Any sexual relations outside of marriage were systematically punished with death.... The consumption of alcoholic beverages ... was another capital crime." Margolin, "Cambodia," in Courtois et al., *The Black Book of Communism*, p. 609.

ness"—to become "new men"—exemplars of "purity, cleanliness, order, total loyalty and obedience."[60]

All of that was calculated to create a class of "worker peasants" who would not only conquer "capitalism" and "imperialism," but economic backwardness as well. So that workers would not be distracted in their enterprise, families were dismantled, with members not to see each other for years, if ever. Demonstrative punishments were meted out arbitrarily—governed by occult "revolutionary" criteria. Unnumbered thousands simply disappeared into the vortex. Product quotas were imposed on regions without accounting or rationale. At the cost of productivity, entire populations would be transferred at will by the revolutionary leadership. They were to be adepts of a demanding revolutionary confession.

This wretched work force was told that out of their individual and collective self-sacrifice, a new Cambodia would emerge. Those who love their nation, would see it "glorious" once again.[61] Pol Pot's Democratic Kampuchea would be a mass mobilizing, nationalist, totalitarian, developmental dictatorship conducted under the auspices of a single party that identified itself only as "Angkar Padevat," the "Revolutionary Organization."

Angkar, "the Organization," was identified with the "nearly mystic omnipotency" that vindicated its right to totalitarian rule. Angkar was reputed to "possess as many eyes as a pineapple," and be "incapable of making mistakes."[62] It was anonymous Angkar that demanded self-effacing deference, unquestioned obedience, and consuming commitment. It was anonymous Angkar that possessed all the transcendent qualities of leadership conceived necessary by the secular religions typical of the twentieth century.

In fact, Pol Pot was Angkar,[63] and in 1977, a decision was made to publicly reveal him as the charismatic leader required by the demands of secular faith. Appropriate devotionals collected around his person. Paintings and heroic statues were commissioned, but in the short time that remained, the effort never fully matured.

Nonetheless, "Angkar," and "Brother no. One," satisfied the requirements of the system. Followers, and nonfollowers alike, obeyed Angkar and were prepared to sacrifice in its service. Angkar was Cambodia, and Cambodia was Angkar. Angkar, mysterious and impersonal, was the object of revolutionary

[60] Becker, *When the War Was Over*, pp. 172, 173, 183.
[61] See ibid., pp. 10, 25, 32, 42, 116, 122, 176, 183, 224.
[62] See ibid., p. 141.
[63] Members of the inner circle of Khmer Rouge leadership used "Pol Pot" and "Angkar" interchangeably. See Ben Kiernan, Introduction to "Planning the Past: The Forced Confessions of Hu Nim," Chandler et al., *Pol Pot Plans the Future*, pp. 227–232.

veneration. It was the "Most Respected and Beloved Angkar," embodiment of the "Most Respected and Beloved Party," that ruled the lives and circumstances of a Cambodia reborn.

The Costs

Between 1975 and 1979, for three years and eight months, the people of Cambodia labored under the ministrations of Pol Pot and the Khmer Rouge. Under the rule of the Communist Party of Kampuchea, more than twenty percent of the entire population of Cambodia perished.[64] With the failure of food production, an untold number died of starvation, neglect, suicide, and abuse. Lack of diligence at labor, evidence of discontent, recurrent absences, and "suspicious" behavior—any and all could earn one a death sentence in what has been aptly called an "indentured agrarian state." Any divergence from the "party line," any quality thought to threaten the political preeminence of Pol Pot, conjectured membership in an "antiparty clique" or in the phantasmagorical CIA, were all enough to earn one a sentence of death.[65]

Anyone not ethnically Khmer was suspect. At the very least, "nonkhmers" were thought lacking in devotion to the revolution. Anyone innocent of Khmer "culture," who spoke a "foreign" language, or who lived a style of life different from that of the Khmer was considered somehow "inferior." After all, they had not created the great civilization of Angkor Wat. They could not understand, nor take pride in the fact that destiny had called upon the Khmer people once again to lead the world to its next stage of development.[66] Those of Chinese, Thai, or Vietnamese origin, Muslim Chams, Laotians, and those belonging to "exotic" hill tribes, could understand none of that. They were not heir to the glories of Cambodia's past, and could not be expected to identify with the anticipated regeneration of the race. The result of all these notions was an "explosive combination of totalitarian political ambition and a racialist project of ethnic purification."[67]

In the subsequent months, thousands upon thousands of ethnic Chinese, Vietnamese, and Laotian Cambodians were sacrificed to Pol Pots prophetic vision of the future. Muslim Chams, their mullahs and their mosques, perished as well. Buddhists, Christians, their priests, and their churches followed. All

---

[64] Estimates vary widely, but that of Ben Kiernan is among the most persuasive. Kiernan, *The Pol Pot Regime*, pp. 456–465.

[65] Chandler, *Brother Number One*, pp. 205–209.

[66] See the discussion in Margolin, "Cambodia: The Country of Disconcerting Crimes," pp. 616–619.

[67] Kiernan, *The Pol Pot Regime*, p. xiv.

"superstitious beliefs" were to be expunged. The belief system of "Democratic Kampuchea" was to be purified of all things foreign.

The homicidal passion of the Khmer Rouge was not to abate. Within eighteen months of the conquest of power, the revolutionary leadership commenced to devour its own. A series of sanguinary purges decimated both the party leadership and its members. The insular leadership of the Khmer Rouge became increasingly paranoid—sacrificing to its pathology the population of entire regions. There were enemies everywhere. Finally, Pol Pot succumbed to his fear of his neighbors—and prepared to engage "socialist" Vietnam in mortal combat. The consequence was the Vietnamese invasion and conquest of Cambodia—and the destruction of the Khmer Rouge government. By the beginning of 1979, Pol Pot's peasant revolution was effectively over. It was left to history to be his judge.

Some have spoken of the entire sequence as some bizarre kind of "red fascism"—others of a "peasantist revolution of the purest sort," giving expression to the irrational violence typical of peasant populist uprisings.[68] For still others, the leaders of the Khmer Rouge revolution imagined Mao's Great Leap Forward and the subsequent Great Proletarian Cultural Revolution as "preparatory for ... the attempt to implement total Communism in one fell swoop." Pol Pot would undertake the attempt in retrograde Cambodia—to become the Marxist-Leninist who would be "enthroned higher than his glorious ancestors—Marx, Lenin, Stalin and Mao Zedong." He would lead humankind to redemption. He would become "a god on earth."[69]

In speaking to revolutionaries so very long ago, Friedrich Engels warned that once one appreciates the power of that Idea that promises an apocalyptic "thousand year reign," one can never abandon it, but "must follow it where it leads, even to death. . . . [That] is the true religion."[70]

Many in the twentieth century were to march behind the guidons of that new religion—without really anticipating the cost. Pol Pot's revolution was but the last in a series that made the twentieth century what it was. No one has yet satisfactorily explained the coming of those "true religions," and it is not certain that we shall see no more of them.

[68] See the entire discussion in Michael Vickery, *Cambodia 1975–1982* (Bangkok: OS Printing House, 1999), chap. 5. The Vietnamese, in justifying their invasion of a fellow "socialist" state insisted on its "fascist" character. Vickery speaks of the sadistic brutalities and the "racism" of the Khmer Rouge as the result of "poor peasant frustrations." See pp. 273, 281, 303.

[69] Margolin, "Cambodia: The Country of Disconcerting Crimes," pp. 577, 630.

[70] Friedrich Engels, *Schelling and Revelation: Critique of the Latest Attempt of Reaction against the Free Philosophy*, in Marx and Engels, *Collected Works*, vol. 2, p. 239.

CHAPTER TEN

Conclusions and Speculations

> Although there were important differences between . . . totalitarian regimes, they drew from a common well of enthusiasm, and shared such heretical goals (or rather temptations) as fashioning "new men" or establishing heaven on earth. They metabolised the religious instinct.
> —Michael Burleigh[1]

The twentieth century tested humanity in ways unanticipated by the prophets and sages of the nineteenth. Of course, there were those who had misgivings about what its reality might be. They reflected on all the calamities that had befallen humankind throughout the ages—ranging from the vast movement of peoples in antiquity that brought barbarians from hither Asia to Eastern Europe, to lay waste to township and field, and smite everyone before them—to the wars that overwhelmed the greatest civilizations of bygone time. They fully recalled the devastation wrecked by Germanic tribes, and the Norsemen, who burned and pillaged, and ruined everything in their path. They also remembered the full sweep of conquest during which Europeans decimated Australian Aborigines and the natives of the Western Hemisphere—and enslaved those of Africa. They understood that millions of human beings could be savaged by the violence of others. They knew full well what human beings were capable of doing to each other at the least provocation. And yet, none of that prepared them for what modern men might do having attained settled governance over others.

Very, very few imagined that a self-selected band of the political faithful might manifest the will, and exercise the power, to enlist untold millions to the task of hammering together a modern machine economy out of agrarian poverty, or march hundreds of kilometers to do battle with opponents superior in numbers and weaponry, and submit to so draconian a dominion that

---

[1] Michael Burleigh, *Sacred Causes: The Clash of Religion and Politics: From the Great War to the War on Terror* (New York: Harper, 2006), pp. xii–xiii, 18, with the last section a quote from Oskar Jaszi supplied by Burleigh.

they would see millions of their own number murdered without resistance. Few imagined that free men would participate in such enterprise with so little protest and, at times, with enthusiasm.

There have been vast undertakings in history. Ancient emperors, hardly remembered pharaohs, and forgotten rulers, have raised massive structures, defensive battlements, ossuaries, temples, and monuments at great cost and corresponding sacrifice. Massed humans have left hearth and home for years on end to undertake strange crusades and explore mysterious places. For all of that, there seems to have been something different in the frightening spectacles of the twentieth century.

Throughout the entire period, in Europe and Asia, everyone, literally without exception, was caught up in undertakings characterized by the prodigal waste, or intentional destruction, of human beings. Millions perished, not because it was necessary to a grand purpose, but because of hubris, monumental incompetence, or because identified as enemies by a belief system imagined impeccably true. Members of the "bourgeoisie," Jews, or "antiparty" elements—or those considered somehow alien or unfit—were marked for murder. Those so marked—the enemies of the systems of which we speak—had few options. They were barred from reconciliation with those who were to decide their fate—because of their class membership or their very antecedents, because of their personal biology, or by the perversity of those who governed.

Humankind has long since become accustomed to the mass destruction of those identified as enemy combatants—and the enslavement of others taken in war. In the past, millions have been put to the sword arbitrarily, because of their ethnic origin or their religious convictions. But it was the twentieth century that managed to bring even more capriciousness and inhumanity to the mayhem. By the mid twentieth century, mass murder came to typify an entire class of political regimes. Even before the coming of the Second World War, millions of citizens were destroyed by those who governed, even though their rulers were nominally at peace with everyone. Untold numbers were threatened with "shunning," incarceration, expulsion, or death—because of membership in a proscribed class, ethnic, or religious community. However prepared those threatened might have been to abandon those identities—to become whatever wished by those who ruled—that possibility was foreclosed. Those afflicted with "counterrevolutionary class consciousness" could do little, if anything, to have themselves restored to good favor. Those so unfortunate as to have "bourgeois"—landlord or capitalist—backgrounds were denied schooling or employment, and were often marked for destruction. Rulers sometimes sentenced them to thankless labor, exiled them, transported them, incarcerated them, and often, if not always, killed them. Finally, those deemed members of a scorned race or despised class could do very little to earn tolerance, much less security. Minimally scheduled for abuse, many, if not most, were ultimately consigned to martyrdom.

In the twentieth century, hundreds of millions of human beings suffered unnatural deaths at the hands of those who governed them. Of course, mass murder has not been unique in history, but its sanction by public rationale—providing motives to rulers, and influencing the behavior of masses—may well be. That such a rationale licenses the systematic destruction of entire groups *within* a community at peace, contributes to the enormity.

That such homicidal public enterprise has behind it the persuasiveness of moral counsel, the force of law, and the power of the state, renders its enormity almost incomprehensible. In such instances, the murder of those the state is expected to protect is not random, but governed by principle, and facilitated by carefully contrived organization. Murder on such scale, supported by public endorsement, and employing public instrumentalities, must necessarily engage the overt or tacit participation of large segments of the community—so that virtually all are made complicit. In substance, in the twentieth, humanity has experienced a century in which governments have sponsored, sanctioned, and created special facilities for the mass destruction of innocent lives. It has engaged almost everyone in the doing. All of which makes the mass murders of the twentieth century perhaps unique in history.

The century opened with politically initiated violence in Colombia that claimed more than 100,000 lives—the result of efforts by contending *caudillos* to attain and sustain power. It involved those in power employing lethal force in order to secure privilege.[2] Towards the end of the century, an estimated 300,000 Ugandans perished under the atavistic rule of Idi Amin.[3] In Burundi, Hutu and Tutsi tribesmen exacted vengeance against each other, sometimes employing the instrumentalities of the state to effect their purpose. The murders were visceral, incited by old hatreds and fueled by contemporary affronts.[4] In Darfur, regional conflict took on the features of mass murder and ethnic cleansing in the government's efforts to retain regional dominance. Throughout Africa, anachronistic political and tribal violence has taken untold lives.

[2] See William Stokes, "Violence as a Power Factor in Latin American Politics," in Francisco José Moreno and Barbara Mitrani, eds., *Conflict and Violence in Latin American Politics* (New York: Thomas Y. Crowell, 1971), pp. 446–469.

[3] See Martin Carney, "Amin's Uganda," *The Nation*, 12 April 1975, pp. 430–435; Whitney Ellsworth, "The Structure of Repression in Uganda," *Amnesty International Release*, 15 June 1978.

[4] See the account in "Sin and Confession in Rwanda" *The Economist*, 334, no. 7897 (14 January 1995), p. 53.

In Latin America, in Paraguay, Uruguay, Argentina, and Chile, there have been episodes of political mayhem on horrific scale.[5] While much of all this has taken on some of the properties of those mass murders emblematic of the twentieth century, they fall short, in significant measure, on one or more dimensions. Often they are better understood as criminal enterprise rather than the result of an effort to realize apocalyptic ends. In none of the object instances was there any systematic effort to provide a public rationale that pretended to vindicate the violence. In all the violence, there was an absence of the justificatory rationale provided by an appropriate political religion.

There were intimations of the future in the prototypical mass expulsion and murder of Armenians at the turn of the twentieth century. The crimes began with the Ottomans—the result of a sensed threat to prevailing power. They continued under the ministrations of revolutionary Kemalists—inspired by a reasonably well formulated ideology of solidarist nationalism and rapid industrial development. Perhaps as many as 1.5 million Armenians lost their lives in the violence that persisted into the new century.[6]

It seems more than coincidental that organized violence against one's own citizens and the appearance of mass mobilizing, developmental ideologies should intersect at the commencement of the twentieth century. The turn of the century experienced the rise of reactive nationalisms, with their transformative passions, and leaders provisioned with powers of life and death.[7] Much of that had been incubating since the French revolution, and the memory of that experience was to inform revolutionary leaders throughout the nineteenth century.[8]

Revolution and Development

By the end of the nineteenth century, José Rizal (1861–1896) spoke, with uncommon passion, if with uncertain program, of a developmental nationalism that would bring the Philippines into the modern world. Originally reformist, his *Liga Filipina* advocated national unity, the expansion of education, and the methodical encouragement of industry, commerce, and agriculture. Rizal

---

[5] See, for example, Richard Arens, ed., *Genocide in Paraguay* (Philadelphia: Temple University Press, 1976).

[6] Richard G. Hovannisian, *The Armenian Holocaust* (Cambridge, Mass.: Armenian Heritage Press, 1980).

[7] See the available data in R. J. Rummel, *Statistics of Democide: Genocide and Mass Murder since 1900* (New Brunswick, N.J.: Transaction Publishers, 1997).

[8] See the insightful account in Michael Burleigh, *Earthly Powers: The Clash of Religion and Politics in Europe from the French Revolution to the Great War* (New York: Harper Collins Publishers, 2005).

spoke of restoring dignity, efficacy, and a future, to a humbled, colonized, people, reacting to the pretense of foreigners.[9] In Cuba, at almost the same time, José Martí (1853–1895) became the advocate of an anti-imperialist nationalism that sought the mass mobilization of his conationals against their oppressors. He sought a regenerate Cuba, making of an oppressed people, "new men," independent and self-confident.

In China, at the turn of the twentieth century, Sun Yat-sen (1866–1925) became the inspired advocate of a coherent and consistent nationalism that sought the reestablishment of sovereign integrity to his motherland. The defense of that restored integrity required rapid, if phased, development of heavy industry that would provide national security its requisite capabilities.[10]

In India, Vinayak D. Savarkar (1883–1966) sought to mobilize Hindus around a developmental program calculated to free his nation from foreign control, and restore it to "its rightful place" among the world's political actors.[11] On the margins, there was the developmental nationalism of Marcus Garvey (1887–1940), who spoke of an imagined industrialized and powerful "Black nation"—to be inhabited by martial Black men who aspired to "empire."[12]

Throughout the period, some reasonably well devised ideologies of reactive nationalism and rapid economic, particularly industrial, development made their appearance. By the time Kemal Ataturk called together his followers, Japan had already covered the initial stages in its transition from an agrarian, to an industrial, economy. Russia and Italy had begun fairly rapid economic development—accompanied by only half formulated ideological impulse. More and more intellectuals, denizens of less developed communities, had become aware that the twentieth century demanded that each community organize itself to meet the challenges that radiated outward from the advanced industrial powers.

It is evident that all such efforts, however well or ill conceived, engaged the most intense emotion among both revolutionaries and those they succeeded in mobilizing. Nationalism, itself, was uniquely affect laden. The identification with a community of similars, in an existential struggle for a secure place in an

---

[9] After the Second World War, Filipino nationalists sought to make Rizal's novels, *Noli Mi Tangere* and *El Filibusterismo*, required reading for everyone in school. Both novels are available in English in a Longman Group edition. Rizal's works were to inspire later nationalists and developmentalists.

[10] For a brief account of the ideology of Sun, see A. James Gregor, *Marxism, China, and Development: Reflections on Theory and Reality* (New Brunswick, N.J.: Transaction Publishers, 1995), chaps. 7, 8, and 10.

[11] For an account of the ideology of Savarkar, see A. James Gregor, *The Search for Neofascism: The Use and Abuse of Social Science* (New York: Cambridge University Press, 2006), chap. 8.

[12] For a brief account of the ideology of Garvey, see ibid., chap. 5.

uncertain world, generated a predictable sense of threat, and inspired an insistence on unquestioned solidarity.[13]

In the first beginnings of the modern world, it became evident that some few European nations had developed the mobility, and the power projection capabilities, to threaten the most remote and long established communities. Among those threatened, there was response—at first tentative—and then insistent. Menaced peoples struggled to make effective reply. Responses ranged from abject submission to violent xenophobia. Within those parameters, the reactions ranged from an archaism that sought hermetic isolation and the restoration of ancient virtues—through selective accommodation calculated to disarm—to swift adaptation to foreign ways—in order to rekindle collective virtue, foster industrialization, enhance politicization, exalt the past, and anticipate a regenerative future.[14]

The stresses that attended such efforts found release in a variety of fashions. Assuagement almost invariably involved action, and a call to action—on behalf of conationals, living and dead, and yet unborn. In the course of meeting individual and collective responsibility, there is the acknowledgment of the need to sacrifice, to labor, to struggle, to endure, and to prevail. There are calls to discipline and commitment. There is call for an affirmation of virtue. There is a fervor akin to that found in the most deeply felt religious experience. One finds all or some of this in the earliest expressions of modern reactive nationalism—in the writings of Kemal, Rizal, Martí, Sun, Savarkar, and Garvey—among all its advocates, known and unremembered. One finds evidence of similar ardor and dispositions in the clear-eyed precepts of German, Italian, and Russian nationalists facing real and imagined enemies more industrially advanced.

Among some of the most important modern revolutionaries, enduring sentiment takes on the unmistakable properties of religion. There is talk of forces that govern life—that afford it meaning, prescribe and proscribe conduct, and define virtue and its absence. Among the most intense, reactive, and developmental nationalism, heroes, saints, and martyrs make their appearance. It is a nationalism that identifies those who betray their calling, not only as selfish, callow, cowardly, and venal, but as heretics, and apostates, as well. In its struggle, it perceives its leaders as providential heralds of a consecrated future,

[13] There is a vast literature on nationalism. John Hutchinson and Anthony D. Smith have put together a collection of readings that provides a range of opinion that is useful. See John Hutchinson and Anthony D. Smith, *Nationalism* (New York: Oxford University Press, 1994). I have found particularly helpful Eugen Lemberg, *Nationalismus: Psychologie und Geschichte* (Munich: Rowohlt, 1964).

[14] See the account in Maria Hsia Chang, *Return of the Dragon: China's Wounded Nationalism* (Boulder, Colo.: Westview Press, 2001), chaps. 4 and 5.

the bearers of grace, members of a sacerdotal order; it generates a liturgy, it catechizes doctrine, fabricates symbols, and becomes the heir of sacred texts. Doctrine transcends the level of the political, and takes on religious properties. In its course, the twentieth century became littered with political parties led by "apostles," "saviors," and charismatics of sundry kinds. They appeared in greatest abundance in Europe between the wars.

During that time, there was the proliferation of Marxist parties, first internationalist, but soon constructing developmental "socialisms" in single countries—in order to break the "encirclement of capitalism." And there were Grey Shirts, and Blue Shirts, and Green Shirts, and Silver Shirts, together with Shirts of Black and Brown, marshalling into seried ranks, those of the National, and the Fatherland, Fronts, the Iron Guards, National Syndicalists, Rexists, the Falanga, and those of the Arrow Cross—all arrayed against foreign threat.

All of these, Marxist and nonmarxist alike, shared significant commonalities. They were all inspired by an ideology considered flawless, chiliastic in intent, moralizing in demeanor, demanding in application, and unmercifully punishing instances of real or perceived, individual or collective, infraction. There were charismatic leaders everywhere, appearing as "captains," "caudillos," or simply as the *Vozhd*, or "Great Leader"—all comfortable in speaking of the "sacralization" of politics, and of the "faith" of members.[15]

All, to some degree or another, were committed to rapid industrialization, in the undisguised effort to construct the ability to project power.[16] Marxists, having undertaken revolution in economically backward environments, very rapidly initiated programs of forced industrialization. Fascists came to power with the sure conviction that a secure future, and the realization of their respective programs, required rapid development—with an emphasis on machine industry for the provision of weapons platforms.[17]

Revolutions of both the left and the right sought rapid and technologically sophisticated growth. What distinguished them for a time were the particular strategies employed. In the past, the abolition or maintenance of private prop-

[15] See, for example, Corneliu Zelea Codreanu, *Guardia di ferro* (Padua: Edizioni di Ar, 1972).

[16] In the past, it was held that generic fascism was a movement that consciously sought to protect the profits of industrialists and financiers by *restricting machine production*, *curtailing technological innovation*, and undertaking a *systematic destruction of inventories*. It is now generally acknowledged that "contrary to a common assertion, economic development was a major goal" of fascist groups. Stanley Payne, *A History of Fascism, 1914–1945* (Madison: The University of Wisconsin Press, 1995), p. 18; see ibid., chap. 14; and Rajani Palme Dutt, *Fascism and Social Revolution* (New York: International Publishers, 1934); see the entire discussion in A. James Gregor, *Interpretations of Fascism* (New Brunswick, N.J.: Transaction Publishers, 2000), chap. 5.

[17] See the discussion in A. James Gregor, *Italian Fascism and Developmental Dictatorship* (Princeton: Princeton University Press, 1979).

erty as an institution was frequently cited as the critical distinction between left and right revolutionary movements and established systems. From the perspective of history it is evident that Marxist systems have been prepared to embrace private property—as well as market modalities—when it served developmental purpose. One need only consider the postmaoist developments in "communist" China.[18] On the other hand, Mussolini was prepared to so attenuate the formal rights of private property in the Italian Social Republic (1943–1945), that any enthusiasts for "free enterprise" that may have collected themselves around his standards could only have been confounded.[19]

In all of that some of these developmental nationalisms crystallized into true totalitarianisms—Marxist-Leninist, Fascist, and National Socialist. Their features were evident—and in the postwar years new members of the class crowded around the survivors.

Developmental Regimes as Totalitarianisms

Considering what rapid economic change and development requires of a community, it is not difficult to anticipate some of the properties that would accompany the process. Major changes in the system of production, no matter the pace, require readjustment on the part of large segments of the population on an unprecedented scale. Urbanization alone, the transfer of populations from familiar rural settings to city life, is traumatic. Traditional norms no longer bind, and familiar conduct is tested by entirely unanticipated circumstances. The historic institutions that advanced those norms and sanctioned those behaviors are hollowed out. A conscious or unconscious effort at their repair, or a search for their replacement, is essayed.[20]

One finds anticipation of all this in the instructive efforts of the Taiping revolutionaries in the China of the middle of the nineteenth century. At the time, China was well into its "century of humiliation." Foreign incursions had weakened the dynasty and humbled the Chinese. Escalating taxes had alienated the peasantry and there was restiveness throughout the land. "Plebian" intellectuals—the marginal figures in a society suffering systemic changes—sought to restore security to themselves, and lost glories to the nation. They chose to attempt that by introducing a peculiar form of Christianity around which all

---

[18] See the discussion in Maria Hsia Chang, *The Labors of Sisyphus: The Economic Development of Communist China* (New Brunswick, N.J.: Transaction Publishers, 2000), chaps. 3 and 4.

[19] See the discussion in A. James Gregor, *The Ideology of Fascism: The Rationale of Totalitarianism* (New York: The Free Press, 1969), chap. 7.

[20] For a more extended discussion of this process, see Gregor, *Interpretations of Fascism*, chaps. 6 and 7.

revolutionaries might collect in unity. It was a politicized religion that consolidated the demanding enterprise.

Between 1851 and 1864, enlisting recruits from the ranks of those displaced by the changes percolating through the nation's economy—the unemployed, alienated literati, migrant artisans, ruined tradesmen, and cashiered military—the Taiping peasant revolutionaries brought developmental intent to a troubled China. There were efforts at the construction of a transportation and communication infrastructure, and the mobilization of labor. Their implausible leader made his appearance as the "younger brother of Jesus," and he pledged those who followed him in obedience and resolve, a "Taiping Heavenly Kingdom," in which they would secure redemption. Obedience, commitment, loyalty, and seamless unity were purchased by invoking a form of a politicized religiosity, apparently conceived functional in a demanding environment of stress and sacrifice. Time and circumstances abbreviated the process, and left only the intimations of a system.

When, at the beginning of the twentieth century, Sun Yat-sen sought to pursue the development of China, following the failed efforts of the Taiping revolutionaries and the Ching reformers, he invoked a redacted Confucianism in the effort to instill among his followers an awareness of the seriousness of life, the virtue of frugality, and the laudability of labor.[21] He clearly understood its instrumental importance in mobilizing the mass support essential for a demanding, collective, and complex project.[22] In a revolutionary mass-mobilizing developmental undertaking, peasant masses would be required to participate in ways never before imagined. Politicized religion was to serve as ancillary to Sun's ideology.

It seems to have been evident to many, if not all, reactive nationalists at the end of the nineteenth, and the beginning of the twentieth, century that economic, particularly industrial, development was crucial to the survival, well-being, and status of their nation. Among the most effective, it was generally un-

---

[21] For a reasonable length of time, Western economists attributed the rapid economic development in Asia—in Taiwan, South Korea, and Japan—to the influence of Confucianism. Sun anticipated them by more than half a century. Although a convert to Christianity, Sun saw Confucianism as a linchpin of his developmental program. See the discussion in Gottfried-Karl Kindermann, *Konfuzianismus, Sunyatsenismus und chinesicher Kommunismus* (Breigau: Rombach, 1963), pp. 30–38; and Tai Tschi-tao, *Die geistigen Grundlagen des Sun Yat-senismus* (Berlin: Würfel, 1931), p. 83. Sun argued, "We must revive not only our old morality, but also our old learning. If we want to regain our national spirit, we must reawaken the learning as well as the moral ideals which we once possessed. What is this ancient learning? ... It is found in the *Great Learning* of Confucius." Sun Yat-sen, *San Min Chu I* (Taipei: China Publishing, n.d.), pp. 41–42.

[22] See Sun's account of his project in Sun Yat-sen, *The International Development of China* (Taipei: China Cultural Service, 1953).

derstood that the process necessitated the urgent accumulation of capital critical for the establishment of domestic industry, for infrastructural construction, for skills and technical training, and for security. Extracting, accumulating, and selectively deploying capital, inevitably would generate tension, restiveness, and resistance. "Surpluses" would have to be wrested from impoverished, reluctant, largely peasant populations. To accomplish that required the appeal to strategies of control. Given the limited governmental resources available, population control could be best accomplished by the inculcation of self-governing principles. Rather than a supervisory system manned by special personnel armed with effective, and expensive, technology, an attempt at control is undertaken through normative conditioning—the fixing of conduct through instruction and by example. Religion, in whatever form it assumes, effectively contributes to the entire process.

Developmental systems, whatever their specific political orientations, seem to find politicized or political religion of singular service. Marxisms, heir to the sacralized systems of Marx and Engels, very quickly put together suitable formularies, with iconic founders, sacred texts, charismatic leaders, sacerdotal parties, myths and liturgies, saints and martyrs. The iteration of such systems on the "Right," throughout the twentieth century, more than suggests that they are not specific to either "Left" or "Right."

In central Europe, involved as it was in a related process of nation building and economic development through much of the nineteenth century, Hegelianism served a multiplicity of purposes—those he intended and those unintended. Hegel expected his thought to help make Germans philosophically sophisticated and pious. He also imagined that it would tend to prompt them to become fastidiously moral, industrious, obedient, frugal, responsible, committed, communitarian, and self-sacrificial. All of that was to be put to purposes Hegel had not envisioned. All of this could be, and was, configured to a variety of ends not necessarily foreseen by the author. By the time Hegelianism contributed to the nationalist and developmental purposes of Giovanni Gentile half a hundred years later, for example, it had taken on the explicit attributes of secular religiosity typically found in modern totalitarianism.

For their part, Ludwig Feuerbach and Moses Hess had taken Hegelianism in another direction. It passed through the prism of Karl Marx and Friedrich Engels—ultimately to conclude, as "Dialectical Materialism," with the undisguised developmentalism of Josef Stalin almost a century later—and the even more distracted form in which it appeared in the forced draft industrialization of Maoist China. The entire devolution ended with Pol Pot, who had little, if any, awareness of the origins of the political faith that moved him and his followers to bring economic ruin and mass murder to Cambodia.

Other than a linear sequence from Hegel to revolutionary developmentalists, there was more in the neohegelianism of Feuerbach that was to influence political evolution throughout the nineteenth and into the twentieth centuries. Everyone acknowledges Feuerbach's influence on the generation of Marx's "materialist conception of history." On the other hand, the impact of Feuerbach's doctrine of "theanthropism" on the revolutionary thought of the period is not as frequently appreciated.

There was much in the theanthropism of Feuerbach that fed into the changes that thrust themselves upon Europe in the twentieth century. Clearly, Feuerbach's activism, his demand that human beings assume responsibility for themselves and their well-being, served the purposes of developmentalism eminently well. But there was more than that.

Feuerbach, in the course of his critique of received Hegelianism, sought to invest humanity with at least some of the attributes of divinity—he sought to render human beings divine. As has been earlier suggested, Feuerbach sought to recover, for humankind, all those transcendent qualities Hegel had assigned the Absolute Spirit. Feuerbach would have human beings, themselves, creators of a life redeemed. Feuerbach had "inverted" the dialectic of Hegel in order to restore to human beings the properties philosophy and religion had alienated. Feuerbach would have humans, as "species beings," together with "history," responsible for the circumstances governing their lives. He argued that all the elements of civilized life, long credited to divinity, in fact, were the products of human enterprise. In a significant sense, theanthropism made human beings, as group animals, not only responsible for their lives, but in some sense, worthy of worship. Their works took on existential significance. Feuerbach had convinced several generations to believe that humankind, in organized community, somehow participated in what used to be spoken of as "God's work."

There was more than activism in Feuerbach's theanthropism. He argued that human beings, as group creatures swept up in goal directed history, created, enhanced, and sustained science, art, and morality—everything of merit. He advanced those notions at about the time that biological *racism* made its first formal appearance. At almost the same time that Feuerbach spoke of humans being responsible for their own world, Arthur de Gobineau made the case that only *some* human beings were divinely creative and equipped to foster and further culture. Richard Wagner, originally animated by Feuerbach's conception of human beings as creative social animals, found plausibility in the arguments of Gobineau.

Gobineau's views afforded emotional depth and cognitive texture to the nationalism Wagner brought to the turbulence of Germany at mid nineteenth century. By the end of the century, Houston Stewart Chamberlain was to assemble all of that in an effort to account for the "foundations" of the modern era. Others were to take what he provided and mold it into a sacralized system of mass mobilization, intended to restore dignity and status to a defeated Germany.

That probably would not have been possible had not Germany found itself challenging the cultural, trade, and colonial dominion of the advanced industrial powers at the beginning of the twentieth century—only to suffer catastrophic defeat in the Great War. In the intellectual and moral denouement that resulted, there was a demand for the creation of those material and spiritual conditions necessary not only for Germany's survival, but its prevalence.

In the unprecedented intensity generated by the demands made by rapid industrialization, solidarity, and dedication, one of the many conditions advanced as necessary for community survival and success was the demand for infrangible unity, for spiritual union—a demand that often found expression in some form of ethnic fraternalism.

In such a crisis environment, there were many prepared to argue that a true sense of community could only be forged of shared traits: common behavior, common language, common beliefs, common aspirations, common allegiance, and common commitment. There were others who confidently traced all that back to common biology—to race or ethnicity.[23]

In trying to understand the ideology that results from the demand for rapid political and economic change, the emergence of racism among its doctrinal beliefs appears to be neither totally incomprehensible nor entirely idiosyncratic. One can trace a similar evolution, for example, in the work of Moses Hess—contemporary of both Feuerbach and Marx. As has been indicated, Hess was a person of transformative influence in the maturation of the thought of Karl Marx. Not only was he credited with converting the liberal Marx to communism, Hess is reputed to have helped give the first Marxism theoretical expression.

After a period of intense intellectual collaboration with Marx and Engels, Hess went on to independently develop his own notions about social change and human history. In the first years of the 1860s, he published his *Rome and Jerusalem*—in which he spoke, once again, as he had in his youth, of history discharging the same tasks as those assigned the Creator—and, like Hegel, he saw God's handiwork in the doings of peoples, of nations, and of states.

Among those peoples, Hess identified the Jews as assigned special responsi-

---

[23] See the discussion in Ludwig Schemann, *Die Rasse in den Geisteswissenschaften* (Munich: J. F. Lehmanns Verlag, 1928), and *Die Rassenfragen im Schrifttum der Neuzeit* (Munich: J. F. Lehmanns Verlag, 1931).

bilities. He saw them charged with the ethical uplift of humanity. To discharge those responsibilities, Hess argued, Jews were endowed with special properties. Attendant to "history's" purposes, Hess insisted that those properties be protected, preserved against debasement or loss. Like Gobineau, he saw the loss of talent the consequent and lamentable result of a loss of a sense of community. Hess was convinced that an unprincipled mixture of Jews and Gentiles, for example, would thwart history's plan. In order to discharge its tasks, and to preserve itself in purity, Hess urged the "Jewish nation" to undertake the development of science and industry in essential isolation, so that the "New Israel" he advocated, wreathed in theanthropic traits, would forever serve as lodestar to humanity.[24] Hess anticipated a process of national development inspired by a clear expression of political religion.

Hess sought to support development through the maintenance of endogamy—within a breeding circle composed of gifted participants, sharing not only common sentiments, but what could only be hereditary endowments, as well. The entire line of argument found in the later work of Hess was to be reinforced by the rise of Darwinism. It can be traced, for example, in the publications of Ludwig Woltmann—who, by the end of the nineteenth century, systematically sought to draw out the implications of a natural science "Hegelianism."

Woltmann, a student of Hegel and of Feuerbach, attempted to fuse all the elements to be found in such works as *Rome and Jerusalem* into a social doctrine of revolutionary consequence. What emerged from the effort was a kind of Darwinian socialism, part Hegel, part Feuerbach, part Hess, part Marx, and part biological racism—all in combination as a "new religion." In the end, by the beginning of the twentieth century, Woltmann became the advocate of a form of biological Nordicism that quickly found audience among people undergoing the stresses of developmental competition, subsequent military defeat, and the consequent efforts to regain positions lost.[25]

Some of these traits here considered, seem to hang together. Among reactive nationalists, the demand for consummate unity, obedience, selfless commitment, and faith suggests a general response to environmental demands. External threats, the loss of status and security, the necessity of accelerated economic, particularly industrial, development, precipitates a search for seamless

[24] Moses Hess, "Rom und Jerusalem," in Hess, *Ausgewählte Schriften* (Cologne: Akademische Verlag, 1962). An English translation is available as Hess, *Rome and Jerusalem* (New York: Philosophical Library, 1958). I have provided a brief account of Hess' views in A. James Gregor, *The Faces of Janus: Marxism and Fascism in the Twentieth Century* (New Haven: Yale University Press, 2000), pp. 158–160.

[25] For a more extensive account of Woltmann's ideas, as they evolved out of traditional Marxism, see the account in A. James Gregor, *Marxism, Fascism, and Totalitarianism: Chapters in the Intellectual History of Radicalism* (Stanford: Stanford University Press, 2009), chap. 3.

unity—however it is to be achieved. One of the contingent forms that search produces is one or another expression of racism.

During the period covering the end of the nineteenth and the beginning of the twentieth century, the impulse to seek homogeneity among many of those who were denizens of communities in reactive crisis, found outlet in some form of racism. There was a tendency to associate community with consanguinity—however consanguinity was understood. Thus, Sun Yat-sen spoke of the Chinese as a "natural" community, united not by force or convention, but by blood. He spoke of the modern emergence of a "new Chinese race." It would be the result of the fusion of related stocks—united by residence, language, religion, custom, and usage—inspired by a history of ancient glories, and imbued with unflagging patriotism. It would be a new race that would create out of an imperiled nation a proud, powerful, industrial China that, once again, would become "the center of the universe."[26]

Over time, before and after the Second World War, lesser figures, such as Marcus Garvey, José Vasconcelos (1881–1959), and V. D. Savarkar, invoked race (in one sense or another) to ensure unity and to energize masses to redemptive purpose. All appealed to lost glories, and national redemption. Among them, there was sometimes more than the suggestion that their very history attested to their intrinsic superiority. Even after racism had been discredited by the horrors associated with the Second World War, Vasconcelos could still advocate the creation of a unified and unifying "cosmic race" that would awaken the *Mestizaje* populations of Latin America to their responsibilities as harbingers of a new, creative "Atlantean" age.[27]

In instances of this sort, the homogeneity sought would be achieved through policies each carrying vastly different consequences in train—some recommending voluntary endogamous breeding, others prescriptive or proscriptive practices, and still others, homicidal "ethnic cleansing."[28] In each case, the intended or serendipitous political purpose would be to instill, among members of a subject population, a religious sense of community that would sustain them through the arduous processes associated with collective redemption.

Similar traits surfaced among revolutionary movements throughout Europe during the interwar years. Among Italian Fascists, the relatively benign

---

[26] Sun Yat-sen, *The Triple Demism of Sun Yat-sen* (New York: AMS Press, a reprint of the Wuchang edition, 1931). Lecture Series I: "Nationalism," sect. 20, p. 20.

[27] See José Vasconcelos, *The Cosmic Race* (Baltimore: The Johns Hopkins University Press, 1979).

[28] In his *Foundations*, Houston Stewart Chamberlain argued for a dynamic, populationist conception of race and race formation—much closer to the notions of Sun Yat-sen and Savarkar than Alfred Rosenberg or Adolf Hitler. See Chamberlain, *Foundations of the Nineteenth Century* (London: John Lane, 1911), vol. 1, pp. 258–297.

form it took was similar to that found in the writings of Sun.[29] It involved a populationist notion of raciation, which conceived races, over time, essentially the product of relative breeding isolation and shared community. Inspired by united purpose, through devoted labor and self-sacrifice, the "new race" was expected to restore to the peninsula the lost glories of antiquity.

Again, the appeal to race was functional in the sense that it helped to create the sense of unity required for development. National Socialism was its pathological, and dysfunctional, expression. Unhappy variants surfaced in Romania's Iron Guard, Hungary's Arrow Cross, and Croatia's Ustasha.

That such developments, however benign or malevolent, were not simply aberrant is attested to by the fact that one can find approximations in the ideologies generally considered "universalistic," and "antiracist." As early as the late 1920s, for example, the Bolsheviks sought revolutionary unity in the "homogenization" of their population—an effort that quickly devolved into a program predicated on a confused "ethnicization"—ethnic cleansing. Thus, by the first years of the 1930s, Stalinist population policy could hardly be identified as class based. Kurds and Koreans, Kuban Cossacks and Chechens, Poles and Finns, Iranians and Balts—irrespective of class provenience or political loyalty—were all selected for incarceration, transportation, and/or mass murder. Millions were punished or destroyed for no reason other than their ethnic or national identities. Once a collective was declared "alien," its individual members each became subject to penalty.

These policies, begun at the very commencement of the Soviet period, continued through and after the Second World War—ultimately involving a program of pernicious antisemitism. They were policies calculated to produce a "homogenization of the ethnic landscape"—an engineered unity that would foster and sustain the programs of the regime. As a consequence, it has been argued that "ethnic cleansing was not a marginal phenomenon of Stalin's terror. Rather it was at the core." The search for ethnic homogenization persisted throughout the years of Marxism-Leninism's consolidation.

Only when the Soviet state was beginning to show unmistakable signs of mortality, did a group of Marxist-Leninist intellectuals make a public case for an ethnically based national policy. They sought to buttress the failing regime by publicly appealing to "ethnogenetic Eurasianism"—an appeal to a form of

---

[29] See the discussion in Gregor, *The Ideology of Fascism*, chap. six. The formal statement of Fascist racism included the insistence that "To say that human races exist is not to say *apriori* that there exist superior or inferior races, but only to say that there exist different human races." Ibid., p. 383. For an interesting account of Fascist racial theory, cf. Aaron Gillette, *Racial Theories in Fascist Italy* (New York: Routledge, 2002). Fascist race theory shared properties with the "populationist conception" of race formation found in the writings of Houston Stewart Chamberlain and Sun Yat-sen.

ethnic unity calculated to provide a biological foundation for the nationalism upon which Soviet socialism, in fact, had always rested.[30]

By the end of the 1980s, Lev Nikolaevich Gumilev (1912–1992) was the doctrinal spokesman for a notion he identified as "ethnogenesis." He collected around himself a number of intellectually sophisticated Soviet authors, recognized throughout the 1970s and 1980s as nationalists and statists, and spoke of the rise, durability, and historic responsibilities of ethnic communities. Whatever else it may have been, Gumilev insisted that his appeal to ethnogenetic Eurasianism was not only fully compatible with the "dialectical and historical materialism" of traditional Marxism-Leninism, but was its "theoretical culmination."[31]

In fact, ethnogenesis supplied the overt expression of a silent component of the developmental nationalism that had always been the inspiration of communist rule. Through much of its history, Soviet intellectuals were under obligation to deplore nationalism and any expression of racism as "antimarxist." "Patriotism"—emotional devotion to the state—was offered as a functional substitute. In retrospect, however, it is clear that Russians had always been, and remained, nationalists—Russian Marxist-Leninists no less so. By the time of the Second World War there was no longer even an effort to maintain any pretense of antinationalism. The war was undertaken as a defense of "Mother Russia." By the time the entire system showed signs of imminent disintegration in the 1980s, nationalism, and "ethnicism," were seen to be its remaining sources of vitality.[32]

In retrospect, it seems clear that whatever the official, prescribed doctrine may have held, both nationalism and some form of racism had been part of the belief system of most Russians, and implicit in the Soviet ideology of development, since the October revolution.[33] Stalin's antisemitism and the wholesale

---

[30] See the documented discussion in Jörg Baberowski and Anselm Doering-Manteuffel, "The Quest for Order and the Pursuit of Terror," in Michael Geyer and Sheila Fitzpatrick, *Beyond Totalitarianism: Stalinism and Nazism Compared* (New York: Cambridge University Press, 2009), pp. 216; cf. pp. 201–227. I have provided a brief account of the "ethnogenesis" of Lev Gumiliev, in A. James Gregor, *Phoenix: Fascism in Our Time* (New Brunswick, N.J.: Transaction Publishers, 1999), pp. 157–161.

[31] Lev Gumilev, *Ethnogenesis and the Biosphere* (Moscow: Progress Publishers, 1990), p. 277; see pp. 9, 29, 56–57, 76–77, 275–276. For a discussion of Soviet ideology during its final phase, see A. James Gregor, "Fascism and the New Russian Nationalism," *Communist and Post-Communist Studies*, 31, no. 1 (March 1998), pp. 1–16.

[32] This spiralled off into a syncretic "National Bolshevism" that sought a synthesis of "fascism" and "bolshevism." See *The Seminal Writings of Alexander Dugin* (London: The Rising Press, 2000), 3 vols., and *The Eurasian Manifesto: The Crisis of Ideas in Contemporary Russia* (London: The Rising Press, 2001).

[33] See the entire discussion in Mikhail Agursky, *The Third Rome: National Bolshevism in the USSR* (Boulder, Colo.: Westview Press, 1987); Yitzhak M. Brudny, *Reinventing Russia: Russian Nationalism and*

deportation of settled ethnic populations prior to, and after, the Second World War, is persuasive evidence of that.[34]

Much the same might be said of doctrinal developments in postmaoist China. Chinese intellectuals, dealing with a community largely composed of homogeneous Han elements, are no longer reticent in appealing to a form of populationist racism, shared with Sun Yet-sen and Chiang Kai-shek, to support the reactive, developmental nationalism that is, and has always been, at the center of China's revolution.[35]

Similarly, Pol Pot invoked the glories of the Khmer past to pursue what has been called a policy of racial "purity," and homicidal ethnic cleansing, in Democratic Kampuchea.[36] The most consistent criteria for discrimination in Pol Pot's Cambodia were ethnic. Only "genuine Khmers" were to be redeemed.

It is not clear if "racism," in whatever form, is a necessary component of totalitarian systems. Certainly, it seems a contingency that arises out of the insistent effort to foster, sustain, and emphasize unity in the community making the transit through rapid development and industrial sophistication. Its appearance would seem to be more than coincidental.

A comparative history of these regimes has not yet been written. We have very little of the conceptual and documentary materials that would make such an effort really effective. Moreover, most of these regimes have endured a relatively brief time. It is difficult to speak of their intrinsic traits, or speculate on the various stages they have traversed or will traverse in the future.

The People's Republic of China is a case in point. It is of analytic interest because together with the residues of a sacralized Marxism and a statist Confucianism, it continues to satisfy most of the property traits characteristics of a twentieth century developmental dictatorship. Some have argued that it has evolved past the stage of frank totalitarianism into a kind of stolid, bureaucra-

---

the Soviet State, 1953–1991. (Cambridge, Mass.: Harvard University Press, 2000), for the period after the Second World War.

[34] By the end of the 1970s and the beginning of the 1980s, antisemitism found expression in common themes. The Jews were made responsible for whatever failures afflicted the system; they were those who corrupted the motherland; and they were unpatriotic. It went so far that some Soviet intellectuals, among other things, were prepared to argue that Jesus was not a Jew. See the entire discussion in Mikhail Agursky, *Contemporary Russian Nationalism: History Revised* (Jerusalem: The Soviet and East European Research Centre, 1982).

[35] See the discussion in Gregor, *The Search for Neofascism*, chap. 9. One of the better accounts of racism in postmaoist China is found in Barry Sautman, "Racial Nationalism and China's External Behavior," presented as a paper before the annual meeting of the Political Science Association in San Francisco in August 1996.

[36] See the account in Ben Kiernan, *The Pol Pot Regime: Race, Power, and Genocide in Cambodia under the Khmer Rouge* (New Haven: Yale University Press, 2002), chap. 7.

tized authoritarianism. Others have argued that it remains totalitarian, however much modified, with a totalitarianism more akin to that of Mussolini's Fascism than that of Stalin's Soviet Union.[37]

None of this can be argued with much confidence. It seems evident that we do not possess a criterial list of necessary and/or sufficient properties that determine entry into the class of totalitarianisms. Further, given the paucity of cases, we know very little of their expected life history, or the distinctive features such systems might assume over time.

At some stage in the life cycle of these systems, for example, they may no longer require the personalistic charismatic leadership once essential to survival and function. The impersonal and bureaucratic unitary party may supply a serviceable alternative. The political religion with which they were sustained may diminish in importance and visibility. How one chooses to identify such a modified system is a matter of heuristics, cataloging requirements, consistency, coherence, and ease of exposition. It is a matter of judgment.

In terms of the data available for analysis, most of the totalitarianisms of the twentieth century self-destructed before they reached the level of maturity of postmaoist China. On the other hand, some, like Kim Jong Il's North Korea, remain unchanging—like a fly in amber. Castro's Cuba remains ill defined to many, perhaps more ineffectual than totalitarian—its goals obscure, its ethnicism absent, its reactive nationalism determinate, its developmentalism abortive.

The most impressive exemplars of the class of reactive, developmental nationalisms as totalitarianisms, either drove themselves into conflicts they had little chance of surviving, much less winning, demonstrated their incompetence until their collapse, or both. As a consequence, we remain unsure about how our treatment of the phenomenon should proceed. The discussion of its defining properties remains abstract, the stages of its life history uncertain, its future elusive. Granted those difficulties, we remain charged with the responsibility of indicating something of the relationship between developmental systems, reactive nationalism, totalitarianism, and political religion.

Totalitarianism and Political Religion

"Totalitarianism" has always been a porous, and contested, concept.[38] No less can be said of "secular or political religion." Cognitive problems are com-

---

[37] See the argument in Gregor, *The Search for Neofascism*, chap. 9.

[38] The literature devoted to the concept of "totalitarianism" is very large. I have found the following useful: Bruno Seidel and Siegfried Jenkner, eds., *Wege der Totalitarismus-Forshung* (Darmstadt: Wissenschatliche Buchgesellschaft, 1968); and Ernest Menze, ed., *Totalitarianism Reconsidered* (London: Kennikat Press, 1981).

pounded when a simultaneous discussion of both is attempted—and the suggestion of a relationship between the two proposed.

Depending on how they are defined, all the elements traditionally associated with both notions have appeared, independently or in constellation, throughout much of recorded history. Historians have acknowledged, and have chronicled, any number of current and past politicized religions—political movements animated by specific, implicit or express, religious convictions. Religious reformers, in all times and places, for instance, have provided illustrative occasions of religious sentiments pressed into political service. More important for present purposes is the fact that the modern period, at least since the time of the French revolution, has witnessed the appearance of a subset of essentially secular ideologies sharing virtually all the emotive, perlocutionary properties of religion. Here those ideologies are identified, specifically, as political religions.

Instances of totalitarianism, on the other hand, are more difficult to identify with much conviction. Clearly, there have been recorded cases in which rulers, and those who serve as philosophic counsel, have sought to influence, if not control, every aspect of the life of subjects. Plato's *Republic* and his *Laws* are almost invariably cited as cases in point.[39] The reference is often dismissed as unpersuasive largely because of the absence of suitable technology that might have made the ancient intention anything other than velleity. Plato's purpose may have been totalitarian, but he seems to have lacked the means.

Certainly, there have been monarchs, and rulers of all and sundry sorts, who have sought total control of their subjects. We characteristically hesitate to call them "totalitarians." It would seem that their control was neither sufficiently effective nor sufficiently inclusive to permit comparativists to comfortably make the ascription.

Totalitarianism would seem to imply not only a disposition to suppress opposition, but a capacity to fabricate and maintain an array of extensive and interrelated organizations calculated to shape the beliefs and behaviors of workers, the military, the young, and women, in all the categories in which they are housed. Totalitarianism would seem to require the technical ability to reach into all aspects of life, individual and collective, in order to indoctrinate subjects to its purposes. The availability of a suitable set of beliefs recommends itself to that end—beliefs established and fostered that provide the norms governing conduct and establishing a public measure of virtue.

In its most mature expression, such a comprehensive code of obligatory conduct rests on a rationale for total control. The intention to exercise total control over a given population, in and of itself, is insufficient to characterize a system

---

[39] Karl Popper, *The Open Society and Its Enemies* (Princeton: Princeton University Press, 1962), vol. 1, "The Spell of Plato," is frequently cited in this context.

as totalitarian. Similarly, history has witnessed any number of discrete systems of religious temper that could not qualify as totalitarian. It is the effective union of totalitarian intent and technological efficacy, together with the availability of a persuasive political religion that appears to produce the totalitarianism with which the twentieth century has made us familiar.

Such a characterization is sufficient to suggest a set of common properties that are intuitively recognizable, and distinguish totalitarianisms from other classes of political systems. Thus, there have been those who have refused to identify Hitler's National Socialist Germany as totalitarian—because some agents and subordinates appeared to operate with considerable discretionary latitude within the system. Others excluded Mussolini's "Corporate State" from the category—because the numbers killed in the course of Fascism's rule were unimpressive. Mao Zedong's China has been sometimes omitted because its governance was unsystematic and inspired by "humane purpose."

The argument here is that there is an abiding similarity, beneath such differences, that warrants identifying some political systems as totalitarian. Nonetheless, whatever the intuitive similarities, it is clear that the criteria for inclusion into the category are not rigorous—identifying one or another political system as totalitarian requires judgment.

Comparative classification of political systems has always been an uncertain affair and probably will always remain so. It is very unlikely that anyone will attempt to "operationalize" the notions—to define "totalitarianism" and "political religion" with sufficient rigor to allow the employment of quantitative, empirical measures. We are left with informed judgment.

Meiji Japan, at the end of the nineteenth century, offers an instantial case for consideration. At that time, Japan, threatened by the military and industrial power of Europeans, very quickly put together a program of political and economic modernization. In the process, the political leadership made recourse to a state sponsored Shintoism—reinvoked, reshaped, and inculcated—as part of the program of general rehabilitation, modernization, economic development, and industrialization. Shintoism provided the rationale for empowering the emperor of Japan with absolute political authority—understood to emanate from his relationship with the goddess Amaterasu.

In 1890, an Imperial Rescript on Education was promulgated in order to instill ethical teachings, "infallible for all ages," among the Japanese—intended to render them obedient, loyal, and patriotic—to be supplemented in 1908 by a Rescript exhorting "thrift and diligence." Together with the Code of Bushido, the "Way of the Warrior," the rulers of Japan, through the collateral support of a rehabilitated Shintoism, had put together a set of sacralized prescriptions calculated to assist in shepherding the united nation from agrarianism into the industrial age. Japan sought modern industry in a search for status as well as the ability to manufacture and deploy modern arms in defense of what were held to be the nation's vital interests.

Allegiance to the emperor was held to be absolute and the nation conceived a specific community of destiny; life became increasingly unitary and serious, individualism abjured, and self-sacrifice and obedience advanced as special virtues. The entire process was sustained and inspired by an ancillary, politicized religion.

The rulers of Japan achieved their purposes by means of the collateral support of a politicized religion—rather than the invocation of a true political religion. As a consequence, the rulers of Japan were prepared to tolerate, both in theory and in practice, a degree of nonconformity absent in what might be held to be "truly totalitarian" systems. What the rulers of Japan sought was more program success and security of tenure, than effective, universal indoctrination. As a consequence, the system that carried Japan beyond the first stages of comprehensive industrialization lacked many of the institutional features of totalitarianism.[40]

As late as the mid 1930s, for example, there were many independent political organizations operative in Japan. Only those explicitly opposed to the government were proscribed. Absent from the prevailing institutions was the single, or unitary, mass mobilizing political party, one of the defining properties of the totalitarian state.[41] While some have chosen to identify the Japan of the first half of the twentieth century as "fascist," and perhaps "totalitarian," the characterization would seem unconvincing.[42]

The history of the revolutionary activities of Sun Yat-sen in premaoist China recommends something of a different, but similarly instructive, analysis. Sun Yat-sen served as the messianic *Tsungli* of his revolutionary party (the Kuomintang), providing it an exclusivist, redemptive, and chiliastic ideology. He spoke unequivocally of control and dominance of the united people of China, mobilized to developmental purpose. Together with what could be legitimately identified as a true political religion, he advocated the appeal to a politicized Confucianism as an adjunct support.

It was that complex system he sought to apply in revolutionary China throughout specific periods of control and dominance. Those periods were defined as intervals of military and tutelary control by his party's armed forces and

---

[40] See the instructive discussion in Paul Brooker, *The Faces of Fraternalism: Nazi Germany, Fascist Italy, and Imperial Japan* (Oxford: Clendon Press, 1991), chaps. 12–15.

[41] See the discussion in Mihail Manoilescu, *Die enzige Partei* (Berlin: Otto Stollberg, 1941).

[42] See the interesting discussion in Brooker, *The Faces of Fraternalism*; and William Miles Fletcher III, *The Search for a New Order: Intellectuals and Fascism in Prewar Japan* (Chapel Hill: The University of North Carolina Press, 1982).

its political cadre—until the preliminary conditions for China's redemption had been achieved. At the conclusion of the "tutelary period" of unitary party rule, the "constitutional period" would commence—in which all the features of pluralistic democracy would be allowed to fully emerge. Thus, one might speak of Sun anticipating "totalitarian," if transient, periods in the history of the regenerative China he sought to lead. How that might proceed is suggested by the economic and political history of the Republic of China on Taiwan after 1949—in which industrial development, under single party auspices, was accompanied by the conjoint, if gradual, articulation of the institutions of political pluralism. In stages, Sun's heirs in the ruling Kuomintang moved from martial and tutelary rule to a functional political democracy.[43]

Certainly, one could identify periods in the history of Kuomintang rule in which it seemed to satisfy the minimum criteria for inclusion into the class of aspiring totalitarian political systems. The heirs of Sun were infused by a political religion, and architects of familiar, system relevant institutions. During the long interwar years on the mainland of China, when its leadership was struggling against domestic insurrection and foreign invasion, totalitarian rule, with all its requisite appurtenances, apparently recommended itself. The final form assumed when Kuomintang rule transferred to Taiwan, on the other hand, whatever the immediate and contributing causes, was essentially democratic—in much the fashion envisioned by Sun.[44] Confucianism was restored as a religious option in an arrangement that increasingly conformed to the requirements common to the civil practices of contemporary democratic polities. How such a system should be classified in history, and for comparative purposes, is a question that allows occasion for principled disagreement.

Similar disagreements attend any discussion of how Hindu nationalism is to be classified. The institutional expression of that nationalism, the Bharatiya Janata Party (BJP), is one of the most popular political parties in India. The ideology of the BJP is clearly redemptive, mass mobilizing, anti-individualistic, and industrializing. The principal theoreticians of *Hindutva* have spoken of unity, self-sacrifice, communitarianism, and enduring nationalist commitment

---

[43] The literature devoted to the economic and political development on Taiwan is abundant. For immediate purposes, see Gregor, *Marxism, China, and Development*, chap. 10, and A. James Gregor (with Maria Hsia Chang and Andrew B. Zimmerman), *Ideology and Development: Sun Yat-sen and the Economic History of Taiwan* (Berkeley: Center for Chinese Studies, 1981). For substantial discussion of the development of democratic institutions and behaviors on Taiwan, see John F. Copper, *Taiwan: Nation State or Province?* (Boulder, Colo.: Westview Press, 1990), *Taiwan's Recent Elections: Fulfilling the Democratic Promise* (Baltimore: University of Maryland School of Law, 1990).

[44] John F. Copper's *Historical Dictionary of Taiwan (Republic of China)* (Lanham, Md.: Scarecrow Press, 2007), contains many instructive inserts in terms of democratic institutions that characterize modern Taiwan.

as the defining virtues of party members. As cultural nationalists, the political ideologists of the BJP favor traditional religious practices—and, as a consequence, have been charged with tendential biases towards a form of exclusivistic totalitarianism.

Quite independent of its animating political religion of rebirth and development, the BJP makes appeal to traditional religion for collateral support. It can be said to seek unity, discipline, and resolution through the indoctrination of its secular religious beliefs, with auxiliary support in traditional religious Hinduism.

As for totalitarianism, *per se*, it has been explicitly renounced by the political leadership of the BJP. When elected to political office, the party has respected all constitutional constraints. The leadership has never advocated single party rule for India. It would be difficult, without studied elaboration, to identify Hindu nationalism, irrespective of its developmentalism, and its appeal to secular and traditional religious sentiment, with the totalitarianism of the twentieth century.[45]

Similarly, irrespective of its rise in the nineteenth century as a reactive nationalism, at no stage in its past or present history can the Israeli political system be characterized as totalitarian. There may well have been those of totalitarian disposition among the many intellectuals who contributed to the articulation of its political inspiration—but the major thrust of its imperatives have been liberal, in the sense that liberalism finds expression in the works of Theodor Herzl.[46]

Like virtually all the nationalisms of the nineteenth, and turn of the twentieth, centuries, Jewish nationalism arose out of the tensions produced by European economic and political modernization. Arguably, at first, Western European Jews were beneficiaries of the changes. Under the influence of the Enlightenment, the French revolution, and the extensive reforms administered by Napoleon, the Jews that found themselves in the most rapidly developing nations were accorded the full rights of citizenship. Even before the end of the eighteenth century, Johann Gottfried Herder had already welcomed the entry of the liberated Jews into the community of nations.[47]

By the middle of the nineteenth century, however, whatever the accrued benefits of emancipation, it was evident to many Jewish intellectuals that their

---

[45] See the discussion and documentation in Gregor, *The Search for Neofascism*, chap. 8.

[46] Other than Herzl's *The Jewish State* in multiple English editions, his *Altneuland, Old New Land* is available in an English edition, published in Haifa, Israel, by the Haifa Publishing Company, in 1960. The latter work clearly testifies to the nineteenth century liberal inspiration of Herzl's political views.

[47] Johann Gottfried Herder, *Ideen zu Philosophie der Geschichte der Menschheit* (Berlin: Aufbau Verlag, 1965), vol. 2, p. 287.

community suffered special disabilities when folded into a larger historical and cultural entity. The intellectual leaders of emergent Zionism had learned from Hegel (as had Moses Hess) that history was made by organic communities acting out dialectic imperatives.[48] Some intellectuals argued that the Jews, as a people, had the same responsibilities as other oppressed nations to seek their own destiny. They saw Jews as featuring the essential traits of an oppressed nation. Like Poles or Armenians, the Jews found themselves infused with a sense of reactive nationalism.

Given such circumstances, there would be every reason to imagine that the revolutionary, nationalist, and developmental ideology of the "new Israel" anticipated by Moses Hess and the first Zionists, would evolve into the sacralized, totalitarian, and single party format followed by other developmental nationalisms in the nineteenth and twentieth centuries. There were intimations of such developments in the years between the Balfour Declaration of 1917 and the founding of the state in 1948, but none achieved sufficient maturity to threaten the essentially democratic design of its founders. Israel made its appearance as a kind of impaired liberal democracy—sharing all the features of nationalism, socialism, and developmentalism that characterized the revolutionary movements of our time.[49]

While falling short of true political pluralism—insisting on the Jewishness of the polity, for example—Israel has allowed individualism, freedom of association, and religious liberty to a degree that would normally be unanticipated in a community under existential threat—and inconceivable in any polity identified as totalitarian.

Many revolutionary movements and regimes have been suggested as candidates for inclusion into the ranks of totalitarianism—particularly immediately after the termination of the Second World War. In the postwar period, when academicians were focused on the developments in the surviving and expanding Marxist-Leninist systems, decolonized Africa provided instances of nationalist, socialist, and developmental regimes that seemed to give every indication of growing into some form of totalitarianism.

Kwame Nkrumah's "socialism" bore all the features of the nationalist and socialist regimes of the interwar years. Inspired by Marcus Garvey, it spoke of

---

[48] "The young national Jewish movement . . . had made the national idea the central concept of its philosophy. Fichte, Hegel, Lagarde and the other leading spirits of the German national idea—they were also our teachers. It was no accident that Theodor Herzl, the genius who founded modern political Zionism, came from German culture to the Jewish national idea." Nahum Goldmann, as quoted in Walter Laqueur, *A History of Zionism* (New York: Schocken Books, 1976), p. 31, n.

[49] For a persuasive account of the evolution of Zionist ideology, see Zeev Sternhell, *The Founding Myths of Israel: Nationalism, Socialism, and the Making of the Jewish State* (Princeton: Princeton University Press, 1998).

restoring the glories of African antiquity, and of economic development as a necessary, preliminary task. It spoke of "proletarian nations" struggling to find equity and place in a world of insecurity and threat.

To achieve its ends, it rejected the liberalism of the advanced industrial states, invoking instead a dominant sense of "community," in which the leader of the single party, without qualification, might speak for all. It spoke of Marxism-Leninism, of discipline, devotion, and selflessness—and there were even intimations of a form of secular religiosity. It imposed a unitary party on a basically tribal population, and had leaders who identified themselves as "Saviors." It spoke of "Negritude" as a kind of ethnic inspiration. Generally spoken of as "African socialism," this kind of doctrine appealed to a host of political leaders in decolonized Africa—and suggested the possibility that analysts might witness the emergence of a true totalitarianism in postwar, decolonized Africa.[50]

In fact the phenomenon was transient and fragile. Most of the regimes that professed to be African Socialist disappeared very rapidly and most of Africa south of the Sahara slid into familiar, traditional authoritarianism—which, however oppressive, satisfy none of the requirements of totalitarianism.

Much the same might be said of "Arab Socialism" which developed at about the same time. For a time it appeared that the form of nationalist socialism that found expression in Europe in the interwar years might make its appearance in at least some of the reactive nationalist Arab states.

Many Arab revolutionaries, as a case in point, found the ideology of Jamael Abdel Nasser attractive. It embodied all the features of the nationalism, developmentalism, and political authoritarianism of the interwar year regimes in Europe—which many Arabs found appealing.[51] Again, although Arab Socialism survived into the twenty-first century in the Syrian and Iraqi regimes of Hafiz al-Asad and Saddam Hussein, it never matured into a system that might confidently be identified as totalitarian. Ultimately, the entire effort was overwhelmed by fundamentalist Islam, to give rise to an entirely different political environment.[52]

In the history of the twentieth century, it would appear that only Marxism-Leninism, National Socialism, and Italian Fascism could fashion true totalitarianisms. Only those systems fully exemplified the union of developmental nationalism, political party dominance, and political religion that serve as recognitors for the class.

[50] See the discussion in A. James Gregor, "African Socialism, Socialism, and Fascism: An Appraisal," *The Review of Politics*, 3, no. 3 (July 1967), pp. 324–353.

[51] An instructive account can be found in Nissim Rejwan, *Nasserist Ideology: Its Exponents and Critics* (New York: John Wiley & Sons, 1974).

[52] Why Islamic republics such as Iran ought not be identified as either "fascist" or "totalitarian" is discussed in Gregor, *The Search for Neofascism*, chap. 7.

Epilogue

The experience of the twentieth century has made it incumbent upon comparativists to speak of totalitarianism and of the forms of political religion that have accompanied it. The phenomenon will always be remembered for the lives consumed in its passage. Hitler, Stalin, Mao, and Pol Pot forever will be enshrined in memory as architects of perhaps unparalleled mass destruction.

Others, like Mussolini, however few the innocent victims for which he is held responsible, will be remembered for the conscious construction of a system that most fully exemplified the traits of totalitarianism. This is nowhere represented better than in the role Fascist intellectuals expected political religion to play in the regime. Fascists fully appreciated the functional utility of religiosity in their system—and however well or ill implemented, the surrogate religion of Fascist Italy best represented the phenomenon.

The Soviet Union, Mao's China, and Pol Pot's Cambodia, on the other hand, pretended to abjure the religiosity that, in fact, was the normative basis of their rule—however transparent the fact, in retrospect. For its part, Hitler's Germany never fully addressed the issue of its religiosity or its totalitarianism. Like the Soviet Union and Maoist China, National Socialists insisted that, as a system of governance, theirs was a new sort of scientifically based "true democracy." As a political system, Hitlerism never fully resolved its uncertain relationship with religion, nor explicitly embraced its totalitarianism. The resolution of all that was remaindered as a postwar task. As a political system, National Socialism featured all the overt properties of sacralized politics, and Alfred Rosenberg fully understood its character—but it was only Italian Fascism that consciously acknowledged the secular religion that was its animus—and shaped institutions and political theater to its totalitarian needs.

None of this is to suggest that the secular religions that companioned totalitarian intent were simply devices calculated to manipulate masses.[53] The evidence is persuasive that both totalitarian leaders and their mass following had faith in the political religions that provided their systems moral impetus.

That is to be distinguished from religious faiths that have become political. Unlike totalitarians, religious fundamentalists press politics into service to further their religious beliefs—rather than invoking companion religious sentiments to achieve profane ends. Totalitarians offer an interpretation of life and history, its existential meaning and goal—all put to the service of national com-

---

[53] This is true even though totalitarian leaders often spoke as though they were so conceived. Stalin, Hitler, and Mussolini all admitted that "masses" required a cult of leadership, mythical and symbolic representations of events, and the security afforded by regular ritual acknowledgment of the role of leadership by the elect.

petitive survival, economic development, and historic accomplishment. Theirs is a political religion. In retrospect, it is impossible to distinguish the faith that inspired the enterprise from the enterprise itself.

What engages attention is the fact that, granted the appalling costs involved, totalitarian systems, nonetheless, managed to garner, organize, and employ a measure of voluntary human energy rarely, if ever, equaled in the history of humankind.

Totalitarianism is far too important a subject to neglect—if for no other reason than the fact that it has exacted incalculable human costs. Other than those murdered in satisfaction of doctrinal imperatives, the least murderous of these systems has transported countless young people to fight and die for a cause the leadership deemed redemptive. Outside of the millions who died to realize Hitler's dream of *Lebensraum* in the East, there were hundreds of thousands of Italians who died on the Russian steppes in pursuit of a strategic goal that never had a chance of success. In the more recent past, thousands of young and vital Cubans fell in Africa, in Angola and Ethiopia, as "new men"—in the forlorn effort to implement the unconvincing social vision of Fidel Castro and flawed strategic purpose of Che Guevara.

Beyond the battlefield, millions were consumed in the forced draft industrialization of the Soviet Union and Mao's China—in their labor camps and in "Great Proletarian Cultural Revolutions." Millions died in the death camps of Hitler's Germany and the killing fields of Cambodia.

Even the least offensive of these systems has exiled thousands upon thousands of citizens to unknown futures, and incarcerated thousands upon thousands more. The totalitarianisms of the twentieth century, that have disappeared into history, have left behind a legacy of destruction and ruined lives unmatched by the tyrannies of the past. Those that have survived the Second World War, given the increasing availability of instruments of mass destruction, continue to threaten security and freedom.

That totalitarianism, in the form we have known it, will be other than a twentieth-century residual in the twenty-first century, is unlikely. Whatever becomes of postmaoist China, it is hard to imagine a return to its homicidal past. The unaltered totalitarianism of Kim Jong Il is clearly unreal in the context of our time. But then, there are vast regions of the globe where populations fester in poverty—obsessed with the conviction that the advanced industrial powers are responsible for their plight. There, one might anticipate almost any form of reactive political response. The prospect of the union of technological lethality, religious fanaticism, and revanchist political purpose is ground for sober reflection.

There is every indication that the twenty-first century will be no less troubled than the twentieth. Militant religions, employing the tools of politics, can easily cause as much human misery as totalitarianism decked in the raiment of political religion. Whatever transpires, it would seem that the twenty-first century will not be easy for anyone.

Index

Index

Absolute, 15, 20, 23–24, 36, 39, 42, 152
Absolute Spirit, 15, 17, 61, 267
Advanced industrial societies, *see* Industrial societies
Africa: Cuban troops in, 283; political and tribal violence, 259; socialism, 280–81
Agriculture, 218–19
Albania, 226–27, 229
Angkar Padevat (Revolutionary Organization), 254–55
Angola, 283
Anthropology, 42, 44–45, 54, 97–98, 173, 225
Antisemitism: of Chamberlain, 192; of Feuerbach, 181; in Germany, 181–82; of Gobineau, 186; of Hitler, 220; of Marx, 177–78; of Rosenberg, 205–6; in Soviet Union, 271, 272–73; of Wagner, 177, 178, 180–82, 187. *See also* Jews
Arab Socialism, 281
Armenians, 260
Art, religion and, 195
Art criticism, 59
Aryan Christ, 210–11, 224n
Aryan languages, 172–73
Aryan races, 173, 183, 190, 191–92, 209, 210, 211–12n. *See also* Germanic race; Nordic race
Asia, *see individual countries*

Atheism: of Bauer, 33; Gentile on, 144, 155; Marx on, 85, 98; scientism and, 131
Axelrod, Pavel, 96

Bauer, Bruno, 30, 31, 33–34
Bauer, Edgar, 30
Belinsky, Vissarion, 91
Berdiaev, Nikolai, 87, 92, 106, 114
Bharatiya Janata Party (BJP), 278–79
Bible of Universal History, 63, 71
Bismarck, Otto von, 188
BJP, *see* Bharatiya Janata Party
Blood myths, 211–12
Bogdanov, A. A., 112–13
Bolshevism, 111, 159, 168–69, 206–7, 216, 231, 271. *See also* Leninism
Boniface VIII, Pope, 118
Börne, Ludwig, 59, 60
Bourgeoisie, 54, 109, 112, 230, 258
Bruno, Giordano, 127n, 132, 135
Burleigh, Michael, 257
Burundi, 259

Cambodian revolution: atrocities, 252–53, 254, 255–56, 283; background, 245–51, 266; Chinese and Vietnamese support, 252; costs, 255–56; economic program, 253–54; ethnic discrimination, 273; ideology, 232, 249, 252, 253–55, 256;

leaders, 232, 253–54, 256; mobilization, 249–50; victory, 245, 252; Vietnamese invasion, 256
Campanella, Tommaso, 132, 135
Capitalism: Engels on, 69–70; Hess on, 77; Marx on, 79–80, 88, 233. *See also* Industrial societies
Carus, Carl Gustav, 173n
Castro, Fidel, 227, 234, 235, 242, 249n, 274, 283
Catholic Church, *see* Roman Catholic Church
Ceausescu, Nicolae, 229–30
Chamberlain, Houston Stewart, 170; on Christ's ethnicity, 195–96, 211n; *Foundations of the Nineteenth Century*, 189–97, 203, 208, 267–68, 270n; on Gobineau, 189n; Hitler and, 200, 203; influence, 188, 189, 198, 203, 268; on Jewish influence, 192, 193, 194, 206n; life and education, 188, 203; on natural laws, 197, 198; on races, 190–93, 198, 212n, 215; on religion, 192–94, 195–97; Rosenberg and, 203, 204, 208; on State, 197–98; on Wagner, 175n, 188, 189–90, 196; World War I and, 197
Charisma, 3, 4, 263, 274
Charles V, Emperor, 119
Chernyshevsky, Nikolai, 91, 100–103; influence on Lenin, 100–101, 107, 111, 168; materialism, 103, 106; *What Is to Be Done?* 100–101
Chiang Kai-shek, 169, 273
China: economic reforms, 264; Great Leap Forward, 250–51, 256; Great Proletarian Cultural Revolution, 235, 250, 251, 256, 283; industrialization, 249, 250–51; Kuomintang, 169, 277–78; Maoism, 169n, 228–29, 234, 235, 247, 250–51; nationalism of Sun Yat-sen, 261, 265, 270; peasant revolution, 242, 243, 247; peasantry, 250–51; population policies, 273; support of Cambodian revolution, 252; Taiping revolutionaries, 264–65; totalitarianism, 273–74, 276

Christ: Aryan, 210–11, 224n; Jewish ethnicity questioned, 195–96, 211n; in Rosenberg's new religion, 210–11
Christianity: Feuerbach on, 38–41; in Germany, 30, 33, 59–60, 119, 174, 180, 193; Hegel on, 176–77, 180n; Hitler and, 223–24; Judaized, 176–78, 180–81, 193–94, 206, 208, 210, 216n; Protestantism, 30, 33, 59–60, 119, 135, 174, 193; racial differences and, 192–94; regeneration, 195–97; Rosenberg on, 210–11; Russian Orthodox Church, 101; salvation, 81; Taiping revolutionaries, 264–65; of Wagner, 180–81, 187; Young Hegelian views, 31–33. *See also* Religion; Roman Catholic Church
Civilizations: Gobineau on, 183, 184, 186; races and, 192
Civil religions, 2, 3–4, 12
Class consciousness, 247
Class relations, 125, 230. *See also* Bourgeoisie; Elites; Peasantry; Proletariat; Working class
Colombia, 259
Communism: Engels on, 65–66; of Feuerbach, 45–46; Hess on, 50–52, 54; Marx and, 82; Mazzini on, 125–26; revolutions, 66–67. *See also* Marxism; Marxist-Leninist systems; Socialism
The Communist Manifesto (Marx and Engels), 83–84, 87, 88, 108
Communist parties, 147, 246, 249. *See also* Marxist parties
Communities: commitments to, 56–57; Fascist view, 167; Herder on, 171–72; Hess on, 53–54, 55; heterogeneous, 217–18, 222; homogeneous, 214, 222, 270–71; individuals and, 57, 158, 170–71; Jewish threat, 206; languages and myths, 171, 172; in National Socialism, 213–14; racial, 270–71; religion and, 139; *Volk*, 171–72, 174, 175–76, 181

Confucianism, 265, 277, 278
Congress of Vienna, 116, 122
Consciousness: class, 247; Feuerbach on, 36, 40, 41–42; Gentile on, 144; Hegel on, 40; Hess on, 52, 53; idealist view, 14; ideological, 231–32; Kant on, 14; Marx's reform of, 76; neohegelian view, 150; shared, 15–16
Corradini, Enrico, 147–48
Corridoni, Filippo, 162
Counterreformation, 119
Croce, Benedetto, 136
Cuba: characteristics of regime, 274; Martí's nationalism, 261; Marxism-Leninism, 227, 229–30, 234; peasant revolution, 242; troops sent to Africa, 283

Darfur, 259
Darwinism, 221, 269
Deism, 11–12n
Democracy: Gentile on, 157–59; in Israel, 280; Marxist view, 247–48
Democratic liberalism, 72
Democratic People's Republic of Korea, *see* North Korea
Developing world: poverty, 283; revolution in, 230, 234, 235–36, 242, 243–44, 246–48, 251
Developmental nationalism, 260–64, 265–66, 269–70, 274
Developmental regimes: political religions, 266; totalitarianism, 264–74
Dialectic: Engels on, 78–79, 78n; Hegelian view, 74, 75, 78–79; of history, 44, 48, 49, 66, 75, 280; Marx on, 73–75; meaning, 74
Dietrich, Otto, 213–14

Eastern and Central Europe, 228, 231, 234. *See also* Europe; Germany
Eckart, Dietrich, 201, 202–3
Economic development, *see* Developmental regimes; Industrialization
Education, 65n, 125
Elites, 48, 108–11, 230, 269
Empiricism, 6–8, 11–13, 16, 42n, 131, 132, 134, 135, 163, 206. *See also* Science
Engels, Friedrich: *Anti-Dühring*, 88–89, 113n; on capitalism, 69–70; *The Communist Manifesto*, 83–84, 87, 88, 108; "The Condition of England," 79; *The Condition of the Working Class in England*, 70n, 83; on dialectic, 78–79, 78n; economic analysis, 65–66, 67–70, 78–79; on German youth, 174; on Hegel, 46n, 60, 61; Hegelianism and, 60–62, 68–69, 70, 76; on history, 60–61, 62–63, 70–71, 79, 84–85, 95–96; *The Holy Family or Critique of Critical Criticism*, 82–83; influence of writings, 88–89; intellectual development, 46, 61–62, 65–67, 70; Kautsky and, 89–90; "Letters from Wuppertal," 59, 60, 63; life of, 59, 66; Marx and, 71–72, 73, 76, 79, 81, 82; on Marxism, 108–9; "Outlines of a Critique of Political Economy," 67–69, 70; on peasantry, 236–37, 238–42, 244, 246n; philosophical writings, 113n; Plekhanov on, 93; realism, 137n; on religion, 33n, 59, 61, 62–63, 95; responses to critics, 88; on revolutions, 256; *Schelling and Revelation*, 58, 61; socialism, 87
England: empiricism, 11–13, 16, 132; Engels in, 65; industrialization, 48–49, 64, 67, 69; liberalism, 18n, 28; revolution predicted in, 49, 64, 65, 66–67, 70n; working class, 65
Enlightenment, 10–11, 119, 170, 206
Epistemology, 13–15, 17–18, 37, 43, 113n. *See also* Materialism
Ethiopia, 229, 283
Ethnic cleansing, 228, 255–56, 270, 271
Ethnogenesis, 271–72

Europe: Communist regimes, 228, 231; imperialism, 262; Jews, 185, 186, 194, 208, 216, 279; poverty, 48, 49. *See also* individual countries

Faith: of Nordic race, 206; in political religion, 3, 10, 122, 282–83. *See also* Religion
Fascism: development, 159; economic policies, 263; Gentile on, 151–52, 164–68; individuals and, 167; intellectuals, 164–69; Mazzini as precursor, 147; as political religion, 164, 167–68, 282; in power, 151, 164; racism, 270–71; totalitarianism, 152, 167, 276, 282. *See also* Mussolini, Benito
Fascisti, 147, 151
Fatherland Association (*Vaterlandsverein*), 175–76
Feder, Gottfried, 204
Ferdinand I, King, 116
Feudalism, 240
Feuerbach, Ludwig, 29, 30; antisemitism, 181; communism, 45–46; critique of Hegelianism, 34–37, 38, 55, 75–76, 267; "Critique of Hegelian Philosophy," 34; *Essence of Christianity*, 35, 37–40, 44, 45–46, 55, 78, 101, 174; Hegel and, 34; Hess and, 54, 55–56; on history, 43–44, 46, 56, 83; humanism, 44–45, 85, 101–4; influence, 43, 101–4, 173, 174–75; influence on Marxists, 45–46, 73–74, 75–76, 107, 173, 267; life of, 34; Marx and, 36n, 45–46, 73–74, 107; materialism, 37–38, 40–42, 44, 55–56, 74, 75; *Principles of the Philosophy of the Future*, 35, 36–37, 41–42, 44, 45–46, 73, 101; reformed Hegelianism, 173, 266–67; on religion, 35, 38–41, 42, 44–45, 78, 97–98, 101, 104, 108, 225; theanthropism, 43–46, 173, 267
Feuerbachianism, 54, 98, 102–3, 107
Fichte, Johann Gottlieb, 178
Fischer, Eugen, 182

France: Indochinese colonies, 245, 246; intellectual influence, 133; Marxism, 246; Napoleon's rule, 29, 116, 117, 170; revolution, 29, 117, 260; revolution of 1830, 29; Vietnam war, 234
Franco-Prussian War, 120
Freedom: Chamberlain on, 197; collective, 123, 124, 158; Gentile on, 158; Hegel on, 18–19n, 19, 20n, 26, 27; Hess on, 51, 53; Mazzini on, 123, 124, 125; National Socialist view, 213–14
French Communist Party, 246, 249
French revolution, 29, 117, 260

Galilee, 196
Garibaldi, Giuseppe, 120–21, 135
Garvey, Marcus, 261, 262, 270, 280
Gentile, Emilio, 226
Gentile, Giovanni: actualism, 152, 154, 155; critique of Marxism, 135–38, 151; *Dottrina del fascismo*, 166–68; in Fascist party, 164; idealism, 137, 138, 146, 152–54; on Mazzini, 115, 139–40, 143–47, 148–50, 155, 164, 165–66; Mussolini and, 161, 163, 164, 166; nationalism, 132, 138, 143, 157; *Origins and Doctrine of Fascism*, 165; philosophy, 134–35, 144–45, 153–54, 155; political views and activity, 142–43, 147–51, 157–59, 164; on politics and philosophy, 143–46; on politics and religion, 152, 155–57; on religion, 130–33, 134–35, 142, 152–53, 154–55; on Risorgimento, 129–31, 132, 133–34, 139, 144, 146, 147–48; support for Fascism, 151–52, 164–68; support for Italian involvement in Great War, 154; writings, 142–43, 150, 164–68
Germanic race: Chamberlain on, 190, 191, 192, 193, 195; creativity, 187; Gobineau on, 183, 186; physical characteristics, 186; regeneration, 195, 196–97; Roman Catholicism and, 193; Rosenberg on, 202; *Urvolk*, 172, 175, 179, 180, 187;

virtues, 179; *Volk*, 171–72, 174, 175–76, 181. *See also* Nordic race
Germanic religion, 179–80, 207–8
Germanic tribes, 185–86
German language, 172–73
German philosophy: Feuerbach's influence, 41; idealism, 14, 16; Kantian, 204, 208; posthegelian, 55; Young Hegelians, 30–34. *See also* Hegelianism
Germany: antisemitism, 181–82; Communist regime, 228; defeat in Great War, 199–200, 268; industrialization, 59; Marxist parties, 89–90; myths, 172n, 176, 179; nationalism, 170, 173, 199, 267–68; peasant wars, 238–39, 240; political and legal change, 30; political reformers, 29–31, 174; Protestantism, 30, 33, 59–60, 119, 174. *See also* Hegelianism; Prussia; *Volk*
Ghibellines, 118
Gioberti, Vincenzo, 129, 133, 135, 138, 139, 140, 144, 165–66
Gobineau, Arthur de: Chamberlain on, 189n; on civilizations, 183, 184, 186; *The Inequality of Human Races*, 182–84; on Jews, 185–86, 189n; on peoples and nations, 186; on races, 173, 182–84, 186, 191n, 215, 267; *The Significance of Race in the Life of Peoples*, 185–86; Wagner and, 182, 184–85, 187, 188
Goethe, Johann von, 178
Great Men, 22
Great War, *see* World War I
Guelphs, 118, 126
Guevara, Ernesto "Che," 234–35n, 243, 252n, 283
Gumilev, Lev Nikolaevich, 271–72
Günther, Hans F. K., 200, 211–12n, 215, 222–23

Hegel, Georg Friedrich Wilhelm: Feuerbach and, 34; goals, 266; on history, 20–22, 43, 46; influence, 16, 22–23, 28, 61, 73; on Jews, 177, 181; liberalism, 29–30; *Philosophy of History*, 1, 46n, 61; *Philosophy of Right*, 31, 34; political writings, 29–30; on religion, 1, 27, 30, 31, 127–28, 176–77, 180n; on State, 1n, 18–20, 24–26; statism, 174; on true knowledge, 17; on true reality, 17–18, 26
Hegelianism: as belief system, 58–59; dialectic, 74, 75, 78–79; elements in common with political religions, 16–18; Feuerbach on, 34–37, 38, 55, 75–76, 267; Hess on, 48; history, 33–34; idealism, 16, 104, 138; influence in Italy, 127–29, 130–31, 133, 134n, 150, 157; influence on Marx, 73, 76; interpretations, 27–28; neo-, 60–61, 62, 73, 76, 79, 84, 157, 266–67; as political religion, 23–28, 266; purposes, 35, 266; reformed, 173, 266–67; State and individuals, 18–20, 24–26. *See also* Young Hegelians
Herder, Johann Gottfried, 170, 171–72, 178n, 279
Herzl, Theodor, 279
Hess, Moses, 29, 30; on capitalism, 77; on communism, 50–52, 54; on communities, 53–54, 55; on consciousness, 52, 53; critique of Hegelianism, 48; economic analysis, 69–70n, 77–78; Engels on, 65; Feuerbach and, 54, 55–56; on freedom, 51, 53; on history, 46–50, 52–53, 55, 56, 76, 268–69; on individualism, 54–55; influence, 266, 268; on Jews, 268–69, 280; Marx and, 49n, 76, 81, 268; materialism, 55–56; on political and economic reforms, 49–51, 63–64, 269; on religion, 46–47, 52, 98–99; religious beliefs, 46, 47; on revolution, 49, 50–51; *Rome and Jerusalem*, 268–69; *The Sacred History of Humankind*, 46; on State, 55; on Stirner, 54

Hindu nationalism, 278–79
Historical materialism, 85–86, 92, 94, 136–37
History: Bauer on, 33–34; critical studies, 33; determinism, 44; dialectic, 44, 48, 49, 66, 75, 280; ends of, 66, 80–81, 82, 84–85; Engels on, 60–61, 62–63, 70–71, 79, 84–85, 95–96; Feuerbach on, 43–44, 46, 56, 83; Gentile on, 145; Great Men, 22; Hegel on, 20–22, 43, 46; Hess on, 46–50, 52–53, 55, 56, 76, 268–69; laws, 92–93, 94–95, 105; Marxist view, 83, 84–85, 92–96, 233–34; Marx on, 46, 75, 80–81, 82–83, 84–85, 94–95; Mazzini on, 145; moral dimensions, 62, 85, 94, 95–96, 99; Oriani on, 128–29; Plekhanov on, 92–93, 99; religion and, 46–47, 52–53, 63, 206, 268; as replacement for religion, 49, 56, 63, 85, 97; responsibilities of races, 215; Rosenberg on, 205, 208, 211–13, 215; Strauss on, 32
Hitler, Adolf: antisemitism, 220; Chamberlain and, 200, 203; church-state distinction, 223–24; imprisonment, 202; intellectual influences, 199–200, 204, 204–5n, 219–21, 222–23; *Mein Kampf*, 220, 221, 222–24, 225; nationalism, 220; party leadership, 199–200; on political religion, 223–24; in power, 204; on propaganda, 220; on races, 222–23; religious elements in writing, 223; Rosenberg and, 200, 201, 202–3, 219, 220–21, 224. *See also* National Socialism
Ho Chi Minh, 242. *See also* Vietnam
Holy Roman Empire, 185–86
Hoxha, Enver, 229
Humanism: of Feuerbach, 44–45, 85, 101–4, 173, 267; Marx on, 76, 98; in Renaissance, 118–19
Hume, David, 11–12, 16
Huss, Jan, 242

Idealism: constructive subjectivism, 14–15; of Croce, 136; of Gentile, 137, 138, 146, 152–54; Hegelian, 16, 104, 138; in Italy, 130, 131, 133, 136, 165–66; religiosity, 132
Ideologies: definition, 6; empirical claims, 6–8; functions, 8; logical and normative claims, 7, 8; political, 11, 263; religious, 6; secular, 6, 8–9, 10; social control through, 231–32. *See also* Political religions
Idi Amin, 259
Imperialism, 242–43, 262
India: developmental nationalism, 261; Hindu nationalism, 278–79
Individualism: of British empiricists, 12–13; critiques of, 132; Fascism and, 166–67; German, 170–71; Herder on, 171; Hess on, 54–55; in National Socialism, 213–14; Rosenberg on, 214n
Indoeuropean languages, 172–73
Indoeuropean races, 191, 192
Indoteutonic (Indogermanic) race, 191, 193
Industrialization: in Cambodia, 253; in China, 249, 250–51; in England, 48–49, 64, 67, 69; in Germany, 59; in Italy, 261; in Japan, 261, 276–77; nationalism and, 265–66, 268, 269–70; peasant revolutions and, 241; in Russia and Soviet Union, 91, 243, 248, 261, 283; strategies, 263–64
Industrial societies: appeal of Marxism, 233, 235–36; contradictions, 67, 69, 78, 81, 233; democracies, 2–4, 10n; Engels on, 65, 67, 69–70; imperialism, 242–43; individual interests, 10n; poverty, 69, 70; revolutions predicted, 49, 64, 65, 66–67, 70n, 230, 233–34, 243; role of religion, 2–4. *See also* Capitalism
Inequality: critics of, 63–64, 65; in industrial societies, 48, 70
Innocent III, Pope, 194
Islamic republics, 3
Israel, 279–80

Italian nationalism: cultural, 172n; of Gentile, 132, 138, 143, 157; interpretations of Risorgimento, 127, 147–48; of Mazzini, 125–26, 148–50, 159, 172n; of Mussolini, 159; organizations, 143, 147–48; of syndicalists, 160, 161–62

Italian Socialist Party, 135, 147, 160, 161

Italy: conditions before reunification, 116–18, 122, 124; foreign interference, 116, 124, 133–34; industrialization, 261; intellectuals, 133, 136, 161–62; localism, 118; Marxism, 120, 135–37, 151; politics of post–World War I era, 147–48, 151; Renaissance, 118–19, 132, 133; reunification, 117, 120, 126, 127, 129; Roman Empire, 117–18, 122, 185, 190; Tripoli war, 160, 161; World War I and, 142–43, 147, 154, 161–62. *See also* Fascism; Risorgimento; Roman Catholic Church

Jahn, Friedrich, 170
Jaja, Donato, 132n, 135
Japan: industrialization, 261, 276–77; Meiji era, 276–77; Shintoism, 276
Jews: Bolshevism and, 206–7, 216; in Europe, 185, 186, 194, 208, 216, 279; Gobineau on, 185–86, 189n; Herder on, 178n, 279; Hess on, 268–69, 280; Marx on, 177–78, 181, 216n; positive views of, 186, 189n, 268–69, 279; as race, 216n; Rosenberg on, 202, 205–7, 208, 216; secular influence, 194; successful, 186n, 194; as threat, 177, 192, 206, 216. *See also* Antisemitism
Judaism: Chamberlain on, 193; Hess on, 46; influence on Christianity, 176–78, 180–81, 193–94, 206, 208, 210, 216n
Justice, 67

Kant, Immanuel, 14, 188, 204, 208
Kautsky, Karl, 89–90, 109, 247–48
Kemal Ataturk, 261, 262

Khmers Rouges, 246, 252–53, 255–56. *See also* Cambodian revolution
Khrushchev, Nikita, 235
Kim Il Sung, 229–30, 231–32, 242
Kim Jong Il, 274, 283
Klopstock, Friedrich Gottlob, 172n
Kuomintang, 169, 277–78

Labor, *see* Working class
Labriola, Antonio, 136–37
Languages, 171, 172–73
Latin America: *Mestizaje* populations, 270; political violence, 259, 260
Leaders: charismatic, 3, 4, 263, 274; Great Men, 22; totalitarian, 4, 274
League of the Just, 64
Lebensraum, 218–19
Left Hegelians, 32, 168, 175. *See also* Feuerbach, Ludwig; Hess, Moses
Lenin, Vladimir Ilyich: on imperialism, 242–43; influences on, 100–101, 107–8, 111; intolerance of opposition, 111–13; leadership of Bolshevism, 111; life and family, 99–100; as Marxist, 107–14; *Materialism and Empirio-Criticism*, 113; in power, 231; on revolutions, 247n; *What Is to Be Done?* 108, 109–10
Leninism: centralized control, 111–13; elites, 108, 109–11; in Italy, 147; as political religion, 113–14, 168–69. *See also* Bolshevism; Marxism-Leninism
Liberalism: agnostic, 156; authoritarian, 166; democratic, 75; English, 18n, 28; Gentile on, 148, 156, 164, 166; of Hegel, 29–30; in Italy, 126, 148, 164; of Marx, 72, 75; of Mazzini, 148–49, 152, 164, 166; nationalism and, 148; in Russia, 91, 112; state authority, 18, 148
Libertarianism, 54–55
Liberty, *see* Freedom
Lin Biao, 251
Lunacharsky, A. V., 112–13
Luther, Martin, 119, 193
Luxemburg, Rosa, 110–11

Manzoni, Alessandro, 131, 133, 135, 144
Maoism, 169n, 228–29, 234, 235, 247, 250–51
Mao Zedong, 228–29, 234, 235, 242, 247, 249
Martí, José, 261, 262
Marx, Karl: on atheism, 85, 98; on Bauer, 34; *Capital*, 88, 91; on capitalism, 79–80, 88, 233; communism and, 82; *The Communist Manifesto*, 83–84, 87, 88, 108; on dialectic, 73–75; economic analysis, 81, 88; *The Economic and Philosophic Manuscripts*, 72–75, 79–82, 98; Engels and, 71–72, 73, 76, 79, 81, 82; Feuerbach and, 36n, 45–46, 73–74, 107; *The German Ideology*, 83, 84; on Hegel, 75–76; Hegelianism of, 73; Hess and, 49n, 76, 81, 268; on history, 46, 75, 80–81, 82–83, 84–85, 94–95; Hitler's references to, 200; *The Holy Family or Critique of Critical Criticism*, 82–83; on humanism, 33n, 76, 98; influences on, 72–73, 76, 81, 268; on Jews, 177–78, 181, 216n; liberalism, 72, 75; on liberation and revolution, 234n, 236–38; life and education, 72, 73; materialism, 75, 82; on peasantry, 236–37, 238, 246n; *The Poverty of Philosophy*, 83; on private property, 79–81, 83, 236–37; on religion, 33n, 85–86, 98; responses to critics, 88; revolutionary commitment, 72; socialism, 87; on working class, 79–80
Marxism: appeal, 233, 235–36; claims, 7–8; critics of, 88; elites, 108–11, 230; Gentile's critique of, 135–38; historical materialism, 85–86, 92, 94; interpretations, 89–90; in Italy, 120, 135–37, 151; knowledge of revolutionaries, 249n; of Lenin, 107–14; Mazzini on, 125–26; of Mussolini, 151, 160–61; peasant revolutions and, 236–44, 246–47; as political religion, 85–86, 96–97, 266; proletariat, 7–8, 230; revolutionary, 227, 230–31, 233–34, 236–39, 246–48; in Russia, 90–91, 96, 110–14; variants, 159; view of history, 83, 84–85, 92–96, 233–34

Marxism-Leninism: departures from traditional Marxism, 232, 236, 242–44, 247–48; peasant revolutions, 242, 243–44, 246–47; as secular religion, 226–30; Western supporters, 235–36, 246, 248. *See also* Maoism

Marxist-Leninist systems: atrocities committed, 235; common doctrine, 226–7; consolidation, 227–32, 271; decay, 232; leaders, 227–28, 229–30; in postwar era, 226–27, 234–35; Soviet, 227–28, 231; treatment of dissidents, 228, 231. *See also* China; Leninism; Soviet Union

Marxist parties, 89–90, 96, 110–14, 263. *See also* Communist parties

Materialism: of Chernyshevsky, 103, 106; of Feuerbach, 37–38, 40–42, 44, 55–56, 74, 75; Gentile on, 135, 144; of Hess, 55–56; historical, 85–86, 92, 94, 136–37; in Italy, 136; of Marx, 75, 82, 137n, 138; monism, 101, 119–20, 206

Mazzini, Giuseppe: economic analysis, 125; Gentile on, 115, 139–40, 143–47, 148–50, 155, 164, 165–66; legacy, 126, 127, 152, 162–63, 165; liberalism, 148–49, 152, 164, 166; life of, 120; Mussolini on, 159–60, 161, 162–63; nationalism, 125–26, 148–50, 159, 172n; on political religion, 121–25, 127, 128, 139–40, 151, 161; as precursor of Fascism, 147, 152; on pre-unification Italy, 116; on religion, 115, 121–25, 135, 145, 155, 165; revolutionary goals, 122–25; on State, 155, 159–60

Mazzinian Republicans, 159, 160
Mazzinism, 127, 128, 129, 152, 157, 159, 164
Mengistu Haile Mariam, 229
Metternich, Klemens von, 116
Middle East: Arab Socialism, 281; Islamic republics, 3

Mind, 15, 17
Miscegenation, 183, 184, 185, 187, 215
Monism, 101, 119–20, 206
Morality: Gentile on, 136; history and, 62, 85, 94, 95–96, 99; Labriola on, 136–37
Mussolini, Benito: evolution of thought, 151, 159, 160–62; Gentile and, 161, 163, 164, 166; leadership of Fascists, 151; life of, 160–61; as Marxist, 151, 160–61; on Mazzini, 159–60, 161, 162–63; national socialism, 162; on peasant wars, 242; in power, 164, 264; on religion, 161; spiritualism, 163–64; support for Italian involvement in Great War, 147. *See also* Fascism
Myths: blood, 211–12; of communities, 171; definition, 209n; German, 176, 179; of race, 209

Napoleon, 29, 116, 117, 170
Narodniki, 91, 99
Nasser, Jamael Abdel, 281
Nationalism: Cambodian, 246; in China, 261, 265, 270; Cuban, 261; cultural, 172, 246, 279; developmental, 260–64, 265–66, 269–70, 274; external threats and, 269–70; German, 170, 173, 199, 220, 267–68; Hindu, 278–79; industrialization and, 265–66, 268, 269–70; Jewish, 279–80; liberalism and, 148; peasant revolutions and, 252; as political religion, 149, 262–63; racial, 198; as religious sentiment, 149, 262–63; Russian, 272; Soviet, 271–72; in twentieth century, 260–63. *See also* Italian nationalism
Nationalist Association, Italy, 147–48
Nationalist parties, 263
National Socialism: community favored over individuals, 213–14; death camps, 283; moral training, 213; as political religion, 169, 225, 282; racial superiority claims, 8; Rosenberg's influence, 200–201, 204–7, 219, 221–22, 225; social philosophy, 213–14; swastika symbol, 209; as totalitarian regime, 276. *See also* Hitler, Adolf
National Socialist German Workers Party (*Nationalsozialistische Deutsche Arbeiterpartei*; NSDAP), 200, 201, 202, 203, 204, 213n
National syndicalism, 147, 162, 163, 263
Nations: Gobineau on, 186; Herder on, 170, 171–72; proletarian, 252
Nature, myths, 209
Nazism, *see* National Socialism
New men, 103, 108, 109, 111, 157, 168, 184, 254
New religion, 99, 209–12, 223
Nietzsche, Friedrich, 200
Nkrumah, Kwame, 280–81
Nordic race: Amorites and Christ's racial origins, 211n; culture, 213, 215; faith of, 206; Gobineau on, 182; Günther on, 211–12n; primordial home, 212; regeneration, 207; Rosenberg on, 205–8, 210, 212–13; in rural environments, 218–19; soul, 205, 212, 214, 217; spiritual traits, 210, 215; superiority, 218, 222, 269; virtues, 214. *See also* Aryan races; Germanic race
Normative claims, 7, 8
North Korea, 229–30, 231–32, 242, 274, 283
Noumenal race soul, 208
NSDAP, *see* National Socialist German Workers Party

Oriani, Alfredo, 127–29, 159
Ottoman Empire, 260

Pantheism, 101, 127–28
Panunzio, Sergio, 142, 168–69
Parties: communist, 147, 246, 249; ideologies, 11; Marxist, 89–90, 96, 110–14, 263; nationalist, 263; religious, 124; single party control, 4
Partito nazionale fascista, 164, 168. *See also* Fascism
Pauperism, *see* Poverty

Peasant revolutions: in China, 242, 243, 247, 264–65; Kautsky on, 247–48; Marxism of, 236–44, 246–47; nationalism, 252; political religion and, 242, 244; successful, 234, 235–36, 242. *See also* Cambodian revolution

Peasantry: in feudal societies, 240; Marx and Engels on, 236–37, 238–42, 244, 246n; Russian, 91, 238

Peasant wars, in Germany, 238–39, 240

People's Republic of China, *see* China

Personality, 222

Philippines, 260–61

Philosophy: Gentile on, 143–46; in Italy, 133; political religions and, 10–16; religion and, 27, 127–28. *See also* German philosophy

Plato, 275

Plekhanov, Georgy Valentinovich: influence, 90–91; life and education, 91–92; Marxism, 92–94, 96–97; political activism, 91–92; religious skepticism, 91

Politica, 143–46, 154

Political religions: definition, 3, 9; in developmental regimes, 266; of Engels, 70–71; faith in, 3, 10, 122, 282–83; foreseen by Woltmann, 225; Gentile on, 152, 154–57; Hegelianism as, 23–28, 266; Hitler on, 223–24; of Kuomintang, 277–78; Marxism as, 85–86, 96–97, 266; Marxism-Leninism as, 226–30; Mazzini on, 121–25, 127, 128, 139–40, 151, 161; of Mussolini, 161; nationalism as, 149, 262–63; peasant revolutions and, 242, 244; political philosophies and, 10–16; in postwar era, 226–27; revolutions and, 55–57, 262; role in twentieth century, xi–xii, 3, 226–27; Rosenberg on, 223, 282; similarities to traditional religions, 3, 9, 10; socialism as, 113–14, 161; totalitarianism and, xii, 5, 274–83; truth claims, 9. *See also* Religion

Political systems: definition, 6; Hegel on, 31; ideologies, 11; overtly religious, 3–4

Political violence, in twentieth century, xi, 257–60

Politicized religions, 3–4, 264–65, 275, 277, 282, 284

Pol Pot, *see* Saloth Sar

Popes, 116, 118. *See also* Roman Catholic Church

Popular sovereignty, 117

Population migrations, 183, 190, 212–13

Positivism, 119, 144, 163

Poverty: in developing world, 283; in industrial societies, 69, 70; Marx on, 234n; of working class, 48, 49, 50, 64, 65

Private property: abolition of, 50–51, 64, 80, 263–64; contradictions, 79–81; criticism of, 64–65, 68; Marx on, 79–81, 83, 236–37; rights, 125, 264

Proletarian nations, 252

Proletariat: class consciousness, 247n; emiseration, 7–8; Engels on, 65; Maoist view, 251; relations with elites, 109, 230; revolution of, 236n, 237–38, 239, 246–48; self-emancipation, 82. *See also* Working class

Property, *see* Private property

Protestantism, 30, 33, 59–60, 119, 135, 174, 193. *See also* Christianity; Religion

Prussia, 31, 188. *See also* Germany

Races: behavioral traits, 215–16, 217; formation, 190–91, 212n; languages linked to, 173; mental abilities, 184, 186; miscegenation, 183, 184, 185, 187, 215; National Socialist view, 8; peoples, 186; physical characteristics, 173, 186, 191, 192–93; purity, 191, 222; religion and, 205–6, 208–10; Rosenberg's racial version of history, 205, 208, 211–13

Racial nationalism, 198

Racial souls, 208–9, 211–12, 214–15, 217, 222–23
Racism: basis, 215; biological, 267, 269; of Italian Fascism, 270–71; scientific, 173, 186; in totalitarian systems, 273; in twentieth century, 270–71. *See also* Antisemitism
Reason: Engels on, 60, 62–63, 94; Feuerbach on, 36, 40, 43; Hegel on, 17, 20, 21; Plekhanov on, 99
Red Khmer, *see* Khmers Rouges
Reformation, 119, 193
Religion: art and, 195; Chamberlain on, 192–94, 195–97; Chernyshevsky on, 101–4; definitional issues, 5n, 6; Engels on, 33n, 59, 61, 62–63, 95; faith, 8, 10; Feuerbach on, 35, 38–41, 42, 44–45, 78, 97–98, 101, 104, 108, 225; functions, 9–10; Gentile on, 130–33, 134–35, 142, 152–53, 154–55; Hegel on, 1, 27, 30, 31, 127–28, 176–77, 180n; Hess on, 46–47, 52, 98–99; history as replacement for, 49, 56, 63, 85, 97; loss of faith, 9, 11; Marxist view, 96; Marx on, 33n, 85–86, 98; Mazzini on, 115, 121–25, 135, 145, 155, 165; Mussolini on, 161; Oriani on, 128–29n; philosophy and, 27, 127–28; Plekhanov on, 97; politicized, 3–4, 264–65, 275, 277, 282, 284; racial differences and, 192–94; relationship to politics, 1–3, 98; Rosenberg on, 199, 205–6, 207–12; secular, 98–99, 105, 107, 113–14; secular surrogates, 8–9; sublation, 15, 97, 98; transcredal, 132–33; Wagner on, 175, 176, 179–81, 187, 196; Young Hegelian views, 31–33, 59–60, 97. *See also* Christianity; Political religions
Religious parties, 124
Renaissance, 10–11, 118–19, 132, 133
Revolutionary syndicalism, 159, 160, 162
Revolutions: communist, 66–67; in developing world, 230, 234, 235–36, 242, 243–44, 246–48, 251; elite leadership, 108–10; Hess on, 49, 50–51; inevitability, 49, 50–51, 55, 65, 66–67, 70, 83–84; Marxist, 227, 230–31, 233–34, 236–39; Marx's commitment, 72; organizing workers, 64; political religion and, 55–57, 262; Russian intelligentsia and, 104–6; Wagner on, 179. *See also* Peasant revolutions
Right, Hegel on, 25
Rights: Gentile on, 158; Mazzini on, 124, 125; private property, 125, 264
Risorgimento: Gentile on, 129–31, 132, 133–34, 139, 144, 146, 147–48; intellectuals, 129, 165; interpretations, 126–31, 148, 159, 164; Jubilee year, 126–27; meaning, 117; relationship to Fascism, 147, 164, 165; role of religion, 120, 130–31, 146; Roman Empire as symbol, 117–18, 122
Rizal, José, 260–61, 262
Roman Catholic Church: competition with secular authority, 118, 119, 134; Counterreformation, 119; defenders, 134; Jewish influence seen, 176–77, 194; political role, 126; popes, 116, 118; reunification of Italy and, 120–21, 130–31, 133; Wagner on, 176. *See also* Christianity
Roman Empire, 117–18, 122, 185, 190
Romania, 228, 229–30, 271
Rosenberg, Alfred: antisemitism, 205–6; Chamberlain and, 203, 204, 208; on Christianity, 210–11; on history, 205, 208, 211–13, 215; Hitler and, 200, 201, 202–3, 219, 220–21, 224; on individualism, 214n; influence on National Socialist ideology, 200–201, 204–7, 219, 221–22, 225; on Jews, 202, 205–7, 208, 216; life of, 201, 202, 203; *Mythus des 20. Jahrhunderts*, 202, 207–9, 216–19, 220–23, 224; new religion, 209–12, 223; *The Philosophy of Germanic Art*, 202; on political religion, 223, 282; on races, 202, 205, 208–9, 211–13, 215–16, 217–19, 222; on

religion, 199, 205–6, 207–12; roles in NSDAP, 201, 202; on science, 224–25; on Truth, 224–25; values, 217–18, 221–22

Rosmini, Antonio, 129, 131, 133, 135, 138, 165–66

Ruge, Arnold, 30

Russia: expatriates in Germany, 203; industrialization, 91, 261; intelligentsia, 92, 99, 104–7, 111, 113; liberalism, 91, 112; Marxism, 90–91, 96, 110–14; *Narodniki*, 91, 99; nationalism, 272; peasantry, 91, 238; social and political change, 90, 91, 104; unrest, 90, 91–92, 100, 105, 112. *See also* Soviet Union

Russian Orthodox Church, 101

Russian revolution, 147, 231, 247. *See also* Bolshevism

Sacralization: of citizens, 9; of humans, 40; in industrial societies, 2–3; of politics, 2, 263; of State, 24–26, 27, 51–52

Saloth Sar (Pol Pot): Chinese visit, 250–51; devotion to, 254; ethnic purification project, 255–56; fall of, 256; leadership of revolution, 249–50, 252; life of, 245–46, 249–50, 251; nationalism, 246

Savarkar, Vinayak D., 261, 262, 270

Schmitt, Carl, 214

Schopenhauer, Arthur, 174–75, 178, 179, 200, 204

Science: empiricism, 6–7, 42n, 119–20, 131; Hitler on, 224; religion and, 9, 119–20; Rosenberg on, 224–25; views of Russian intelligentsia, 106–7

Scientific racism, 173, 186

Scientism, 119–20, 131, 144, 206

Secularism, 118–19, 134. *See also* Political religions

Self-fulfillment, 217–19, 222

Self-interest, 10n

Semitic peoples, 185. *See also* Jews

Sensory perceptions, 36, 37–38, 41, 43, 56, 144. *See also* Empiricism

Shintoism, 276

Social Democratic Party, German, 89–90

Social Democratic Party, Russian, 96, 110–14

Socialism: African, 280–81; Arab, 281; Darwinian, 269; Engels on, 65; of Garibaldi, 120–21; of Hess, 54; of Marx and Engels, 87; Mazzini on, 125–26; Plekhanov on, 93–94; as political religion, 113–14, 161; revolutionary, 161; Saint-Simonians, 120–21, 125; scientific, 93, 235; secular, 114; totalitarian states, 114; World War I and, 162. *See also* Communism; Marxism

Socialist Party, Italian, 135, 147, 160, 161

Sombart, Werner, 216n

Sorel, Georges, 89, 161

Soviet Union: antisemitism, 271, 272–73; ethnogenesis, 271–72; industrialization, 243, 248, 283; nationalism, 271–72; patriotism, 272; population policies, 271, 272–73; relations with China, 247n; satellite states, 228, 231; Stalin's leadership, 227–28, 231, 235, 243, 247, 248–49; World War II and, 272. *See also* Leninism; Marxist-Leninist systems; Russia

Spaventa, Bertrando, 133, 135, 166

Spinoza, Baruch, 53

Spirit: Engels on, 60, 61; Gentile on, 130, 133; Hegel on, 17, 20, 21–22, 23–24; idealist view, 15; Mazzini on, 145; Mussolini on, 163–64; Oriani on, 128; World, 21–22, 47, 60, 70, 98

Spirito, Ugo, 169n

Stalin, Joseph, 227–28, 231, 243, 248–49, 272–73

Stalinism: Cambodian revolution and, 249; French intellectuals and, 246; ideological orthodoxy, 231; oppression, 235; as political religion, 169; population policies, 271; "socialism in one country," 247

State: Chamberlain on, 197–98; Fascist, 167–68; Gentile on, 146, 149–51, 155–57, 158–59; Hegel on, 1n, 18–20, 24–26; Hess on, 55; immanence, 146, 149, 158; liberal view, 18, 148; Mazzini on, 155, 159–60; nation as, 149, 158; Oriani on, 128; relations with individuals, 18–20, 24–26, 146, 149–50, 156–57, 158; religion and, 156–57; responsibilities, 51–52; sacralization, 24–26, 27, 51–52
Statism, 159–60, 173, 174
Stirner, Max, 30, 54, 177n
Strauss, David Friedrich, 30, 31, 32–33, 59, 60, 127
Sun Yat-sen, 261, 262, 265, 270, 273, 277–78
Swastika symbol, 209
Syndicalism: national, 147, 162, 163, 263; revolutionary, 159, 160, 162
Synoptic Gospels, 32, 33

Taborites, 242
Taiwan, 278
Technological change, 64. *See also* Industrialization
Terrorism, 91–92, 100
Theanthropism, 43–46, 97, 173, 267, 269
Totalitarianism: characteristics, 4–5, 274, 275–76; of Chinese regime, 273–74; classifying regimes, 276–81; control of population, 5, 275–76; definition, 4, 274, 275–76; of developmental regimes, 264–74; of Fascist State, 152, 167, 276, 282; human costs, 283; leaders, 4, 274; legacy, 283; political religion and, xii, 5, 274–83; socialism as, 114; Soviet, 169; warnings about, 114
Truth: Gentile on, 154, 156; human salvation in, 45; of Marxism, 110–11; Mazzini on, 123n, 124n; in political religions, 9; possessed by Lenin, 112–13; Rosenberg on, 224–25; of sensory perceptions, 37, 41. *See also* Empiricism
Turkey, 260, 261

Uganda, 259
Ulyanov, Alexander, 100
Urban centers, 218–19, 252
Urvolk, 172, 175, 179, 180, 187. *See also Volk*
Utilitarianism, 103, 107, 114, 132

Vanguards, *see* Elites
Vasconcelos, José, 270
Vaterlandsverein, *see* Fatherland Association
Vico, Giambattista, 132, 133, 135, 140
Victor Emmanuel, King, 120
Vietnam: Cambodia and, 246, 252, 256; Marxists, 234, 235, 242; wars, 234, 235
Volk, 171–72, 174, 175–76, 181. *See also* Germanic race; *Urvolk*

Wagner, Richard: antisemitism, 177, 178, 180–82, 187; "Art and Revolution," 176, 179; "The Art Work of the Future," 176; Chamberlain's study of, 188, 189–90, 196; on Christ's ethnicity, 211n; Feuerbach's influence, 174–75; Gobineau and, 182, 184–85, 187, 188; Hegelianism and, 174; influences on, 174–75, 184–85, 187, 188; on leadership, 178–79; patriotism, 175–76, 178–79, 267; political mobilization, 187; on races, 187, 267; on regeneration of humanity, 176, 178, 179, 180, 181, 195, 196; on religion, 175, 176, 179–81, 187, 196; "Religion and Art," 180–81, 187; on revolution, 179; themes of musical works, 179–80
Weitling, Wilhelm, 45, 64–65, 81, 82
White Russians, 203
Woltmann, Ludwig, 89, 199, 221n, 225, 269
Working class: education, 65n; exploitation, 77, 83–84; Marx on, 79–80; poverty, 48, 49, 50, 64, 65; Russian, 90, 91; self-externalization, 77, 78, 79; virtues, 65; wage labor, 83n. *See also* Proletariat
World Spirit, 21–22, 47, 60, 70, 98

World War I: Chamberlain's reaction, 197; effects, 147, 199–200, 268; Italy and, 142–43, 147, 154, 161–62; Marxist view, 233; socialist views, 161–62
World War II, 226, 227–28, 234, 248, 272

Young Hegelians, 30–34, 59–60, 76, 82, 95, 97

Zionism, 279–80

Lightning Source UK Ltd.
Milton Keynes UK
UKHW010606120519
342513UK00010B/733/P